Stalin and the French Communist Party 1941–1947

STUDIES OF THE RUSSIAN INSTITUTE

COLUMBIA UNIVERSITY

Stalin and the

French Communist Party

1941–1947

by ALFRED J. RIEBER

COLUMBIA UNIVERSITY PRESS

NEW YORK AND LONDON 1962

The transliteration system used in this series is based on
the Library of Congress system with some modifications

Copyright © 1962 Columbia University Press
Library of Congress Catalog Card Number: 62–17354
Manufactured in the United States of America

The Russian Institute
of Columbia University

THE RUSSIAN INSTITUTE was established by Columbia University in 1946 to serve two major objectives: the training of a limited number of well-qualified Americans for scholarly and professional careers in the field of Russian studies, and the development of research in the social sciences and the humanities as they relate to Russia and the Soviet Union. The research program of the Russian Institute is conducted through the efforts of its faculty members, of scholars invited to participate as Senior Fellows in its program, and of candidates for the Certificate of the Institute and for the degree of Doctor of Philosophy. Some of the results of the research program are presented in the Studies of the Russian Institute of Columbia University. The faculty of the Institute, without necessarily agreeing with the conclusions reached in the Studies, believe that their publication advances the difficult task of promoting systematic research on Russia and the Soviet Union and public understanding of the problems involved.

STUDIES OF THE RUSSIAN INSTITUTE

To John J. Rieber

Acknowledgments

IT IS IMPOSSIBLE to acknowledge adequately the great debt I owe to a large number of people who contributed so much in so many ways to the completion of this work. Most of all it is difficult to thank Philip E. Mosely enough for his help and encouragement. Professor Mosely suggested this topic to me and guided the manuscript through every phase of its development. Shephard B. Clough, Mario Einaudi, Geroid T. Robinson, Henry Roberts, Alexander Dallin, and Zigmundt Gasiorowski offered many very helpful criticisms. I hope I have taken full advantage of these. Thomas T. Hammond read the first four chapters at an early stage of the work and made many useful suggestions. Gray C. Boyce gave freely of his encouragement and aid at a critical moment in the writing of the book.

In France I was under a particular obligation to His Excellency Michel Debré for the opportunity to consult him and to meet many French officials who discussed the problems of French Communism with me. Robert Aron made the supreme gesture of scholarly assistance by sharing with me all the unpublished sources in his possession which he was using for his book *Histoire de la Libération de France.* I am deeply indebted also to all those who submitted to interviews, of whom only a few are listed in the bibliography. I would also like to thank those who opened many doors to new avenues of research and personal contacts in France, especially to Pierre Racine, Pierre Pascal, and David I. Goldstein for their tireless efforts on my behalf. Guy Lemmonier and Paul Barton gave liberally of their time and knowledge to help me clear up obscure points and find informative people.

The staffs and librarians of the following libraries were extremely helpful and patient in their efforts to satisfy my requests: Bibliothèque de Documentation Internationale Contemporaine, Bibliothèque Nationale, Columbia University Libraries, Hoover Institute and Library, Northwestern University Library, and the Lenin State Library of the USSR. I take great pleasure in expressing my appreciation to Helen Bajan of the Columbia University Press editorial department and Miss Louise Luke of the Russian Institute for their invaluable help in preparing the manuscript for publication. Finally, to my wife, Edith, I owe that immeasurable debt to one who shared all the burdens and few of the joys of writing a book.

The research for this dissertation was made possible by grants from The Ford Foundation in 1955–56 and from the Inter-University Committee on Travel Grants in 1958–59.

A.J.R.

Contents

Abbreviations

PCF	Parti Communiste Française
PRL	Parti Républicain de la Liberté
PTT	Poste, Télegraph et Téléphone
RGR	Rassemblement des Gauches Republicaines
SFIO	Section Française de l'Internationale Ouvrière.
STO	Service du Travail Obligatoire
UDSR	Union Démocratique et Sociale de la Résistance
UPRA	Union Patriotique Républicaine Anti-Fasciste
WFTU	World Federation of Trade Unions

SOURCES

Affiches CBN	Affiches. "Provinces," "Paris." Collection de la Bibliothèque Nationale.
BDIC	Bibliothèque de Documentation Internationale Contemporaine, "La Libération en province."
SCCR	Ministère de l'Interieur. Service Central des Commissariats de la République. Bulletin sur la situation dans les régions et les départements.
SFO	Ministerstvo Innostrannykh Del SSSR. Sovetsko-frantsuzskie otnosheniia vo vremia velikoi otechestvennoi voiny, 1941–1945: Dokumenty i materialy.
Correspondence	Ministry of Foreign Affairs of the USSR. Correspondence between the Chairman of the Council of Ministers of the USSR and the Presidents of the U.S.A. and the Prime Ministers of Great Britain during the Great Patriotic War of 1941–45.

Stalin and the French Communist Party
1941–1947

Introduction

FROM 1941 to 1947 the Soviet Union, the United States, and Great Britain became allies in order to defeat Hitler and reconstruct war-torn Europe. The inherent difficulty of these joint undertakings was further complicated by the widely divergent views held by the leaders of the Soviet Union and the Western democracies concerning the most basic questions of government and society. During the war the uneasy alliance was held together by the demands of the struggle for survival against a common enemy—Nazi Germany. After the war there was no longer a bond of immediate common purpose, and the great-power coalition broke up on the question of rebuilding a new Europe on the ruins of the old.

The disappointment and disillusionment which accompanied the end of wartime cooperation gave rise to many questions concerning the goals of Soviet foreign policy. Were Soviet war aims limited to attaining territorial security for the USSR in Eastern Europe? Did the Soviet leaders equate postwar security with frontier rectifications and friendly relations with "capitalist countries," or with the destruction of all capitalist states, the establishment of dictatorships of the proletariat everywhere—the triumph of world revolution? Had the Soviet leaders modified or abandoned their belief in the doctrine of world revolution, or did they still maintain their adherence to it? What role did the local Communist parties play in carrying out the short-term and long-range foreign-policy aims of the Soviet Union? The purpose of this study is to shed some light on these problems.

The foreign policy of the USSR is unique in one respect. Soviet national interest and the brand of revolutionary Marxism which

Moscow endorses are defended not only by Russian Communists but by millions of people, in almost every country of the world— the members of the Communist parties. Therefore, in tracing the pattern of Soviet foreign policy there is good reason to compare the activities and policy statements of local Communist parties with those of the Soviet Union. In order to make clear the long-range aims of the Kremlin's foreign policy, it is useful to make this comparison between Soviet policy and that of a Communist party outside the area controlled by the Soviet Union.

Two factors have led to a choice of the French Communist Party as the subject of this study. From 1941 to 1947 the French Communists were one of the largest and most active groups supporting Soviet aims in western Europe. France was, next to Germany, the most powerful highly industrialized state on the Continent, and the Soviet leaders were deeply interested in strengthening its resistance to Hitler and in influencing its postwar development.[1]

This study will be primarily concerned, then, with the interaction between the policies of the Soviet Union and those of the French Communist Party in order to discover whether or not they were at all times consistent, similar, and revolutionary. This study also seeks to show how effective the French Communist Party was as a political force in France. What were its strengths and weaknesses as a group which professed to champion international communism and French national interests? Finally, there will be an attempt to draw some general conclusions about the strategy and tactics of Soviet foreign policy during one of the most critical periods of Soviet history.

[1] See, for example, the analysis of the significance of the decline of France as a capitalist power in E. Varga, "Pravitel'stvo Lavalia i polozhenie Frantsii," *Mirovoe Khoziaistvo i Mirovaia Politika*, Nos. 5–6 (May–June, 1942), especially p. 24.

CHAPTER I

The Soviet Policy: "Unity of Action"

THE GERMAN invasion of the Soviet Union on June 22, 1941, was a crucial turning point in the history of world communism. Not since the darkest days of the Civil War in 1918 had Soviet Russia been faced with so dire a threat to its existence. During the four-year period of war that followed, the first task of the Soviet leaders was to defeat and to destroy the enemy. To attain this goal, no sacrifice was too great for them. If they failed in this mission, there would no longer be a Communist Soviet Russia.

After the German invasion of Poland and the declaration of war by Great Britain and France in September, 1939, the Soviet leaders had tried to remain neutral. Acting on the terms of the secret protocol of the Nazi-Soviet pact, the Soviet Union occupied eastern Poland and incorporated these and other territories into the USSR. Criticisms of Germany disappeared from the Soviet press, and Moscow began to negotiate a series of agreements with the Nazis involving the fate of Eastern Europe. In 1940 and 1941, as relations between Berlin and Moscow deteriorated, Stalin tried desperately to avoid being pulled into the "imperialist war." German leaders and Soviet historians later admitted that the USSR loyally carried out its onerous economic obligations to Germany.[1]

With the German attack, the Soviet view of the war changed radically. From "the struggle of predatory imperialist nations over the control of world markets" it was transformed overnight into "a

---

[1] Institut Marksizma-Leninizma pri TsK KPSS, *Istoriia velikoi otechestvennoi voiny Sovetskogo Soiuza 1941–1945* [History of the Great Patriotic War of the Soviet Union 1941–1945], I, 395, 402–4. See also Beloff, *The Foreign Policy of Soviet Russia 1929–1941*, II, 376–83; Dallin, *Soviet Russia's Foreign Policy, 1939–1942*, pp. 66–69; and Rossi (Tasca), *The Russo-German Alliance, August 1939–June 1941*, pp. 196–99.

great patriotic war of freedom-loving peoples against fascism." Moscow discontinued its hostile line of propaganda toward the Western democracies and the governments-in-exile of the countries under German occupation. Yet, it was not immediately clear what new policy the Soviet Union intended to follow in its relations with the United States, Great Britain, France, and other anti-Nazi governments. Would the Soviet leaders seek aid from the "capitalist camp"? If so, would acceptance of material assistance mean a basic change in Soviet foreign policy? To what extent would the USSR cooperate with the West, and what implications did the new line have for their future relations?

As the Communist parties of Europe began to adapt themselves to the situation caused by the German invasion, their relations with the German occupation forces and their own governments-in-exile changed. After having supported the war at the very outset in September, 1939, the French Communists were soon thrown into great confusion by the Soviet stand against the war, and their policy remained uncertain until Raymond Guyot returned from Moscow on September 20, 1939. Thereafter, the Communists denounced the Anglo-French "fomenters of war" and endorsed the Soviet invasion of eastern Poland.[2] By February, 1940, large numbers of Communists were being arrested, deported, and imprisoned for "anti-national" propaganda. After the armistice of June, 1940, and General de Gaulle's appeal to carry on the fight, the Communists denounced both the "collaborationists" and the "resisters." They repeated again and again the slogan, "One party alone struggles for peace. It is the Communist Party."[3] There was a small French Resistance movement at work by June 22, 1941, but the Communist Party organization had taken no part in it. Though this attitude was not popular among many militants, and despite many individual deviations from it, the Party leadership did not waver in its stand.[4] This French Communist line fitted in well with the Soviet aim of keep-

[2] Rossi (Tasca), *Les Communistes français*, pp. 45–52.
[3] *L'Humanité*, No. 58 (July 1, 1940) [Paris?], clandestine edition. All issues of *L'Humanité* up to August 16, 1944, No. 317, are clandestine.
[4] For some suggestive comments on activities of the Communist Party in the period between the Armistice of June, 1940, and the German invasion of the Soviet Union in June, 1941, see Werth, *France,* pp. 187–98.

ing out of the war and letting the "rival imperialist groups" exhaust each other in combat.

The German attack on the Soviet Union opened up many exciting possibilities for the French Communist Party. In adapting to the new circumstances, did the Party answer the needs of the embattled Soviet Union, or did it develop its own aims independent of Soviet foreign policy? The lack of clear answers to these questions was reflected in the uncertainty and hesitation that surrounded the first meetings and negotiations between the Soviet Union and the local Communists on the one hand and the Western, democratic, anti-Nazi forces on the other.

Moscow's first interests were in obtaining military supplies from the West and in persuading the British to open a second front, to recognize the Soviet boundaries as they were in June, 1941, and to agree to territorial changes in Eastern Europe.[5] The British and the Americans soon found out that the Soviet leaders were rude and demanding until the Soviet views on these matters were accepted in their entirety. After Stalin's early appeals to Churchill for an immediate second front were denied, the Soviet leader warned that the absence of a second front was "playing into the hands of our common enemies" and "that the Soviet Union will be either defeated or weakened" if it did not receive relief from the West.[6]

At the same time it was not clear whether the Soviet Union intended to cooperate with the West on a limited and short-range basis to win the war or on a long-range basis that would ultimately modify Moscow's aim of spreading world revolution. Consciously or not, the Soviet leaders encouraged speculation on their motives. While they reasserted their adherence to "Lenin's legacy," they did not openly state their intention of establishing world communism. Instead, they extolled the economic and social achievements of the

[5] For a discussion of these early negotiations see Feis, *Churchill, Roosevelt, Stalin,* especially pp. 15–17, 26–29, 33–34. See also the collection of Soviet documents, Ministry of Foreign Affairs of the USSR, *Correspondence between the Chairman of the Council of Ministers of the USSR and the Presidents of the U.S.A. and the Prime Ministers of Great Britain.* 2 vols. Hereafter cited as *Correspondence* I, II.

[6] *Correspondence,* No. 3, Stalin to Churchill, July 18, 1941, I, 13; and No. 12, September 13, 1941, I, 24.

Soviet regime, a theme which was consistent with their patriotic and nationalistic wartime propaganda.[7]

In addition to improving relations with the United States and Great Britain, the Soviet government tried to establish good relations with the anti-Nazi governments-in-exile, including the representatives of the nucleus of a French government-in-exile that had formed around General Charles de Gaulle in London. This was not an easy task because of the conflicting views of the United States and Great Britain on the role of De Gaulle in the future of France.

A New Communist Policy toward Free France

The German attack on the Soviet Union made it possible for members of the French Communist Party to be good Frenchmen as well as militant Communists. On July 3, 1941, Joseph Stalin made his famous appeal to all "freedom-loving peoples." "It is impossible," he began,

to consider the war with fascist Germany as a usual war. It is not only a war between two armies. It is instead of that a great war of all the Soviet peoples against the German-Fascist army. The goal of this people's patriotic war against the fascist oppressors is not only to liquidate the danger threatening our country but also to help all the people of Europe, suffering under the yoke of German fascism. In this liberating war we will not be alone. In this great war we will have close allies in the peoples of Europe and America, including the German people. . . . There will be a united front of peoples, standing for freedom against enslavement and the threat of enslavement on the part of the fascist army of Hitler.[8]

Thus, the Communist battle cry of the 1930s was revived: "The united front of peoples against fascism." Under this slogan the Soviet press exhorted the "enslaved peoples" to show their hatred toward the conqueror by strikes, open revolt, and guerrilla war.

[7] For a typical endorsement of "Leninist" social and economic policies see "Pod znamenem Lenina—Doklad tov. A. S. Shcherbakova," *Mirovoe Khozia-istvo i Mirovaia Politika* [World Economy and World Politics], Nos. 1–2 (January–February, 1942), 9–11, 18. The publication of *Propagandist* was resumed after a brief interuption in March, 1942 in order to step up the flagging ideological work. For a content analysis of *Propagandist*, 1942–1943 see David J. Dallin, The *Changing World of Soviet Russia*, New Haven, 1956, pp. 197–202.

[8] *Izvestiia*, July 3, 1941.

"The graves of Europe," it declared, "are changing into powder kegs. The more victories gained over Hitler, the more enemies will rise up before him as a result of these victories. Conquering half Europe, fascism has found itself inside a ring of deadly hatred." [9]

The French Communist Party responded to this appeal immediately. Its new battle cry combined Communist and patriotic slogans: "Today if you are not for the USSR, then you are against France; 1789–1793: The people hang traitors and drive out the foreigners, Frenchmen! Remember." The first reaction of the Party was to urge all-out support for the heroic peoples of the Soviet Union in their fight against the Fascist barbarians. This assistance should take the form of a "National Fighting Front for the Independence of France." The Party did not come out in open support of General de Gaulle and the British until some weeks later.[10]

In addition to its dramatic appeal to the "peoples," the Soviet government set about extending diplomatic recognition to all European governments-in-exile that were active or potential allies in the struggle against Germany. According to the Soviet documents, on August 8, 1941, representatives of General de Gaulle first broached the subject of establishing "informal relations" between the Free French movement and the Soviet Union. Moscow was willing to "establish official relations with De Gaulle along the same lines as those between De Gaulle and the British government." [11] The Free French movement did not have a formal executive committee meeting until September 24, 1941, when the Comité National Français (CNF) was formed. Two days later the Soviet Union recognized De Gaulle as "chief of all the Free French" and stated that

The Soviet government is ready to enter into relations with the Defense Council of the French Empire, created October 27, 1940, in all questions relative to collaboration with the overseas territories placed under his authority. [It] is ready to lend aid and assistance to the Free French in the common struggle against Hitlerite Germany and its allies. At the same

[9] *Ibid.*, July 5, 1941.

[10] Rossi (Tasca), *La Guerre des papillons*, pp. 190, 211, plate XIX.

[11] Ministerstvo Inostrannykh Del SSSR, *Sovetsko-frantsuzskie otnosheniia*, No. 1, I. M. Maiskii to the Commissariat of Foreign Affairs, August 8, 1941, p. 43; and No. 3, Letter from V. M. Molotov to Stafford Cripps, August 15, 1941, p. 45. This collection hereafter cited as *SFO*.

time [it] makes use of this opportunity to underline the firm resolve of
the Soviet government [and] to assure the full and entire restoration
of independence and grandeur of France once the joint victory over the
common enemy has been achieved.[12]

The Soviet press began to print the full texts or excerpts of
General de Gaulle's speeches. It also stressed the General's considerable following in France and in the United States. Wildly
exaggerating, it estimated that De Gaulle had an army of 100,000
men under his command.[13] Direct criticism of the Vichy government in the Soviet press came later. By April, 1942, the government
organ *Izvestiia* was attacking almost daily the "shameful capitulation of Pétain before Germany" and "the Hitlerite lackeys at the
head of the Vichy government." Laval was denounced as the
"French Quisling." [14]

The Soviet press was extremely careful to avoid pointing up
the particular exploits of the French Communists and identified the
underground forces by the terms "French patriots," "anti-Fascist
elements," or, occasionally, "French partisans." It denied allegations
that the Resistance in France was made up only of Communists.[15]
This was in accordance with the aim of fostering national "unity of
action" and solidarity against the common enemy, and the Soviet
press followed the same line in its comments on resistance movements in other countries, including Yugoslavia, Poland, Belgium,
and Norway.

From the beginning, General de Gaulle hoped that the Franco-
Soviet relationship would grow into something far more lasting and
important than a wartime agreement. He considered close contact
with the Soviet Union "useful because the Soviet Union and France
are continental powers and therefore have other goals and problems
than the problems of the Anglo-Saxon [*sic*] countries which are primarily sea powers." [16] He asserted the necessity of a Franco-Soviet

[12] *Ibid.*, No. 6. Letter from Maiskii to Charles de Gaulle, September 26, 1941,
p. 47.
[13] *Izvestiia*, September 25, 1941.
[14] *Ibid.*, April 16, 17, 18, 19, 22, 1941.
[15] *Ibid.*, August 30, September 20, 1941.
[16] *SFO*, No. 2, S. Vinogradov to the Commissariat of Foreign Affairs, August
10, 1941, p. 44.

alliance "from political as well as other points of view." [17] By April, 1942, De Gaulle was "already prepared to undertake a study of the question of the conclusion of an agreement between the USSR and France on postwar cooperation." [18]

Part of De Gaulle's eagerness to woo Moscow and obtain an alliance with the Soviet Union arose from his practical difficulties with the British and later the Americans. In his policy of building a strong and independent France, he hoped to strengthen Franco-Soviet relations as a counterweight to British influence on the Continent. He complained constantly to Soviet diplomats about the "underhanded Anglo-American policy." He accused the United States of a "secret plot . . . with Pétain according to which Pétain promises not to surrender the fleet and its bases in North Africa to the Germans and the United States promises Pétain not to allow De Gaulle in North Africa." He followed up his accusations with a lengthy note to the United States and the Soviet Union, entitled "Washington and Vichy," which discussed the alleged plot in detail and stressed the dangers it would create for the future stability of Europe. The main object of the United States and Great Britain was, De Gaulle maintained, "to preserve a strong Germany against the USSR and France."

To gain Soviet support, De Gaulle emphasized that "now the French people think little of the Americans and the English—they look to . . . the Soviet Union." [19] With his limited armed forces De Gaulle could make only a splendid gesture to give the Soviet leaders tangible proof of French sympathy with their cause at a crucial moment. In December, 1941, at the height of the battle of Moscow, he offered to transfer a French division from Syria to the Russian front. The Soviet Union quickly accepted.[20] After run-

[17] *Ibid.*, No. 18., Maiskii to the Commissariat of Foreign Affairs, January 29, 1942, p. 60.
[18] *Ibid.*, No. 25, A. Vyshinskii to the Commissariat of Foreign Affairs, April 13, 1942, p. 71.
[19] *Ibid.*, No. 17, A. Bogomolov to the Commissariat of Foreign Affairs, January 22, 1942, pp. 58–59 and p. 512, note 6.
[20] *Ibid.*, Nos. 11, 17, Bogomolov to the Commissariat of Foreign Affairs, December 9, 1941, p. 51, and January 22, 1942, p. 59.

ning into both logistical difficulties and British opposition, the project had to be abandoned.[21]

The Soviet leaders gave a cool reception to De Gaulle's continental theory and his many complaints against the Western Allies. They underlined the need to win the war now and think of the future later. They urged him to strengthen his relations with Britain because

now it is essential to prepare the second front in Europe, since only the active liberation of all French territory from the German occupation and the struggle with Germany will create the conditions necessary for the solution of all complicated questions.[22]

Not only did they hint that France was militarily incapable of playing a major role in the war at that time, as the abortive transfer of the Syrian division had shown, but they were uncertain about the political views of De Gaulle himself.

The Soviet ambassador in London, I. M. Maiskii, stated that De Gaulle favored a strong executive government for postwar France with "a corporative parliament" made up of various professional groups in society and which would settle the economic and social problems while the executive decided questions of a military and political nature. "Thus one finds in this program," Maiskii reported, "many elements of fascism in the Italian style." He concluded that "though the general political mood of De Gaulle is characterized by tendencies toward a modernized Bonapartism, he does not have rigid political views." [23]

In sum, in this early period Soviet policy toward De Gaulle was cautious. De Gaulle and Free France were as yet unknown quantities in the political and military sphere. Moscow was unwilling to commit itself to any unilateral support of a small and untried force which was deeply embroiled in quarrels with the Soviet Union's Western allies.

[21] *Ibid.*, Nos. 18, 19, Maiskii to the Commissariat of Foreign Affairs, January 29, 1942, p. 59, and February 3, 1942, p. 61.
[22] *Ibid.*, No. 17, Bogomolov to the Commissariat of Foreign Affairs, January 22, 1942, p. 59.
[23] *Ibid.*, No. 18, Maiskii to the Commissariat of Foreign Affairs, January 29. 1942, pp. 60, 61.

The Crisis of the Summer of 1942 and the Appeal to the West

Early in 1942 the Soviet Union was forced to appeal for immediate aid from its Western allies to offset its severe military reverses. The German spring offensive inflicted a series of disastrous defeats on the Red Army. In May, Von Mannstein unleashed his offensive in the Crimea. In June, Von Bock broke through the Russian lines between Kursk and Kharkov, and the Red Army fell back 500 kilometers in an almost disorderly retreat. Voronezh and Rostov fell, and besieged Sevastopol capitulated. The Soviet situation on the southern front had reached the decisive stage. The Wehrmacht broke into the North Caucasus in August, and on the ninth Maikop and its oil wells were seized by the Germans.

To Soviet leaders it was imperative to bring about the mounting of large-scale attacks against the German Army in Western Europe in order to draw off some of the enemy divisions from the eastern front. They again sought to convince the only powers which could organize and carry out such a diversion, the United States and Great Britain, that it was necessary to land on the Continent and establish a second front. It was with this purpose in mind that Soviet foreign Minister V. M. Molotov visited London and Washington in May and June, 1942.[24] Stalin had set the stage for the discussion by his May Day speech:

Peoples of all freedom-loving countries look to the Soviet Union as the force capable of saving the world from the Hitlerite plague. Among these freedom-loving countries first place is occupied by the United Kingdom and the United States of America, to which we are bound by ties of friendship and alliance and which are giving our country more and more military aid against the German-Fascist invaders.[25]

At first it appeared that Molotov had succeeded brilliantly in his mission. On June 11, 1942, a White House communiqué stated, albeit ambiguously, that a "full understanding was reached with regard to the urgent tasks of creating a second front in Europe in

[24] *Correspondence,* No. 40, Stalin to Churchill, April 22, 1942, I, 44–45.
[25] *Izvestiia,* May 1, 1942.

1942." [26] This declaration was greeted in Moscow as "having a colossal historical significance for the international relations of all freedom-loving countries." The Soviet leaders assumed from the word-. ing of the communiqué that "the political, economic, and military strength of the USSR, the United Kingdom, and the United States is now directed toward the decisive, common, basic task—to defeat the Hitlerite war machine on the European Continent in the course of 1942."[27] The Russian people were told that the war would end in 1942.[28]

The optimism of the Soviet leaders waned as the German offensive pushed forward relentlessly during the summer months. Stalin wrote Churchill in July: "I state most emphatically that the Soviet government cannot tolerate a postponement of the second front in Europe until 1943."[29] Near the height of the military crisis in August, the Soviet press began, for the first time, to appeal urgently for a second front.

All the freedom-loving peoples of the world are united against Hitlerite Germany. But the main burden of the struggle, the main weight of the war up to this time, has been carried alone by the Soviet Union during the course of thirteen months. In Europe at present there are no second fronts. Hitler will be destroyed on the day when all the strength of all peoples and powers actively enter the struggle.[30]

The press hammered at this theme for a solid month. It quoted at great length demands for a second front in the British and the American press and cited the statement of André Philip, a French Socialist closely associated with General de Gaulle, that any landings in France would receive "strong support from the French population."[31] This well-timed campaign began a few days before the first visit to Moscow of Winston Churchill, and it continued

---

[26] Hull, *Memoirs*, II, 1174. If this wording was meant to confuse the Germans, it also misled the Soviet leaders.

[27] *Izvestiia*, June 12, 1942. The Soviet government maintained that the communiqué contained "commitments to open a second front," *Correspondence*, I, 385, note 23.

[28] *Izvestiia*, June 21, 1942.

[29] *Correspondence*, No. 57, Stalin to Churchill, July 23, 1942, I, 56.

[30] I. Ermashev, "Razgrom nemetskikh imperialistov v voine 1914–18 gg." [The Defeat of the German Imperialists in the War, 1914–18], *Izvestiia*, August 1, 1941.

[31] *Ibid.*, August 4, 1942.

until the British leader made his report on the mission to the House of Commons. The French Communists conducted a similar propaganda drive in their press, which, though it began earlier than that of the Soviet press, spanned about the same period of time.[32]

The Soviet government was deeply disillusioned by Churchill's visit, which came at a time when the Soviet military situation was extremely serious. Churchill explained to Stalin that, after an "exhaustive Anglo-American examination of the problem," the "British and American governments did not feel themselves able to undertake a major operation in September, which was the last month in which the weather was to be counted upon." He also explained that there were only enough landing craft to put ashore and maintain six divisions on the French coast, and that such an operation would constitute a great risk for the success of a larger landing next year. Stalin disagreed with Churchill's view and told the British leader that everyone must take risks in war. Stalin believed that "troops must be blooded in battle." How else, he asked, could one learn their capabilities?[33]

Stalin was especially disturbed because he had assumed that "the decision to open a second front in Europe in 1942 was reached at the time of Molotov's visit to London and found expression in the agreed Anglo-Soviet communiqué released on June 12 last." Stalin was also deeply concerned over the effect on the Soviet home front of the decision to postpone a cross-channel invasion. He reiterated the Soviet view that

the opening of a second front was designed to divert German forces from the eastern front to the West, to set up in the West a major center of resistance to the German-Fascist forces and thereby ease the position of the Soviet troops on the Soviet-German front in 1942. . . . It will be readily understood that the British government's refusal to open a second front in 1942 in Europe delivers a mortal blow to Soviet public opinion, which had hoped that the second front would be opened, complicates the situation of the Red Army at the front, and injures the plans of the Soviet command.[34]

[32] See especially L'Humanité, No. 168 (June 23, 1942), No. 173 (July 31, 1942), No. 175 (August 14, 1942), and No. 178 (August 28, 1942). By September there were few if any references to the need for an immediate second front.

[33] Churchill, The Second World War, IV, 478–79.

[34] Correspondence, No. 65, Stalin to Churchill, August 13, 1942, I, 60–61.

At the same time Stalin was angered that the British had decided, in the face of strong German air and naval forces, to discontinue temporarily the sending of convoys to the northern Soviet ports.[35] Even while appealing for aid from the West, the Soviet leaders were deeply suspicious of their allies' motives.

The Development of Franco-Soviet Relations

During that desperate summer of 1942 the Free French alone could not substantially aid the Soviet Union. However, the growing prestige of De Gaulle and the activities of the Resistance movement in France were factors in the anti-Nazi struggle which Moscow could not ignore. While Foreign Commissar V. M. Molotov was in London in May, 1942, he had a lengthy conversation with General de Gaulle. Each man has given a slightly different version of the talks. De Gaulle emphasized Molotov's willingness to support the Free French, even in their disagreements with Great Britain and the United States. In his record of the discussion Molotov was not so specific in his offers of Soviet aid as De Gaulle indicated.

Both men agreed on the need for a second front in Europe immediately. De Gaulle complained that the Western Allies treated the Free French as a purely military organization and ignored their political qualifications. He criticized the British for not allowing Free French officers to land in Madagascar after the occupation of Diego Suarez. "Such a position by the British and the Americans in relation to the Free French movement was causing puzzlement in France, where people were beginning to doubt the significance of this movement, since it could not defend the interests of the French people." What measures could the Soviet Union take, he asked, to help the Free French in Madagascar?

Molotov replied that "the Soviet government wished to see the sovereignty of the French people fully reestablished and France restored in all its former greatness and glory." He added that "at first the Soviet government would show its interest in this question [of Madagascar] to the British and American govern-

---

[35] *Ibid.*, No. 57, Stalin to Churchill, July 23, 1942, I, 56.

ments, and further measures might be taken after it became clear what the consequences would be of such a declaration of interest in this question by the Soviet government."[36] De Gaulle interpreted this to mean that the Soviet Union was ready to support his efforts to reestablish the unity of the French Empire in general and, in particular, to play a role in "the administration of Madagascar, where the Anglo-Saxons [sic] were in favor of excluding us." [37]

When De Gaulle raised the question of Soviet interest in French domestic policies, Molotov "answered in categorical form that the Soviet government considers that the internal regime of France is the affair of the French people, who themselves will choose the system and government which will guarantee the happy and enlightened future of France. The Soviet government will not interfere in the internal affairs of France." [38] De Gaulle interpreted this to mean that "no foreign government, including that of the Soviets, should turn the allegiance of the Resistance movements in France away from General de Gaulle." Again, according to De Gaulle, Molotov ended the conversation by declaring that "my government is the ally of those in London and Washington. It is essential for the war that we collaborate closely with them. But with France Russia desires to have an independent alliance." [39] Neither this nor any similar statement appears in the Soviet documents.

In the eyes of the Soviet leaders, De Gaulle was now important enough to receive assurances of Soviet support and sympathy. However, was not De Gaulle giving these verbal declarations a much broader significance than they deserved? There is nothing to show that Moscow ever mentioned its interest in the Madagascar question to the Western Allies. It surely did not go beyond this. When the newly appointed French representative in Moscow, Roger Garreau, asked Moscow "to examine the question as to what extent the Soviet government could use its influence on the Allies in the interests of France," Andrei Vyshinskii simply replied that

[36] SFO, No. 29, Notes on the conversation of Molotov and De Gaulle, May 24, 1942, p. 80.
[37] De Gaulle, Mémoires, II, 248.
[38] SFO, No. 29, Notes on the conversation of Molotov and De Gaulle, May 24, 1942, p. 81.
[39] De Gaulle, Mémoires, II, 248.

"the position of the Soviet government in relation to France is well known to the National Committee—we could not think of reorganizing the world without the participation of France." He pointed out that the best indication of the Soviet attitude toward Free France was its willingness to accept De Gaulle's offer to send a French squadron of fighter planes to the Russian front! [40] At best these were minor concessions.

However, the Soviet leaders were beginning to realize that De Gaulle was a serious, if as yet only potential, military and political factor in the common struggle. They began to revise their estimate of his possible contribution to the war effort. On July 14, 1942, De Gaulle issued a proclamation changing the name of his organization from Free France to Fighting France. He wanted to demonstrate that the French were still in the battle. The Soviet Union was delighted with this move.

This was not a simple change of names, but a consecration of that military unity which will rally French patriots who are gathering their armed strength throughout France . . . and who will lead the struggle on its territory. Unity is the guarantee of the liberation of France, which still has its say in the international arena.

De Gaulle's political views for postwar France were also praised. There was favorable Soviet comment on the agreement between De Gaulle and the "patriotic organizations operating in occupied as well as unoccupied France . . . which specified that the sovereign will of the French nation will find its fulfillment in the National Assembly, which will be elected by free suffrage and will determine the future government structure." The Soviet press concluded that "the Fighting French movement, led by the head of the French National Committee, General Charles de Gaulle, has strengthened its international ties and this has promoted, in remarkable measure, the consolidation of the national strength of France." [41]

In August, 1942, these words of support and approval were given practical application. French Communists in Moscow, who until

[40] *SFO*, No. 28, Notes on the conversation of Vyshinskii and Roger Garreau, May 20, 1942, p. 78.
[41] L. Volynskii, "Frantsuzskii narod splachivaet svoi sily" [The French People Unite Their Strength], *Izvestiia*, July 29, 1942.

this time had avoided all contact with the representatives of Fighting France, began to visit Roger Garreau. The first visitor was André Marty, a member of the Political Bureau of the French Communist Party. Marty vigorously praised De Gaulle and offered to put himself entirely at the disposition of the French delegation to develop Gaullist propaganda in the USSR. Later Marty, chafing at his inaction in the USSR, expressed a desire to participate in the organization of the Resistance in continental France. He asked if the French National Committee would help him to return to France. Garreau was convinced that this support, given with the blessing of the Kremlin, marked an important change in relations between the French Communist Party and General de Gaulle.[42]

The Soviet government took a more official step toward enhancing De Gaulle's prestige in September, 1942, when it approved the change in the name and powers of the Free French movement. The Soviet Union agreed with and recognized the following definitions:

Fighting France. All the French citizens and territories which do not accept the capitulation and which, by all means at their disposition, contribute wherever they may be to the liberation of France through the common victory of the Allies against Hitlerite Germany and all its accomplices in Europe.

French National Committee. Directing organ of Fighting France, having the sole right to organize the participation of French citizens and territories in the war and to represent French interests to the government of the USSR, notably in the cases where the latter are affected by the conduct of the war.[43]

The Soviet Union recognized the French National Committee only after similar action by the Western Allies and in more or less similar terms.[44]

Direct and well-coordinated joint action of De Gaulle and the Soviet leaders in foreign policy was difficult because of the Anglo-American distrust of the Free French leader. Stalin had stated that the United Kingdom and the United States "occupied first place"

[42] Telegram from Roger Garreau to the National Committee in London, September 1, 1942, Moscow, as quoted in De Gaulle, *Mémoires*, Documents, II, 363–64.

[43] *Ibid.*, Documents, II, 371, Text of the Franco-Soviet agreement of September 28, 1942. SFO, No. 41, Communiqué of the Soviet Government and the French National Committee, p. 97.

[44] De Gaulle, *Mémoires*, II, 337–38, 340.

in the Soviet alliance system. Therefore, when disputes arose between De Gaulle and the Western Allies, Moscow avoided becoming deeply involved. Stalin was particularly anxious to avoid antagonizing his allies by supporting De Gaulle in the North African and Syrian crises. However, he was careful not to disregard altogether De Gaulle's sensitivities.

In August, 1942, there was a particularly sharp exchange between the British and the Free French over the administration of Syria. In reply to De Gaulle's message informing him of the dispute, Bogomolov transmitted the message "that his government was disposed to help the [French] according to its means." [45] There is no evidence that Moscow went beyond this purely verbal affirmation of support to the French cause.[46] Any Soviet intervention in the quarrel would have incurred the anger of one of the Allies without resulting in any corresponding advantage to the Soviet Union. If the Soviet government had been forced to take a stand on this issue, there is little doubt that it would have chosen to support Great Britain.

The Soviet government employed similar tactics during the dispute which threatened to disrupt Free French unity in North Africa. As in the past, the Gaullists tried to convince Moscow that the Soviet Union ought to intervene on the side of the Free French in North Africa because the State Department of the United States was plotting to make a deal with the Vichy regime which would lead to collaboration with the Germans and the creation by the Americans of a reactionary government in postwar France. As before, the Soviet leaders did not rise to the bait. For them these French tactics were clearly provocatory. Vyshinskii reiterated to Garreau that "our position should be well known." As for the understanding between the Americans and Darlan, Vyshinskii made it clear that "we look at it from the point of view of whether it is useful in the struggle with Germany, that is most important now. We consider that any sort of action which can weaken the German strength is justified." [47]

[45] *Ibid.*, II, 23. The date for this message was September 11, 1942.

[46] The Soviet press reported the Franco-American clash by quoting from British news-agency bulletins. It made no editorial comment.

[47] *SFO*, No. 47, Notes on the conversation of Vyshinskii and Garreau, February 1, 1943, pp. 108–9.

When there appeared to be some doubt in the minds of the Western leaders as to the Soviet position on Darlan, Stalin wrote to Churchill and Roosevelt: "As for Darlan, I think the Americans have made skillful use of him to facilitate the occupation of North and West Africa. Military diplomacy should know how to use for the war aims not only the Darlans but the devil and his grandmother." [48] Why were the Western powers concerned about the Soviet position when, according to the Soviet documents, the Free French received no encouragement from Moscow? Certainly the Soviet press had taken a detached view of the situation throughout the crisis. When Darlan was assassinated in December, 1942, *Izvestiia* simply stated that "history will hand down an impartial sentence on Admiral Darlan." [49]

However, in London De Gaulle believed the Soviet Union was more serious in its intentions to intervene. According to his sources, Moscow, relying on reports from Ambassador Maxim Litvinov in Washington about "Roosevelt's intention to become the arbiter between the French factions, was becoming quite worried (*éprouvait des sérieuses inquiétudes*) about this American tendency to seek a predominant position." Bogomolov explained that his country, "engaged in a death battle against the invader, could not actually intervene in a direct manner, but that it also disapproved of the policy of the Anglo-Saxons [*sic*] and that it would know how to oppose it as far as possible (*à la limite*)." [50]

The only evidence from a third source that the Soviet leaders were concerned about the North African imbroglio is a statement attributed to Molotov in a private conversation. He is reported to have said that he was puzzled over the Allied actions in North Africa and indicated that the Soviet Union was deeply interested in the fate of French Africa. [51]

Stalin was unwilling to interfere in the Allied diplomacy in North Africa, and he endorsed American policy. If his subordinates made some contrary remarks in private and dropped vague hints to the

---

[48] *Correspondence*, No. 89, Stalin to Churchill, November 27, 1942, I, 80; see also a differently worded message with the same meaning in *Correspondence*, No. 58, Stalin to Roosevelt, December 14, 1942, II, 44.

[49] *Izvestiia*, December 26, 1942.

[50] De Gaulle, *Mémoires*, II, 36.

[51] Feis, *Churchill, Roosevelt, Stalin*, pp. 90–91.

Free French in London which led De Gaulle to conclude that Moscow was on his side, so much the better for Stalin. Stalin could gain the appreciation of the Western Allies for his public support of their policy and secure the admiration of the French for his sympathy with their views.

In Moscow in the summer of 1942, Stalin told President Beneš of Czechoslovakia what he really thought about the advisability of openly supporting De Gaulle. Beneš made a gallant plea for Soviet recognition of the Comité National Français as the government of France. It was explained to him that in principle the Soviet government approved such an action, but that the opportune moment for it had not yet come. The Red Army had an urgent need for military aid from the United States and Great Britain. In view of the attitude of these two governments toward General de Gaulle, the Soviet government did not believe it could force their hand at this time. The question could be opened, Beneš was told, after the establishment of the second front.[52]

Soviet Policy and "Unity of Action" in the Resistance

Aside from securing aid from the Western Allies, there were other possibilities which Stalin could not overlook for obtaining military support against Nazi Germany. Since the invasion of the Soviet Union, the Communist parties of Europe had thrown their forces into the struggle already being waged by the anti-Nazi underground movements in occupied Europe. This fact and the entrance of the United States into the war raised new hopes in occupied Europe that resistance was no longer futile but, rather, necessary to hasten the coming liberation. Could not the Soviet leaders expect this growing internal opposition to Hitler to help the embattled Red Army? Was it not possible that guerrilla warfare and sabotage, such as that carried on by Red partisans behind the German lines in western Russia, could spread to all Europe? Had not Stalin declared that "the graves of Europe are turning into powder kegs"?

[52] Telegram from Maurice Dejean, National Commissar of Foreign Affairs, to De Gaulle, August 7, 1942, as quoted in De Gaulle, *Mémoires*, Documents, II, 348.

Recent evidence from Soviet sources shows clearly that organizational links between various European Communist underground movements had been established even before the German invasion of the Soviet Union.

In early 1941 a special section of the French Communist Party called "Work among the Germans" was set up to bring about "extensive cooperation not only with German and Austrian anti-Fascists, but with Polish, Czech, Hungarian, Rumanian, Yugoslav, and Bulgarian patriots who happened to be in France." According to Soviet historians, this organization "demonstrated the profound sense of internationalism among Communists of various nationalities." Similar contacts were established between "patriots" of east and southeast European countries. "In Germany itself comradely cooperation developed between the German Communist underground and the toilers of various nationalities." At the same time the German Communist Party

directed all its members who were in France to join the ranks of the anti-Fascist front. Subsequently the center of the German Communist Party in Toulouse sent several German Communists to Paris to participate in the struggle against the Hitlerites [and one of these] was authorized by the Central Committee of the KPD to direct the anti-Fascist activities of German Communists in France.[53]

The immediate purpose of this international network was to protect the remnants of Communist organizations against Nazi persecution. However, after the German attack on the Soviet Union the loosely knit European Communist underground could be reactivated to carry on the kind of coordinated struggle against Hitler which Stalin wanted and encouraged.

One of the thorniest problems the Soviet leaders encountered in encouraging mass resistance to the Germans in occupied Europe was the unwillingness of some local Communists to work with the democratic forces against the common enemy. For example, Stalin was deeply disturbed by the tendency of the Yugoslav Communist Party under Tito (Josip Broz) to develop an independent policy and ignore or denounce the underground organization of the Royal

[53] Archiv des Institut für Marxismus-Leninismus beim ZK der SED. Fond Nachlässe, CXX/1020, as cited in *Istoriia velikoi otechestvennoi voiny*, p. 328.

Yugoslav government-in-exile. As early as February, 1942, Stalin sent the following message to Tito:

Study of all the information you sent gives one the impression that the adherents of Great Britain and the Yugoslav government have some [justification] for suspecting the partisan movement of acquiring a Communist character and aiming at the Sovietization of Yugoslavia. Why, for example, did you need to form a special Proletarian Brigade? Surely at the moment the basic immediate task is to unite all anti-Nazi currents, smash the invaders, and achieve national liberation.[54]

On March 5 Tito received another rebuke from Stalin, one which revealed more clearly some of the Soviet leader's reflections on the international situation:

The defeat of the Fascist bandits and liberation from the occupier is now the basic task and is above all other tasks. Take into consideration that the Soviet Union has treaty obligations with the Yugoslav king and government, that any open actions against them would create new difficulties in the common war effort in relations between the Soviet Union and England and America. Do not consider your struggle only from your own national point of view, but from the international point of view of the English-Soviet-American coalition. Strengthen your positions in the people's liberation struggle and at the same time show more elasticity and ability to maneuver.[55]

Apparently in reply to Tito's message that the Chetniks were class enemies and fence-sitters, if not outright collaborators with the enemy, Stalin wrote in April:

It is certainly necessary to unmask the Chetniks to the people, complete with documentary proof, but for the present it would be politically opportune for you to do so through a general approach to the Yugoslav government, emphasizing that the Yugoslav patriots who are fighting have a right to expect support for any Serb, Croat, Montenegrin, and Slovene fighters who are waging a struggle either in Yugoslavia or abroad on the basis of a National Liberation Partisan Army.[56]

The Soviet press gave no hint of encouragement to Tito. It did not mention his name throughout 1942, and it referred only incidentally to the Yugoslav Communist Party. This was in part a rebuke and in part a reflection of the Soviet campaign to minimize

[54] Dedijer, *Tito*, p. 178.

[55] *Borba* [The Struggle], March 23, 1950, as quoted in Armstrong, *Tito and Goliath*, p. 27.

[56] Dedijer, *Tito*, p. 179.

its actual influence over foreign Communist parties, as well as to emphasize the common effort of all anti-Hitlerite forces. As we shall see, the Soviet leaders favored "unity of action" in the French Resistance, and yet in France, as in Yugoslavia, the Party was at first reluctant to establish close contacts with the non-Communist forces.

The Soviet leaders were also disturbed by the tendency of some underground groups to conduct a passive resistance against the Nazis. These forces built up their military strength and avoided clashes with the enemy, waiting until the arrival of Allied troops should enable them to attack the rear of the German Army. From the early days of the German invasion, Moscow vigorously denounced this policy as "fence-sitting" and at every opportunity encouraged the development of a partisan movement in the occupied countries which would carry the fight to the enemy with vigor and dispatch. Especially during the wave of Soviet defeats in the summer of 1942 the Soviet leaders appealed eloquently for an active struggle against the Nazis throughout Europe.

In August, 1942, the Soviet press noted that "the partisan struggle, above all in Yugoslavia, is turning into a total people's war against the enslavers. . . . The occupying powers are obliged to consider the partisan movement in Yugoslavia as a very serious force." [57] Some months later the praise for Yugoslavia swelled to a tribute. "The Yugoslav people . . . are giving an example to all the enslaved peoples of Europe." [58] The great merit of the Yugoslavs was that they understood that it was "indispensable to strike at the rear of the occupiers, to take the offensive against them with complete determination, precisely at that moment when the Germans had both hands tied on the Soviet-German front." [59]

By October, 1942, Moscow claimed that other peoples were following the example of Yugoslavia. Hilary Minc declared that the

[57] D. Ikhok, "Narody okkupirovannykh stran v bor'be za svoe osvobozhdenie" [Peoples of Occupied Countries in the Struggle for Liberation], *Izvestiia*, August 7, 1942. See also I. Ermashev, "Narodnaia voina v Iugoslavii" [The People's War in Yugoslavia], *ibid.*, August 2, 1942.

[58] D. Petrov, "Geroicheskaia bor'ba iugoslavskikh partizan" [The Heroic Struggle of the Yugoslav Partisans], *ibid.*, October 16, 1942.

[59] E. Gerö, "Rost osvoboditel'nogo dvizheniia v okkupirovannykh stranakh" [The Growth of the Liberation Movement in Occupied Countries], *ibid.*, October 21, 1942.

Polish partisan movement had become widespread and "constitutes a great danger for the German occupiers." [60] In Norway, resistance was reportedly growing into "a powerful partisan movement of the Norwegians directed against the occupiers." A Norwegian underground paper was quoted: "The time for passive resistance has passed. Military preparedness and active participation in the war for the fatherland for humanity is the task of each Norwegian." [61] The Soviet press also maintained that by October, 1942, there were 30,000 Greek partisans in action.[62]

Moscow also noted "the transfer of the partisan movement to countries where any partisan struggle had been considered impossible, for example, France." It admitted that the partisan movement had appeared in France only during the spring of 1942 and in the form of small and weak detachments; yet it was now "expanding rapidly under skillful leadership." For the Soviet Union it was especially significant that heretofore passive sections of the population were resorting to active resistance.

Many anti-Hitlerite political figures in France, stunned and disorganized by the fall of the country and by the government of Laval-Pétain, took up a temporizing position for a long time. . . . But the mass of people did not wish to temporize, . . . and the political leaders who did not want to lose contact with the masses went along.[63]

To encourage all partisans, the Soviet press indicated that active resistance would grow "as the situation demands and in line with the objective conditions," and it added that "in spite of the terror and the lack of a second front, the people are going forward." [64] The Soviet leaders acknowledged the importance of this activation of the Resistance in their slogans for the twenty-fifth anniversary of the October Revolution: "A salute to the peoples of Europe struggling against the Hitlerite imperialism! Patriots of European coun-

[60] Hilary Minc, "Zlodeianiia gitlerovtsev v Pol'she i osvoboditel'naia bor'ba pol'skogo naroda" [The Crimes of the Hitlerites in Poland and the Liberation Struggle of the Polish Nation], *ibid.,* October 15, 1942.
[61] V. Shtern, "Ne slomlen dukh norvezhskogo naroda" [The Unbroken Spirit of the Norwegian Nation], *ibid.,* October 18, 1942.
[62] Ikhok, "Grecheskii narod prodolzhaet bor'bu [The Greek People Continue Their Struggle], *ibid.,* October 28, 1942.
[63] Gerö, "Rost osvoboditel'nogo dvizheniia v okkupirovannykh stranakh," *ibid.,* October 21, 1942.
[64] *Ibid.*

tries, rise up to the struggle for your freedom from the Fascist yoke! Overthrow the Hitlerite tyranny!" [65]

One aspect of this Soviet propaganda theme received little publicity in the Moscow press, but was mentioned in the French Communist press and in private conversations between Soviet and Free French diplomats. This was the Communist idea of unleashing a mass insurrection of the enslaved peoples of Europe. No mere partisan diversion, this spontaneous rising would force the Germans to withdraw units from the eastern front; perhaps more important in the eyes of the Soviet leaders, it might encourage the Allies to risk an early landing on the Continent. The large-scale disruption of German transportation and communication lines and the demonstration of solidarity and sympathy by the peoples of Europe would be an open invitation for the Western Allies to intervene. If this idea had the fault of being totally unrealistic, it had the merit of seizing the imagination of some Resistance forces and inspiring them to great efforts.

About the time that Churchill arrived in Moscow in August, 1942, Soviet Deputy Foreign Minister V. G. Dekanosov engaged De Gaulle's representative, Roger Garreau, in a lengthy conversation. Later Garreau reported his recollections:

After having expressed his sympathy for Fighting France, [Dekanosov] indicated that the French people ought not to wait for the arrival of outside help to unleash the active struggle against the oppressor. He cited the example of Yugoslavia. An insurrection throughout France would serve, he said, as the signal for a rising of all enslaved Europe and would hasten the desired intervention of the English and the American forces.[66]

According to the Commissar of Foreign Affairs, Maurice Dejean, in a message transmitting Garreau's report to De Gaulle, there was strong evidence that, "failing a general offensive of the Allied forces in the West, the Soviet government, subjected to the formidable pressure of the German armies, ardently desired an insurrection of the enslaved countries." [67]

[65] *Pravda* and *Izvestiia*, October 28, 1942.
[66] Telegram from Dejean to De Gaulle, August 13, 1942, as quoted in De-Gaulle, *Mémoires*, II, 353.
[67] *Ibid.*

Even when this idea failed to materialize, Stalin continued to emphasize the close connection between the opening of the second front and the strengthening of the Resistance movements. In November, 1942, he laid the Germans' great "tactical successes" during the spring and summer to their ability "to create a great preponderance of strength in the southeastward offensive," and pleaded for Allied action to "pull off just sixty German and twenty satellite divisions" as a step that would mark the beginning of the end for Germany. He warned that "the lack of a second front against Fascist Germany can end badly for all freedom-loving countries, including those of our Allies." Stalin emphasized that the "peoples of Europe are in complete sympathy with the members of the coalition and are ready to give them great support." [68]

The French Communists and "Unity of Action"

Though the response of the French Communists to the Soviet policy of "unity of action" was at first sluggish, it rapidly became enthusiastic. It was not until May, 1942, almost a year after the German invasion of the Soviet Union, that the well-known Gaullist secret agent Remy (whose real name was Gilbert Renault) met an important member of the Communist paramilitary underground forces in France, known as Colonel Drumont or Joseph (his real name was Beaufils). Both men were interested in establishing closer relations between their respective Resistance groups. Joseph explained that the Communist groups needed arms, ammunition, and military specialists.[69] According to Jacques Soustelle, an early and close associate of De Gaulle, this meeting resulted in the establishment of an information network between the Communists in France and the Free French in London and "the acceptance in principle" by the Communists of the establishment of a unified chief-of-staff of the north, or occupied, zone of France under the control of London. The secret services in London would finance this network and also the Communist paramilitary forces. It is evident that the Soviet

[68] "Doklad predsedatelia gosudarstvennogo komiteta oborony tovarishcha I. V. Stalina" [Report of the Chairman of the State Committee of Defense Comrade I. V. Stalin], *Izvestiia*, November 7, 1942.

[69] Renault, *Mémoires*, I, 448.

leaders approved of the arrangement. A few days before the Remy-Joseph meeting, Andrei Vyshinskii told Garreau that the authority of the French National Committee depended on "the extent to which [the Committee] can unite the popular masses under its leadership, [and] the extent to which its basis is broad and solid." [70]

This stage of "unity of action" with the French Communist Party was something less than General de Gaulle desired in order to forge a united French underground behind him. Therefore in September, 1942, he told A. Bogomolov in London:

> If tomorrow some one of the leaders of the French Communist Party came to me with a single declaration of their readiness to fight together with me against the Germans, I would accept it. I want to unite all Frenchmen who wish to fight against Germany. [70]

Clearly, the Soviet leaders were of the same mind, and less than three weeks later, on November 15, 1942, the French Communists agreed to incorporate their paramilitary forces into the Forces of Fighting France. (FFC).

Yet, it was not until two months after this that Fernand Grenier, former Communist deputy in the French Chamber of Deputies and member of the Central Committee of the Party, arrived in London, bringing with him the formal adherence of the Communists to Fighting France for the duration of the war. "As for what happens after the liberation of France," Grenier added, "that is not the present question." In conversations with De Gaulle and Soustelle he stressed the need for cooperation among all the elements of resistance, no matter what their political views. He urged the formation of a government led by both Giraud and De Gaulle. Then he insisted that Louis Marin, an outstanding conservative republican statesman, be brought to London. He even admitted that the Communist paramilitary forces welcomed into their ranks former members of such French Fascist groups as the Croix de Feu. [72] That very month the Soviet press announced that "the Communist Party,

[70] SFO, No. 26, Vyshinskii to the Commissariat of Foreign Affairs, May 9, 1942, p. 75.

[71] Ibid., No. 40, Bogomolov to the Commissariat of Foreign Affairs, September 26, 1942, p. 95.

[72] Soustelle, Envers et contre tout, I, 390; II, 20. Grenier, C'était ainsi, p. 131, does not mention Marin or the Croix de Feu.

participating in the single national front, has officially joined the Fighting French movement." [73]

After this the French Communists closely followed Moscow's lead in stressing the need for "unity of action" among all resistance movements in Europe. They came out in support of "the glorious General Mihajlović" whose "Young Partisans [sic] are inflicting cruel losses on the Fascist enemy." [74]

The French Communist leaders also tried to answer the Soviet demand for a more active Resistance. By March, 1942, the Party had stepped up its efforts to increase the number of its paramilitary formations. "Everywhere," the clandestine press exhorted, "patriots must constitute groups of Francs-Tireurs et Partisans [FTP] to make life miserable for the occupying forces, and must carry on a guerrilla war which, from the armistice line to the farthest corners of the country, will give no respite to the enemy." [75] Though the Party did not officially and publicly support a policy of terrorist attacks against the Germans, some of its militants looked with favor upon such tactics. For example, the Communist leader Joseph told Remy that it was necessary to kill German officers in order to get their arms. When Remy questioned him about the resulting reprisals, Joseph replied: "At the announcement that five or ten of ours have been shot, we will enroll fifty to a hundred new volunteers in the Francs-Tireurs et Partisans." [76] This attitude was not unusual.

In its propaganda the French Communist Party fully echoed the Soviet proposal for an early and general insurrection in France. "A *levée en masse* of the French people to free our country will naturally bring in its wake a liberating army of English and American soldiers and soldiers of General de Gaulle's Free France." [77] Thus, the Party urged: "It is necessary to fight with all means; it is necessary to get arms by all means; it is necessary to recruit

[73] Monin, "Krasnaia armiia sozdala fundament" [The Red Army Established the Foundation], *Bol'shevik,* No. 2 (January, 1943), p. 78.

[74] *L'Humanité,* special number (August–September, 1942).

[75] *Ibid.,* special number (March, 1942).

[76] Renault, *Mémoires,* I, 449.

[77] *Cahiers du Bolchévisme,* first and second quarters, 1942, "L'Heure du combat," pp. 7–8. This clandestine edition of the *Cahiers* was published with a false cover and title page which read *Mémoires de Napoléon, Le Vol de l'aigle.*

among the patriots for the new FTP." [78] At the same time, the French Communists reacted vigorously against the attempt of the Germans to deport French laborers by helping to organize in cooperation with five other Resistance groups a massive strike of railroad workers in Lyon. "The interests of France urgently demand," they stated, "that we not deliver to collapsing Nazism new hostages and the working force to delay its destruction." [79]

Despite its vigor, the French Communist propaganda for resistance à l'outrance achieved only a modest military effect. The practical response to the many Communist appeals was not energetic. The Party leadership was particularly disturbed by the attitude of those Party members who were following a "fence-sitting" policy. It accused them of remaining "criminally inactive at the time when everything commands action." "It is not," the leadership continued, "a question of an isolated case, and we could cite numerous factories, railroad stations, and other enterprises where the militants conducted themselves in the same way." [80]

The Party called for elimination of "fence-sitters," an obligatory enlistment of 20 percent of Party effectives in the FTP, and the condemnation of the "criminal negligence of certain responsible members" which resulted in all too numerous arrests. "Squealers" who "through lack of courage tell the police everything they know" are treated with too great "liberalism" by "too many members of the Party." [81]

This type of stinging attack was pressed hard into December and January, 1943, by the Party's leading theoretical organ. For the Communists the present danger was too great to permit idle speculation on the future, and the Party denounced "certain comrades who are preparing 'plans' for tomorrow and come to the conclusion that at the present time there is no need for action . . . the organization of forces cannot be separated from immediate action." [82]

[78] *L'Humanité*, No. 181 (September 25, 1942). The Party continued to appeal for a great struggle "whose accentuation will contribute to hasten the formation of the second front." *Ibid.*, No. 182 (October 2, 1942).

[79] Rossi, *La Guerre des Papillons*, p. 263.

[80] *La Vie du Parti*, November, 1942, pp. 4–5.

[81] *Ibid.*, pp. 6–8.

[82] *Ibid.*, December, 1942, p. 6.

This furious onslaught, plus the continued urgings of the leadership, did not succeed in turning France into a battlefield. By August, 1943, Benoît Frachon of the Political Bureau of the French Communist Party was forced to warn the rank and file of the Party:

First, it is necessary to reject firmly the false idea that sees the national insurrection being born one fine day on the order of some committee or other and that assumes the need to wait for that day calmly without doing anything, under the wrong headed pretext of "not wearing down one's strength." Those who defend this concept, which ends up in inaction, in demoralizing fence-sitting, show an absolute failure to understand the problems of a national insurrection.

Agitation, strikes, and demonstrations were, he continued, a way of orienting the masses toward "more decisive action." "Those who devote themselves to bringing them to a halt under the pretext of 'saving their strength,' turn their back on the insurrection." Frachon concluded that "daily action is an imperious necessity in preparation for the tasks which will face the working class in the popular uprising." [83]

While demanding greater efforts from its militants, the Party also urged non-Communist forces to swing into action. When the German Army overran the southern, or unoccupied, zone of France in November, 1942, the French Communists issued an appeal to the French Army of the Armistice. This armed force, left to the Vichy regime after the armistice of June, 1941, was dissolved officially by Vichy when the Germans occupied the southern zone. Although the Communists could hardly have approved of its politics, they exhorted its members to "organize yourselves, form Corps Francs guerrilla units, and take to the hills, preparing yourselves for a guerrilla war; take inspiration from the glorious example of General Mihajlović and make the enemy pay dearly for the occupation of the soil of our beloved France." [84]

Despite the initial practical difficulties, the French Communists

[83] *L'Humanité*, No. 240 (August 15, 1943).

[84] *Ibid.*, No. 191 (December 4, 1942). For the organization of the Resistance elements in the Vichy Army (ORA) see Ministère de l'Information, *Notes, Documentations et Etudes,* LXVI, No. 225 (January, 1946), "Esquisse d'une histoire de la Résistance française," 5.

took up their new role with alacrity and skill. This was partially due to the presence in the USSR of Maurice Thorez, secretary-general of the Party, who remained in Moscow from the autumn of 1940 to late 1944. Until 1944 he occasionally spoke on Radio Moscow, and during 1944 he made regular broadcasts to France.[85] His close collaborator and the second in command in the Party, Jacques Duclos, remained in France. There is no evidence that either Thorez or Duclos opposed Soviet leadership during the war or that there was any disagreement between the two on tactics during this period. The presence of Thorez in Moscow and of Duclos in France helped to assure unity of outlook and action between the French Communists and the USSR. Confirmation of this can be found in the almost complete identity of views in the Soviet and the French Communist press during this period.

A second factor which contributed to the acceptance by the French Communist Party of the appeal for "unity of action" was the absence of a strong representation of the traditional French Right in the underground. There were only individual moderate political leaders such as André Mutter, Louis Marin, and Joseph Laniel. True, after the dissolution of the French Army of the Armistice in November, 1942, the Organisation de la Résistance et de l'Armée (ORA) was created. This force was made up largely of conservative army officers, but it was a purely military formation which had no avowed political program. The characteristics of the Resistance, in so far as they can be generalized in so varied a movement, were Leftist, reformist, and even revolutionary.[86]

The Right either supported Pétain or was inactive, completely demoralized by defeat and occupation. General de Gaulle himself could be considered a man of the "Right." However, by 1942 he rejected the Third Republic and spoke out in favor of consulting the French people on the future political structure of France. In one sense he was a rebel and had no ties with the old regime. His attitude was symbolized by the now famous phrase "The national insur-

[85] Thorez, Un grand Français, passim.
[86] Boris Mirkine-Guetzévitch, "La Pensée politique et constitutionnelle de la Résistance," in Michel and Mirkine-Guetzévitch, eds., Les Idées politiques, pp. 40–41.

rection is inseparable from the national liberation." [87] Thus, De Gaulle was the ideal rallying point for all the resistance movements, including the Communists.

The French Communists had to endorse "unity of action" because they relied for military supplies on contacts with Fighting France or with British Intelligence. Neither of the latter groups would have been willing to supply the Communists if the Party leadership had been responsible for disrupting a common effort against the Germans.

Despite the pronouncements of the Soviet press, France gave no evidence prior to 1944 of a massive resistance such as that in Yugoslavia or even those in Greece and Poland. One problem was that of Communist leadership. The able and courageous head of the Communist-dominated FTP, Charles Tillon, a member of the Political Bureau of the Party, did not have Tito's power and prestige, and his activities were strongly influenced, if not dictated, by other Party leaders. However, he hoped to emulate the Yugoslav leader and, though this was to become evidence only in 1944 and again in 1952, he favored a more active and independent line than did Thorez and Duclos. His inability to combine military prowess with political control over the Party hampered his attempts to form a large Communist underground army.[88]

A second obstacle lay in the situation of the French Army of 1939–40, which, unlike many of the Yugoslav units, had surrendered and had for the most part been deported to Germany. It was difficult for the French Resistance in general and the Communists in particular to get hold of quantities of arms and munitions. There were also great geographical handicaps to a successful resistance movement, let alone a widespread guerrilla war. Until November, 1942, the northern, or occupied, half of France offered no natural retreats or fortresses from which large-scale underground units could attack and in which they could take refuge from German armor and aircraft. There were neither immense tracts of forest, as in Poland, nor rugged mountainous regions like those of Yugoslavia. After the southward expansion of the occupation zone in November,

[87] De Gaulle, *Discours,* II, 45.
[88] Interview with Pierre Hervé.

1942, a slow and danger-strewn process of organizing a large maquis began in the southern zone. One such redoubt, at Vercors, claimed a force of 30,000 men by March, 1943. This group and others like it formed the Armée Secrète, the military counterpart of a non-Communist Resistance front in the south. The Armée's strategy, contrary to that of the FTP, was to build up large concentrations in the mountainous areas in order to establish bases from which to harass the Germans during the Allied landings.

Lastly, most of the French youth remained indifferent to the call of the maquis until 1943, when the Germans began drafting young Frenchmen to work in German factories. By comparison, in other countries many of the partisan recruits left their homes to join the underground fighting because of the physical dangers they ran by remaining at home. There were no large-scale massacres in France, except of Communists, until 1944. However, it cannot be denied that there were other motives for inaction, motives that were deeply rooted in the French political and social structure. The Party itself faced up to this serious situation when it declared, in late 1942 and early 1943, that there simply were not enough FTP to carry on the struggle with full force.[89]

On the Eve of Stalingrad

By the end of 1942 the short-term aims of Soviet foreign policy were clear. The USSR was appealing for "unity of action" of peoples and governments in the war against Nazi Germany. It had established diplomatic relations with the governments-in-exile, as well as in signing treaties of alliance with the United States and Great Britain. Moscow was urging the various Communist parties to cooperate with all democratic elements in the Resistance and in the exiled governments. In all these ways it sought to rally military and political support for its life-and-death struggle. The demands and appeals for active assistance reached a climax in the summer of 1942, when the USSR was in serious military straits. Stalin wanted a second front or, lacking that for the time being, insurrection against the German army of occupation. Though neither mate-

[89] *La Vie du Parti*, December, 1942, p. 6, and January, 1943, p. 7.

rialized, Stalin continued to insist on their importance and emphasized that the growth of the Resistance would bring closer the day of the Allied landings.

The Soviet leaders showed considerable caution in furthering their political interests. They attempted to cultivate De Gaulle without antagonizing the Western Allies. Stalin did not challenge openly the Anglo-American dealings with a representative of the Vichy government, Admiral Darlan, in North Africa. In part the Soviet reluctance to recognize De Gaulle's cabinet as the provisional government of France was due to Roosevelt's opposition. After all, the second front and military supplies still came first.

The long-range aims of the Soviet and the French Communist policies were not as clear. The Communist cooperation with the West was marked on all levels by restraint, if not distrust. Neither the Soviet nor the French Communist leaders had publicly renounced their avowed revolutionary aims. Though the French Party promised allegiance to De Gaulle and the Soviet Union endorsed this, the French Communist press continued to give a predominant place to the victories of the Red Army and to Stalin's policy statements. Furthermore, from the outset the French Communist definition of "unity of action" was limited in time—"until the liberation." It gradually became apparent that it was also limited in scope; the Communist forces refused to unite or merge with other groups if that meant giving up their separate identity or organization. Much like the Soviet Union in its relations with the Western governments, the French Communist Party did not surrender or limit its freedom of action.

Was the Soviet or the French Communist policy undergoing a fundamental change, and was the evident suspicion of the West just a residue of antipathy? Or was the new Communist line a temporary expedient destined to last only for the duration of the war, and were the misunderstandings with democratic leaders evidence of lasting basic differences between two political systems?

CHAPTER II

The Superficial Friendship

THE SOVIET VICTORY at Stalingrad in the winter of 1942–43
enabled the Soviet leaders to raise their sights above the goal of
national survival and to embark on a more flexible and more ambitious foreign policy. For the first time since the beginning of the
war, the Soviet leaders began to discuss publicly the political aspects of the conflict. In January, 1943, a Soviet commentator
warned that

to neglect the demands of politics for "purely" strategic interests is
fraught with dangerous consequences, a fact which the Patriotic War
again underlines. The strategy of the Red Army grows out of the basic
demands of politics. Strategy is obliged to proceed from the political
situation.

Then he quoted Lenin in support of his position:

The philistine does not understand that war is a "continuation of politics," and that is why he limits himself to "the enemy attacks," "the
enemy is invading my country," not finding out which classes and which
political goals cause wars.[1]

It was clear to Moscow that the enormous pressure of the military
defeats had been lifted. Now was the time to begin considering
Soviet war aims with an eye to preventing any repetition of the
German attack. The great victory at Stalingrad, together with the
failure of the Allies to mount a second front in 1943, strengthened
the position of the Soviet leaders in the diplomatic sphere. How
could Moscow take advantage of this situation? Would the Soviet–
Free French relationship change?

The strong Soviet posture encouraged the Communist parties in

[1] E. Razin, "Lenin o sushchnosti voiny" [Lenin on the Nature of War],
Bol'shevik, No. 1 (January, 1943), pp. 47–48.

Europe to step up their military and political activities, resulting in the growth of the partisan movements and the rapid expansion of Communist influence in the occupied countries. The governments-in-exile were obliged to take a fresh look at this new and powerful factor. New political combinations began to emerge, and the position of the French Communist Party was profoundly affected.

The great importance of these questions for Europe in 1943 underlined a radical change which had taken place in the power status of the local Communist parties and of the Soviet Union itself. The fact that political agreements between Communists and non-Communists were now inescapable indicated that the Second World War was bringing about a basic realignment of political forces in Europe.

The USSR and the Western Powers

Throughout Europe the Communists carried on their policy under the slogan of "unity of action." The Soviet leaders still needed massive military assistance from the West; the need for a second front had not diminished. Stalin was greatly disturbed when he learned from Churchill in February, 1943, that a second front was envisaged only for the late summer of 1943. Stalin wanted

the opening of a second front in the west at a date much earlier than the one mentioned. So that the enemy should not be given a chance to recover, it is very important, to my mind, that the blow from the west, instead of being put off until the second half of the year, be delivered in spring or early summer.[2]

Stalin was also displeased by the slow progress of the Anglo-American campaign in North Africa. Because the Allies had not pressed the Axis army in Tunisia, the Germans had been able, he asserted, to transfer thirty-six divisions from Western Europe to the eastern front. Although the Soviet leader welcomed the plans to invade Sicily, he pointed out that such an offensive "can by no means replace a second front in France."[3]

[2] *Correspondence*, No. 114, Stalin to Churchill, February 16, 1943, I, 95.
[3] *Ibid.*, No. 129, Stalin to Churchill, March 15, 1943, I, 106.

Allied economic aid to the USSR once again suffered a severe setback in the spring of 1943 with the decision, because of German naval superiority in Norwegian waters, to postpone the sending of new convoys to the Soviet Union until September, 1943. Stalin was again dismayed at what he condemned as a "catastrophic cut in the delivery of strategic raw materials and munitions to the Soviet Union." [4]

Because of the continued need for Western aid, it was necessary for the Soviet Union to make concessions to Western public opinion, even if these were more apparent than real. The most spectacular of Moscow's obeisances to the cause of inter-Allied unity was the disbanding of the Communist International. On May 23, 1943, it was announced that the Comintern had been dissolved and all its members freed of their responsibilities to that organization. The purpose of this symbolic act was made clear in the conclusion of the statement:

The Executive Presidium of the Communist International calls upon all supporters of the Communist International to concentrate their strength in all-out support of and participation in the war of the liberation of peoples and of governments of the anti-Hitlerite coalition for the quickest destruction of the deadly enemy of the workers—German fascism, its allies and satellites.[5]

Several days later, Stalin explained further the significance of the dissolution. The decision, he said, was a "correct one" because "it makes easier the organization of a common onslaught of all freedom-loving nations against the common enemy—Hitlerism." The dissolution

unmasks the Hitlerites' lie that "Moscow" interferes deliberately in the life of other countries as if to "bolshevize" them. It unmasks the slander of the enemies of communism in the working class that the Communist parties of various countries act, not in the interests of their people, but as though at the orders of others. . . . It makes easier the work of the freedom-loving peoples by uniting the progressive forces of their countries, irrespective of their political affiliations and spiritual tendencies, in one national freedom camp—for the expanding struggle against fas-

[4] *Ibid.*, No. 138, Stalin to Churchill, April 2, 1943, I, 112.
[5] *Pravda*, May 23, 1943.

cism. It makes easier the work of the patriots of all countries in uniting all freedom-loving people in one international camp for the struggle against the threat of world domination of Hitlerism, clearing the path to the organization in the future of the well-being of peoples on the basis of their equal rights.

All these factors when taken together, Stalin concluded, will "lead to the further strengthening of the United front of allies and other United Nations." [6]

It is not yet possible to determine on the basis of documents whether or how far the dissolution of the Comintern affected the relationship between the Soviet Union and the Communist parties of Europe. In the light of the propaganda and actions of those parties after the event, it would appear that the formal loosening of ties did not bring with it any change in that relationship. As we have seen, the occupation of most of Europe by Hitler forced various Communist parties to find new ways to link the European underground movements and to coordinate their activities. As a matter of fact, the Comintern lost much of its original significance in 1937, when many of its personalities, such as Otto Kuusinen, and presumably most of its functions were transferred to a special section of the Communist Party Secretariat in Moscow. The Soviet announcement simply enabled the local parties to declare, as did the French Communist Party, that the dissolution "shows up clearly the lying character of the Hitlerite allegations about the so-called 'Bolshevization' of the various countries . . . and underlines what the Communists have never stopped repeating, namely, that they do not impose by force from the outside a regime not of the people's choice." [7]

While the Soviet leadership strove, through dissolving the Comintern, to reassure its Western allies of its sincere desire to cooperate with them for the sole purpose of winning the war, Moscow continued to press for other and stronger action by them against Ger-

---

[6] "Otvet tov. I. V. Stalina na vopros glavnogo korrespondenta angliiskogo agentstva Reitera" [Comrade I. V. Stalin's Answer to the Question by the Chief Correspondent of Reuter's English Agency], *Izvestiia*, May 30, 1943.

[7] *La Vie du Parti,* June, 1943, p. 1. See John A. Armstrong, *The Politics of Totalitarianism,* New York, 1961, pp. 155–156 for the effects of the dissolution on the Comintern staff.

many. On the second anniversary of the German attack, *Izvestiia* proclaimed that

the balance of power has shifted in the course of the war in our favor and in favor of our allies. But this is not enough for victory. Now all depends on whether our allies make use of the favorable conditions for the creation of a second front on the Continent of Europe, for without a second front the victory over Hitlerite Germany is impossible.[8]

This point was urged even more sharply on Allied statesmen at the Foreign Ministers' Conference at Moscow in October, 1943. The agenda for the meetings was discussed in an exchange of messages between the Big Three. "The Russians," said Churchill, "made one suggestion and one suggestion only—'the consideration of measures to shorten the duration of the war against Germany and her allies in Europe.'" The Soviet Union made three proposals in this connection: an invasion of northern France; an invitation to the Turks to join the Allies; a request to Sweden to provide air bases for the Allies. At the conference, according to Eden, "the Russians were completely and blindly set on our invasion of northern France. It was the only decision in which they took an absorbing interest." [9] When the Soviet representatives were informed that the invasion of the Continent was planned for the spring of 1944, they were very pleased.[10]

At the Moscow Conference, Soviet leaders made what appeared to be their second major concession to Western opinion by signing the Four Power Declaration on General Security. By it the signatories pledged themselves to establish an international organization to keep the peace, renounced the use of military force to change the goverments of the liberated countries and in general signified their willingness to cooperate in international affairs. The Soviet press emphasized two results of the conference: "the decision and the will of the peoples of the three great countries to carry on the cause of the struggle with the German-Fascist bandits to the end,

[8] "Dva goda otechestvennoi voiny Sovetskogo Soiuza" [Two Years of the Patriotic War of the Soviet Union], *Izvestiia*, June 22, 1943.
[9] Churchill, *The Second World War*, V, 284, 285, 288. See also Deane, *The Strange Alliance*, pp. 8, 16.
[10] Deane, *The Strange Alliance*, pp. 18–19.

to hasten the defeat of the enemy"; and "the aspiration of the peoples of the Allied countries toward a further solidarity of strength against the common enemy and toward cooperation in the postwar period in the interests of peace and the security of peoples." [11]

The question must be raised again whether the Soviet commitment to postwar cooperation was a significant concession to the Allies, and especially to the Americans. It has already been pointed out elsewhere that Stalin believed that the purpose of an international organization should be limited to preventing a resurgence of fascism and to rehabilitating the war-torn countries. In general, the Soviet leaders were not at all enthusiastic about the international organization.[12] Did the Soviet leaders support only this type of limited cooperation? What did they expect from the West in return?

At the Teheran Conference in November, 1943, Moscow defined cooperation in terms of an overwhelming Allied invasion of northern France. The Russians bitterly opposed all of Churchill's proposals for nibbling away at "Fortress Europe" by keeping up the pressure on the Germans in Italy, Yugoslavia, and the Aegean Sea. Stalin "believed that north or northwestern France was the place for Anglo-American forces to attack. . . . It would be a mistake to send part of the Allied forces to Turkey and elsewhere and part to southern France." In a private conversation with Churchill, Stalin was even more insistent and darkly hinted that "if there was no big change in the European war in 1944, it would be very difficult for the Russians to carry on. They were war-weary. He feared that a feeling of isolation might develop in the Red Army." [13]

Soviet concern for "unity of action" in the Resistance and for cooperation with the West seemed to rest on considerations of military necessity, but it had a strong political motivation as well. Each

---

[11] "Znachenie Moskovskoi Konferentsii" [The Meaning of the Moscow Conference], *Izvestiia*, November 2, 1943.

[12] Fuller, "Soviet Policy in the United Nations," *The Annals of the American Academy of Political and Social Science*, CCLXIII (May, 1949), 142–43.

[13] Churchill, *The Second World War*, V, 352–55, 380; *Foreign Relations of the United States, Diplomatic Papers: Conferences of Cairo and Teheran*, pp. 489–95.

new gesture toward cooperation, as in dissolving the Comintern and agreeing to participate in a postwar international organization, not only mollified the United States and Great Britain but also opened the way for greater Communist activity in the occupied countries under the guise of participation in a truly patriotic struggle. The USSR further encouraged this trend by entering into closer relations with the governments, such as those of France and Czechoslovakia, which were willing to accept cooperation with their own Communists or with the Soviet Union or both, while its relations with the governments-in-exile of Greece, Yugoslavia, and Poland— governments which did not or would not accept cooperation with the USSR—deteriorated. Though the Soviet definition of cooperation varied to some degree from country to country, it usually included the participation of Communists in the government-in-exile under the slogan of "governments of national unity." The amount of pressure the Soviet Union was willing to exert to gain advantages for the Communists varied according to the geographical location of the country, the military position of the Red Army, and the attitude of the Western Allies.

From Stalingrad to the invasion of France in June, 1944, Soviet and local Communist activity in Eastern Europe entered a more dynamic phase, in sharp contrast to the course of Franco-Soviet relations. By mid-1944 events in Eastern Europe were beginning to foreshadow clearly the enormous political changes which would result from the war. The traditional ruling circles in many countries had once regarded the USSR with fear and disdain and had persecuted the local Communist parties. Now the Red Army was about to overrun their frontiers in great strength with the nuclei of Communist governments in its baggage trains. The power of Western Europe had declined, and the United States was unable or unwilling to assert its power in Eastern Europe.[14] The Soviet insistence on an increased share of influence in Eastern Europe was the result of growing Soviet power in the area. Between Stalingrad and the Allied landings in Normandy, Soviet policy toward France was

[14] Mosely, "Hopes and Failures," in Kertesz, ed., The Fate of East Central Europe, pp. 57–58.

influenced by the fact that unless the Allies failed to open a
second front, the Soviet Union would have no way of directly influencing or hastening the return of the Free French to France.

The Soviet Union and Fighting France: Superficial Friendship and Basic Disagreements

Officially and publicly the Soviet leaders continued to give moral
support to De Gaulle's efforts to recapture for France a place in the
sun. However, they did not support him as much as he had expected
and in some cases not even as much as they had promised. During
the De Gaulle-Giraud controversy in North Africa, Stalin followed
a policy of cordial restraint in his dealings with the French and the
Western Allies. De Gaulle insisted that his rivalry with Giraud for
leadership of French North Africa had caused a rupture between
him and the United States, and he wanted to know the Soviet position on the matter. He was informed that "the policy of the USSR
involved support or sympathy with all anti-Hitlerite forces which,
in one way or another, are taking an active part in the struggle
against Hitlerite Germany." De Gaulle was "obviously displeased"
by the answer and noted that "if Giraud took complete power in
France, then France would become a weapon of the reactionary
French circles and . . . the result would not be advantageous for
Russia." Again Moscow turned down this gambit and replied that
"without the unity of all anti-Hitlerite forces, whatever differences
they may have between them, a powerful front of the Allies in
this colossal war could not be created." [15] At the same time, the
Soviet press stressed the importance of the unity of all Frenchmen
without supporting either of the rivals.[16]

Stalin considered the establishment, on June 3, 1943, of the
Comité Français de la Libération Nationale (CFLN) a triumph for
his North African policy. This body, the new executive organization

[15] *SFO*, No. 55, Bogomolov to the Commissariat of Foreign Affairs, May 11, 1943, p. 132.

[16] See, for example, Monin, "Krasnaia armiia sozdala fundament" [The Red Army Established the Foundation], *Bol'shevik*, No. 2 (January, 1943), pp. 79–80; *Izvestiia*, March 16, 1943, merely noted the exchange of messages between De Gaulle and Giraud concerning their agreement in principle to work together in the National Committee.

of Fighting France, was made up of supporters of De Gaulle and Giraud. Moscow wanted to recognize the Committee at once, but Churchill intervened, explaining to Stalin that the Western Allies were not prepared to take such action and that unilateral recognition by the USSR "would reveal a difference of view between the Soviet government and the Western Allies, which would be most regrettable." [17] Stalin was disturbed by the message because

from the moment of the French surrender General de Gaulle had headed the anti-Hitler forces of France and the struggle of the French patriots united around Fighting France. Since, however, the British government requests that the recognition of the French Committee be postponed and through its ambassador has given the assurance that no steps will be taken in this matter without consulting the Soviet government, the Soviet government is prepared to meet the British government halfway.

Stalin stressed "the Soviet interest in French affairs" and requested "timely information" on Western intentions toward De Gaulle.[18]

The Soviet leaders told the French about this disagreement with the West in order to show that Moscow favored De Gaulle. But they did this in such a way as to prevent De Gaulle from driving a wedge between the West and Moscow. On June 23, 1943, Vyshinskii invited Garreau to the commissariat and told him that the Soviet government was prepared to recognize the Committee, but had to defer to the wishes of London and Washington, which opposed recognition. The same day the London radio announced that the North African crisis had been settled. General Giraud was to command the military forces of Fighting France and De Gaulle was to control civil affairs.[19] This meant that the United States and Great Britain no longer had any reason to delay recognition of the Committee. Since there was now no basis for disagreement between the West and Moscow over recognition, there was not much point in the Gaullists using the information Vyshinskii had given them to put diplomatic pressure on London and Washington.

[17] *SFO*, No. 60, A. Kerr to V. M. Molotov, June 15, 1943, p. 152; No. 65, Molotov to Kerr, June 19, 1943, p. 164; No. 69, Kerr to Molotov, June 23, 1943, p. 168; and *Correspondence*, No. 164, Churchill to Stalin, June 23, 1943, I, 136.

[18] *Correspondence*, No. 166, Stalin to Churchill, June 26, 1943, I, 139–40.

[19] *SFO*, No. 71, A. Vyshinskii to the Commissariat of Foreign Affairs, June 23, 1943, p. 171.

In August 1943, when the United States and Great Britain recognized the French National Committee, Moscow declared that the Committee represented "the interests of the French Republic" and was "the only executive organ and the only qualified representative of all French patriots in the struggle against Hitlerism." This Soviet definition of the Committee's powers was more generous than that of the Western Allies.[20] At the same time Molotov reiterated that the USSR had tried unsuccessfully to persuade the British and the Americans to recognize the Fighting French earlier and that the West also had delayed the departure of a Soviet representative to Algiers. However, Molotov concluded, in both cases the Soviet view finally prevailed. The French representative in Moscow could only reply, "You are our savior." [21]

Despite the satisfactory outcome of this incident for Moscow, Molotov complained to the Americans that the Soviet Union was "little informed on what is happening in North Africa" and wanted to send Bogomolov to Algiers as its representative. He was also disturbed by the information that the United States wished to postpone the arrival of a Soviet representative in North Africa.[22] According to Andrei Gromyko, Secretary Hull insisted that the presence of Bogomolov in Algiers "would strengthen the agitation of the De Gaullists against Giraud." [23] The Soviet leaders were, in fact, more concerned with obtaining information about the political situation and establishing contact with the important group of French Communists in Algiers than with encouraging De Gaulle against Giraud. Similarly, during the negotiations for an armistice

[20] De Gaulle, *Mémoires*, II, 137. The statement of the United States government read: "The Committee is recognized as the administrator of the overseas territories which are placed under its authority." It further specified that this communiqué "did not constitute the recognition of a government of France or of the French Empire by the United States." Great Britain, after having again expressed the same sentiments as those in the first part of the American declaration, added: "In the eyes of Great Britain the Committee is the organ qualified to exercise the conduct of the French effort in the war." *L'Année politique, 1945*, pp. 25–26.

[21] *SFO*, No. 91, Notes of Molotov on conversation with Schmidtlein, August 26, 1943, p. 192.

[22] *Ibid.*, No. 76, Notes of Molotov on conversation with W. Standley, July 1, 1943, p. 177.

[23] *Ibid.*, No. 78, A. Gromyko to the Commissariat of Foreign Affairs, July 5, 1943, p. 179.

with Italy, Moscow was eager to send its representatives—in that case, Vyshinskii and a Moscow-trained Italian Communist, Palmiro Togliatti—to Italy so that they could report on the political situation and instruct the Italian Communists.[24]

During the negotiations for the surrender of Italy, the Soviet leaders continued to flatter De Gaulle and give him verbal encouragement, though they were careful to avoid involvement in his disputes with the Western Allies. De Gaulle was irritated that the French had not been represented at the acceptance of the Italian capitulation and that they had not been consulted on the armistice terms.[25] Moscow did not intervene in the misunderstanding. It did attempt to appear as the champion of French interests at high-level conferences to which the French were not invited. During the October Conference of Foreign Ministers in Moscow, Bogomolov assured De Gaulle that not only was the Mediterranean Commission or Advisory Council for Italy a Soviet idea, but that his government was demanding that France be invited to become a member of it.[26] This simply was not true. Eden originally proposed the appointment of the commission, defined its duties, and urged the immediate inclusion of France in it; and Churchill first proposed French membership to Stalin.[27]

The Soviet government had several claims to make against Italy and was anxious to secure French support for them. On November 29, 1943, Vyshinskii, appointed to the Advisory Council for Italy, assured De Gaulle of his government's desire to work closely with the French in order to "perpare the creation in Italy of a democratic regime capable of getting Italy into the war against Germany and of leading the country toward a peaceful destiny." He further ex-

[24] Kogan, *Italy and the Allies*, p. 59.

[25] For the Western position see Churchill, *The Second World War*, V, 136, and Hull, II, 1428. For General de Gaulle's position see his *Mémoires*, II, 137–40.

[26] De Gaulle, *Mémoires*, II, 192.

[27] Hull, *Memoirs*, II, 1284. The Commission had the duty of watching over the control machinery in Italy which would enforce the terms of surrender. Greece and Yugoslavia were, according to the original proposal, to be added to the Commission at a later date. *Correspondence*, No. 178, Churchill to Stalin, August 30, 1943, I, 152. Stalin agreed, *ibid.*, No. 179, Stalin to Churchill, August 31, 1943, but was willing to postpone French participation when President Roosevelt expressed doubts on the matter. *Ibid.*, No. 185, Stalin to Churchill, September 8, 1943, I, 157.

pressed his hope that the French Committee would not consider the USSR one of the powers which would intervene to prevent the complete independence of the Committee's authority in its dealings with the French people. Vyshinskii said that, in Stalin's personal opinion, no European question could be regulated without the participation of France. The Soviet representative felt himself in agreement with De Gaulle on the relations between their countries and the United States, on the need to prevent German aggression, and on the Italian problem. Concluding his conversation, Vyshinskii reiterated that it was the Soviet Union which had taken the initiative in bringing the French into the Mediterranean Commission.[28] Beyond misleading the French as to who were their real friends, the Soviet government made no further attempt at this time to win De Gaulle over to its side. The Soviet leaders hoped that the French would see some advantages in working with them on the commission. They could not afford to promise the French anything concrete because this might irritate the Western Allies at a time when the long-promised second front seemed about to materialize.

Despite these Soviet assurances to De Gaulle, the course of Franco-Soviet relations was not smooth. The USSR was concerned with the problems of France's role in the final victory and in the postwar settlement, and with the French attitude toward Soviet relations with Poland. In January, 1944, when President Beneš of Czechoslovakia returned from Moscow, he told De Gaulle that Stalin had openly expressed an attitude of reserve toward the CFLN. The Soviet leaders, according to Beneš, were not sure of the evolution of French politics. They were asking whether the two opposite groups of Pétainists and resisters would neutralize and paralyze the nation's policies. This very uncertainty about the future of France, Beneš said, had led him to go to Moscow, for Czechoslovakia could no longer count on the lasting recovery of its former ally.[29]

[28] Note of the cabinet of General de Gaulle on the subject of the conversation with Mr. Vyshinskii on November 23, 1943, as quoted in De Gaulle, *Mémoires*, Documents, II, 603–6.

[29] Note on the conversation of President Beneš with General de Gaulle and René Massigli on January 2–3, 1944, as quoted in De Gaulle, *Mémoires*, Documents, II, 616.

Soviet concern over the future role of France increased with the development of a more ramified and independent Gaullist foreign policy. As early as May, 1943, Bogomolov asked De Gaulle how he regarded the Soviet-Polish conflict. The French leader explained that he "was interested in the existence of a free, independent Poland, but, on the other hand, France was also interested in Russia's having the best strategic frontier in the west and, of course, on the Baltic coast." He implied further that "if he came to power, then France, without doubt, would support Russia on the frontier question in the spirit of the Curzon line." [30]

The Soviet leaders may not have been reassured by these words, because they were disturbed by certain aspects of French policy toward Poland. An especially sharp blow for Moscow was the transfer by the French Committee to the Polish government in London of the important gold reserves which the State Bank of Poland had entrusted to the Bank of France in September, 1939. Bogomolov protested vigorously to De Gaulle: "The Soviet Union raises a formal protest against the transfer of Polish gold to the refugee government in London." He then bluntly informed De Gaulle that "the latter will not be the government of Poland tomorrow." [31]

Meanwhile, at the Teheran Conference, unknown to the Free French, Stalin expressed grave reservations about De Gaulle's ability to direct the future course of French policy. He bitterly denounced the French ruling class for "helping our common enemy Germany by making available French ports, materials, machines, etc., for the German war effort." The trouble with De Gaulle, Stalin said, was "that this [his?] movement had no communication with physical France, which should be punished for its attitude during this war. De Gaulle acts as though he were the head of a great state, whereas, in fact, it actually commands little power." [32]

Throughout the conference Stalin and Molotov played up the collaborationist role of the French and insisted at one point that after the war France must be stripped of its colonial empire. "It

[30] SFO, No. 55, Bogomolov to the Commissariat of Foreign Affairs, May 11, 1943, p. 133.

[31] De Gaulle, Mémoires, II, 208. The transfer was made in March, 1944.

[32] Foreign Relations of the United States, Diplomatic Papers: Conferences of Cairo and Teheran, p. 484.

would be not only unjust but dangerous," Stalin continued, "to leave in French hands any important strategic point after the war." Lebanon, Dakar, and Bizerte were suggested as points of importance, but, above all, in Stalin's words, "France should not get back Indo-China." [33]

Furthermore, the Soviet leaders now began to receive information concerning De Gaulle's views on the postwar political structure of Europe which increased their suspicions of his role as the possible future leader of France. Gromyko reported from Washington that the State Department considered De Gaulle's recent political position "less radical" and less strongly anti-Vichy than in the past. Consequently, according to Gromyko, anti-Gaullist Frenchmen in America

fear very much the postwar plans of the Americans and English with regard to France. They believe that specific influential circles in the United States (the State Department and financial circles) nourish the hope that they will succeed in bringing France into the American economic sphere of influence due to the industrial backwardness of France. These circles also consider that the United States should apply pressure to bring France into the Anglo-American political sphere of influence.

Far more menacing to Soviet interests was Gromyko's report that "a plan for the creation of a postwar bloc of European countries, including France, Belgium, Holland, Spain [and] Italy, is being worked out in the State Department. According to its supporters, this bloc should be controlled in every possible way by the United States and Great Britain." [34]

In February and March, 1944, as this disquieting information was being received in Moscow, General de Gaulle came out in favor of an organization of the states of Western Europe which could be extended eventually to the Arab countries of the Near East. Any idea of a European bloc or federation was anathema to the Soviet leaders. At the Moscow Conference in October, 1943, Molotov had denounced Eden's idea of an East European federation as a British attempt to revive the *cordon sanitaire*. The Western bloc would

[33] *Ibid.*, pp. 485, 509. See also pp. 514, 568–69.
[34] *SFO*, No. 130, Gromyko to the Commissariat of Foreign Affairs, February 25, 1944, p. 241.

mean, in essence, a counterweight to Soviet power in Eastern Europe and the possible revival of the *cordon sanitaire,* though much farther to the west. Bogomolov was instructed to seek a clarification of De Gaulle's plan, and, in Moscow, Dekanosov pressed Garreau to explain its details. The French Communists attacked the idea immediately.[35]

On February 8, 1944, the Soviet leaders found further justification for their suspicions about a Western bloc in the Anglo-French financial agreement and protocol on mutual aid. Vyshinskii expressed surprise that the French had not informed the Soviet government on the course of the negotiations and that a political as well as an economic agreement had been signed. In replying, Garreau added fuel to the smoldering resentment by complaining that "not all the members [of the French National Committee] held similar views about the Soviet Union and that there are many people who do not sympathize with the Soviet Union namely because it is Soviet." Vyshinskii sharply retorted that "if the French Committee is going to have its policy toward the USSR conducted by these Vichyite influences, . . . then the French Committee, above all, will be the loser." [36]

The French representative in Moscow, Roger Garreau, by virtue of his distrust and dislike of the United States and Great Britain, played an important role in arousing Soviet suspicions of American policy. He not only continued to denounce the Western Allies, but insisted that the French Committee was under great pressure from the Americans and British, "who had at their command the means to determine its fate." [37]

As a result of these developments, the Soviet Union began to protest against what it considered a marked reluctance on the part of the British and the Americans to consult with Moscow on matters concerning France. Following a statement by Eden in the House of Commons dealing with the administration of liberated French territory, the Soviet government charged:

[35] *La Vie du Parti,* February, 1944, p. 14. Also see below, p. 77.
[36] *SFO,* No. 128, Vyshinskii to the Commissariat of Foreign Affairs, February 12, 1944, pp. 239–40.
[37] *Ibid.,* and No. 131, M. Sergeev to the Commissariat of Foreign Affairs, March 6, 1944, p. 245.

it is clear that two governments, the British and the United States, will act together on the question of the administration of French territory after its liberation, excluding the Soviet government from participating in this affair. In this way the declaration of Mr. Eden contradicts what was agreed between the three governments at the Moscow Conference. Moscow demanded a clarification of the British point of view.[38]

Finally, there was a disagreement between Moscow and De Gaulle over relations with the Italian government of Marshal Pietro Badoglio. The Soviet government, unlike De Gaulle, offered no opposition to the monarchical regime in Italy in order to assure "the union of all anti-Fascists for the war of liberation from the Axis." When, in a conversation with Bogomolov, General de Gaulle explained that French claims on Italy were based on the need for military security, Bogomolov returned to the offensive in typical Soviet fashion by protesting the publication in *L'Echo d'Alger* of a military map which represented the Polish frontiers as those of 1939.[39]

The Soviet diplomats tried to shrug off all these difficulties by maintaining that "unity of action" was necessary above all. For example, when Dekanosov and Garreau were discussing the problem of the extreme reserve which had arisen in the relations between the two governments, the Soviet Deputy Minister brushed the annoyance aside with the following sentiment:

What is essentially important for the two Allied countries is a common will to exert all their efforts on the internal and external planes to hasten the liberation of Europe, annihilate Hitler, and reestablish France in its power [which is] indispensable for the equilibrium of the world.

He added that the Soviet attitude toward France has been clear and had never wavered since

the day after the German aggression. Often, even though it had had to take into account certain circumstances, to avoid hurting the sensitivity of its two great allies, to abstain from giving us all the support which we would have liked to receive and which it would have been happy to be able to grant, these were only measures of adaptation to temporary

[38] *Ibid.*, No. 133, Memorandum of the Soviet Government to the British Government, March 25, 1944, p. 251.

[39] Note of the cabinet of General de Gaulle on the subject of his conversation with Mr. Bogomolov on April 28, 1944, as quoted in De Gaulle, *Mémoires, Documents*, II, 633.

circumstances of a policy which basically and essentially never failed us in a time of need.[40]

Yet these statements of general policy could not obscure the divergences in diplomatic activity between the USSR and France. This, indeed, was the primary difficulty between the two governments. The Soviet Union was not willing to transform its words of good will into actions in the field of international politics. By the spring of 1944 Dekanosov's explanation of this attitude as a Soviet desire to avoid antagonizing the Western Allies was becoming an outdated excuse, for the West was drawing closer to De Gaulle. It was in fact this very rapprochement which looked to Stalin suspiciously like a Western bloc. In Moscow in September, 1943, after General Petit, head of the French military mission, had thanked Stalin profusely for some minor Soviet concessions to the French, the Soviet leader replied "that France would recover in the future and then the French would adopt another tone." [41] Stalin was never one to entertain any illusions about the political value of gratitude.

The French Communists and De Gaulle

When the French Communist Party took a stand on any international issue, it invariably supported the Soviet position. The Party showed special concern over the outcome of the disagreement between De Gaulle and Giraud. In February, 1943, after the French National Committee in London had proposed a new basis for co-operation, the Party asked "that the agreement concluded between De Gaulle and Giraud lead to some concrete decisions and to a renewal of a single leadership of all the French forces fighting against Hitler outside the metropolitan area, because France demands the union of all her sons in the struggle against the enemy and against the traitors." Within France the Party expressed its "hope" that De Gaulle would be the sole political leader and Giraud the military leader of the Fighting French.[42] From his distant vantage point in

---

[40] Telegram from Garreau to CFLN in Algiers, Moscow, March 31, 1944, as quoted in *ibid.*, Documents, II, 621.

[41] *SFO*, No. 103, Notes on conversation between Stalin and Petit, September 15, 1943, p. 210.

[42] *L'Humanité*, No. 202 (February 2, 1943), No. 211 (April 1, 1943).

Moscow, Maurice Thorez expressed disappointment that "the recent interview at Casablanca between General Giraud and General de Gaulle does not seem to have solved all problems. Furthermore, as long as there is no complete unity, with a single commander of the French military forces, the organization of the new army cannot seriously move ahead." [43]

At the same time Giraud released twenty-seven Communists who had been imprisoned in the Maison Carrée in Algiers. One of the Communists was quoted in the Soviet press as having stated that "the unity of all Frenchmen is the best instrument of struggle against Hitlerism—the mortal enemy of France. Most of all, we wish this unity, and now, when we find ourselves free, we will exert all our strength in order to unite all Frenchmen under one banner." [44] Thus, both the French Communists and the Soviet government brushed aside any opportunity to weaken De Gaulle by splitting his support in North Africa.

To further its own plans, the Party preferred to see the politically indifferent Giraud in command of the military forces. Just how this situation could be advantageous to them was demonstrated during the liberation of Corsica, in September, 1943.[45] Despite the Communist support of separate military and civilian leadership, the Party never committed itself to endorse Giraud as a rival to De Gaulle. Its purpose was to further "unity of action" and to split the French Resistance. In any case, with his record of allegiance to Marshal Pétain, Giraud was hardly the man around whom the Party could rally.

Even before Soviet recognition of the French Committee, the French Communist Party "pledged to De Gaulle and Giraud its firm will to support the French Committee of National Liberation by all means in its power, in the indispensable task of unifying the military forces." [46] The Party greeted the Soviet announcement of recognition as a demonstration of "how complete was the Soviet rupture with the clique of Vichy traitors." The Party concluded

[43] Thorez, *Oeuvres*, Book Five, XIX, 155.

[44] *Izvestiia*, March 8, 1943. For the negotiations leading to the release of the Communists see Bonte, *Le Chemin de l'honneur*, pp. 466–68.

[45] See below, p. 86.

[46] *L'Humanité*, No. 233 (July 15, 1943).

that "for all Frenchmen the CFLN is the real government of France." [47] Immediately after this expression of support the French Communists began their agitation for representation in the Committee.

Along with its practical support of Soviet policies, French Communist propaganda extolled the USSR as the liberator of mankind and the savior of France. The tenor of this propaganda was set by Maurice Thorez in his articles in both the Soviet and the French clandestine press. He denounced Laval as the man who had nullified the Franco-Soviet treaty and doomed France to defeat in 1940. However, the "cowardly and traitorous" German attack on the Soviet Union, "the invincible citadel of liberty, progress, and the grandiose future of all mankind," had been the beginning of the end for Laval. The French people, "their enthusiasm kindled by the victories of the Soviet Union," were organizing a growing resistance against the invader. "All of France," Thorez maintained, "is rising against Hitler and Laval." In his recipe for liberation Thorez skillfully blended Communist and nationalist ingredients. In 1942, for example, he appealed to the French peasants:

As for the Communists, everyone knows that they are ruthlessly persecuted by Hitler because they do not want France to be subservient to the Third Reich and because they are firm supporters of the National Front for the Independence of France, because with all their heart and soul they want the liberation for which the proud and courageous soldiers of the Soviet Union are fighting. [48]

After the Soviet victory at Stalingrad Thorez emphasized increasingly that "the victorious offensive of the Red Army is bringing closer the national insurrection" in France. At Stalingrad, he continued, "it was not just the fate of the Soviet Union which was at stake, but also our fate, that of France and all humanity." Therefore, he concluded:

Each Frenchman renders homage to the Red Army . . . to the genius of its supreme commander, Stalin. Every Frenchman is profoundly grateful to the Soviet people, united . . . around its government, around Stalin. Because each Frenchman knows well the very valuable assistance which

[47] *Ibid.*, No. 244 (September 3, 1943).
[48] Thorez, *Oeuvres,* Book Five, XIX, 130, 138.

the Red Army, by virtue of its brilliant offensive, has rendered to the cause of the liberation of France.[49]

In sum, the French Communists loyally toed the Party line set down in Moscow. Despite their agreement to cooperate with De Gaulle, the French Communists continued, in the face of Gaullist opposition, to press for acceptance of their own policies. If the Communists could increase their power and prestige within the French Resistance, then Stalin could count on strong support from them in his relations with General de Gaulle.

By mid-1944 Stalin still regarded De Gaulle as the best man to lead the French Resistance against the enemy. He had given some verbal and diplomatic support to the French National Committee and also had encouraged the French Communist Party to cooperate with De Gaulle. It would have been futile and even foolhardy for the Soviet leaders to sponsor a French national front centered on Thorez and Marty in Moscow. The organization would have withered away, with no prospect of winning any concessions from General de Gaulle. The best way for the USSR to influence French policy remained to support De Gaulle and the "unity of action" in the Resistance movement. However, the cooperation between Moscow and De Gaulle had clearly defined limits. The Soviet leaders were not willing to go much beyond the Western Allies in their support of De Gaulle. They did not offer him any concrete proposals for political cooperation in Europe. They did not try to bring him into the inner councils of the Big Three. Their main purpose was to make it easier for the French to rally their armed forces against the enemy, to increase Soviet prestige among the French people, and to facilitate the efforts of the French Communists to capitalize on their new-found prestige as a leading factor in the Resistance.

[49] *Ibid.*, pp. 142–43.

CHAPTER III

The Communists Prepare for the Liberation

SINCE mid-1941 the French Communists had, as we have seen, pressed for a vigorous war effort and the earliest possible uprising against Germany, along the lines indicated by Moscow. By 1943 they were prepared to do much more than this; their growing prestige and power had made them a political force to be reckoned with. How could the French Communists exploit their position to influence De Gaulle's foreign policy and to shape the political, economic, and social reconstruction of France?

The Communists needed to secure representation in the executive body of the Fighting French movement, the nucleus of a future French government. They also would have to bolster their strength in France by broadening their appeal to the French people and by reestablishing the shattered unity of the French trade-union movement. At the same time, the Party had to expand its own military and propaganda activity. If the Party were successful in pressing the broad line of "unity of action" and republicanism, it could expect to win numerous converts and sympathizers to its side, with the net result of an enormous expansion of Communist influence and power.

The French Communists Enter De Gaulle's Government

Direct participation of the Communist in the central bodies of the Gaullist overseas Resistance did not come about until November, 1943. It came then as a result of General de Gaulle's desire to give his government a more broadly democratic base. Partly in order to counter Allied, and especially American, criticisms of the lack of representative character of his support, De Gaulle had inaugurated a Consultative Assembly at Algiers, to consist of representatives of the Resistance, former deputies who had not voted to give full powers to Marshal Pétain, representatives of Overseas France, and other groups. In the Assembly the twenty-seven Communists in a total of 102 included André Marty, who had recently arrived from Moscow, Fernand Grenier, who had left France for London early in 1943, Etienne Fajon, Florimond Bonte, and François Billoux, all of whom had been released from a Vichy prison in Algiers.

The Communists, however, were not satisfied with their minor share in the direction of the external Resistance. They had been agitating for representation in the far more important policy-making body, the French Committee of National Liberation (CFLN), which had been created on June 3, 1943, to provide an executive branch for the Fighting French movement. The Committee had gradually taken on the form of a provisional government for liberated French territories.

De Gaulle himself was in favor of bringing the Communists into the Committee, and in August, 1943, he asked Grenier to participate. The answer was "Yes," under the conditions that De Gaulle should accept a five-point Communist policy statement and that the Communists would choose the men who were to represent them and also the posts in which they were to serve.

The five-point program stipulated:

(1) the demand to devote all efforts and resources of France and the Empire to the war by forming a powerful anti-Hitlerite army and by arming the patriots in France;

(2) the punishment of all traitors already in the hands of the French Committee and a purge of the public administration of postwar France;

(3) the development of a democratic political and social program for postwar France;

(4) the satisfaction of the legitimate aspirations of Overseas France;

(5) the growth of the role of France in the common struggle of the Allies.[1]

It is significant that the most specific Communist demands were aimed at winning the war and preventing any compromise arrangement with the anti-Communist Vichy regime. Neither of these aims was objectionable to De Gaulle. His dispute with the Communists arose over their insistence on being represented in the policy-making committees, each consisting of three or four men, which ran the administrative departments, or commissariats. This often meant that the Communists were asking for the secretary-generalships of the embryonic ministries. Rather than have representatives of the Communist Party in each commissariat, De Gaulle preferred to offer them the portfolio of a single commissariat.[2]

The Communists accepted this proposal, but they still insisted that, as Grenier put it, "it is the delegation of our Central Committee at Algiers which, following the customs and principles of our Party of the French workers' movement, would designate those among us who would be part of the French Committee of National Liberation." De Gaulle ignored the message and offered Grenier himself the portfolio of the Commissariat of Industry, Commerce, and Agriculture or, if he wished, of Food Supply. The Central Committee reiterated its position and expressed "its regrets that the reorganization of the Committee had been undertaken with methods contrary to the traditions of democracy."

Again ignoring the Communist reply, De Gaulle reorganized the commissariats without the Communists. The latter tried another approach by asking that the Commissariat of Information be given to Etienne Fajon and that another commissariat be created especially "for the coordination of contacts with France." However, they continued, if De Gaulle still insisted on offering them Industry, they would accept it if its powers were expanded to include "the

---

[1] *L'Humanité*, No. 258 (November 15, 1943).

[2] Interview with Michel Debré, former member of the Delegation of the French Committee to metropolitan France and the Commissar of the Republic at Angers. According to Grenier, the Party was willing "eventually to participate in the CFLN on the condition that it or its delegates exercise power and not merely serve in a consultative capacity." Grenier, *C'était ainsi*, p. 173.

pure and simple confiscation of the property of all persons who fall under an order of sanction" and of "enterprises and lands of those who sabotage production."[3] De Gaulle was silent, but it was clear why he refused to accept these proposals. He was the Communists' most formidable rival for control of the Resistance. If he submitted to their demands on this question, he would be setting a dangerous precedent. The Communists would take advantage of his weakness to make further demands. They would try ultimately to force him to share his power with them. Also, the Communists were asking for very important positions. The Commissariat of Information would give them some control over contacts with the internal Resistance; the Commissariat of Industry, as defined by them, would enable a Communist to conduct a political purge in the North African economy and later in the French economy.

The Central Committee made one last attempt to break De Gaulle's position. It nominated Lucien Midol as Commissar of Industrial Production and Etienne Fajon as Commissar of Public Health.[4] When, after some time, the Party had received no reply from De Gaulle, it unleashed a determined propaganda campaign against what it called the "anti-democratic methods" of choosing members of the Committee.[5] In February, 1944, the Central Committee sent a ten-page letter to the French Committee in which it condemned the "anticommunism" manifested by "certain elements which claim to be of the Resistance." It criticized the policies of the French Committee in the military and intelligence fields.[6]

These tactics were to no avail, and meanwhile the Party was losing valuable time by pursuing the argument. The moment for the liberation of France was approaching. It would be to the Communists' advantage to be in the provisional government when the Allies landed in France. Therefore, in April, 1944, Fernand Grenier and François Billoux accepted, on behalf of the delegation of the Central Committee in Algiers, the posts of Commissar of Air and Commissar of State, which had just been offered to them by Gen-

---

[3] Soustelle, *Envers et contre tout*, II, 449–50.

[4] *L'Humanité*, No. 259 (November 19, 1943).

[5] See, for example, *L'Humanité*, No. 261 (December 1, 1943) and No. 262 (December 3, 1943).

[6] Soustelle, *Envers et contre tout*, II. 451.

eral de Gaulle. The basis of their acceptance was still the five-point program. At the same time the delegation of the Central Committee published an assurance that the "entrance of the Communists into the government engages the entire French Communist Party." [7]

From this time until May, 1947, the Communists remained a government party. During these three years they continued their tactic of bringing pressure to bear on the head of the government in order to get control of the key ministries. They failed because De Gaulle and his successors did not break with the precedent set in April, 1944.

Besides participating in the French Committee and the Consultative Assembly, the French Communists hoped to increase their power in the provisional government by persuading De Gaulle to accept their plan for the new administrative structure to be set up in France during the period of liberation. In late 1943 and early 1944 the Communists, in private conversations with other political groupings and with the representatives of General de Gaulle, urged that the departmental committees of liberation should form the basis for the local provisional governments of France. The creation of these committees had been suggested originally in London in the spring of 1943 during discussions between the representatives of the Resistance movements and the Special Services of Fighting France. As defined at that time, the committees were to unite the Resistance groups on the local level in order to show the Allied forces their cohesion and their representative character.[8]

Immediately after these discussions the Communists had opened a campaign to secure majorities in as many local committees as possible. Each Resistance group having a departmental organization was allowed to send one delegate to the departmental committee. Reports from France clearly showed that the Communists were especially active throughout France in extending their Party organizations to entire departments, thus multiplying the number of front organizations under their control.[9] There are numerous doc-

---

[7] *L'Humanité*, No. 288 (April 7, 1944).

[8] Interview with M. Debré. The Communists presented their proposals on the committees to the Consultative Assembly in January, 1944. Assemblée consultative provisiore, *Journal Officiel, Documents*, January 18, 1944, p. 11. Henceforth cited as *JO*.

[9] *L'Observateur*, August 28, 1952.

umented cases of the Party's activity. One of the most important organizations was the rapidly growing Front National (FN), with its paramilitary auxiliary, the Francs-Tireurs et Partisans Français (FTP). The FN was the only Resistance movement which had widespread influence in both the occupied and the unoccupied zones. Its ideology and propaganda were similar to, if not identical with, the Communists', and the command posts in the political and military branches were exclusively in the hands of leading Communists. A report by a Gaullist secret agent revealed that,

Considered a few months ago as nonexistent, the Front National is appearing in most of the departments without it being possible to determine whether it really had troops and whether these were organized. Except in the large centers, where its existence is comparable to that before the war, the situation is similar to that of the Communist Party, which says it is everywhere and makes use of the exploits of the Francs-Tireurs et Partisans Français as proof of its activity.[10]

The Communists also created several other groups which tried to organize patriotic women, youth, lawyers, and other professional classes, and which claimed to be independent of Communist control. Then the Party demanded representation for each of these organizations in the departmental committees. It is difficult to say how successful these tactics were in spreading the influence of the Communists, because there has been no systematic study of the composition of all the committees. A superficial analysis would be misleading; there were many circumstances which could at any time during the occupation shift the balance of power within these organizations. For example, one would have to know whether a certain decision was made by the entire committee or by the executive bureau. If the bureau took action, were all its members present? Often the absence of a single member might be the decisive factor in establishing a Communist majority.

The activities of the Paris committee demonstrate how difficult it is to judge the extent of Communist influence in a departmental committee merely on the basis of the majority of its total membership. The Paris organization, formed in October, 1943, counted

---

[10] Report No. 4 of F. Closon (Fouché), dated 1/4/44, Courrier-Documentation-Diffusion, Bureau Central des Renseignements et d'Action, as quoted in Hostache, *Le Conseil,* p. 290.

seven Communists among its eighteen members, but the Communists had three of the six members on the important executive bureau. The Communists had originally tried to pack the committee with representatives of a large number of their front groups, and only the strong intervention of the Gaullist delegates in France defeated this plot.[11]

According to one non-Communist member of the Paris committee, the Communists' dynamism and ceaseless activity were extraordinary. It was they who organized the meetings of the executive bureau in the house of a militant, provided bodyguards for the members both coming and going, and insisted upon editing the tracts for distribution to the people.[12] It can be imagined how much more difficult it was, under occupation conditions, for the entire committee than for the executive bureau to meet. It is, then, not surprising that decisions of the Paris committee were often made, in effect, by the tireless Communist members of the executive bureau.[13] Still other factors must be considered in an attempt to estimate the Communist influence in the departmental committees. The size, membership, and life span of a single committee varied greatly during the period of German occupation. Some committees never had representatives of all the eligible Resistance organizations in their department. Others were broken up by the Germans and reconstituted later.

Several committees were enlarged either in the process of reconstitution or in the normal course of the growth of the Resistance movements. The Communists held majorities in Seine-et-Oise and Isère only after these committees were enlarged in the spring of 1944. The committee in Corrèze was expanded in September, 1944, to include eleven members of six organizations controlled by the Communists. With some support from those representing non-Com-

---

[11] Report No. 2 of Closon. *Ibid.*, p. 306.

[12] Interview with M. Henri Bourdeau de Fontenay, former representative of Ceux de la Libération on the departmental committee of the Seine, later Commissar of the Republic at Rouen, and now Directeur Général of the Ecole de l'Administration Nationale.

[13] There were reports from France that the Communists sometimes commanded majorities at meetings of some departmental committees because of the laxness of the others or their inability to attend. See Report of Jacques Bingen, dated December, 1943, Archives de la Délégation, and Report No. 4 of F. Closon, annex No. 3, n.d., as quoted in Hostache, *Le Conseil*, p. 207.

munist groups, the Party could then muster a majority of the twenty-seven members.[14] In the department of Cher there were, possibly, seven Communists among the sixteen members; yet the executive bureau was composed of one member each from the Communist Party, the Radical-Socialist Party, and the patriotic militia. Since the Communists were very active in the formation of the militias, it is quite possible that they had a majority on this executive bureau.[15]

Despite this sampling of cases, it seems unlikely that the Communists dominated anything approaching a majority of the seventy-one departmental committees that had been established before the liberation of France. However, General de Gaulle's agents in France were deeply concerned over the Communist campaign. They urged the French National Committee to utilize the departmental committees to a maximum and to send them directives "in order not to leave the initiative to others"—that is, to "the most dynamic elements, the Communists and the Front National." [16]

Though perhaps they could not control the departmental committees, the Communists believed that they could infiltrate these bodies and wield considerable influence in them. In the short term the Party could use this influence to spread its power locally and also to bring pressure to bear on General de Gaulle's national provisional government. The creation of local Resistance committees was a standard partisan device in Eastern Europe, ultimately aimed at guaranteeing Communist power in the countryside. From the short- and long-range viewpoints the French Communists had good reason to propose the departmental committees as a basis for the local provisional government of France. For the same reason it is clear why De Gaulle rejected the Communist proposals and published his own plan for provisional local government during the period of liberation.

The ordinance of January 10, 1944, was characterized by a highly centralized structure, one which could be easily controlled from the

---

[14] *L'Écho de Corrèze,* September 15, 1944.

[15] *Bulletin Officiel, Comité Departemental de Libération de Cher* (Bourges, 1945), issue dated September 7, 1944.

[16] Report No. 4 of F. Closon as quoted in Hostache, *Le Conseil,* p. 305.

top, where De Gaulle's power was unchallenged. Article One prescribed the division of the metropolitan territory into regional commissariats corresponding to the Vichy regional prefectures. The representative of the central power in these areas would be (Article Three) the Commissar of the Republic, named by decree on the proposal of the Commissariat of the Interior. His broad powers were described in Article Four.[17]

This ordinance was later supplemented by another which officially confirmed promises that De Gaulle had made to the Resistance movement in 1942 on the rapid reestablishment of republican institutions in liberated France. Undoubtedly he was influenced in his decision to issue such reassurances by the fear that the Allies, the United States in particular, were suspicious of his motives and were still planning to govern France temporarily with a military administration.

In April De Gaulle took a further step toward making sure that the departmental committees would not entrench themselves in power permanently. On April 21, 1944, the French Committee published an administrative order which specified that the French people would determine the future institutions of France through decision by a national constituent assembly to be elected within a year after the complete liberation of the country. Republican institutions would be reestablished before the elections, and, at the local level, municipal councils would be reorganized on the basis of those elected before September 3, 1939, excluding collaborators. In special cases (lack of a quorum or council collaboration with the Germans) the prefect, with the advice of the departmental committees of liberation, would complete or replace the membership. As soon as the general councils began functioning, the departmental committees would disappear.[18] Thus again De Gaulle deprived the Resistance elements of an opportunity to play a decisive role in the provisional administration of liberated France.

The Communists, as a governmental party, were obliged to accept the decree which frustrated their efforts to secure a more

---

[17] De Gaulle, *Mémoires*, II, 554.
[18] *L'Année politique, 1945*, pp. 431 ff.

"democratic" system. Undaunted, they presented a list of their candidates for the posts of prefect and Commissar of the Republic.[19]

The process of appointing the powerful representatives of the French Committee was actively carried out in a manner different from that specified in Article Three of the ordinance of January 10, 1944. One reason was that the Commissar of the Interior, Emmanuel d'Astier de la Vigerie, was consistently supporting the Communist position and was to become a "Progressive," or fellow-traveling deputy, after the war. The selection of candidates was actually carried out in secret by two members of the general delegation of General de Gaulle in France, an intelligence and liaison organization which sent delegates to get in touch with and supply the metropolitan Resistance. The two members were Alexandre Parodi, the delegate-general and Michel Debré, the future commissar, senator, and premier.[20] In making their selections they adhered to the unwritten rule that there would be neither a Communist commissar nor a Communist prefect in a maritime or border region or department.[21] The French Communist Party was assigned two prefectures, Haute-Vienne (Chaintron) and Loire (Monjauvis).[22] Known Communist sympathizers were named Commissars of the Republic in three areas: Yves Farge at Lyon, Jean Cassou at Toulouse, and Raymond Aubrac at Marseilles. It is possible that this was done, as Alexander Werth has suggested, to overcome difficulties in potential trouble spots.[23]

To complete preparations for the administration of liberated France, it was necessary to appoint certain administrative officials, especially secretaries-general of the ministries, who would take over and direct their respective departments in Paris until the commissar could arrive from Algiers. These posts were important because no one could foresee how long the liberation of Paris or of some of the provinces would take. There was also a possibility that a short period of time might intervene between the German withdrawal and the Allied occupation of certain areas. In such cases the

---

[19] Interview with M. Debré.
[20] De Gaulle, *Mémoires*, II, 177.
[21] Interview with M. Debré.
[22] Henry, *Histoire*, p. 346.
[23] Werth, *France*, p. 221.

secretaries-general would have a great deal of power, in the absence of their chiefs.

The internal Resistance was anxious to be consulted on the appointments to these posts. In fact, its representative body, the Conseil National de la Résistance (CNR) wanted to name the secretaries-general. De Gaulle rejected this proposal, but his agents did take the desires of the CNR into consideration. In order to satisfy the Party, Parodi even went so far as to propose two Communist secretaries-general. They were Marcel Willard, for Justice, and Henri Wallon (a Communist sympathizer), for Education.[24] De Gaulle at first opposed even this concession, but finally approved it.

The participation of the French Communists in the CFLN helped to fulfill one goal of Soviet foreign policy—the unity and close cooperation of all anti-Hitlerite forces. The party was represented in the Consultative Assembly, in De Gaulle's cabinet, and in the provisional local administration for liberated France. However, it had not secured from De Gaulle any concessions on the structure of the provisional administration of France. De Gaulle had invited the Communists into the government to strengthen his own internal and international position—in effect, to make prisoners of the Communists in the government by binding them to a moderate and responsible position, and to assure support of his government by the French working classes, thus enabling France to carry through its reconstruction rapidly.[25] Unity of the external Resistance had been achieved formally, but the Communists had not as yet gained any practical advantage from it. The Party was trying to remedy this state of affairs by pressing for implementation of its five-point program by the French Committee. During the negotiations with De Gaulle and after its entrance into the government, the Party constantly explained and elaborated its views.

[24] Dansette, Histoire, p. 60.
[25] These arguments were made by De Gaulle and his associates during this period and afterward. See De Gaulle, Mémoires, II, 150; Soustelle, Envers et contre tout, II, 338–39; Mutter, Pourquoi faut-il dissoudre le parti communiste?, p. 5.

The French Communists Demand Arms for the Resistance

As early as November, 1942, the French Communist partisans sent a letter to De Gaulle in Algiers saying, "We ask you to send us arms necessary to intensify the struggle against the German occupiers." By August, 1943, the tone of their appeal had become desperate: "The absence of sufficient arms is forcing us to limit our action against the Germans." [26] "The situation demands that the CFLN organize arms shipments to the patriots and partisans." [27] The Communist clandestine press noted with bitterness that "in France we see that the FTP, who alone are fighting, do not receive arms, whereas organizations which do nothing receive them. This is a scandal which must be ended." [28]

The most influential advocate of sending more arms to the metropolitan Resistance was the fellow-traveler Commissar of the Interior in the De Gaulle cabinet, Emmanuel d'Astier de la Vigerie. In November, 1943, speaking in an official capacity, he stated, "France has no arms. It is necessary to shout it out loud: The French lack arms. It is astounding to note the indifference of the great powers in this regard." [29] D'Astier was often able to exploit for Communist purposes his role as commissar because his allegiance to the Party was unknown or unproven. Sometimes his methods were extremely clever. For example, at the end of December, 1943, he sent the following telegram to De Gaulle:

French opinion profoundly disturbed by silence General de Gaulle and BBC and by absence material aid for deportation struggle. Rising wave of resentment against Anglo-Saxons [*sic*] risks turning against FFC if chiefs refuse order total struggle. Any delay in helping movements to form redoubts and to assist deserters [from the labor draft] will disorganize Resistance, will cause loss of esteem of FFC, and will involve impossibility of interior struggle. In this case empty country will not partici-

[26] Letters of the FTP to General de Gaulle dated November 23, 1942, and August 6, 1943, as quoted in Godunov, *Bor'ba,* pp. 92–93. See also *Les Lettres françaises,* September 13, 1947.

[27] *L'Humanité,* No. 233 (July 15, 1943).

[28] *L'Humanité,* No. 186 (November 26, 1943) [Var], central clandestine edition of the southern zone.

[29] *L'Humanité,* No. 260 (November [?] 1943).

pate in war and will condemn its chiefs and allies, to Communist advantage.[30]

The Communists also brought pressure on the government by accusing those in power of preventing arms shipments to France by their petty machinations.[31] This charge was taken up with more effect by D'Astier, who attacked the Bureau Central des Renseignements et d'Action (BCRA), De Gaulle's intelligence service, which was responsible in large measure for the transportation and distribution of agents and money to the internal Resistance. D'Astier accused it of being particularly harmful to the Resistance.[32] Then he endeavored to have this agency removed from De Gaulle's control and subordinated to someone who was first and foremost a military man and whose interest in politics was slight. In December, 1943, at a meeting of the executive Action Committee of Fighting France, D'Astier supported a motion of General Henri Giraud which proposed subordinating the intelligence group to the military commander.[33] Apparently the Communists believed it would be easier to obtain arms from Giraud than from the politically more astute De Gaulle.

Though this plan failed, D'Astier continued his efforts to disrupt the operations of the bureau or to bring it under his control as Commissar of the Interior. According to Soustelle, he attempted to stir up rivalry and ultimately to cause a breach between Colonel Dewavrin (known in the Resistance as "Passy"), of the London branch of the bureau, and Soustelle, who controlled the branch at Algiers.[34] In this case his intrigues failed, but they appeared to have borne fruit elsewhere. On March 3, 1944, a decree of the French Committee specified that the Commissar of the Interior would

make use of all the competent services through the intermediary of the Direction Générale des Services Spéciaux [the new name for the Bureau des Renseignements] concerning action in France. In this way

---

[30] D'Astier, *Les Dieux*, pp. 18–19.
[31] *L'Humanité*, No. 261 (December 1, 1943).
[32] D'Astier, *Les Dieux*, p. 92.
[33] Soustelle, *Envers et contre tout*, II, 324.
[34] *Ibid.*, II, 342.

he can have communicated to him all papers and documents of all types emanating from these services or proceeding to them and concerning action in France.

He has the right to order the dispatch of civil missions to France. The relations with the Resistance organizations are equally under his jurisdiction. Plans relative to military action and susceptible of affecting relations with the Resistance organizations or of having political repercussions will be brought to the attention of the Commissar of the Interior. In case he objects to these decisions, the Action Committee will be called on to discuss the question.[35]

About this same time the clash between Passy and D'Astier reached a climax, and D'Astier announced that he would resign if his rival did not. Passy was relieved of his post.[36]

Both these Communist victories, at first sight overwhelming, proved to be hollow. The March decree remained a dead letter. Passy was attached to General Koenig's chief of staff in London and became even more influential, while D'Astier's influence in the French Committee declined rapidly. For example, with the appointment of André le Troquer as Commissar of the Liberated Metropolitan Territories in April, 1944, D'Astier was relieved of all responsibility for the conduct of affairs in liberated France. Ironically, the same decree by which Le Troquer was nominated also brought two Communists into the government.[37]

The significance of the Communists' campaign to have arms shipped to France and to discredit the intelligence bureau lies in their disagreement with the government over what the policy of resistance actually involved. As we have seen, the French Communists and the Soviet Union had a similar concept of resistance. The Party's attitude was most forcefully summarized in its adoption of Danton's famous revolutionary battle cry, "De l'audace, encore de l'audace, toujours de l'audace!" [38]

General de Gaulle and his followers were, on the contrary, opposed to this interpretation. For them the Resistance was to serve four distinct purposes: a source of military intelligence; a means for conducting certain well-planned and militarily useful acts of

---

[35] D'Astier, Les Dieux, pp. 105–6.
[36] Ibid., p. 107.
[37] De Gaulle, Mémoires, II, 569.
[38] L'Humanité, No. 257 (November 12, 1943).

sabotage; a transmission belt of hope and Allied propaganda; and a potentially powerful striking force to be used in support of an Allied landing on French soil. As early as the fall of 1941, De Gaulle denounced the indiscriminate assassinations of German troops, and he constantly attempted to prevent isolated acts of terror that would result in terrible reprisals.

It was this great difference of opinion as to the purpose of the Resistance that led to so many disagreements between De Gaulle and the Communists. The Communists attacked the liaison groups with France because they did not send enough arms and because the arms which did arrive were "stockpiled" by agents of De Gaulle's Délégation Générale for later use. The Gaullists protested that they had insufficient means to send massive arms shipments and that arms were being fairly distributed.[39]

The French Communists and the Creation of a "Popular" Army

As the first point in their five-point program the Communists had demanded the creation of a "new, popular French Army." In an article in *Pravda* Maurice Thorez outlined the Communist concept of the mass army. He pointed out that the French Committee had more than enough men and resources "to put more than one million men rapidly on a war footing." This new force, "a truly national army," should "play an important role in the offensive action of the Allies and no longer be considered an auxiliary and supporting force." Thorez insisted that a large-scale recruiting campaign would "boldly show confidence in the people." It was clear, he continued, that the defeat of 1940 had been caused by "the caste spirit, the mistrust of the people, the routine and narrowness" of the great military chiefs, "who were ignorant of the rules of modern warfare." On the other hand, he admitted that many officers had fought well for Fighting France and should continue to do so in the new French Army. "The criteria should be firmness, courage, and ability, but also absolute devotion to France and to the Republic." The revital-

[39] For one specific instance of a sharp exchange of views along these lines, see the Pascal Copeau–Jacques Soustelle dispute over distribution of arms in the south of France. Soustelle, *Envers et contre tout*, II, 302–3.

ization of France, Thorez maintained, must be based on the rapid liberation of the nation. "And that, to a great extent, depends on us, on our own efforts." [40]

Therefore, Thorez in Moscow and the French Communists in France urged agreement between De Gaulle and Giraud in order to bring about the creation of "a truly national army, the Army of the French Republic, which tomorrow will admit into its ranks the soldiers without uniforms who make up the FTP, [and] the Armée Secrète." [41] In Algiers, Fajon and Billoux insisted that the "new French Army" be formed from a fusion of the regular forces and the Resistance groups. They further insisted that the new army include special parachute units for immediate use in France. According to them, the army should be under a military commander, separate from the civilian government. Fajon concluded his report by warning that "a small army will delay French independence and diminish France's role in the war and in the peace settlements." [42]

According to the Party, its demand for a popular army was closely tied in with the essential problem of French foreign policy, which was "the maintenance of the unity of France and the restoration of her greatness." The Communists took note of President Roosevelt's statement that "liberty will be equal to the efforts which have been dedicated to it." They concluded that "the only guarantee of national independence is the formation of a powerful national army." They further justified their stand by quoting remarks from the American press. They cited, for example, Colonel Robert McCormick, owner of the Chicago *Tribune,* who had suggested that the United States should maintain bases in certain foreign countries after the war in order to guarantee American military security. *The New York Times,* they continued, had expressed a belief that the United States would be obliged to intervene with troops "in order to avoid chaos . . . in the countries of liberated Europe." Such violations of national sovereignty, the Party concluded, could not be tolerated, and there must be no reason for their occurrence.

[40] Thorez, *Oeuvres*, Book Five, XIX, 170–73.

[41] *Ibid.*, p. 155, and *L'Humanité*, No. 233 (July 15, 1943).

[42] Fajon and Berlioz, *La France*, pp. 16–19, and *L'Humanité*, No. 287 (April 1, 1944).

France must be strong and stable.[43] It is not surprising that the French Communists, like other Frenchmen, were very sensitive to suggestions that France was no longer a great nation. They berated Prime Minister Smuts of South Africa for his remark, made a few days after the Teheran Conference, that France had ceased to be a great power. "We ought to show him," they cried, "and also the whole world, that the French people remain a great people which intends to earn, arms in hand, the right of France to be reestablished in its liberty, its independence, and its greatness." [44]

The Communist pleas for more arms and for a large and powerful army were well adapted to serve the immediate needs and the long-range goals of Soviet foreign policy. The French Communists were trying to encourage a more vigorous war effort. They also hoped to undermine the traditional anti-Communist officer corps, and they sought to infiltrate the ranks of the army with disciplined Communists who had received their training in the underground. A large army, the Communists thought, would guarantee the right of the French to govern themselves during and after the period of liberation without any interference from outside. If this new army were to cooperate in the short run with the legally established and universally recognized provisional government, it would not run the risk of being attacked by the West, as the Home Army in Poland was being destroyed by the Red Army. Through "unity of action" the new army could preserve and strengthen itself during the liberation and could be prepared at a later date to help the Communists, either by remaining neutral in a struggle for power or by actively supporting a Communist coup.

The French Communists and the Purge

The second point in the Communist program was an immediate purge of Vichy officials already in the hands of the French Com-

---

[43] Michel and Guetzévitch, Les Idées politiques, "Des observations du parti communiste sur le projet d'un programme commun presenté par le parti socialiste à la Résistance, 25 avril 1944," p. 231.

[44] L'Humanité, No. 263 (December 10, 1943). Similar comments, ibid., No. 264 (December 15, 1943).

mittee and a future purge of the public administration in liberated France. The Party demanded the execution of several men in particular. One was the former Vichy Minister of the Interior, Pierre Pucheu, who had handed over to the Germans as hostages some forty Communists, who were later executed as a reprisal. After the Allied landings Pucheu crossing to North Africa, where he was seized by the Free French and imprisoned. The Communists carried on a prolonged attack against him and others:

As for the criminals who are in the hands of CFLN, they ought to be killed. The French rejoice to see that Peyrouton [a Vichy minister], Flandin [former Vichy foreign minister], and Tixier-Vignancourt [extreme Rightist deputy, supporter of Vichy] have joined Pucheu and Bergeret in prison; this is the first act of justice, but the blood of our martyrs demands that Pucheu, condemned to death by the French Resistance, be punished swiftly. . . . France expects much from the CFLN because it sees in it the government of the French Republic.[45]

Pucheu was closely identified with Marshal Pétain, and the Party saw in his execution a symbol of an absolute rupture between Vichy and London or Algiers. They feared that some other alternative was in the air: "Pétain has tried in the recent period to play a comedy designed to set himself off from Laval. The fact remains that the two wretches are indissolubly associated in terms of treason." [46] Commenting on the Pucheu trial, the Party made it clear that it attached great political importance to a verdict of guilt.

As for the Pucheu trial, it has brought to light the swinishness and cynicism of this criminal, who has tried to transform his trial into an operation of dividing the forces of the Resistance, using, as all Hitlerites do, the argument of anticommunism.

The Vichy traitors believed up to the last moment that Pucheu would benefit from a special measure and would not be executed.[47]

No "special measures" for Pucheu, the Communists insisted, and none for Pétain. They rejoiced that the gap was widening between the Marshal and the General. However, they were never wholly

[45] La Vie du Parti, January, 1944, p. 11.
[46] Ibid.
[47] Ibid., February, 1944, p. 13.

convinced that it was wide enough or permanent enough. In the eyes of the Party, Pucheu's execution was also a warning to all those who tried to dissociate their anti-Communist activities from the stigma of collaboration. The Communists were determined to bring about the destruction of the Vichy regime, and the purge of leading Vichyites would forestall any last-minute attempt by De Gaulle and Pétain to come to an agreement in order to prevent civil strife in France. Such turmoil would open the way for the Communists to take over positions left vacant by those who had been purged and would frighten those who had collaborated or done nothing during the occupation. The Communists could and did blackmail such people for political purposes. The purge, then, was an important part of the Communist plan to increase Party control over the institutions of French life.

The French Communists and the Political Reformation of France

The third proposal of the Communists was to prepare a democratic political and social program for postwar France. Perhaps the most complete presentation of their views was contained in the commentaries prepared by the French Communist Party on the common program for the Resistance which had been drawn up by the Socialists.[48]

The Party's memorandum commented first on the political problem. The provisional government was a "makeshift organ which should be replaced as soon as materially possible—that is, about two months after the return of the prisoners of war and deportees." The radical moral regeneration of the country could not, it was argued, come only from above, but must be the result of a popular movement. This would, in turn, assure the Allies that the French delegates to international organizations were representing the wishes of the people.[49] The Party favored the convocation of a National Constituent Assembly and rejected out of hand a proposal to submit to a plebiscite a constitution drawn up by "experts." Elections

[48] Michel and Guetzévitch, Les Idées politiques, pp. 217–36.
[49] Ibid., p. 220.

should be secret, direct, and equal, with each deputy representing the same number of voters. All citizens over eighteen years of age, including women, would be granted the right to vote.

After the rejection of its more radical proposal for placing all local power in the hands of the departmental committees, the Party supported the proposal for creating local commissions under the Commissariat of the Interior, based on the party representation in the Chamber of Deputies of 1939. These organs would administer the liberated territory temporarily. Only Paris should have a different and more "equal" representation through *arrondissement* delegations selected by universal suffrage on the basis of the type of proportional representation used in 1935–36. These proposals would ensure, in the words of the Communists, that "the patriotic delegations [would] have as short an existence as possible; there should be an early election of municipal and general councils." [50]

The deputies who had voted full powers to Marshal Pétain or who had abstained or been absent from the vote of July 10, 1940, must, the Communists insisted, be denied the right to participate in the National Assembly. They also wanted the purge of Vichy elements extended to include certain sections of the police in addition to the leaders of the administration.[51]

In large measure, the Communists had accepted the ordinance of April 21, 1944, which was published after the Party had entered the government. Their supplementary proposals were not of an extremist character. The adoption of their electoral plan for Paris would, of course, increase their representation in the capital. Lowering the voting age might be expected to increase their proportional strength in the national electoral returns. However, these gains were on a constitutional and parliamentary level. Actually, the Party did not try to put forward an alternative to the rapid reconstitution of the municipal councils or to the creation of temporary commissions, based on the 1939 representation in the Chamber of Deputies, to administer the liberated territories. Yet

---

[50] *Ibid.*, p. 223.

[51] Most of these political proposals had already been made to the French Committee by the Communists in a letter of February 7, 1944. See *ibid.*, p. 297, "Lettre du parti communiste français (comité central) aux membres du CFLN, 7 février 1944."

the Communists were fully aware that their strength in the country had greatly increased since the parliamentary elections of 1936. The Communist Party preferred to abandon certain parts of its political program rather than jeopardize the position it had already acquired in the government.

It is also clear that in this, as in its proposals for the new economic structure of the country, the Party was much concerned with the impression its proposals would make on moderate opinion in France. Just as important was the Party's desire to prevent instability and chaos in the days which would follow the liberation, in order to avoid any intervention by the Anglo-American forces. Its concern with wooing moderate public opinion and preserving internal stability was to exert a strong influence on its actions during the liberation.

The Communist's Economic and Social Program

The Communist Party's economic and social proposals had some important political ramifications which went unnoticed at the time. The Party demanded the liquidation of "trusts"—especially of the large banks, whom they identified with the "trusts"—which had dominated the prewar economy; the punishment of traitors; and the confiscation of the property of collaborators and of all war profits. The Communists proposed to use the capital thus acquired to raise the living standards of the masses. First they would give back to the peasants the capital that "the trusts had taken away from them." Compensation would be paid to peasants who had been prisoners of war, and in general the protection and consolidation of peasant property against the pressure of "finance capital" would be assured. From the same funds an immediate increase in salaries and wages would also be granted. The Party further proposed the use of the confiscated property for pensions, for relief to small rentiers, and for the repair of war damage. The Communists suggested that the collection and administration of these funds be carried out by "local commissions of patriots." [52]

[52] *Ibid.*, p. 229.

The Communists envisaged the establishment of an Economic Council, with representatives from the workers, the technicians, the middle class, and the peasants, which would have control over the allocation of raw materials and would manage stockpiling "to prevent sabotage." The Communists favored creating a modern machine-tool industry, increasing the work of the extractive industries, and modernizing transportation. Finally, the Communists suggested the creation of a National Committee of Trust Surveillance and a Commission for the Control of Companies, whose task it would be to supervise and control the production and distribution of gas, electricity, and other sources of power. They did not explain how these safeguards were to be defined or what the extent of their activities would be.

These proposals were obviously directed toward using the capital of the "national enemies," who in most cases could be identified with the more important "class enemies," to better the lot of the "patriots," who were either "class comrades" (the workers) or important potential allies (the peasants). The addition of the rentiers and the middle class to the list of proposed beneficiaries was important for electoral reasons. The vagueness of the proposals offered the possibility of enlarging or reducing the scope of confiscation and awards according to the needs of the moment. The French Communist effort to increase state control over the French economy was similar to actions later taken by the Czechoslovak and the Yugoslav Communists.[53] A national economy directed from the center could be more easily infiltrated by the Communists than a decentralized one. This was in fact what happened in France as well as in the East European countries.

The French Communists Propose a New Foreign Policy

The Communist attitude toward the postwar international situation was stated clearly. France was to seek a rapprochement with the nations of Eastern Europe. According to Thorez, "tomorrow the old Franco-Russian friendship will be one of the best guarantees

---

[53] Ducháček, "Czechoslovakia," in Kertesz, ed., *The Fate of East Central Europe,* p. 186; Dragnich, "Yugoslavia," *ibid.,* p. 363.

of the security and independence of France." [54] The Communists also insisted that there should be no "retreat to the Atlantic." There had been indications, they warned, that the French had little interest in Central Europe and did not want to form alliances with the East. Any French foreign policy which neglected close ties with Eastern Europe showed a complete ignorance of the geographical, military, and demographic situation of France. There was evidence of this, the Party declared, in the "well-proven" fact that "it took the so-called Atlantic powers from four to six years to come to the aid of France with a land army." [55] More specifically, the Communists attacked De Gaulle's idea of a Western, or Atlantic, bloc. This concept, they charged, "risks restoring inopportunely certain outdated formulas on the 'imperial retreat.'" [56]

It was no secret, the Party insisted, as to who was the champion of French interests in Europe. In 1943, on the anniversary of the Russian October Revolution, the Communists had declared that "a France deprived of a solid alliance with the USSR could only fall under a foreign influence which would place its independence in danger." They concluded that a Franco-Soviet alliance was "indispensable," "necessary," "imperative." [57]

Pierre Hervé made this point quite clear in his widely read *Rapport Chardon*. He indicated that "the balance of Europe can be founded only on collaboration with the USSR," and concluded that France had no desire to become an American bridgehead or "dominion." [58] The Communists developed this propaganda line with special emphasis during the visit of President Beneš of Czechoslovakia to the USSR in December, 1943. They indicated that a Franco-Soviet alliance would "serve for France as a guarantee of its restoration to the ranks of the great nations." [59]

In their note of April, 1944, to the Socialists, the French Communists also defended Soviet interests against a revival of combinations in Central Europe which would either prevent the USSR

---

[54] Thorez, *Oeuvres*, Book Five, XIX, 175.
[55] Michel and Guetzévitch, *Les Idées politiques*, p. 232.
[56] *La Vie du Parti*, February, 1944, p. 14.
[57] *L'Humanité*, No. 252 (October 15, 1943).
[58] Michel and Guetzévitch, *Les Idées politiques*, "Rapport Chardon," p. 383.
[59] *L'Humanité*, No. 266 (December 24, 1943).

from playing a role "equal to its merits" in Europe or block the development of "democracy in Central Europe" by denying economic and social rights to the population. They declared that European combinations created for such purposes would only result in a resurrection of German imperialism.[60]

Lastly, the Communists pointed to the danger of relying too heavily on the United States because

postwar world policy hangs a good deal on the results of the presidential elections in America; the Congressional resolutions voted in the United States in favor of participation in the postwar international organizations were events that, as *The New York Times* said, should not be exaggerated; actually, the United States at best would be inclined not toward forming a united states of the world but, very simply, toward an empirical trial of various solutions of international questions according to the needs [of the moment].

The Communists added that, even within a united states of the world, difficulties would immediately arise between the United States and France over such problems as the breaking up of the trusts and the social reforms inaugurated in France in 1936. They rejected the idea of a superstate by asserting that "nothing guarantees us that these economic forces which opposed the 1936 reforms will not tomorrow control several of the greatest countries of the globe." They concluded: "Let us not forget the power of the isolationists. It was these isolationists who manifested their power for two years in preventing the second front from becoming a reality in spite of the interests of peace, justice, and respect due to solemn agreements." [61]

The Communist attitude toward postwar Germany was more vague. According to the Party, the problem would devolve upon the United Nations. Whatever the tendencies of the new government in Germany, the French ought to support those currents which wished to modify the concentration of trusts and destroy the "remnants of the feudal landed society." It is interesting to note that the Soviet Union had not as yet made its position on Germany publicly known.

The immediate tasks for France, the Communist note to the So-

[60] Michel and Guetzévitch, *Les Idées politiques,* p. 233.
[61] *Ibid.,* p. 234.

cialists concluded, were to guarantee its territorial independence, to reject any outside interference in its destiny, to punish the Fascist war criminals, and to participate in a security system designed to prevent a renewal of German aggression, a system "implying, above all, a firm entente with the strongest continental power in Europe." [62] Avoiding any mention of ideological considerations, the Communists demanded that postwar French policy be guided by considerations of continental military power. They based their analysis on the lessons of the past, not the possibilities of the future. The past that they drew upon was, of course, purged of certain inconvenient memories such as the Nazi-Soviet pact, and it raised the ghost of a vengeful Germany even before the body had been put to rest. Yet the appeal did not lack a certain attraction for those Frenchmen who were constantly reminded by the Party of the strained historical equation: Tannenberg and the Marne, Soviet neutrality and the Ardennes.

French Communist Proposals and Soviet Policy

The Soviet Union gave slight and indirect support to the French Communist five-point program. In commenting on the activities of the French Consultative Assembly in Algiers, a Tass dispatch praised the activities of the "most prominent political and social activists in the Assembly," who were nearly all Communists or fellow-travelers. Tass noted the "series of urgent problems" which were discussed; the only ones mentioned were the four points in the French Communist program on which the Party had taken a firm stand.[63] The report in the Soviet press implied that the Soviet government considered that the most important goals of French domestic and foreign policy were the creation of a national French Army "without full dress," the purging of the administration and

---

[62] *Ibid.*, p. 235.

[63] *Pravda*, June 1, 1944. The political figures mentioned were the Communists Marty, Bonte, Fajon, Mercier, Berlioz, Midol, Pierre Bloch, and Pourtalet; the Radicals Pierre Cot, Marc Rucart, and Paul Giacobbi (who was not a Communist sympathizer); the Socialist Vincent Auriol (who also was not a sympathizer); and Raymond Aubrac. The Tass dispatch did not mention the Communist plank on self-determination of the overseas peoples, but the Communists themselves had not developed their views on this point.

army of Vichy elements, the development of a democratic political and social program for France, and the increased action of France in the common struggle of the Allies.

The French Communist demands for a new government policy appeared to be moderate, patriotic, and democratic. They were not, as Lenin's "April theses" had been, a public blueprint for revolution. The French Communist Party program had the merit of appealing to republican elements in France and in exile.[64] Politically, the French Communists offered few innovations and, except for the purge, no radical ones. Economically and socially, there were to be more important changes. National wealth was to be to some extent redistributed, and the toiling classes would participate more directly in the management of the national economy. The social structure of the officer corps was to be drastically altered. A significant change would have to be made in French foreign policy. France would have to base its European security on a firm alliance with the Soviet Union and could not enter into or create any European bloc that would exclude the USSR. Though this program did not mention Communist plans to take power, its adoption might well have brought about revolutionary changes in French society that could have paved the way for a Communist coup. The Communists did not discuss these long-range implications publicly until after the liberation of France.

[64] A not uncommon attitude was that of Indomitus (Philippe Viannay), who indicated that there could be cooperation with the Party. He added, "what would be serious, what would be irremediable, is if you would like to impose your point of view by violence. In our eyes, as in those of the majority of Frenchmen, you would lose all the prestige that you have acquired by your courage. We accept discussion with you, but in legality. Illegal action must be ended with the war." Indomitus, *Nous sommes les rebelles,* quoting an article by the author in *Défense de la Liberté,* October 25, 1943.

CHAPTER IV

The French Communists in the Resistance

ACTING under the slogan of "unity of action," the French Communist Party was more successful in spreading its influence and increasing its power in the Resistance than within the French National Committee. The advantages of the Communists over other Resistance groupings helped the Party to secure a strong position within the anti-Nazi underground. After June, 1941, the Communists supported, as we have seen, a program of total resistance to the German invader. It must be noted that they were not the only Frenchmen willing to die or risk reprisals for their underground activities. However, the other resisters did not constitute a large and well-organized body of men with a sharply defined ideology. They could not harness and direct to their own ends the hatred that reprisals engender in an occupied population. The Party was able to do this because of its well-disciplined and tightly organized character and because the Communist ethic of revolution subordinates all considerations, moral and material, to attaining its goals.

The French Communist Party was the only prewar political party which maintained its identity and cohesion throughout the occupation period. The other parties and even the trade-union movements had been badly shaken and disorganized. Some of their leaders, such as Léon Blum and Marx Dormoy, the Socialists; Paul Reynaud and Georges Mandel, the moderates; Edouard Daladier, the Radical; and Socialist Léon Jouhaux of the Confédération Générale du Travail (CGT), had been arrested, deported, or killed. Others, such as Edouard Herriot and Jules Jeanneney, had retired from the political scene; a few, such as René Belin of the CGT and Paul Faure of the Socialists, supported or sympathized with Marshal Pétain's regime. The formerly bold and patriotic Right was, with few exceptions, Pétainist or silent. In every other party except the Communist many deputies had voted full powers to Marshal Pétain.[1] Some of these, it is true, later joined the Resistance, but in most cases not until the German invasion of the unoccupied zone in late 1942 had demonstrated how bankrupt the Vichy policy was.

By contrast, many members of the French Communist Central Committee stayed in hiding and remained active during three or four years of war. Though Thorez had fled to Moscow, Bénoît Frachon, Charles Tillon, and Jacques Duclos remained in Paris; Georges Marrane and Léon Mauvais were in Lyon.[2] Driven underground before the German invasion, the Party had been thoroughly reorganized. At the end of 1940, while speaking to a meeting of the Communist leaders of the illegal Party organization, Jacques Duclos outlined the new Party structure in France.

We must introduce iron discipline. . . . We have to reorganize the entire system of our underground work. . . . The rank and file of the Party should be put into groups of three men, including the chief. He will guide the three-man cell directly. Each member of the cell will maintain ties with the chiefs of two or three groups, in no case more than that. Such a nucleus will, on the whole, form the primary unit of our organization. . . . On a higher level there will be sections, sectors, and regions set up on the same principle. . . . In this way, we can coordinate our work but at the same time keep to a minimum the contacts between Party members. . . . Then it will be impossible to destroy the organization as a whole, even if one or another of its parts is wiped out.

The Party organization of the Paris area was created along these lines, and then similar groups were set up all over France.[3] It was

[1] All Communist deputies had been forced out of the Assembly by the time this vote was taken in June, 1940.

[2] Interview with Pierre Hervé. For Marrane's activities see Morgan, *Yves Farge*, p. 58. Together with Mauvais and Grenier, Eugène Hénaff and Henri Raynaud of the Central Committee escaped from the French police in June, 1941, and remained at large in France. Grenier, *C'était ainsi*, p. 85.

[3] Godunov, *Bor'ba*, p. 37.

this organization which carried on the Party's work during the German occupation as well.[4]

Despite the handicaps forced on them by a precarious existence in the underground, the Communists carried on their recruiting and organizational activities. As one Soviet source explained, "work among laborers, peasants, and former members of trade unions is also carried out through the organization of the French Communist Party . . . which in underground meetings frequently has reestablished its cadres in the occupied as well as the unoccupied zone."[5]

Side by side with its political organization, the Party created a tightly knit paramilitary force also based on the principle of decentralization. Not long after the Armistice of June, 1940, the Central Committee selected a group of Communists to set up a special military committee in order to "unite and train cadres necessary for the organization of an army, adapted to the conditions of illegal work [under] the Fascist terror." In September, 1941, after the German invasion of the Soviet Union the Central Committee created the National Military Committee, which "united the FTP and conducted all the military activities of the French patriots."[6]

The organization of the Francs-Tireurs was based on a fighting group composed of two detachments. Each detachment consisted of three men. One was led by the group adviser, and the other by the deputy group adviser. Three groups formed a platoon, three platoons a company, and three companies a battalion. Depending on their location, the battalions were combined and their action was coordinated on a departmental scale by an executive committee of three men. In turn, the departmental executive was subordinated to the interdepartmental committee of three. Crowning the edifice of this military underground was the National Military Committee itself, which was divided into three sections—intelligence, medical, and arms and munitions; it also published its own newspaper, *France d'Abord*. The staff of the committee was composed of Marcel

---

[4] *La Vie du Parti* (Dijon), September, 1944, p. 16.

[5] Vasil'eva, "Frantsuzskii narod v bor'be," *Mirovoe Khoziaistvo i Mirovaia Politika,* No. 8 (August, 1942), p. 26.

[6] Godunov, *Bor'ba,* pp. 41–42.

Prenant, Laurent Casanova, Eugène Hénaff, Georges René Raoul, and Charles Tillon.[7]

The Communists have claimed that their first partisan detachments were formed in Haute Vienne in April, 1941—that is, before the German attack on the USSR. Their claim is valid, but only because the Communist commander in the area, Georges Guingouin, disobeyed Party orders and set about organizing resistance against the Germans. To Communist eyes, his lack of discipline was unforgivable even though its results were laudatory. From the beginning the Communist partisans did not have enough arms, one rifle to every ten or twelve men being the rule. According to Soviet figures, there were, by the end of 1943, 7,000–8,000 FTP in Haute Savoie, 20,000 in Cantal and Haute Loire, and 200,000 throughout France.[8]

The increase in the Party's prestige and in its ability to recruit large numbers of Frenchmen for its armed groups was aided substantially, though unwittingly, by the Vichy government and the German occupation forces. The propaganda of Pétain's "French state" attempted to identify the Resistance with the Communists in order to discredit the movement among conservative or moderate circles.[9] This policy had the unexpected result of helping to advertise the French Communist Party. A Frenchman who read both

[7] *Ibid.*, pp. 55–57. The Soviet author does not name Charles Tillon as the fifth member of the Committee because the book appeared after the public disgrace of Tillon at the hands of the Central Committee. Actually, during the liberation the Party extolled Tillon as the "director" of the National Military Committee. See below, p. 149.

[8] Godunov, *Bor'ba*, pp. 61, 64–66. Recently two Soviet historians have claimed that in 1943–44 a number of Soviet prisoners of war who escaped from German concentration camps in France formed partisan detachments and edited a clandestine Russian-language newspaper, *Sovetskii Patriot,* organ of the Central Committee of Soviet Prisoners. Without stating the exact numbers of the guerrilla forces, they maintain that two groups of battalion strength were responsible for killing 3,500 Germans! By 1944 thirty-five "detachments" were said to have been operating on French soil and in contact with the French Communists. There is no evidence from the French Communists, other Resistance groups, the Vichy police, or the German occupation authorities to substantiate these reports. The only extant copies of the newspaper *Sovetskii Patriot* are said to be in the Central Party Archive of the Marx-Lenin Institute and are therefore unavailable to me. Kokorin and Struchkov, "O boevoi deiatel'nosti," *Voprosy Istorii,* No. 3 (March, 1960), pp. 89, 90, 94.

[9] See, for example, *Revue de la Presse Communiste, Information de l'Etat Français,* August, 1943.

the legal press and the illegal Communist tracts found them in agreement on one fact, the omnipresence of the French Communists in the anti-Vichy and anti-Nazi struggle.

The Nazis' arbitrary tactics in dealing with the people of occupied France enhanced Communist opportunities for mass action. By the end of 1942 the German economy had begun to feel the effects of the drain on its manpower. At first the Germans called for volunteers and promised good pay and the exchange of French prisoners of war for workmen who signed up to go to Germany. When this plan failed to generate any positive response in France, the Germans organized the Service du Travail Obligatoire (STO), which, as its name implies, was a forced labor draft. All Resistance movements fought the draft with all means at their disposal, but Yves Farge, a Communist sympathizer, became the head of the important Comité d'Action contre la Déportation (CAD).[10] This organization provided money, false papers, and, when possible, places of refuge for the young men who fled the impending draft, and, as a result, many of the non-Communist refugees from the labor draft joined armed groups of resisters dominated and led by Communists.[11]

In sum, the French Communists had the advantages of a well-organized clandestine force, an uncompromising attitude in the struggle against the enemy, and the combination of their own and the enemy's propaganda machines spreading the word of Communist preponderance in the underground struggle. These advantages gave the Communists the opportunity not only to develop their own activity but also to take a leading role in creating front organizations which, while Communist-dominated, enlisted large numbers of non-Communist resisters.

The Front Organizations

The most famous and active of these was the Front National, which was, as we have seen, a broad rally of widely diverse political

---

[10] The activities of the CAD were extensive. It issued, for example, over 500,000 sets of false papers. Michel, *Histoire*, pp. 93–94. See also Ministère de l'Information, *Notes, Documentations et Etudes*, LXVI, No. 225, "Esquisse," 6.

[11] The author was personally acquainted with several cases.

elements led and controlled by members of the Communist Party. The FN delighted in parading the names of François Mauriac, Monseigneur Chevrot, Georges Bidault, and Frédéric Joliot-Curie, then a Socialist, on the roster of its executive committee. Many Frenchmen joined the FN who would never have considered becoming members of the Communist Party. The Party took advantage of this fact by using the FN to carry out certain actions which it could not have performed without being suspected of trying to seize power in France. The liberation of Corsica was the most striking example of this Communist tactic.

The Resistance in Corsica had been united in 1941 by a representative of General de Gaulle; and the FN, led by two Communists, Arthur Giovoni, the political chief, and François Vittorio, the military chief, had agreed to serve under his command. In March, 1943, the Gaullist leader was captured and killed by the Italians. Soon afterward the FN committee, with a three-to-two Communist majority, entered into direct relations with General Giraud, who in June, 1943, had become commander in chief of the Free French Army. In this capacity he had control of the Special Services, or military intelligence forces. Without discussing the situation in Corsica with General de Gaulle, Giraud carried out the arming of the FN on his own initiative.[12] Meanwhile the Communists had sent their former deputy from Alpes-Maritimes, André Pourtalet, from France to Giraud in Algiers, and before leaving for Africa he had met Giovoni in Nice. The result of these military and political maneuvers was to concentrate power in the hands of the Communists, who, by controlling the FN, controlled the distribution of the arms sent by Giraud and also monopolized communications with Algiers. No other elements of the Resistance were able to get in touch with the French Committee, and so they accepted the instructions of the FN as representing the wishes of the entire Committee.[13]

---

[12] De Gaulle, *Mémoires*, II, 141. Giraud claimed, "Since the decapitation of the Fighting French, the FN is practically the only organization of resistance capable of entering immediately into action." Giraud, *Un Seul But*, p. 246.

[13] De Gaulle's own cousin, Henri Maillot, joined the committee of the FN under the illusion that he was carrying out De Gaulle's intention. De Gaulle, *Mémoires*, II, 141.

The surrender of Italy on September 8, 1943, precipitated a series of dramatic events in Corsica. Giovoni, who had just returned from a secret interview with Giraud, ordered the seizure of Ajaccio. The rising was almost immediately supported by regular French forces. Giraud had informed De Gaulle of the situation, and the order to liberate the island bore the signature of both leaders. Corsica was rapidly occupied by troops from North Africa. However, it became evident that the Communists were exploiting their originally strong position to gain political control. Improvised local authorities were set up in most of the towns. And, since elections to these bodies were often carried out by acclamation in the public square, the Communists were assured of heavy representation in local government bodies.[14] The French Committee immediately appointed and dispatched Charles Luizet as prefect of the liberated department and General Mollard as military governor. Although there was no opposition to the new authorities, the Communists continued to occupy a position that their numbers alone would not have warranted.[15]

The Communists in Moscow and in France greeted the liberation of Corsica as a vindication of their methods. In *Pravda* Thorez wrote that the Corsican events "show how one should act . . . to take the initiative everywhere, to launch the first attack on the occupation forces, to prepare the best conditions for the debarkation of our soldiers and the Allied military forces." The uprising "also showed the firm discipline and organization of the Francs-Tireurs, imbued with the spirit of order, supported by the population, and capable of bringing to their senses those Vichyites who would plunge the country into civil war." [16] The FTP in Ajaccio had not waited for the Allied landings, the Party declared, and there had been no fence-sitting.[17] After stating, incorrectly, that the new prefect had been designated by the French Committee in accord with the FN, *L'Humanité* went on to prophesy that "when the general

---

[14] Soustelle, *Envers et contre tout*, II, 283. See also the similar views of Socialist André Philip as quoted in De Gaulle, *Mémoires*, II, 146.

[15] Soustelle, *Envers et contre tout*, II, 283.

[16] Thorez, *Oeuvres*, Book Five, XIX, 173.

[17] *L'Humanité*, No. 249 (October 1, 1943)

uprising is carried on in the whole of France, such designations will also be made in accord with the Resistance groups." The departmental committees will play "a role of the first order in the selection of new leaders." [18]

As a matter of fact, as Thorez himself admitted, the liberation of Corsica was in no sense an example for the liberation of the mainland.[19] The island was of no strategic or economic significance to the Germans, and even if they had tried for prestige reasons to retain it, the Allied air and sea power could have prevented that. It is significant, moreover, that although the Communists used the front organization to help liberate Corsica, they did not attempt to make the FN the nucleus of the departmental government. If the Party intended to set a precedent in the Corsican affair, it was clear that the front organization in liberated France would be used to influence the provisional government without trying to replace it immediately.

The Communists were not content to have the FN occupy first place among the mass underground organizations, but tried to make it the basis of a unification of all the Resistance movements in France. If they could keep the control and direction of this united front of the Resistance in their hands, they would have a powerful bargaining point in any negotiations with De Gaulle over the composition of the future government of France. Their first move was to infiltrate non-Communist organizations with crypto-Communists or Communist sympathizers. Often these men were elected as representatives of their organizations to important executive, military, or other coordinating committees. If the Communists had been able to place enough men in these important positions, they might have brought about unity from the top. In any case, the Party considered that such a possibility was worth a great effort.

The Communists scored a notable success in their penetration of the Mouvements unis de la Résistance (MUR), a large non-Communist mass political organization of the Resistance which had

---

[18] *Ibid.*, No. 251 (October 8, 1943).
[19] Thorez, *Oeuvres*, Book Five, XIX, 173.

been created by a fusion of three smaller groups in March, 1943.[20] The extent of this infiltration was not known until after the liberation, but there were some signs of it even during the clandestine period.[21] For example, by infiltrating the MUR and other organizations, the Communists succeeded in gaining a strong position in the Conseil National de la Résistance (CNR). This body had been created by the almost legendary Jean Moulin (known as Max or Rex) in order to coordinate the activities of the Resistance and to prove to the Western Allies that the French underground was united behind General de Gaulle; it was to have been a representative organ of the various internal Resistance movements, political parties, and free trade unions.[22]

A representative of the MUR to the Conseil was Pascal Copeau, a Communist sympathizer, who was the delegate from the leftist intellectual group, Libération-Sud. Copeau was also selected to be a member of the permanent bureau of the Conseil. As a representative of a non-Communist mass organization on the important bureau, he was in a key position to influence the general policy of the Resistance. The Communists had other supporters in the Conseil, also representing non-Communist organizations. Louis Saillant, who represented the CGT, was sympathetic to the Party at this time and became a pro-Communist apologist after the liberation. Jacques Debrû-Bridel, representing a political party, The Fédération Républicaine, was also a member of the FN. Though never a Communist, he was an opportunist who often adhered closely to the Party line. The Soviet press quoted his articles, published in the clandestine

---

[20] These groups were Libération-Sud, Combat, and Franc-Tireur. The latter should not be confused with the paramilitary bands of the FN, which were the Francs-Tireurs et Partisans Français. The paramilitary group of the MUR was the Armée Secrète. Later two other groups, Ceux de la Libération and Ceux de la Résistance, merged with MUR to form the Mouvements de la Libération Nationale. For a convenient summary of the complex subject of the organization of the Resistance, see Ministère de l'Information, Notes, Documentations et Etudes, LXVI, No. 225, "Esquisse," and Hostache, Le Conseil, Chapter III.

[21] The numerical strength of the pro-Communist wing of the MUR/MLN was revealed at the first congress in January, 1945. See below, p. 215.

[22] Moulin was also responsible for the creation of the MUR and for the organization of the General Delegation of General de Gaulle in France. He presided over the first meeting of the Conseil National. The Germans arrested him in June, 1943.

paper of the FN, *Front National,* as representative of Resistance opinion. Two acknowledged Communists were in the Conseil, Pierre Villon (Ginsburger) of the FN and André Mercier, who represented the Party itself.

Most important of all, the five-man permanent bureau was composed of Villon, Copeau, Saillant, Maxime Blocq-Mascart (delegate of the Organisation Civile et Militaire), and Georges Bidault (representing a political party, the Démocrates Populaires), who was elected president of the bureau after Moulin's arrest.[23] Despite the fact that the Communists and their sympathizers had a majority in the bureau, they did not succeed in dictating their policies to the other organizations of the Resistance. However, because of its strong position, the Party resisted any attempts to create a potential rival to the Conseil, especially one which was made up solely of Resistance groups and excluded political parties.

As early as 1943 Pierre Hervé, secretary-general of the MUR but still a loyal Communist, condemned the idea of a monolithic Resistance party as an attempt to create "a single bourgeois party with a demogogic revolutionary wing" which, "as in Germany, would fight against the former so-called republican parties." The transformation of the Resistance into a party, Hervé concluded, could only lead to a decline in the dynamism and mass appeal of the movement. Already he saw signs of "fence-sitting" and political

[23] It is only fair to note that Saillant and Copeau could not always be depended upon by the Communists. They were criticized occasionally by the Party and sometimes did not vote with the Communists in the Conseil. See the report of Bingen, February, 1944, M/B Archives du Bureau des Renseignements et d'Action de Londres (BRAL), as quoted in Hostache, *Le Conseil,* pp. 164–65. Hostache cites the unanimous personal testimony of all the non-Communist members of the Conseil that Saillant was not completely committed to the Party at this time. On the other hand, it must also be noted that Georges Bidault has been accused of flirting with the Communists in the Conseil in order to increase his prestige. Claude Bourdet of Combat, a constituent member of MUR, claimed that Bidault insisted on setting up the bureau of the Conseil and was supported by the Communists. He also blames Bidault for having made the Conseil what it was not originally intended to be—a directing committee of the Resistance. This action, Bourdet maintained, wrecked the attempt of the Resistance groups to form a unified movement which would have been free of the "rotten old parties." See Bourdet, "La Politique intérieure de la Résistance," *Les Temps modernes,* Nos. 112–13, special number, "La Gauche," p. 1860, and Werth, *France,* pp. 196–97, who quotes a conversation he had with Bourdet on this matter.

infighting, when the real need was to follow the example of the FN, which "boldly carries on a policy of national union; it calls for initiative on the part of the masses; it moves into towns and villages; it strongly urges immediate action involving the broadest segments of the population." [24]

The only kind of unity outside the Conseil which the Communists favored was the fusion of all Resistance groups into the FN. By infiltrating the other Resistance groups, the Party hoped to bring about this unity before, during, or after the liberation of France.

This is why the FN refused to join the other seven large Resistance movements in forming the Comité Central des Mouvements de la Résistance. The main goal of the Comité Central was to create a national organization imbued with a new reforming, patriotic spirit which would be free of the taint of party politics or parochial interests. Though the Comité central established a few important commissions, it was not able to unify paramilitary formations in the northern zone.[25] Its power was never great, and one of the principal reasons for the organization's dissolution was the refusal of the FN to join it.

In early 1944 the non-Communist Resistance groups appealed again to the FN to draw up a constituent charter of a Union Nationale de la Résistance Française. This new organization was to be a federation of all Resistance groups, with the CNR as the supreme organ for the unification of the political forces; its immediate goal was to be that of coordinating all efforts at mass action, sabotage, the struggle against deportation, and armed resistance against the invader and the Vichy militia.

The FN rejected these proposals again, but this time Villon presented the Communist viewpoint on unity and action in the Resistance. His long and detailed analysis showed clearly that the Communist demands for unity meant complete acceptance of party leadership and doctrine.

[24] "Rapport Chardon," late 1943, as quoted in Michel and Guetzévitch, *Les Idées politiques,* pp. 107–9.
[25] Two of the most important of these commissions were the Comité d'Action contre la Déportation, under the Communist sympathizer Yves Farge, and the Comité d'Action Immédiate, under the Communist sympathizer Marcel Degliame-Fouché. For the activities of the latter see below, p. 94.

First, Villon criticized the other groups for their failure to cooperate in the creation of the departmental committees of liberation. "In practice the local leaders of the MLN [MUR] are opposed," he charged, "to forming such a departmental committee of liberation at Limoges; the functioning of the [committee] of the Pas-de-Calais is blocked by the absence of the representatives of OCM [Organisation Civile et Militaire] and Libération-Nord." Then he accused them of fence-sitting: "Since last summer the manifesto of the CNR has been appealing for an open struggle against the enemy and the traitors. The manifesto of the CNR calls especially for the struggle against Darnand's militia. However, in the Côtes-du-Nord 'Libération' is against hunting down militiamen and claims it is necessary to wait until the militia strikes first and that perhaps a good reprimand would be enough." [26]

Villon rejected the proposal to adopt a common name for all the Resistance; it would "permit . . . those movements which temporize to hide their inaction behind this common name which united them to the active movements." He also opposed the exclusiveness of the proposed arrangements. "In creating a National Union of the Resistance for the Resistance movements only, we would eliminate the central syndicates and the [political] parties and political tendencies; we would facilitate the crystallization of an antagonism between the 'young' movements and the 'old' parties, an antagonism which cannot but lead to slowing up the union and action of the patriots in the country."

The Communists would not have benefited from the establishment of a National Union, since they would have been in a one-to-seven minority. The Party wanted a unity that would contribute to the growth and development of its power. This was evident from Villon's counterproposals to the non-Communist groups. He assured them that "the FN is a supporter of the *total union* of all patriots in one organization. With all its might it has struggled from the beginning to unite in its midst all patriots, whatever their origin, their political opinions, or their beliefs. . . . For three years it has never missed an occasion, above all after the formation of the CNR,

---

[26] *Documents édités par le comité directeur du FN,* June, 1944, No. 4, "Lettre de P. Villon, 4 avril, 1944," p. 5.

to appeal to the other movements to join with it." Villon then defined unification on Communist terms:

(1) that a single movement should have one *leadership which has given proof of its political farsightedness* and of its ability to lead the popular masses into action. This means that such a leadership cannot be composed of any kind of movement with a few hundred members which offsets by its vote the proposition of a movement which has been able to rally hundreds of thousands of adherents, so that the partisans of inaction offset the voices of the partisans of immediate action. It is necessary, on the contrary, that those who were mistaken in the past reenter the ranks and strive to win their stripes.

(2) this presupposes a common doctrine . . . of the Resistance . . . [which means] that it is necessary to know if everyone is for the *immediate struggle in all forms*. It is necessary . . . that all the elements which compose it be convinced that what the FN did Corsica was right and that it is possible in continental France. This common doctrine ought to be based. above all, on a *common confidence in the people*. . . .

Finally, according to Villon, the organization of the movement must rest on the right of the masses to take the initiative and even to replace "incompetent leaders."

The French Communist Party wanted to create a monolithic front organization in France which would be similar to the AVNOJ in Yugoslavia or the Fatherland Front in Bulgaria. It wanted this organization to adopt a program of total and active resistance to the Germans. Such a front would be able to dominate the CNR and play an outstanding role in the liberation of France, and could thus be in a position to demand important concessions from De Gaulle. The FN and the Communist Party were not strong enough to force the other groups to accept their plans, and there was no external power which would support the Party. Consequently, unity was never achieved in the French Resistance, but we have some idea of what it might have been like if the Communists had been in a position to enforce it.

The Military Resistance

The Communists combined similar tactics of infiltration with daring and luck to gain control of the most important military co-

[27] *Ibid.*, pp. 6–8, emphasis as in original.

ordinating committee of the Resistance. The Comité d'Action Militaire (known as COMIDAC and, after May, 1944, as COMAC), one of the committees of the CNR, was established in the spring of 1944 in order to unite and direct the clandestine struggle. It was composed of three men, only one of whom was originally a Communist, the ubiquitous Pierre Villon. However, by May, 1944, two of the three members were Communists. The complex process by which the party came to control COMAC reveals much of its organizational and tactical skill in infiltration. It also demonstrates that much of the Communist success in the underground was due to the willingness of its members to run the risks of remaining in France while others left to accept responsible but safer posts in Algiers.[28]

In March and April several events occurred which gave the Communists a majority in the executive committee of the MUR. First of all, the executive bureau of one of the major constituent groups of the MUR, Combat, was greatly altered at this time. Claude Bourdet, the civil representative of Combat to the MUR, was arrested. Maurice Bertin-Chevance, the military representative to the MUR, Guillain de Bénouville, and Henri Frenay, of the Combat executive bureau, were called to Algiers. Bénouville left a note which proposed Georges Rebattet (known as Cheval) as military representative and Henri Ingrand as civilian representative of Combat to the MUR executive committee. This procedure was challenged by Jacques Baumel, secretary-general of the MUR, who asked for a meeting of Combat. The delegates of Combat elected Cheval to replace Chevance and Degliame to replace Bourdet. In the meantime Ingrand had withdrawn, having accepted an appointment as Commissar of the Republic, offered to him by De Gaulle. Degliame took Bourdet's place in the Conseil, as well as in the

[28] In an interview Pierre Hervé maintained that Communist success in the MUR was not so much the result of intrigue as of the lack of skill, organizational ability, and even courage on the part of the Gaullists. He claimed to have joined Combat without, and in fact against, Party orders. Though the Party distrusted him throughout the war, it nevertheless considered him *"fidèle."* Similarly, Degliame-Fouché stated that he joined Combat, not on Party orders, but because he could not get in touch with the Party in the southern zone. Granet and Michel, *Combat,* p. 97.

MUR. He had been a Communist before the war, and it was erroneously believed that his views had changed.

Communists or their sympathizers now had a majority in the executive committee of the MUR, consisting of Pierre Hervé, Copeau, and Degliame against Robert Lacoste and Antoine Avinin. Cheval had already taken over Chevance's post as MUR representative to COMAC in February in preparation for the latter's departure. Degliame quickly supported the replacement of Cheval in COMAC by Maurice Kriegel-Valrimont, a crypto-Communist, and this was approved by the MUR executive committee in May. The Communists now had a majority of two to one in COMAC.

The Communists insisted that COMAC should be the organ of command of the military Resistance, just as the Conseil should be the policy-making body in the political field. In fact, they had supported this viewpoint before they secured control of COMAC, and many of the other Resistance groups agreed with them. It became clear that the internal Resistance wanted to control its own military forces when, in March, 1944, General de Gaulle created the Forces Françaises de l'Intérieur (FFI). The leader of the external Resistance hoped to give a formal organization to the irregular partisans in France by "obligatorily including all underground troops, prescribing that they be organized in so far as is possible in military units conforming to regulations—sections, companies, battalions, and regiments—and deciding that the officers who had command of them would take temporarily the ranks which correspond to the numbers of effectives under their orders." [29] De Gaulle also wanted to place the FFI under the command of the National Committee in London. The Resistance wanted to make these forces responsible to COMAC.

The Délégation of General de Gaulle persuaded the CNR to sign the agreement of March 10, 1944, which clearly defined the powers and responsibilities of the internal military Resistance. According to this document, an Executive Committee of the Resistance Movements was to be established, to consist of representatives of various Resistance groups and two civilian delegates from London. Its

[29] De Gaulle, *Mémoires*, II, 256.

military branch, a Comité Militaire National, would be established, with one delegate from the northern zone, one from the southern zone, one each from the Organisation de la Résistance et de l'Armée (ORA) and the FTP, and, finally, the national military delegate (DMN). The agreement specified that the external Resistance was responsible for the military command, which was to be exercised in a decentralized fashion. The internal Resistance was responsible for its own centralized military organization.[30]

This was the arrangement which De Gaulle favored. However, the Comité Militaire National was never created, and COMAC refused to dissolve its chief of staff's organization or to give up its right of command. The failure to implement the agreement was due to the attitude of the Conseil. It is not clear to what extent the Communists influenced this decision, but it is likely that they were quite active in opposing the new organization. They certainly would not favor a centralized organization controlled from London, one which would decrease their influence and hamper their independence.

The moribund agreement of March 10 was replaced by instructions from the Conseil which directed COMAC to assume "supreme command of the FFI"—that is, for organizing them, arming them, preparing them for combat, and directing their immediate action until the debarkation. Afterward it was to command operations behind the lines, but not those connected with the front lines.[31] General Chaban-Delmas, the DMN, accepted these conditions, while realizing that COMAC could not effectively enforce its orders because of its lack of liaison with the rest of France.[32] At the same time General de Gaulle made other preparations to coordinate the actions of the internal Resistance. In April, without consulting the Conseil, he created a command of the FFI in London and placed General Koenig at its head. Supreme Allied Headquarters recognized this command and by June 12 had assigned several American officers

[30] "Note sur la Résistance," by General Jacques Chaban-Delmas, as quoted in Hostache, Le Conseil, p. 393.

[31] Procès-verbal of CNR and directive number 9, May 22, 1944, to COMAC, as quoted in Hostache, Le Conseil, p. 395.

[32] Dansette, Histoire, p. 45. Opinion expressed by General Chaban-Delmas in a conversation with the author.

to Koenig's chief of staff. The inevitable clash between the COMAC and Koenig commands broke out after the Allied debarkation, when the Communists attempted to assert their influence over the FFI.

By May, 1944, COMAC had made good its claim to command the internal military Resistance, and the Communists had won control of this military committee. These two developments had a widespread effect on the organization of the military forces of the Resistance on the eve of the Allied landings.

In May another unexpected and tragic event redounded to the benefit of the Communists. Pontcarral, the chief of staff of COMAC and a non-Communist, was arrested by the Germans. A meeting of COMAC was held to elect his replacement. Kriegel had definite orders from the executive committee of the MUR to support General Bloc-Dassault if the FTP (Villon) proposed him. If this nomination were not made, then he was to propose Cheval. Villon said nothing. Jean de Vogüé nominated Cheval, who, as inspector of the maquis for both zones, was known to him. Villon was noncommittal. Kriegel suddenly proposed Alfred Mallaret-Joinville, a Communist. Vogüé could not very well insist on his own nominee for the military representative of the southern zone if the civil representative of that zone on COMAC refused to endorse him, and Joinville was unanimously elected.[33] This change was to bring others in its turn.

The chiefs of staff of most of the regional organizations of the Resistance had not yet been named, and it was Joinville's task to do this. At Toulouse, Limoges, Marseilles, and Montpellier his Communist appointees were installed. The arrest of Coquoin (Lenormand), a representative of Ceux de la Libération and commander of the FFI in the Paris region, gave Joinville the chance to replace him, not by André Mutter, who was the head of Ceux de la Libération, but by Rol-Tanguy, a Communist.[34] The result of this particular appointment was to be felt at the liberation of Paris.

Communist infiltration of the MUR had another far-reaching effect on the organization of the military Resistance. As rumors grew of the approach of D-Day, the MUR executive committee decided

---

[33] Interview with M. Georges Rebattet (Cheval).
[34] Soustelle, *Envers et contre tout*, II, 375; Mutter, *Pourquoi faut-il dissoudre le parti communiste?* p. 4.

to name two men to serve in a special executive capacity during the liberation period. Since it would obviously be impossible for the MUR bureau to direct the fighting, it was agreed that these men would be the delegates from the two largest constituent organizations; thus, Degliame of Combat and Copeau of Libération-Sud were chosen. Degliame then pointed out that since he was in agreement with Copeau on political matters, he would occupy himself with military affairs. In this way he encroached on the activities of Cheval, who had remained the military delegate of Combat. Yet Degliame retained his position as the civil representative of Combat to the Conseil.[35] On the eve of the invasion both Degliame and Copeau interfered directly in the appointment or replacement of two zonal commanders in the south, and they attempted to discredit the local commander in Marseilles, who was a member of the Organization de la Résistance et de l'Armée.[36]

Thus, on the eve of the Allied landings the Communists or their sympathizers controlled the majority on COMAC, the COMAC chief of Staff, several regional commands of the FFI, many important local commands, such as Paris and Toulouse, and the special military representative of the MUR in the southern zone.

The Communists wanted unity of all the internal Resistance military forces under the command of COMAC, but their own FTP refused in most cases to serve under the command of a non-Communist delegate or of a military representative of General de Gaulle. The FTP retained their individual units up to and after the Allied landings. In December, 1943, De Gaulle's regional military delegate from Lyon, Polygone, had reported, "The FTP are opposed to the creation of mixed teams for reasons of security." [37] In April, 1944, the regional chief of the maquis in zone R¹ (Lyon) wrote to Soustelle that the FTP were criticizing the Armée Secrète as fence-sitters and counterrevolutionaries and therefore refused to unify with them. He added, "I do not have any contact with this element of the Resistance, and consequently I am chief of the Forces Fran-

---

[35] Interview with M. Rebattet.
[36] Soustelle, *Envers et contre tout*, II, 248, 426.
[37] *Ibid.*, II, 361.

çaises de l'Intérieur (FFI) in name only." [38] The regional delegate, Droite, in zone R⁴ (Toulouse) wrote of the "total impossibility of getting in touch with the responsible FTP chiefs." [39] The inspector of the maquis of the northern zone, Brozen, expressed concern over the "separatism" of the French Communists.[40]

The demand by the French Communist Party for unity of action in the Resistance assisted it in its infiltration of other organizations. It was also an appeal to the other groups to accept Communist political and military leadership in the underground. As long as that appeal went unanswered, the Party and its front groups preserved their own freedom of action and their independent organizations. The Communists did not reject cooperation with external Resistance and with other groups of the metropolitan Resistance. They simply avoided tying their hands to any specific policy except that of killing Germans and "traitors."

These tactics give rise to a few questions about the motives of the Party. Was the Party planning to use its great strength and influence in the Resistance to seize power during the chaotic period of the liberation? Were the Communists conserving their independent organization in order to take over control of France? Did the Party expect to capitalize on a rapid German withdrawal from France in order to set up its own administrative and military control before the Western Allies and the Fighting French troops could occupy the areas evacuated by the German Army? How, in sum, did the Communists propose to use their strength?

[38] *Ibid.,* II, 363. France was divided into twelve military regions, A, B, C, D, M, P, and R¹–R⁶. At the head of each region were a regional and a departmental chief, usually designated by COMAC with the advice of their chief of staff, Pontcarrel, and their military adviser, General Bloc-Dassault of the ORA. Rogé (Lt. Col. Etienne), "L'Organisation des FFI," in Bourdet, ed., *Annuaire de la Résistance,* p. 105.

[39] Soustelle, *Envers et contre tout,* II, 364. By 1944 General de Gaulle had his own organization for the internal Resistance, parallel to that of COMAC. For each of the twelve military regions he nominated a regional military delegate (DMR); each of these men had a geometrical pseudonym. Their task was to supply the Resistance, and later to coordinate the action of the FFI with the invasion forces. There was also a national military delegate (DMN), General Chaban-Delmas, and two zonal military delegates (DMZ), Colonel Ely for the north and Maurice Bourgès-Maunoury for the south. Bourdet, ed., *Annuaire de la Résistance,* p. 105; Granet, "Dessin," *Revue d'Histoire de la Deuxième Guerre Mondiale,* No. 1 (November, 1950), 62–63, and Michel, *Histoire,* p. 105.

[40] Soustelle, *Envers et contre tout,* II, 364.

The National Insurrection: A Program

For the period before the liberation of France the only evidence that can serve as a basis for answering these questions is the Communist Party's propaganda and its instructions to its militants. It might be argued that such published materials are misleading and that the Communists acted on instructions different from those which they printed for the world to read. However, because of the peculiar conditions that prevailed in France under the occupation, there was a limit to how secret a plan could be and yet remain effective. Since the Communists were widely scattered throughout France in small bands or cells, it was extremely difficult to inform these groups of the Party line even through the medium of the clandestine press. It was an even greater challenge to bring these groups under the necessary discipline of continuous propaganda. If the Party leaders had regularly sent out two sets of instructions, urging two different policies, the result would have been only confusion and bewilderment at the local level. Proper planning and coordination of illegal Party action were difficult enough in normal, peaceful conditions. In wartime and under occupation, to implement such action would have been too complex, for it would have involved plotting against both the Germans and the men of Vichy on one hand and the other Resistance groups on the other hand.

The Communists stood unequivocally for a national insurrection or a revolution in France, but a revolution against what or whom? The idea of a national uprising had originated, not with the French Communist party, but with General de Gaulle. His slogan, "national liberation is inseparable from national insurrection," was quoted *ad nauseam* by the Party. De Gaulle intended to direct this insurrection against the French "state" of Marshal Pétain. Was the Communist concept of the revolution different from that of De Gaulle?

The first set of published instructions to the Party militants, dated April 15, 1943, was entitled "General Directives for the Preparation of the Armed Insurrection." It focused attention on preventing the German labor draft from draining France of its "most active elements," and the Party demanded that "all Frenchmen of all social ranks" participate in this supreme effort. "Women should demonstrate in the stations, lie down on the rails to prevent the departure of trains of deportees. . . . Similarly, officials should falsify the lists of deportees, make the files disappear, and furnish the patriots with identification papers and food tickets," and so forth.[41]

The militants were also

to intensify sabotage, destroy machinery, set fire to factories and enemy depots, derail trains [and,] in order that the enemy may be paralyzed, to develop the armed struggle against him and against the traitors, to form new groups of armed patriots fighting in the example of the FTP. The duty of all the leaders of patriotic organizations, on the regional as well as the local level and in the public services, is to give their activity this precise orientation and to overcome at any price the resistance or lack of understanding which could prevent the realization of these tasks. It is by *fighting, by struggling without waiting,* that the people of France ought to prepare for the national insurrection, which will demand of all militants that they know how to show proof of initiative and that they have the courage to shoulder their responsibilities.[42]

In order to encourage widespread adherence to the ranks of the active resisters, the Party claimed that the Germans planned to intern in concentration camps all Frenchmen between the ages of fifteen and sixty-five as a measure to forestall a rising of the population. "This measure envisaged by the Boches," the directive continued, "obliges every Frenchman to choose between combat for the liberation and the concentration camp, which ultimately means starvation or the firing squad." The Germans and their Vichy "valets" could be prevented from carrying out this monstrous plan, the Communists explained, by several decisive moves: First, by "coordination between all patriotic organizations, which should prepare to recruit the population at the time of the rising, [and] the groups of reserve officers as instructors of the masses." Second, "without waiting for orders from central organs of the Resistance, the local leaders should, at the moment of the Allied landings, (a) mobilize their forces and alert the population; (b) unleash a general strike; (c) kill or take prisoner the militiamen, police, and gendarmes of Vichy who try to stop the French in order to intern them"; and (d) "occupy the public buildings, prefectures, town

[41] *L'Humanité,* No. 214 (April 15, 1943). The general directive was endorsed by Thorez in *L'Humanité.* See Thorez, *Oeuvres,* Book Five, XIX, 162–67.

[42] *L'Humanité,* No. 214 (April 15, 1943).

halls, central post and telegraph offices, radio stations, etc., turn out the representatives of Vichy, and replace them by delegations of patriotic groups, who will take in hand the management of food supply and public administration." [43]

The clandestine Communist press continued to issue these instructions until the liberation of the greater part of France had been achieved. It denied vigorously German and Vichy propaganda that the Communists were planning a proletarian revolution. "They are trying," the Party warned, "to spread the belief that the Communists march alone and are preparing 'their revolution,' whereas what we are preparing with all patriots is the national insurrection." [44] Party leaders denounced the often clumsy efforts of the Germans to deceive Frenchmen with false copies of *L'Humanité* urging the workers "to form a Communist government which will rally to its support the enthusiasm of a Union of People free from capitalist domination. . . . Long live the French Soviet Republic!" [45] We have seen that the French Communists and the Soviet spokesmen denied that the Resistance was dominated by the Communists; and French Communist leaders criticized overenthusiastic militants who were hatching their own plans for liberation. The object of this propaganda was to encourage the unity of all Frenchmen in order to overthrow the Vichy government. According to the Party, the supporters of Pétain were the targets of the national insurrection.

Some of the more outspoken Communists in the Resistance even expressed strong fears that the Gaullist movement was infected by germs of fascism, which, if not checked at the liberation by a national uprising, might spread under the protection of the Allied armies to all France. As Pierre Hervé, the *enfant terrible* of the Party, explained in one of his "Reports of the Thistle," many resisters rallied behind De Gaulle for very special reasons, but "this does

[43] *Ibid.*

[44] *La Vie du Parti*, May, 1943, p. 12.

[45] The crude counterfeit was printed as *L'Humanité*, No. 286 (February 15, 1944). It was denounced by Duclos in *L'Humanité*, No. 283 (March 15, 1944). An exposure of the false number hardly requires an expert. The quality of the paper is different from that of any other clandestine issue of *L'Humanité*, the numbering is incorrect, and the masthead is not an accurate reproduction of the original.

not imply mystic belief in the personality of a chief." Fearing that the "new men" in De Gaulle's entourage were laying plans to take power at the moment of liberation, Hervé warned that "no attempt to set up a dictatorship could be made without the authorization of the 'occupying' armies. . . . There is no way to avoid domination by foreign armies camping on our soil except to promote and depend on the self-reliance of the masses." [46] There were few, however, who openly expressed such doubts about De Gaulle.

A less pointed emphasis on the anti-Fascist rather than anticapitalist character of the insurrection was inherent in the famous "order of insurrection" prepared by Emmanuel d'Astier de la Vigerie in the autumn of 1943. This short plan of action described D-Day as the "decisive crisis which should lead not only to the liberation of territory but also and above all to the disappearance and the punishment of the Vichy regime and its accomplices." D'Astier's definition of the insurrection is of particular significance.

The insurrection should take place in the short lapse of time which will intervene between the departure of the Germans (or the moment of their decisive weakness) and the arrival of the Anglo-Saxons. The insurrection has as its goal: (1) to paralyze in every conceivable way the German defense apparatus and the exercise of power by Vichy; at the same time it is a question of making impossible any attempt at the return of Pétain (which is possible) or of Laval (which is thought about, but appears problematical); (2) to eliminate and to replace in a few hours all the important executive officials; (3) to assure in a few hours the revolutionary punishment of treason, conforming to the legitimate desire of the militants of the Resistance for reprisals; (4) to give, by forcible and mass demonstrations, a popular and democratic base to the provisional government, and thus to assure the international recognition of the *de facto* government of General de Gaulle.

D'Astier concluded by discussing the question of the punishment of traitors. He suggested that departmental lists be drawn up of "the most notorious traitors whose summary execution would be considered by the whole population as an act of justice (surely appealing to public opinion in general and not merely to the more radi-

[46] "Rapport Chardon," January, 1943, as cited in Michel and Guetzévitch, *Les Idées politiques,* pp. 126–27. Hervé's pseudonym in the Resistance was Chardon (Thistle).

cal opinion of the militants of the Resistance). After agreement and
on D-Day, the accused will be immediately arrested and shot." [47]
One of the most straightforward and precise definitions of the
revolution, this "order of insurrection" aimed at a total destruction
of the Vichy regime and a mass demonstration of support for the
government of General de Gaulle.

In general, the Communist attitude on the revolution against
Vichy was shared by several groups and many individuals in
France who were non-Communist.[48] Other Resistance groups were
equally anxious to bring about a revolution in French politics which
would introduce a new spirit and new men into the ruling class.
The Vichy bureaucrats were to be replaced by the men of the
underground.[49] This interpretation of the Communist position on
the national insurrection left one question unanswered until the
liberation: Why did the Party resist the integration of its armed
forces into the FFI?

Communist Unity and the Trade-Union Movement

Besides infiltrating the political and military Resistance, the Communist Party sought to increase its influence in the trade-union
movement. As in their contacts with other Resistance groups and
with the French Committee, the Communists encouraged cooperation and unity of all trade-union elements on their terms in the
common struggle against the enemy. They succeeded in reunifying

---

[47] Abetz, *Histoire*, pp. 337–38. The same document was published in *Ecrits
de Paris*, August, 1950, by Louis Rougier.

[48] See, for example, the opinion of Ceux de la Libération-Vengeance, which
stated on the eve of the liberation that "no hesitation is possible; the Resistance
ought to take power from the first hours of the liberation." *La France Libre,*
August 5, 1944, as cited in Michel and Guetzévitch, *Les Idées politiques,*
p. 363.

[49] See, for example, the opinion of Libération-Nord, which appealed to the
French National Committee to "rely on the pure elements in the nation and
to surround itself immediately with men who represent the will of the liberation of the nation . . . the Resistance movements." *Libération-Nord,* April 20,
1943, as cited in Michel and Guetzévitch, *Les Idées politiques,* p. 260. *Franc-
Tireur* stated that it was the men of the Resistance "who . . . ought to provide
the Republic with its leadership élite; it is they who ought to remake France."
Franc-Tireur, July 14, 1944, as cited in Michel and Guetzévitch, *Les Idées politiques,* p. 260.

the trade-union movement in such a way that Communist influence in French labor organizations was greatly increased.

A split in the CGT between the *unitaires*, or Communist wing, and the *confédérés*, or non-Communist wing, had occurred after the conclusion of the Nazi-Soviet pact and the invasion of Poland by the Red Army in September, 1939. After the German invasion of the USSR the Communists established contact with the *confédéré* faction. During a long period of negotiations it was decided to re-unify the two wings of the CGT in a single trade-union organization. When the executive, or confederal, bureau was convoked in May, 1943, Communist members participated for the first time since 1939. In the small town of Perreux the two factions signed an agreement which set down the conditions of unity. Under these arrangements the two factions agreed to return to the trade-union framework of September, 1939; to establish a confederal bureau with a representative of the two factions—non-Communists (*confédérés*) and Communists (*unitaires*)—at the prewar ratio of six to three; and to reorganize the syndicates on the local and regional level in accordance with the proportion of representation that each faction had had before the war.[50]

By the time of the liberation the slow process of reunification had almost been completed. However, as early as July, 1943, some significant differences had again arisen between the two factions over the program of the CGT. The Communists wanted to enlarge the powers of the shop stewards, notably in matters of hiring and firing. They supported the election of the stewards by all the workers. To supplement these changes, the Communists wanted to suppress the committees of organization, which had been established by a Vichy decree to formulate rules for industrial operations, plan the distribution of raw materials, and suggest prices to the government. The Communists opposed any transformation of the economic system, merely demanding the elimination of trusts (if effective, this would actually increase the number of owners of private property) and the confiscation of the industrial properties of collaborators. In sum, the Party wanted to increase the power of the workers in the field of economic planning and to strengthen the hand of

[50] *Ibid.*, p. 178.

elective shop stewards. At the same time it wanted to lull moderate public opinion and did not, unlike its Socialist counterpart, demand extensive nationalizations.[51]

There was no complete unity of views on other matters, for the Communists insisted on retaining their separate clandestine trade-union newspaper, *La Vie Ouvrière*, in which they continued publishing their opinion on postwar problems even after the unification of the two factions had been achieved.

The Communist gains in the trade-union field were solid but not spectacular. They had recaptured their prewar position in the CGT, and they were able to continue under clandestine conditions their separate organs of propaganda and agitation. The war, the occupation, and the German labor draft had considerable disrupted the organizational pattern of the CGT, especially on the local level. The well-organized and well-disciplined Communist Party cells in the labor field were able to exploit their newly won positions to great advantage. This was done to some extent in the local reorganizations before the liberation, and on a much more extensive scale afterward.

The Communist Clandestine Press

Widespread as they were, Communist activities in the government, the Resistance, and the trade unions would have been less significant if the Communists had been unable to make Frenchmen aware of their gains. Therefore, the Party never neglected the propaganda field. In general, the Communist clandestine press was a large, vociferous, and influential element in the Resistance. *L'Humanité* published 317 numbers of its clandestine edition during the

---

[51] *Ibid.*, p. 190. The Socialists wanted to keep the Committees of Organization for a short period of time in order to avoid serious economic dislocation and probable chaos. They favored the election of shop stewards by the unions in order to avoid rivalry between the two representatives of the workers' interests. Hiring and firing powers would be entrusted to public employment offices, in which unions would take a decisive part. A labor inspector would approve dismissals after having consulted with the trade unions. The Socialists thus opposed both mass elections, in which demagogy and intimidation would prevail, and shop stewards who would be responsible to no specific organization, but would wield enormous powers over the workers.

occupation. Some of the larger Communist or sympathizing papers were *La Marseillaise* (Marseilles), *Le Patriote* (Lyon), *Le Patriote du Sud-Ouest*, *L'Echo du Centre*, and *Rouge Midi*. As this brief selection shows, even during the occupation the Communist press was nation-wide. Some of the clandestine papers had been prewar stalwarts of the party, but many others had not, and these papers tended to adopt names that evoked the spirit of patriotism and nationalism.

No reliable circulation figures are available for the clandestine period, and it is impossible to make a clear distinction between the titles and the circulation figures of the Communist papers which existed during the clandestine period and those which were created afterward. Though there was ample opportunity for the Party to establish new papers after the liberation, the great dailies had already won their spurs in the Resistance. This gave them a considerable advantage over their newer competitors of the same political orientation. It seems likely that the Communists' post-liberation press consisted mainly of papers which had been published in the underground and was proportionately as large and as important as their clandestine press.

Of course, circulation during the Resistance period was severely restricted, and it was low even in the early days of the liberation because of the paper shortage. The figures of the Ministry of Information show that the Communist press in 1944 was authorized to publish 1,598,000 copies, or 15.2 percent of the total number of French newspapers. If the FN papers are included, the Communists controlled thirty-one daily papers, which were authorized to publish over 20,000 copies each and issued in all 2,815,000 copies, or 26.8 percent of the French press.[52] These figures contrast sharply with those of 600,000 or 4.6 percent of the French press, attributed to the Communists in 1939.[53] A Soviet source reports that in the Paris region the Communists printed more pamphlets and throwaways (a

[52] Mottin, *Histoire*, p. 31.

[53] *Ibid.*, pp. 37–38. The ministerial figures were calculated on the basis of three sources—the report of the prefect, the accounts of the printer (SNEP), and the amount of paper authorized by the government to be issued to each newspaper. It is impossible to determine exactly how many papers out of these totals were actually sold.

total of 430,000) during the occupation than in a similar time period before the war.[54]

It can be safely assumed that the Communist clandestine press had a circulation proportionately larger than the legal Communist press had had in 1939. Many of the readers before and after the liberation were not members of the Party, and the Communists made special efforts to persuade them to join one of the front organizations. The clandestine press became an important element in the Communist drive for "unity of action" among all classes of French society.

The French Communists on the Eve of Liberation

On the eve of the invasion of France the Communists were entrenched in all the important centers of Free French political, social, and economic life. For the first time in its history the Party held cabinet responsibilities. Friend and foe alike recognized its strong position in the Resistance. The Party was beginning to recapture its former status in the trade-union movement. Its clandestine press was active and aggressive. The Communists had achieved their successes under the slogan of "unity of action." Their current policy was to cooperate with all anti-Nazi elements of the Resistance. In each case the degree of their cooperation depended upon distinctive factors. The French Communists were committed to support the French Committee of National Liberation as the government of France, but it was not easy for them to give up the freedom of action which they had enjoyed in the opposition days. Since the Party wished to remain in the government, it had to abandon some of its own cherished plans in the face of De Gaulle's opposition. The Communists did not have their way in the cabinet dispute or in the planning of administrative arrangements for post-liberation France, nor did they have control over official military contacts with metropolitan France.

Their new status as a "governmental party" did not prevent the Communists from criticizing the government or from putting pressure on De Gaulle to adopt new policies. The Communists maneuvered with Giraud and against Passy, but they never allowed them-

[54] Godunov, Bor'ba, p. 38.

selves to be trapped too far out on the limb of intransigent opposition. Their verbal attacks and their political manipulations were always couched in terms of greater efficiency and "unity of action" against the common enemy.

Within the internal Resistance the Communists were again committed to support a joint effort against the occupiers. The Party did not conduct private wars against non-Communist groups, but joined the Conseil National de la Résistance, and in some measure participated in the establishment of local commands of the French Forces of the Interior. Again, this commitment did not prevent the Communists from sometimes carrying out an independent policy. The Party refused attempts at organic union which would have placed its own supporters in the minority, and it favored unity only on Communist terms. To increase its chances for the control of the Resistance, the Communist Party conducted a very successful policy of infiltrating other organizations.

The short-term objectives of these tactics were, first of all, to organize and move into action the human and material resources of Free France against Hitlerite Germany; secondly, to make certain that the provisional government of France would be republican, anti-Pétainist, and socially progressive, would govern France immediately after the evacuation by the German Army, and would include members of the Communist Party; thirdly, to eliminate from organized French political, social, and economic life the representatives of anti-Communist, anti-Soviet collaborationist elements; and, fourthly, to increase Communist influence in the army, in the trade unions, and in the press, while at the same time winning supporters of the Party among the broad masses of the people. The Communists assumed that France would have to be united before it could be led, and, therefore, the Party's short-range program did not include plans to seize power. Unity on Communist terms could not be imposed by force from the outside, and in 1944 France was not ready to rally voluntarily to the hammer and sickle. Thus, for a limited historical period the Communists would have to take their stand under the Cross of Lorraine.

CHAPTER V

Soviet Policy from Normandy to Yalta

DURING THE PERIOD between the Allied landings in France and the Yalta Conference of February, 1945, the struggle against Germany entered its decisive phase, and now it was doubly important for the United States, Great Britain, and the USSR to coordinate their military assault upon the heart of Fortress Europe. With the end of the war approaching, it was more necessary than ever for the great powers to consider carefully the settlement of the many problems which had developed in Europe during six years of war, occupation, and civil strife.

There was the question of the postwar control of Germany and future of Eastern Europe. What would be the political composition of the new governments of Europe? There was also the problem of creating a strong and stable international organization to keep the peace. Though the answers to these momentous questions were often set down by the Big Three alone, the interests of other countries, such as France, could not be ignored. Soviet relations with General de Gaulle were conducted against the background of the final campaign against Hitler and the discussions on the reorganization of Europe. The relations between the French Communists and De Gaulle were also in large measure determined by these questions.

The Grand Alliance and the Illusion of Unity

In the opinion of the Soviet leaders, the opening of the second front and the Yalta agreements were important landmarks of Allied cooperation. Stalin greeted the opening of the second front with enthusiasm. "One cannot but acknowledge," he said, "that the history of warfare knows no other similar enterprise that equals it in breadth of conception, enormity of scale, and high skill of execution." He concluded that "history will record this deed as an achievement of the highest order." [1] The Soviet leaders were convinced that the invasion was a sign of good faith, and, as a result, "unity of the Allied governments has never been so close." [2] In his speech on the anniversary of the Revolution, Stalin indicated that "what must be regarded as a new factor in the war against Hitlerite Germany this past year is that . . . the Red Army has not been operating against the Germans singlehanded, as was the case in previous years, but in combination with the forces of our Allies." After praising the "consummate skill" with which the invasion had been planned and launched, he declared that now "the task is to keep Germany gripped in this vise between the two fronts. This is the key to victory." [3] A day later the Soviet leader reiterated this view: "The Red Army and the armies of our Allies have taken up their initial positions for the decisive offensive against the vital centers of Germany. Now the task is to crush Hitlerite Germany within the shortest possible time, through a determined onslaught of the armies of the United Nations." [4]

The Soviet Union also took an active part in the Dumbarton Oaks Conference for the creation of a United Nations Organization. In evaluating the work of the conference, the Soviet press declared that, just as the destruction of Hitler required the unity of the Big Three, so "strengthening and guaranteeing of postwar peace and security from the encroachments of new instigators of war requires the maintenance of friendship and collaboration of the great democratic powers in the interest of all peoples of the world." [5] The

[1] *Pravda*, June 14, 1944.
[2] "Tri gody otechestvennoi voiny Sovetskogo Soiuza" [Three Years of the Patriotic War of the Soviet Union], *ibid.*, June 22, 1944.
[3] "Doklad Predsedatelia Gosudarstvennogo Komiteta Oborony tovarishcha I. V. Stalina" [Report of the Chairman of the State Committee of Defense of Comrade I. V. Stalin], *ibid.*, November 7, 1944.
[4] *Ibid.*, November 8, 1944.
[5] "Mezhdunarodnoe obozrenie" [The International Review], *ibid.*, August 27, 1944.

Soviet Union pledged itself to support "with all its strength" the task of establishing an international organization.[6] Stalin restated the Soviet view in his speech on the twenty-seventh anniversary of the October Revolution.

An equally striking indication of the solidarity of . . . the United Nations is to be seen in the decisions of the Dumbarton Oaks Conference on postwar security. There is talk of differences between the Three Powers on certain security problems. Differences do exist, of course, and they will arise on a number of other issues as well. . . . The surprising thing is not that differences exist, but that they are so few and that . . . in practically every case they are resolved in a spirit of unity and cooperation between the three Great Powers. . . . It is known that more serious differences existed among us over the opening of the second front. But it is also known that these differences were resolved in a spirit of complete accord. . . . What is characteristic of this conference is not that certain differences were revealed there, but that nine tenths of the security problems were solved at this conference in a spirit of complete unanimity. That is why I think that the decisions of the Dumbarton Oaks Conference are to be regarded as a striking indication of the solidity of the front of the anti-German coalition.[7]

Stalin also stressed the importance of unity and cooperation among the Big Three within the framework of the United Nations in order to prevent a revival of German imperialism. He pointed out that Germany would be disarmed after the war. "However," he added, "it would be naïve to think that she will not attempt to restore her might and launch a new aggression. It is common knowledge that the German leaders are preparing for a new war." The only way to block this resurgence of militarism was, in Stalin's words, "to establish a special organization made up of representatives of the peace-loving nations for the defense of peace and the maintenance of security."[8]

Since cooperation among the Big Three continued to be important to the USSR, the Soviet leaders wanted to gain Allied approval

---

[6] "Kontury mezhdunarodnoi Organizatsii Bezopasnosti" [Outline of the International Security Organization], *ibid.*, October 11, 1944, and also "Mezhdunarodnoe obozrenie," *ibid.*, October 15, 1944.

[7] "Doklad Predsedatelia Gosudarstvennogo Komiteta Oborony tovarishcha I. V. Stalina," *ibid.*, November 7, 1944.

[8] *Ibid.*

of their policies in Eastern Europe. Nevertheless, this did not prevent the USSR from increasing its pressure on the non-Communists in the area. In fact, "for East Central Europe the crucial year was 1944, which saw the conclusion of several armistices and the installation of massive Soviet power, backed by Communist parties and the Soviet secret police, in most of the area." [9]

Limitations of Soviet Policy in Western Europe

What of Soviet policy toward France during this critical year? Was there a possibility that the Soviet Union could bring any pressure to bear on France? In the absence of a second front, were the Soviet leaders planning to destroy Germany in the field and conquer all of Europe? After the war Soviet analysts claimed that in 1944 the Soviet Union "was in a position, with its own forces alone and without the assistance of its allies, to occupy the whole of Germany and to liberate France." [10] According to this interpretation, "the émigré circles (including the pretender to the role of French dictator, De Gaulle) . . . began to demand from America and England the immediate opening of a second front, not so much to crush the Germans as to struggle against the popular masses and the internal Resistance movement." [11] Even more bitterly it was maintained that "by opening the second front in June, 1944, the ruling circles of the United States and Great Britain tried to block the entrance of the Soviet Army into France and the other countries of Western Europe." [12]

Are these statements an accurate reflection of Soviet plans in 1944? Did Stalin regard the second front with suspicion and hostility because he saw in it an attempt to prevent the Red Army from reaching the Atlantic? In the light of the available evidence, it is not possible to give final answers to these questions. However, the evident pleasure manifested by the Soviet leaders at the opening of

[9] Mosely, "Hopes and Failures," in Kertesz, ed., *The Fate of East Central Europe,* p. 66.
[10] Stalin, *Kratkaia biografia,* p. 180.
[11] Deborin, *Mezhdunarodnye otnosheniia,* p. 248.
[12] Godunov, *Bor'ba,* p. 119.

a second front makes it difficult to believe that Moscow secretly opposed the landings in France. What the Soviet Union would have done had the Allies not landed is a matter of pure speculation.

A consistent feature of Soviet foreign policy is always to leave two lines of conduct open. The situation in 1944 is no exception to this pattern. The Soviet Union could have signed a separate peace treaty with Germany on the basis of a new partition of Eastern Europe into spheres of influence, or it could have continued the war in the hope of crushing Germany and occupying Western Europe. In the event of a Soviet conquest of all of Europe, the French Communist Party would have played a decisive role in the future of France.

As Stalin himself admitted, the Allied landings put an end to speculation on this matter. After June, 1944, the Soviet Union could no longer hope to influence directly the struggle for power in France. Writing to the Yugoslav Communist Party in May, 1948, Stalin asserted:

Even though the French and Italian Communist Parties have so far achieved less success than the CPY, this is not because of any special qualities of the CPY, but mainly because . . . the Soviet Army came to the aid of the Yugoslav people, crushed the German invader, liberated Belgrade, and in this way created the conditions necessary for the CPY to achieve power. Unfortunately, the Soviet Army did not and could not render such assistance to the French and Italian Communist parties.[13]

This was not the first time a Soviet source admitted the importance of the Red Army as a factor in Soviet foreign policy. In a history of France during the Second World War a Soviet historian, A. Manusevich, declared:

The political conditions in France were complicated by two important circumstances: (1) the dominating military strength in the country was the British and American army, and (2) the De Gaullist elements occupied the ruling position in the country by relying on their connections with the Allies.[14]

Stalin's regret that the Soviet Army had not helped the French Communists to achieve power clearly reveals the Soviet aims for

---

[13] Royal Institute of International Affairs, *The Soviet-Yugoslav Dispute*, CPSU to CPY, May 4, 1948, p. 51.
[14] Manusevich, *Bor'ba*, p. 111.

France during this period. Because the Red Army did not drive the Germans out of France, the Soviet Union could not force De Gaulle to share his power with the French Communists.

If this were true, why did Moscow not offer De Gaulle some political inducements in order to show him how advantageous it would be for France to cooperate closely with the USSR? We have already seen that suspicion of De Gaulle's political views and deference to the wishes of the Western Allies played a large part in Moscow's reluctance to support the Free French leader. In a conversation with General Petit, Stalin had hinted at an even more deep-seated motive for the attitude of reserve displayed by the Soviet government toward De Gaulle: "France would recover in the future and then the French would take another tone." It was only when Stalin and De Gaulle came face to face in November, 1944, that the Soviet leader made it clear exactly what he expected from the French and what he was willing to give in return.

Up to that time Moscow continued its efforts to convince the French that their liberation and future security depended on close relations with the USSR. As Moscow put it, the "heroic struggle of the Soviet people, . . . the victories of the Red Army, and the bankruptcy of the legend of the 'invincibility' of the German military machine—all this awakened in the French the faith in the possibility of victory over the eternal enemy of France." Pressure on Germany from the east, the Soviet Union asserted, had forced the Nazis to deport French laborers to Germany, a factor which also encouraged resistance.[15]

The Red Army victories over the *Wehrmacht* compelled Hitler in 1943 and 1944 to transfer twenty-two divisions from France and Belgium to the east. The Soviet leaders claimed that these forces either were never replaced or were replaced by second-rate garrison and non-German troops. "So, by its victories the Red Army contributed to the success of the partisan movement in France, bringing close the day of deliverance of the French from the Hitlerite yoke." Then the Soviet Union attacked those who had opposed the Communist tactics in France: "Those people, groups, and or-

[15] Kozlovskii, "Osvoboditel'naia bor'ba," *Bol'shevik*, No. 15 (August, 1944), pp. 54–55, 56–57.

ganizations which called upon the French to 'sit tight' . . . brought real harm to the task of the anti-Hitlerite struggle. . . . Behind this cowardly advice can be seen the fear and terror which brought France to catastrophe in 1940." In sum, the Soviet Union berated the French for not having followed the lead of Soviet foreign policy in 1940 and from 1941 to 1944. There was, however, one more chance to make good the past errors, for the fight was not over. "The many millions of French people can help shorten the war by their strength. The united, powerful anti-Hitlerite army of France ought to play a significant role in bringing closer the hour of the complete destruction of Hitlerism." This policy could be achieved in only one way: "Unity and solidarity in the ranks of the French, coordination of their actions, and mobilization around common national problems are indispensable to success in the struggle for the renascence of France. Lack of national unity was one of the basic causes of the catastrophe which befell France in 1940. The strengthening of unity will be the basic condition of victory." [16]

On the diplomatic level Moscow continued to discourage the French from appealing for Soviet support against the United States. Molotov emphasized that the second front and the Soviet offensive

have special significance for France. . . . It is important that these events produce the maximum desired result. In these circumstances the agreements on [joint] action of the principal Allies, the United States, Great Britain, and the USSR, are of primary importance. . . . Our position cannot but depend to some extent on the position of our principal Allies, the Americans and the English.

Then, characteristically, Molotov complained to Garreau that the Soviet Union was not kept informed about the negotiations between De Gaulle and the Western Allies concerning the administration of liberated France. While the French representative fumbled for an answer, Molotov assured him that "the French could not doubt that the Soviet Union values highly the significance of the rebirth of France, deeply understands the interests of the French people, and feels profound sympathy for [France]." [17] Obviously,

---

[16] *Ibid.*, pp. 57, 60.
[17] *SFO*, No. 145, Notes on the conversation of V. M. Molotov and Roger Garreau, June 9, 1944, pp. 275–76, and No. 147, M. Sergeev to the Commissariat of Foreign Affairs, June 10, 1944, p. 282.

short of a statement by Stalin, no reassurances beyond such evasive platitudes could be expected.

The Soviet government also attempted to convince the French that it was championing their interests in the inner councils of the Allies, especially by supporting French membership in the European Advisory Council (EAC). When, in July, 1943, Eden had suggested the creation of an organization to study questions arising from the cessation of military activities in Europe, he had proposed that France be a member "if it recovers its influence." Roosevelt had opposed French participation on a permanent basis because "it would only hamper the work of the commission if we now included in it at this stage representatives of various groups or various committees." Therefore, when the EAC was set up at the Moscow Conference in October, 1943, its permanent membership consisted of the United States, Great Britain, and the Soviet Union, though other countries were to be invited from time to time to participate in sessions dealing with questions of interest to them. During these preliminary discussions the Soviet Union was not opposed to French membership in the permanent commission, but it accepted the Western position on this matter.[18]

In September, 1944, the French began to press actively for a permanent voice in the EAC.[19] The British and the Americans agreed that a French representative should be allowed to participate in the discussion of the German problem. The Soviet Union not only agreed to this, but also wanted to discuss permanent French membership on the commission, which it favored.[20]

Why was the Soviet Union concerned at this time with inviting France to become a permanent member of the EAC? Stalin was receiving disquieting reports concerning the policy of his Western Allies toward De Gaulle. Gromyko telegraphed from Washington that the Americans did not want to invite the French to the commission until all major questions had been decided. This was par-

[18] Ibid., pp. 524–25, note 40.
[19] Ibid., No. 161, Letter from A. Kerr to A. Vyshinskii, September 11, 1944, Supplement II, Notes on the exchange of opinions between Foreign Minister A. Eden and Commissar of Foreign Affairs of the GPRF, R. Massigli, on the question of the European Advisory Commission, pp. 305–6.
[20] Ibid., No. 174, Note of the Soviet Government to the British Government, October 26, 1944 (delivery date), p. 318.

tially true. However, Gromyko gave a sinister interpretation to this policy.

The position of the Americans is explained partly by the fact that they are trying to gain concessions from the French, including the acquisition of [military] bases in French possessions. In addition to Dakar and Casablanca, the Americans are endeavoring to acquire other bases, in particular in Indo-China . . . and New Caledonia. In addition, the Americans are trying to put pressure on De Gaulle regarding the Spanish question. They consider that De Gaulle occupies a . . . negative position as regards Franco and are trying to reconcile them.[21]

At the same time Garreau revealed that for the past two or three months Eden had been saying that the Soviet government was not well disposed toward the French Committee and that "the disinclination of the Soviet government to have the CFLN participate on an equal footing with the Three Powers in the discussion of [the German armistice]" was the main obstacle to French aspirations.[22] The Soviet Union was disturbed because it had not been fully consulted on the recent negotiations between the Western Allies and De Gaulle. In a display of pique Moscow informed the British government that it could not express any opinion on the final draft of the agreement between the French Committee and Great Britain on the liberated territories because "the substance of the French recommendations was not transmitted to the Soviet government by either the British government or the CFLN."[23] In Soviet eyes these isolated developments must have appeared suspiciously like an attempt to turn the course of French foreign policy away from Moscow. This explains why the Soviet leaders were anxious to bring France into the EAC and also why they were disturbed when the United States and Great Britain decided suddenly to recognize the French Committee as the provisional government of France. Molotov informed Churchill that this hasty action by the West would make it look as if the Russians were "the ones who were obstruct-

[21] Ibid., No. 165, A. Gromyko to the Commissariat of Foreign Affairs, October 17, 1944, p. 311.

[22] Ibid., No. 156, Sergeev to the Commissariat of Foreign Affairs, August 8, 1944, p. 297.

[23] Ibid., No. 158, Letter from Vyshinskii to Kerr, August 15, 1944, pp. 300–301.

ing recognition, whereas they . . . would have recognized [it] long ago, but had deferred to the American and British wishes."[24]

However, General de Gaulle had no intention of allowing the Western powers to determine his policy. He insisted that "French interests do not correspond with the interests of England to the extent that the interests of Belgium and Holland do. Therefore, the French government will not arrive at any serious agreement with England [along political lines]. Furthermore, the French government does not want to sign an agreement with England which excludes the Soviet Union." If it were agreeable to the Soviet government, De Gaulle suggested, he and his ministers would like to visit Moscow to discuss mutual relations.[25]

De Gaulle had first asked to meet Stalin in March, 1943, but there had never been any favorable response.[26] Now Stalin seized this opportunity to extend an invitation to De Gaulle.[27] His action coincided with the Big Three invitation to France to become a fourth permanent member of the EAC and to sign the United Nations Declaration. Soviet attempts to discover De Gaulle's real reason for wanting to see Stalin were turned aside by the disarming reply that Marshal Stalin's invitation had been so "unexpected" that the French were not prepared to sign any agreements and wanted merely to establish contact.[28]

While De Gaulle was flying to Moscow in early December, 1944, the Soviet leaders publicly claimed credit for inviting the French to become a member of the EAC and emphasized the outstanding role that the USSR had played in the liberation of France.[29] The implication was that the Soviet Union had already done its share in

---

[24] Churchill, *The Second World War*, VI, 249. Nevertheless, the Soviet government made it clear in its official recognition of the French Committee as the provisional government that the Western Allies were setting the pace on this matter.

[25] SFO, No. 181, A. Bogomolov to the Commissariat of Foreign Affairs, November 8, 1944, pp. 324–25.

[26] *Ibid.*, No. 51, Bogomolov to the Commissariat of Foreign Affairs, March 30, 1943, p. 121.

[27] *Izvestiia*, November 18, 1944.

[28] SFO, No. 192, F. Guseev to the Commissariat of Foreign Affairs, November 22, 1944, p. 335.

[29] "Mezhdunarodnoe obozrenie," *Pravda*, November 26, 1944.

supporting France, and now it was the turn of the French to endorse Soviet policy.

De Gaulle did not take the hint. He attempted to negotiate with
Stalin on the basis of *quid pro quo* and he puts his cards on the
table at the very beginning of the talks. France wanted a secure,
natural frontier and a Franco-Soviet political agreement. This
meant, according to De Gaulle, that "the Rhine River ought to be
the final barrier in the east against the German threat." He conceded that the Ruhr might be placed under the control of an
international regime, but the rest of the Rhineland to the south
of it ought to be annexed by France. In return De Gaulle asserted
that the Oder-Neisse line should be the western frontier of Poland
and that the French had no serious objection to the Poles annexing
East Prussia.

On the frontier issue "Stalin said that the Anglo-American troops
conducted military operations in this area against the Germans . . .
[and] that he considered that it was necessary to hear the opinion
of the English and the Americans, and without them such a question
could not be decided." In reply to De Gaulle's statement that the
Western Allies would not always be on the Rhine, "Stalin said that
the last two wars showed that the strength of the continental
powers was not great enough to restrain Germany. Without the aid
of the English and the American forces it would be difficult to defeat Germany. . . . Though the English and the Americans are
situated far from the Rhine, they are close enough to have played
an important role in the attainment of victory. Such is the lesson
of two wars." When De Gaulle protested that an international
regime for the entire Rhineland would make France dependent
upon the Allies, Stalin retorted that "all governments are dependent
upon one another. It is nice to have high mountains for a frontier,
but that does not decide the issue." [30]

Stalin agreed that an international coalition against Germany had
been a good and necessary development, but he allowed Molotov to

[30] *SFO*, No. 197, Notes on the conversation of Stalin and De Gaulle, December
2, 1944, pp. 339–47. See also slightly differently worded version in De Gaulle,
Mémoires, III, 365, Memorandum of Roger Garreau on the conversation of
General de Gaulle and Marshal Stalin, December 2, 1944.

discuss the practical questions of a Franco-Soviet agreement in private conversations with Georges Bidault. Molotov immediately made it clear that "agreements are inseparable from the discussion of concrete questions of Soviet-French relations." More specifically, what was France's attitude toward Poland?

According to Molotov,

the Soviet and French governments ought to do something to bring their points of view on . . . the Polish question closer together. . . . Why does not the French government exchange official representatives with the Polish committee? He cited the example of England and the USSR, which established relations simultaneously with the Yugoslav Committee of National Liberation and the Yugoslav royal government, and showed that an exchange of official representatives between Paris and Lublin would make easier the preparation of an agreement of mutual aid and would further the common task of the Allies.

When Bidault said that the question required study, Molotov bluntly informed him that "in the opinion of the Soviet government the question of a pact with France was linked to the solution of the question of Franco-Polish relations along the lines of official contact between the Polish Committee of National Liberation and Paris." Moscow did not expect De Gaulle to break relations with the Government-in-exile; nor did it expect an identity of views between the Soviet Union and France. However, "if the French cannot take a step forward in these relations, then the effectiveness of the political basis of the treaty is in doubt." [31]

De Gaulle was willing to promise only that after the liberation of Poland France would use its influence with all the Poles to persuade them to unite, accept the suggested frontier changes, and establish close ties of friendship with the Soviet Union and France. Stalin considered De Gaulle's attitude a confirmation of his suspicions concerning the dependence of French foreign policy on the Western Allies. In answer to De Gaulle's lengthy explanation of the French position, he remarked laconically, "What is the Western bloc?" and then ironically apologized for putting De Gaulle on the spot. Thus did Stalin imply that failure of the French to move closer to the

[31] *SFO*, No. 199, Notes on the conversation of Molotov and G. Bidault, December 5, 1944, pp. 349–54.

Soviet position on Poland was proof that France was associated with a Western bloc which aimed at thwarting Soviet policy in Eastern Europe.

Stalin also believed that it was important for the fulfillment of Soviet policy in Poland to gain French support.

Historically, France has always been a friend of Poland and its independence. It may be said that France was the protector of Poland's independence. In this respect its policy happily differed from the policies of the other powers. The Poles know and understand this. Stalin said that he thought that the present policy of France would happily differ from the policies of America and Britain. Stalin said that he counted on it.

If the traditionally great influence of France in Poland were used to encourage the Communists, there would be no united Western front against Sovietization of Poland; the democratic opposition in Poland would be weakened; and the Polish government-in-exile would be deprived of its only ally on the Continent.

De Gaulle would go no further than before: "When all Poland is freed, then it will be clear what the mood of the Polish people is." He added that "the French are satisfied by the way in which the Soviet government is conducting its policy with all the German satellite governments. The French wish to act in accord with the Soviet government." [32] For Stalin these assertions were an insufficient guarantee on which to base a treaty of alliance.

Stalin tried to break the diplomatic deadlock by using an unexpected message from Churchill to put pressure on De Gaulle. Churchill suggested that a tripartite treaty of alliance be drawn up between Great Britain, the Soviet Union, and France. The French were informed that "Marshal Stalin considers this idea of Churchill fully acceptable and believes that its realization would be advantageous for [the USSR] and France." De Gaulle, deeply disturbed, argued that between France and the Soviet Union there were no such disagreements as between France and Great Britain.

---

[32] *Ibid.*, No. 202, Notes on the conversation of Stalin and De Gaulle, December 6, 1944, pp. 359–64; De Gaulle, *Mémoires*, III, 368–71, Memorandum of Roger Garreau and Maurice Dejean on the conversation of General de Gaulle and Marshal Stalin, December 6, 1944.

He emphasized the need for a purely Franco-Soviet alliance on the basis of common interests.

Stalin agreed that a bilateral pact between the Soviet Union and France would be advantageous for the French. "Stalin said that he ought to speak freely and excuse himself, but several governments are preventing France from carrying on an independent policy, and the pact would help them to conduct a hundred-percent-independent policy." Of course, he added with a deft touch, a trilateral agreement with England might be better, though it would take a month or more to arrange the negotiations.

Could De Gaulle afford to return empty-handed from Moscow, humiliated by failure to obtain a treaty of alliance without the adherence and approval of his onetime British protector? Stalin offered him an alternative. "Let the French do us a favor and we will do them one. Poland is a factor in our security. . . . Let the French accept representatives of the Polish Committee of National Liberation in Paris, and we will sign a bilateral agreement. Churchill will be offended, but that cannot be helped." [33]

Stubborn and defiant, De Gaulle refused to be blackmailed. Though he agreed to receive some of the leaders of the Lublin Committee, he informed them that France would not exchange official representatives with Lublin. Furthermore, he even rejected the Soviet and Polish demand that at least an announcement be published of the exchange of unofficial representatives.[34] When it became clear that De Gaulle was prepared to leave Moscow without a treaty, the Soviet leaders agreed, after a night of feverish negotiations, to accept an unofficial exchange of representatives between Paris and Lublin which would be announced publicly only on the day the French representative arrived in Poland.

Aside from suggesting half-jokingly that De Gaulle should not put Thorez in jail, "at least not yet," because he was a good French-

---

[33] SFO, No. 207, Notes on the conversation of Stalin and De Gaulle, December 8, 1944, pp. 378–80. See also slightly differently worded version in De Gaulle, Mémoires, III, 379, Memorandum of Roger Garreau on the conversation of General de Gaulle and Marshal Stalin, December 8, 1944.

[34] SFO, No. 208, Notes on the conversation of Molotov and Bidault, December 8, 1944, p. 383, and Catroux, J'ai vu tomber le rideau de fer, pp. 15–16.

man, Stalin did not raise any questions about French internal politics. In contrast to the treatment Mikolayczyk and even Beneš had received in Moscow, the Soviet leader did not use the French Communist Party as a bargaining point.

The Treaty of Alliance and Mutual Assistance between the USSR and France was signed on December 10, 1944, and ratified several weeks later by both governments. The section of most potential significance was Article Three, which read:

The High Contracting Parties undertake also, after the termination of the present war with Germany, jointly to take all the necessary measures for the elimination of any new threat coming from Germany and to prevent such actions as would make possible any new attempt at aggression on her part.[35]

The Soviet Union was quick to indicate that the importance of this article would depend on the future development of Franco-Soviet relations. *Pravda* stressed that the German problem was always important for both the USSR and France. One of Hitler's prime goals in preparing his aggression had been to isolate these two natural allies, and "history has given many examples of how disastrous this isolation has been for the interests of France and for the interests of the peace of Europe." *Pravda* deplored the sabotage of the Franco-Soviet Treaty of 1935 by "French reactionary circles."[36]

The Soviet government evidently hoped for French cooperation in settling the future of Germany, even though it was still unwilling to have a zone of occupation assigned to France, or to accept France as a fourth occupying power. Even more, Moscow intended this treaty to become a symbol of the emancipation of French foreign policy from a purely Western orientation. Some years later a Soviet historian summed up this attitude when he wrote, "It is understood that the position of France [as a great power] will not be stable and firm until France . . . establishes close links with those countries of the world whose policies and interests are very close to the interests and needs of French security." [37]

[35] The treaty was published in *Pravda*, December 18, 1944. An English translation can be found in Rothstein, ed., *Soviet Foreign Policy*, II, 194.

[36] "Vazhnyi shag v razvitii sovetsko-frantsuzskikh otnoshenii" [An Important Step in the Development of Soviet-French Relations], *Pravda*, December 18, 1944.

[37] Manusevich, *Bor'ba*, pp. 103–4.

In France the Communists welcomed the treaty with enthusiasm. Duclos emphasized that the alliance did not constitute "the least interference in domestic French politics, which are exclusively France's affair." The USSR, he declared, was the true guarantor of French independence. Anti-Sovietism had been the real cause of the defeat of 1940, and the failure to rely on the Franco-Soviet Treaty of 1935 had led to four years of occupation and the loss of national sovereignty. France still had to fight for its independence because, Duclos concluded, if France had not fought from 1940 to 1944 and resisted the enemy, "France would not be where it is today." [38]

Thorez, echoing these sentiments, also boasted of the situation in Eastern Europe: "In these troubled times how can we ignore the calm, the perfect order which reigns in these countries which the Red Army has liberated from the Hitler yoke?" This meant, according to Thorez, that "in all these countries the word belongs to the people and to the people only. In all these countries democracy is restored because Stalin favored it." [39] The French Communists, like the Soviet leaders, wanted to avoid any interference by the West in France's domestic policies, while entrusting France's future "greatness" to the renewed alliance with the USSR.

Through its propaganda campaign and the treaty of friendship and alliance, the Soviet Union attempted to encourage the formation of a new French foreign policy, one less dependent on America and Britain and more in accord with Soviet policy. To this same goal the Communists in France also devoted both the power and the prestige which they had harvested from their role in the national insurrection.

[38] Duclos, "Notre Politique," *Cahiers du Communisme*, New Series, No. 2 (December, 1944), pp. 3–4.

[39] Thorez, *S'unir, pour vaincre le Fascisme*, pp. 8–9. This was the text of Thorez's speech of December 14, 1944.

CHAPTER VI

The Liberation

IN THE FIRST three months of the liberation of France the Communist program for a national insurrection was put to the supreme test. Would the French Communists continue to co-operate with General de Gaulle, or would they try to exploit their strong position in the underground to seize power? Did the French Communist interpretation of "unity of action" in France continue to parallel that of the Soviet Union? Was French Communist action consistent with the French Communist clandestine program? Despite marked differences in the attitudes and actions of Party leaders on the local and national level, Communist action followed a clearly defined pattern throughout France. This pattern hewed closely to that laid down by the Party leaders before the liberation.

The French Communists and Military Cooperation

After June 6, 1944, the principal purpose of the 70,000 FTP was to seek out and destroy the enemy and to cooperate with the Allied armies.[1] The FTP attempted to liberate territory lying behind the German lines, disrupt German communications and transportation, and replace the Vichy administration. They also strove to arouse and organize the population in order to harass the Germans in their retreat and demonstrate the allegiance of all Frenchmen to the French National Committee and to General de Gaulle.

Communist propaganda urged the Party militants and the front organizations to fight with all means at their disposal. It exhorted the FTP to attack both the German troops and the hated Vichy

[1] The number of FTP is given by De Gaulle, *Mémoires*, II, 252, 254, and confirmed by D'Astier, *Les Dieux*, p. 154.

militia of Joseph Darnand, to cut German supply and communication lines, and to disorganize industrial production by widespread sabotage and a general strike.[2] Finally, they were to prevent the Vichy state from assisting the German forces by disorganizing its administrative apparatus.[3] The Party warned again that "those who do not subordinate everything to these demands are unworthy of leading the action of the patriots."[4] Leaflets, newspapers, and wall inscriptions appealed to everyone to "Unite! Arm! Fight!" [5]

Every Communist publication carried detailed orders to some part of the population. For example, the peasants were encouraged to form patriotic militias in every village, to fight the Germans and prevent the delivery of food to the enemy. They were instructed to destroy or mix up immediately all enemy road markers and directional signals, to derail enemy trains by removing sections of the track, to sabotage train signals, to cut telephone lines, especially underground ones, to bar roads with felled trees, and to destroy bridges. Finally, they were urged to attack Darnand's militia and also small enemy posts and isolated cars.[6]

The Communists were anxious to make the uprising truly national. The FTP command stated in its brochure "How to Make War":

In order to mount a national insurrection, it is necessary for the entire nation to participate. That does not mean that this insurrection must take

[2] These instructions were in accord with the preconceived Allied plans, Green, Blue, Violet, and Turtle. "Green" was to paralyze rail transport in France for two weeks while the beachhead was being established; "Blue" was to sabotage the central electrical stations; "Violet" was to destroy telegraph and telephone communications; "Turtle" was to prevent the rapid movement of German reserves, especially Panzer units, from reaching the beachhead area. De Gaulle, *Mémoires*, II, 225.

[3] *L'Humanité*, No. 302 (June 6, 1944), No. 303 (June 15, 1944), and No. 304 (June 16, 1944); *L'Avant-Garde*, June 15, 1944.

[4] *L'Humanité*, No. 303 (June 15, 1944). The Party realized and admitted that all members were not aware of "the new situation, do not yet understand it, and because of this fact continue their petty routine instead of applying themselves with boldness to the new tasks. It is necessary to combat all tendencies toward fence-sitting, routine, rigidity . . . and continually to adapt our methods of struggle to the changed conditions." *La Vie de la MOI* (Mouvement Ouvrier International), June, 1944, p. 8. The Party insisted further that, "as in the past, there are some militants who, in spite of all the changes in the situation, are not adapting themselves to the new demands. If they do not change quickly, such comrades ought to be relieved of their responsibilities." *Ibid.*, p. 9.

[5] *L'Humanité*, No. 303 (June 15, 1944).

[6] *La Terre*, July, 1944.

place everywhere at the same date. . . . The insurrection should not
and cannot be that of such-and-such an organization, but must be that
of all the patriots.[7]

The Communists tried to infuse the population with the traditional spirit of revolution: "Let us decree the *levée en masse* for
revenge, for liberty, and for the independence and greatness of
our country." [8] They called for the formation of patriotic militias
of armed minutemen in every city block, section, factory, and
town. The patriotic militias were assigned a leading role in the
liberation of French territory behind the German lines.

Guerrilla units can presently occupy a town and momentarily liquidate
the power of Vichy. If the masses are not ready to participate with arms
in this occupation in order to make it lasting, or if this action remains
limited to one town instead of spreading rapidly to a region so large that
the enemy's troops cannot contain it, there is a risk that the liberation
will be only temporary.[9]

This does not mean, the Central Committee asserted, that one should
not fight in any case, for "each battle weakens the enemy." The
Party insisted that the patriotic militia was needed to defend the
liberated territory because it was "the form of organization of mass
armed struggle capable of meeting this military necessity." [10]

The Communist leaders, especially Maurice Thorez, urged the
national and local organizations of the internal Resistance to take
the lead in directing the insurrection. Broadcasting from Moscow,

[7] As quoted in Nardain, *Les FTPF*, p. 43.

[8] *L'Avant-Garde*, June 15, 1944.

[9] *La Vie du Parti*, Paris, July, 1944, p. 10.

[10] These Communist instructions closely resembled in spirit, if not in fact,
the Cayman plan of General de Gaulle. De Gaulle, *Mémoires*, Documents, II,
689, "Le plan 'Caiman,' " dated Algiers, May 16, 1944.

"I. *Goal to attain:* Various plans have already set actions of sabotage to be
carried out in the whole of the territory in the course of the battle of France.

"But, in addition to these instructions, the forces of the interior ought to move
directly into battle at the moment of the debarkation of the Allies in liaison
with the Allied forces, having as their aim the liberation of entire zones of
territory.

"II. *Principal zones of action:*

(1) Southwest-Center (quadrilateral: La Rochelle-Clermont-Ferrand-Foix-
Bayonne). While attacking and, if possible, destroying the enemy forces wherever they are found in this zone, the forces of the interior will seek as objectives:

(a) the opening, to the advantage of the Allies who have landed on the
Mediterranean littoral, of the axis Alès-Clermont-Ferrand, permitting their
passage to the west of the Rhone corridor."

Thorez declared that "the precise moment of the armed insurrection will naturally be fixed by the responsible organization of the national Resistance acting on the spot." In commenting on this speech, *L'Humanité* maintained that

It is for the CNR, the supreme organ of the Resistance in France, to carry out these responsibilities; on this subject it cannot be said too often that there must be an end to certain methods which tend to restrict the authority of the CNR, composed of responsible representatives of the Resistance, on the part of the general delegation of the CFLN, which is composed of officials carrying out the letter, and not always the spirit, of their approved instructions, but without . . . giving proof of the freedom of spirit and the sense of responsibility which the situation demands of the militants of the Resistance.[11]

During the period of actual fighting, Thorez emphasized, local initiative would be even more important. He encouraged the patriots to act "without waiting for orders from above, which may arrive too late or not at all." [12]

For the most part the Communists on the local level carried out these instructions with energy and skill, in cooperation with the Allied forces and other Resistance groups. In Brittany, where the activity of the FFI was of great and immediate importance to the beachhead operations, the combined forces of the Resistance, 30,000 strong, carried out a brilliant and successful operation. Taking advantage of the favorable terrain, these united and well-armed groups lived up to the highest expectations of the Resistance and the Allies.[13] The non-Communist commander of the FFI in Brittany, Colonel Eon, later declared, "I always found the FTP inspired by a will to fight and a hatred of the Germans which surpassed that of any other unit formed by any other organization." [14]

There was the same degree of responsible unity and discipline in Zone D (North), which included the departments of Maine, Côte d'Or, Saône-et-Loire, Haute Savoie, Doubs, Jura, and the territory of Belfort. A strong concentration of between 22,000 and 25,000 FFI, including the FTP groups "Haute Marne" and "Jura" (Com-

---

[11] *L'Humanité*, No. 298 (May 26, 1944).

[12] Thorez, *Le Parti*, p. 5.

[13] De Gaulle, *Mémoires*, II, 281–82; Churchill, *The Second World War*, VI, 28; Michel, *Histoire*, pp. 110–11.

[14] Robert Aron, *Histoire de la Libération*, p. 112.

mandant Chazeau), carried out Plan Green at the moment of the Allied invasion. Then they waited until the general retreat of the Germans became evident before putting Plan Red, the guerrilla war, into action. They timed their action perfectly to coordinate with the convergence of the United States Third Army and the First French Army near Dijon on September 11, 1944.[15]

To the south in Auvergne the Communists and the ORA signed an agreement on July 14 for cooperation in liberating the area. Even before this a handful of FTP near Vercors had sacrificed themselves to try to save their non-Communist comrades. The Communists and non-Communists also cooperated in an effort to develop some mountain redoubts in Auvergne, but, unknown to them, Algiers never agreed to the plan.[16] As a result, the massacre at Vercors became a tragic symbol of failure to coordinate the external and the metropolitan Resistance.

In Isère the FTP and the Armée Secrète formed a united front during the liberation, and in Drôme the FTP held up the retreating German divisions for thirty-six hours while waiting for the American armored forces.[17]

In the department of Ain the FTP served under the command of the departmental chief of the Armée Secrète, Colonel Romans-Petit. A man high in the estimation of General de Gaulle, Romans-Petit did not report any difficulties in discipline or command in his area.[18] In the west there was much the same pattern. In the Dordogne 10,000 volunteers, divided into three groups of the Armée Secrète and three of the FTP, cooperated closely to liberate most of the department before the arrival of regular Allied forces.

In neighboring Charente the FTP group, which with two groups of the Armée Secrète totaled 4,000 men, acted in similar fashion to liberate the north of the department. Bordeaux and Angoulême fell to a combined force of the Armée Secrète and the FTP under the command of General Adeline of the Armée Secrète.[19] In September

[15] "Les Maquis de Bourgogne et la jonction Leclerc-De Lattre," pp. 2–3. Text from the unpublished notes of Claude Monod (known as Colonel Morait), regional chief of the FFI, "Des maquis à l'armée régulière."

[16] Robert Aron, Histoire de la Libération, pp. 270–71, 281, 289, 296.

[17] Ibid., pp. 520, 524.

[18] Romans-Petit, Les Obstinés, pp. 140, 165, 208–9.

[19] Adeline, La Libération, pp. 28, 35–38.

Adeline, who was in command of all these groups, accepted the FTP offer of full cooperation in the formation of new units and incorporated them into the twenty-third Division, intact but in the minority. The FTP forces in the Gironde-Charente-Dordogne area helped in the blockade of La Rochelle and Royan. In reply to a question by the Germans during the surrender negotiations at Royan, the French delegate replied, "All the FFI, whatever their political, religious, or racial beliefs may be, are united by the same ideal: to liberate their country. The FTP are the FFI, they obey the same command as the other elements which have been formed in the maquis." [20]

In Haute-Vienne the command of 8,750 FTP, 4,100 men of the Armée Secrète, and 1,050 men of the ORA was held jointly by the famous Communist "prefect of the maquis," Colonel Georges Guingouin, and the chief of the Armée Secrète, Jean-Humbert Jolly. The latter, writing after the war, maintained that there was complete agreement and full cooperation between his forces and those of the FTP.[21]

The French Communists Take Unilateral Action

Even while the Communists were carrying on the fight within France, Party leaders continued to criticize the policy followed by De Gaulle in arming and supplying the Resistance. In one case the Communists became involved in a wrangle with De Gaulle over his failure to send assistance to a non-Communist Resistance force which was besieged on the plateau of Vercors in the Dauphiné. After November, 1942, some elements of the French Army of the Armistice (the Organisation de la Résistance et de l'Armée) and later a maquis of the Armée Secrète had occupied the plateau

[20] *Ibid.*, p. 73.
[21] Statement and letter of Jolly as quoted in Guingouin, *Nouvelle.* The figures on the armed strength are from *Franc-Tireur,* September 30, 1952, and came originally from an interview of Guingouin and researches of a former officer in the Armée Secrète, Roger Dauphin. See also Guingouin, *Libération,* p. 16. The FTP in Lot were originally financed by the Armée (*Franc-Tireur*) and included many sons of the local industrialists. Statements by Albert Houillon, editor-in-chief, *Journal d' Alsace,* and G. Enserguieux, ex-commandant of the FTP and militant Socialist, in Guingouin, *Nouvelle,* pp. 27, 28; also interview with Roger Dauphin, and interviews with several persons in Limoges.

and turned it into a well-protected redoubt.[22] The inter-Allied chief of staff in London decided in 1942 to create a "fortress" there which would serve as an interior bridgehead at the moment of the invasion of France.[23] There were about 3,000 men of the FFI in the Vercors area in July, 1944, when the Germans attacked in force. Supplies and an American commando unit were parachuted to the FFI. The FTP of the region were not represented on the plateau because they preferred to remain mobile.[24]

While the battle was raging, the Communist leaders in Algiers opened an attack against the provisional government for not sending more aid to the Vercors area. Marty criticized the government in the Consultative Assembly.[25] Two days later Fernand Grenier, Commissar of Air, published a blistering note to De Gaulle dissociating himself from the government's "criminal policy," demanding that those responsible for failure to support Vercors be punished, and proposing the immediate formation of an air corps.[26] De Gaulle was furious and forced Grenier to write a letter of apology. The Communist Commissar complied, as he later said, "in the sole interest of maintaining the unity of the combatants." [27] Although the Communists failed in this and other attempts to harass De Gaulle into parachuting more arms to the internal Resistance, they continued to demand more arms for the underground until long after the liberation of Paris.[28] In fact, they charged that "the FTP were being deprived, mostly by the DMR and the agents of

[22] Tanant, Vercors, pp. 18–19, 27. The author was chief of staff of the Vercors ORA. The preface and endorsement are by General Descour (nom de guerre, Bayard), commander at Vercors and chief of the FFI in the Isère. The details are supported by Lemoine, Vercors; the author was chief of staff of the Vercors FFI.

[23] Tanant, Vercors, p. 23, the orders of General Delestraint; De Gaulle, Mémoires, II, 279.

[24] Tanant, Vercors, pp. 202–3. Remnants of the Vercors group later contacted the FTP in lower Dauphiné. See also Parti Communiste Français, Des témoins parlent, p. 6.

[25] Assemblée consultative provisoire, JO Débats, July 25, 1944, pp. 242–43.

[26] The full text of Grenier's letter in Parti Communiste Français, Des témoins parlent, p. 10.

[27] Ibid., p. 12. See Soustelle, Envers et contre tout, II, 409–10; the author blames Grenier for not organizing the air forces that had already been authorized by the Committee of Action. See also Catroux, Dans la bataille, pp. 398–99.

[28] L'Humanité, No. 307 (July 1, 1944), No. 310 (July 15, 1944), and No. 316 (August 15, 1944).

the BCRA, of arms and money which were supposed to be distributed impartially to the entire Resistance." [29] The Gaullist leaders, on the other hand, remained suspicious of how the Communists were planning to use these arms.

In certain sections of France, such as Paris, Limoges, Toulouse, Marseilles, and the department of Loire-et-Cher, Communist activities have given rise to speculation that the Party was trying to seize power in France rather than fight the Germans. Some obscure incidents, which have never been satisfactorily explained, occurred in these areas.

The situation in the Limoges area (including the departments of Haute-Vienne, Lot, and Corrèze) throws some light on the motivations behind the Communist policy. On June 6, 1944, the German Second Panzer Division, *Das Reich,* left Montauban to rejoin the defenders of the Atlantic Wall in Normandy. As part of Plan Turtle, the FFI were to harass and delay this unit on its northward march. The task was carried out very effectively, for it was only on June 18 that battered remnants of the division reached Alençon.

On their own initiative, the Communists planned to seize the three prefectures of Cahors, Tulle, and Limoges through which the Panzer division was to pass. On the evening of June 6, FTP units attacked the German barracks in the town of Tulle, and a battle raged for two days.[30] Units of the Armée Secrète, which were encamped in the vicinity of the town, did not move.[31] When strong German armored units arrived on June 9, the maquis withdrew. The Germans hanged 120 hostages and deported one-half of the remaining population of the town. According to Colonel Guingouin, he then received from the Communist representative of the Central Committee in the southern zone, Léon Mauvais, the order to occupy Limoges. Guingouin refused to comply, stating that he believed the town would suffer the fate of Tulle or be completely leveled, as Oradour-sur-Glane had been. Then a member of the FTP of Corrèze attempted to assassinate Guingouin, only to be cap-

---

[29] *La Vie du Parti,* August, 1944, p. 14.
[30] *La Corrèze,* No. 33 (July 14, 1956), special number on Tulle. See also *L'Echo de Corrèze,* October 24, 1944.
[31] Bourdelle, *Départs,* p. 9. The author was an inhabitant of the town, a hostage of the Germans, and hostile to the Communists.

tured, forced to sign a confession, and promptly executed.[32] Two
months later Guingouin tried to unite all the Resistance units in
the area, but Mauvais forbade the action.[33] It has been maintained
that only the timely intervention of the Armée Secrète prevented
the FTP from trying to seize Cahors also.[34]

What was the meaning of these Communist moves? Was it to
seize control and establish a "Yenan"? The timing of the Communist
attacks shows up the weakness of the seizure-of-power theory. If
the Party really intended to take control of the area, why did it not
wait until the German Panzer division had passed through the
towns? The lightly armed FTP had no chance to hold populated
areas against German armor. After the Germans had passed by,
it would have been an easy matter to occupy the public buildings
without fear of being attacked. If the Communists were trying to
seize power, why did they abandon Tulle without a fight against the
German reinforcements? Why did they order the occupation of
Limoges after it had become apparent that they could not hold
even a smaller town, such as Tulle, against German opposition?
If they were not trying to take power, what was their purpose?

The Communist liberation of important towns in the path of
the *Wehrmacht* had the effect of directly involving the civilian
population in the conflict. The people of a town which had been
freed from the enemy would be more likely to join the Resistance
at that moment than at any other time before the liberation. For
this there were two reasons. There was always the chance that the
Germans would attempt to recapture the town, especially if it
was a road junction or rail hub. The fear of reprisals would force
the male population either to fight the invader or to flee the
town—if possible, with their families. They would be likely to join
the FFI in order to protect themselves and escape massacre; it

[32] *Franc-Tireur*, October 1, 1952.

[33] *Ibid.*; though Colonel Guingouin, a Communist, had violated discipline by
refusing to carry out the orders of the Central Committee, he was not publicly
chastised until 1952, when he was expelled from the Party. *L'Humanité*,
January 21, 1952.

[34] Interview with M. Dauphin. Another source reported that in this same area
the FTP attempted to bring pressure on a non-Communist Resistance group,
the Comité de Résistance (Group Verny), to fuse with them. See Parazines,
"Notes sur la Résistance," p. 13. The author was a militant Socialist.

might then be possible for them to liberate enough additional territory so that the enemy could not "contain" them. In the second
place, the arrival of the Resistance forces was an obvious sign of the
coming liberation. This would win over certain fence-sitters and
even collaborationists, for this would be their last opportunity to
"clear" themselves.

In sum, the FTP action was designed to carry out one of the
tasks assigned by the Communist leaders: "to multiply everywhere
groups of action and combat in order to organize militarily the
entire able-bodied population." In fact, the Party leaders emphasized that "the decisive role of the FTP and the whole of the FFI
will consist of brigading the rising masses and leading them to
combat." [35] Of course, many Frenchmen who had fought in the
Resistance from the outset (not the Communists, however, for
sometimes they benefited directly from the support of these "last-
minute resisters") were very bitter about the timing and motives of
the late-comers. For example, at the beginning of a battle at
Montluçon between the Resistance and the Germans, the Armée
Secrète counted 600 men, and the FTP group, 70. At the end of
several days' engagement the Armée had lost 200 men and had 400
left, while the FTP, which had also suffered casualties, had grown
to 1,200 men.[36] The FTP were recruiting as they fought. Nowhere
did they do this more successfully than in the Paris region, where,
it has been estimated, there were between 20,000 and 30,000 FFI
on the eve of the conflict for the city.[37] By the day of liberation the
number had doubled.[38]

Limoges was not the only area in which Communist actions
aroused suspicion as to their intentions. In the department of Loire-

[35] *L'Humanité*, No. 271 (January 15, 1944).

[36] Interview with M. Dauphin, who participated in this engagement.

[37] Dansette, *Histoire*, p. 51, cites 20,000 as a realistic figure, but also quotes
the official figures of 35,523 on p. 50. Taittinger, . . . *Et Paris ne fut pas
détruit*, p. 139, mentions 30,000, of whom only 475 were fighters and only a
third of these were armed. As Vichy mayor of Paris, he was violently opposed to
the rising, and his figures must be viewed with caution. Koenig estimated a
core of 30,000 armed men. De Gaulle, *Mémoires*, II, 705, Report of General
Koenig to General de Gaulle, dated London, August 22, 1944. De Gaulle himself mentions "25,000 armed men." *Ibid.*, II, 293. The number of small arms
probably did not exceed 1,800 rifles and 240 machine guns. Dansette, *Histoire*,
p. 52.

[38] Massiet, *La Préparation*, p. 83.

et-Cher a dispute broke out between the regional military delegate,
Marcel Matron, and the departmental chief of the maquis, Lieu-
tenant Colonel de la Vassière (known as Valin); the latter had
been appointed by the CNR and COMAC, with the support of
the departmental committee of liberation. Each man claimed exclusive command of the troops in the department, and the quarrel had not been settled by the time of the Allied landings. Except
in the Salbis area, the FTP frankly refused to follow the lead of the
other armed groups, the ORA and the maquis of Libération-Nord,
which finally accepted the command of De Gaulle's military delegate. General Koenig tried to end the disagreement, first by naming
a new departmental commander and again by dispatching an American colonel to settle the dispute. Throughout July the FTP refused
to accept any compromise.[39]

By this time the dispatches of the "War Office" (the Allied liaison
group on the spot) had relayed disquieting reports of Communist
terror and pilfering of arms. The arrival of American forces on the
scene resolved most of these problems, though for some time thereafter the FTP continued to resist unification with the FFI, and,
according to some reports, they "retained their arms" after demobilization.[40]

It is likely that the disagreement over the command of the
departmental forces was initiated by personal jealousies and complicated by the dispute between the command of the FFI, in
London, and COMAC. Quite possibly that part of the FTP group,
especially in the south, was exceeding instructions by hoarding arms
and terrorizing the local population. As we have seen, such actions were roundly denounced by the organs of the Communist
press. Though there continued to be difficulties with some members
of the FTP, there was no fighting in the department between Communists and non-Communists.

Occasionally the local Communists replaced a Gaullist official
with one of their own candidates—for example, the mayor of Dinan
—or refused to accept a Gaullist military delegate, as in Montpellier,
because he had been parachuted into France and had not fought

[39] Guillaume, *La Sologne*, pp. 234–35.
[40] *Ibid.*, pp. 237, 238, 253, 258.

in the Resistance.[41] However, such cases were extremely rare considering the size of the liberated areas and the chaotic conditions in which the struggle was being carried on.

The Battle for Paris

The situation in Paris was more serious and more complex. The question of how best to liberate the capital had caused sharp disagreement between COMAC and the supreme command of the FFI in London. COMAC, supported by the Communist Party and some other elements in the CNR and in the Paris Committee of Liberation, wanted to turn Paris into a battlefield by trying to block a German withdrawal through the city. They envisaged the building of barricades, street fighting, and the liberation of the capital by the Parisians before the Allied forces could arrive on the scene. General de Gaulle and his Delegation, as well as the more moderate members of the Conseil and the Paris committee, feared that this would lead to the destruction of Paris. They wanted to harass the enemy without provoking him into a house-by-house defense of Paris. This reasoning was in line with Allied military strategy, which hoped to by-pass the capital in order to avoid what might have been a severe battle inside Paris.

These different conceptions of the insurrection pointed up the dispute which had long been brewing between General Koenig's FFI command in London and COMAC. Koenig's staff issued the order: "Slow up the guerrilla warfare as much as possible, form isolated groups rather than large detachments, break contact [with the enemy] when that is possible, while waiting until we are in a position to carry out numerous parachute drops." COMAC reacted swiftly and contrarily: "Continue the hit-and-run guerrilla warfare to the maximum extent with armed units against the lines of enemy communications." [42] This disagreement was at the heart of the crisis over the liberation of Paris.

The Communist position in the military and political Resistance was strong in Paris. The five-man executive bureau of the Conseil in-

[41] Robert Aron, *Histoire de la Libération,* pp. 256, 325.
[42] Dansette, *Histoire,* p. 46.

cluded Villon, a Communist; Copeau, a Communist sympathizer; and Saillant, who by this time was moving closer to the Communist position. The departmental committee of the Seine had an executive committee for Paris, the Comité Parisien de la Libération (CPL) with an executive bureau of six members. Three of these were Communists or "extremists": André Tollet, of the Union of Syndicalists; Carrel, of the FN; and Georges Maranne, president, a member of the Communist Party. The commander of the FFI in the Ile de France was Colonel Rol-Tanguy, a Communist. In the Seine region Colonel de Margueritte (*nom de guerre*, Lizé), a career officer highly regarded by General de Gaulle, was commander. His second in command was Commandant Raymond Massiet (*nom de guerre*, Dufresne), an extremist. Finally, of course, there was COMAC with its majority of two Communists out of three.

At first the Resistance was in general agreement on the liberation of the city. The CPL agreed with COMAC that "before all France and the world, it is indispensable that the capital, whose liberation will symbolize the decisive turning point in the new campaign of France, shall not stand by passively during the liberation." [43]
The Communists went much further. In June they refused to agree to the evacuation of old people and children; they demanded that the insurrection be unleashed when the Germans tried to deport the male population, and they supported the establishment of courts-martial during the insurrection.[44] However, the various movements unanimously agreed to form *arrondissement* committees, having the same representation as the CPL bureau, which would infiltrate the local administrations, form the patriotic militias, and prepare for the occupation and proper functioning of the city halls until the election of new municipal councils.[45]

To prepare for the coming battle, the FN began to form patriotic

[43] Procès-verbal of the CPL (n.d.). *Ibid.*, p. 59.
[44] *Ibid.*, pp. 59–60.
[45] *Ibid.* Parodi of the Delegation had an agreement with the military commission of the CPL to permit the occupation of government buildings on his orders by government forces, the Gardes de Paris (future Gardes Républicaines), and the fire department. Villon thought that these groups, which had served the Vichy regime, should not have the right to occupy the buildings. See the procès-verbal of COMAC, August 9, 1944, as quoted in Hostache, *Le Conseil*, p. 441.

militias in Paris.[46] The Communists tried to secure control of these paramilitary formations by setting up a departmental council of the militias with representation for four organizations dominated by the Party: the Front National, the Union of Syndicalists, the Union des Femmes Françaises (UFF), and the Fédération de l'Union de la Jeunesse Patriotiques (FUJP). This plan was forestalled in the CNR.[47]

While recruiting, the Communists were anxious to begin the insurrection as soon as possible. On July 1, 1944, L'Humanité exhorted the people of Paris to organize grandiose demonstrations for the national holiday, to encourage manifestations in front of the city halls, and to go out on strike. Duclos called upon all the people, not just the FFI, to rise against the enemy and to take an example of self-sacrifice from the Soviet people.[48]

The arrest of several workers who participated in these demonstrations brought new appeals from the Party's newspaper to launch a protest strike. Party militants within the unions stepped up this agitation, and on August 10 the Union of Syndicalists issued an order to all railroad workers in the Paris region: "For the total and definitive liberation of our country, strike."[49] On August 15 the Committee of Liberation of the Paris Police, of which the Front National de la Police was a vociferous minority, ordered a general strike. The text of the order carried an appeal and an order by Colonel Rol-Tanguy to the police to help the FFI "kill all those who . . . continue to serve the enemy."[50]

The often hasty and furtive retreat of the Germans through Paris, the growing food crisis, the mounting excitement, and the rapid circulation of fantastic rumors added fuel to the smoldering situation in the capital. The Communists exerted great pressure on their moderate colleagues in the Conseil, COMAC, and the CPL to issue a call to arms. Then the Communists tried to precipitate an uprising by plastering the walls of Paris on August 19 with three tracts

[46] *La Vie Ouvrière*, No. 210 (June 5, 1944).

[47] Note on CCMP from CNR to COMAC, July 31, 1944; COMAC Archives, as quoted in Hostache, *Le Conseil*, p. 434.

[48] *L'Humanité*, No. 307 (July 1, 1944).

[49] *Ibid.*, No. 311 (August 11, 1944).

[50] The leaflet is reproduced in Dansette, *Histoire*, annex document 15, pp. 479–80.

emanating from three different sources, all of them controlled or heavily influenced by the Communists. An appeal of the CGT (and the CFTC) called for a general insurrectionary strike; the Chief of Staff of the Paris region of the FFI proclaimed a general mobilization; and the Communist deputies of the Paris region appealed for the insurrection of all Parisians. Even in this appeal, however, the Communists claimed to be acting in the names of the CPL and General de Gaulle.[51]

All Resistance groups in Paris now moved into action. While the Delegation of General de Gaulle and the armed forces under its control occupied the principal national government buildings and installed Charles Luizet as prefect of police, the FTP seized several city halls (in Montreuil, Lilas, and Bondy). Though there were local excesses in the transfer of power and much confusion in the transmittal of orders, the Communists did not intervene in the occupation of the government buildings by the representatives of the provisional government, nor did they attempt to countermand the administrative orders emanating from the Delegation.

The clash between the Communists and the Delegation came over the question of a truce in the fighting. The German forces did not undertake a systematic repression of the insurrection, and they were willing to take advantage of the good offices of the Swedish consul to negotiate a truce with the Resistance. The moderates in the Resistance and Alexandre Parodi, then the national military delegate (DMN) of General de Gaulle, favored a general truce to spare the city from useless destruction. The Communists disagreed violently. Villon declared:

It is not a question of holding the public buildings, but of carrying out the guerrilla warfare everywhere, in Paris as elsewhere. . . . It is shame-

---

[51] *L'Humanité*, No. 316 (August 15, 1944). The Party tract read: "*We summon the people of Paris and of its great suburbs to the liberating insurrection. All to the fight!* Such is the duty imposed on the entire population of the Paris region in application of the directives issued for the Department of the Seine by the Paris Committee of Liberation and for the greater suburbs by the Departmental Committee of Liberation of Seine-et-Oise and of Seine-et-Marne, acting under the auspices of the National Council of Resistance and under the authority of the provisional government of the French Republic, which is presided over by General de Gaulle." Jacques Duclos (pref.), *L'Insurrection parisienne, 19 août–26 août, 1944*, p. 12.

ful to let divisions pass through Paris in retreat which are going else-where to devastate other parts of France. . . . We are there to lead the people, to teach them to fight, to rip up paving stones, to raise the barricades.[52]

Villon proposed instructing the Parisians by loud speakers to or-ganize if they wished to fight, and to attack the enemy; to evacuate the public buildings if these could not be held; and to order the FFI to harass the enemy in Paris and, above all, at the approaches to the city so that the enemy would not enter.

Outvoted in the executive bureau, Villon took the fight to the full meeting of the Conseil. There he argued that the truce would cut off Paris from the rest of the nation.

Tomorrow there would be the impression that the Parisians had given up the fight while other Frenchmen were continuing the struggle. . . . Agreement with the Germans was not possible. The CNR would take the responsibility of disarming the population. . . . Finally, it was inadmis-sible to say that Paris would be protected and also to abandon the large workers' suburbs to the Germans, to divide the Paris region into two parts.

Villon was strongly supported by Pierre Hervé and Auguste Gillot. The latter declared:

We are faced by a new maneuver of the enemy. It is necessary to expose it; one does not have confidence in the word of Hitlerites. It seems that they are afraid of the Parisian population. . . . The Resistance is not victorious because it has taken several buildings. It is necessary to carry on guerrilla warfare. . . . The CNR ought to show that it is in agreement with the words of General de Gaulle, "national insurrection is inseparable from national liberation." The fight cannot be stopped forty-eight hours after it has been unleashed. Paris wishes to make its contribution to the liberation of the country, so that France can get the recognition of rights which certain allies seem still to contest.

It was impossible, he concluded, for the Communists to accept the truce.[53]

The Communists were supported by Colonel Rol-Tanguy and

[52] The procès-verbal of the CNR (bureau ?), session of August 20, 1944 (9 A.M.), Dansette, *Histoire*, p. 488.

[53] Procès-verbal of the CNR, session of August 20, 1944 (2:30 P.M.), extract Dansette, *Histoire*, pp. 491–95.

Colonel de Margueritte, a non-Communist.[54] When the moderates proclaimed the truce in the name of the Conseil, the Communists immediately denounced it.

To allow the Boches to leave Paris with all their forces means leaving to the broken-down soldiers their long-range cannon, their V-1's to bombard Paris; it means separating Paris from the populous suburbs; it means Paris betraying the suburbs; it means fulfilling the wish of the Boches: to divide the French and wipe out the laboring population of Greater Paris, whom they hate and fear; it means giving free rein to the cowardly intrigues of all those who are animated by the hatred of the people. *People of Paris, your organizations call you to fight. Those who have been fighting for three years* in the ranks of the FFI cannot *stop fighting while even one Boche remains at liberty on the soil of the capital. Practice guerrilla warfare, attack the Boches everywhere you can. Remain united until the victory, to greet the Allies fighting. Forward, Paris! Crush the Boches! No quarter until victory!*[55]

After gaining twenty-four hours, Parodi agreed on August 21 to break the truce officially, but the Communists were not satisfied and demanded a public denial of the truce posters. Finally a compromise was adopted in the Conseil which prevented the Resistance from splitting asunder on this question, and the French underground closed ranks to welcome the liberating army of General Leclerc with an outward manifestation of great unity.[56]

Communist Goals in the First Phase of the Liberation

Communist tactics during the liberation revealed how closely the Party followed both its preconceived plan and the requirements of Soviet policy. In the military sphere the French Communists did their utmost to injure the enemy and to prevent the Germans from retreating in good order, able to fight again. The Communists were

---

[54] Massiet, *La Préparation*, p. 141.

[55] Full text dated August 20, 1944, as quoted in Dansette, *Histoire*, pp. 497–98.

[56] The moderator between the two views was Saillant, who, though opposed to the truce, was not willing to see the Conseil split over the question of denouncing it. See procès-verbal of the plenary session of the Conseil. August 21, 1944 (5 P.M.), as quoted in Dansette, *Histoire*, p. 504.

willing to sacrifice their most active members in the battle, and they urged their forces to spare no effort in attacking the enemy. The Soviet Union noted and praised the activities of the French partisans.[57] For the first time Soviet commentators singled out the FTP for special commendation. Ilya Ehrenburg wrote that "the liberation of France was begun not only by the soldiers of the expeditionary corps, but also by the Francs-Tireurs falling upon the communications of the enemy." [58] The Soviet press stressed the "organized character" of the partisan movement, which it attributed to the leadership of the Conseil; it reported that large areas of France were already under the control of the FFI. It concluded that this development was of "great help to the Allies."[59]

Besides its military effect, the Communist policy of audacity was aimed at raising the prestige of the Party to new heights. In July, 1944, after Communist attacks on the Germans in the Limousin, a Communist newspaper in the area declared: "In the formidable struggle that the French people have carried on for their liberation, the Communists were always to be found in the advanced guard. Hundreds of thousands of our men fell for the sacred cause; thousands were sent to concentration camps, to prison, endured torture; but tirelessly our party continued the battle." [60] A month later Jacques Duclos asserted: "Certainly there have been many difficulties to overcome, but we can say that no other party, no other Resistance group, has done what we have done; none has dedicated so much effort and so many militants to the cause of the liberation of the nation." [61]

The attempt of the Communists to prove themselves the leaders of the Resistance gave rise to numerous myths which embittered many non-Communist resisters.[62] For example, Communists invented

[57] In almost every issue of *Pravda* and *Izvestiia* during the months of June and July there was a Tass dispatch on the actions of the French underground.

[58] Ilya Ehrenburg, "Bitva Frantsii" [France's Battle], *Pravda*, June 11, 1944.

[59] *Ibid.*, August 18, 1944.

[60] *Le Travailleur du Centre et du Centre-Ouest*, July, 1944.

[61] Duclos, *Les Communistes dans la bataille*, p. 7.

[62] Each reference to the FFI in *L'Humanité* was followed by the phrase "of which the FTP were the élite" or "the best." The Communist paper baptized itself "the soul of the Resistance" and "the leading newspaper of the Resistance." See *L'Humanité*, August 26, 1944.

the myth of "the Party of the 75,000 firing-squad victims." [63] Another myth was that the German commander of Paris had surrendered to both General Leclerc and Colonel Rol-Tanguy.[64] Finally,
the Communists claimed not only that Paris had freed itself but
also that the Party had been largely responsible for that victory.

Though the Communists were concerned with questions of prestige and military necessity, they had important political reasons for
unleashing the Paris insurrection. At the moment of the Allied landings in Normandy it was still not clear what kind of administration
would be established in liberated France. The United States government had given up its plan to administer France through SHAEF
only in April, 1944, but this was not widely known.[65] Long before
the liberation the Communists had been critical of the attitude of
the United States government toward the French National Committee, and they continued to stress the importance of rapidly recon-
stituting the civil authorities in France. Therefore, the Communist
Party "greeted with joy" Secretary of State Hull's declaration concerning the civil administration of France "because it clearly means
that our American allies are planning that the civil administration
of France will not be exclusive of the CFLN but under its direc-

[63] The figure alone was cited in a proclamation of the Union of Syndicats of
the Paris region, the Communist Party, the FN, and the FTP on August 20,
1944: "Union so that the sacrifice of the 75,000 Parisians shot at Chateaubriand,
at Mont Valérien, and elsewhere will not have been in vain. They died for the
nation." As quoted in Dansette, *Histoire*, annex document 31, p. 498. The Communists later spoke of themselves as "the party of the firing-squad victims."
Duclos. *Les Communistes dans la bataille*, p. 6. Soon the two items became
fused, and the Communist Party became "the party of the 75,000 firing-squad
victims." Careful examination of the Communist press has revealed that the
Party has published only 176 names of this claimed total. See *Agence France
Presse*, September 12, 1947. Furthermore, the official figure on atrocities presented by the Bureau of Research on War Crimes at Nuremberg for all France
was 26,600. Viret, *Les 75,000 fusillés communistes*, p. 12.

[64] During the surrender ceremony, Kriegel-Valrimont, representing COMAC,
insisted that the act of surrender bear the name of Colonel Rol-Tanguy as well
as that of General Leclerc. To avoid an unpleasant incident, this was agreed to.
No change was made on the German commander's copy, however. Therefore,
the addition of Rol-Tanguy's name to Leclerc's copy had no legal value, but its
propaganda value was enormous. The press and radio ignored the technicality
and gave the people the impression that the German Army had surrendered to
the Second Armored Division and the FFI. Colonel Rol-Tanguy, militant Communist and veteran of the Spanish Civil War, had become a national hero.
Dansette, *Histoire*, p. 387.

[65] Pogue, *The Supreme Command*, pp. 140–47.

tion." However, the Communists questioned Hull's use of the phrase "the sovereign will of the French people conforming to the constitutional laws of the French Republic."

Is it a question of hoisting into power again the dishonored parliamentarians who voted for Pétain and Laval in July, 1940, or who, through cowardice, abstained from taking part in the vote? Is it a question of forcing upon us the politicians à la Camille Chautemps who did so much harm to France and who prepared the way for the men of the capitulation of June, 1940?[66]

Though the State Department had already published a statement denying "the absurd reports . . . which are evidently inspired, endeavoring to create the impression that this government upon the liberation of France intends to deal with Vichy regime," the Communist suspicions of American intentions only increased.[67]

On June 12, after a conversation with Ambassador John G. Winant in London, Ambassador Gusev reported, "Winant did not explain what kind of administration would be [established] in liberated French territory, but from his words it is clear that it will be the AMGOT." [68] In Moscow Roger Garreau declared that "the actual administration of France is in the hands of AMGOT . . . and the American and British troops are allowing former collaborationists and Vichyites to carry on their functions." [69]

At the same time General de Gaulle telegraphed Henri Queuille and René Massigli that General Eisenhower's declaration to the French people "in principle introduced AMGOT into France." The next day the French Information Agency was authorized to state that "at present no agreement exists between the French and Allied governments concerning the cooperation of the French administration and the Allied armies in the liberated territories of continental France." [70] What were the Americans planning to do?

[66] *La Vie du Parti*, clandestine, May, 1944, p. 14.
[67] Goodrich and Carroll, eds., *Documents on American Foreign Relations*, "False Rumors of Possible Future Collaboration between the United States and the Vichy Regime, Statement of the Department of State, March 21, 1944," p. 671. See, for example, *L'Humanité*, No. 304 (June 16, 1944).
[68] SFO, No. 147, F. Gusev to the Commissariat of Foreign Affairs, June 12, 1944, p. 286.
[69] *Ibid.*, No. 150, M. Sergeev to the Commissariat of Foreign Affairs, June 17, 1944, p. 288.
[70] Robert Aron, *Histoire de la Libération*, pp. 73, 76.

When in August the United States government recognized the administrative rights of the provisional government of the French Republic over the liberated territory of France, the Communists admitted this was "appreciable progress," but they demanded that the provisional government be recognized *de jure* as the government of France:[71] "He who considers himself a friend of France ought to recognize the provisional government of the French Republic." [72]

The Party was disturbed about the anti-Communist propaganda emanating from Vichy and denounced it as an intrigue designed to split the Resistance. Against the possibility of an attempted restoration of Vichy, "the only position that Frenchmen who are concerned with the future of their country can adopt," the Party insisted, "is that of a massive rallying around the CFLN, which . . . must be considered the government of the French Republic." [73] "The national insurrection is," Marty declared, "the only way to avoid the intrigues *à la Darlan* which always fascinate certain individuals." [74]

The Soviet press also warned against the machinations of Marshal Pétain's entourage, which it asserted, was planning "to play a role in the liberation of France. Is that not why Pétain declared, in his answer to the German evacuation demand . . . , that he would not abandon Vichy and would rather stay there as a prisoner" than flee to Germany? The Soviet Union scorned the " 'repenting of the sinners,' collaborationists with the occupiers, who are now ready to settle down in the new France." Moscow charged that men such as Georges Bonnet and Anatole de Monzie had sponsored a plan to restore a republican regime in France without breaking off collaboration with Germany. The Soviet Union was convinced that, despite these intrigues,

the French people know the worth of the traitors, those who gave up the country to be desecrated by the Hitlerite bandits. Now the whole country is enveloped by a great agitation; the patriots of France are mobil-

---

[71] *La Vie du Parti*, August, 1944, p. 6.
[72] *L'Avant-Garde*, July 20, 1944.
[73] *Cahiers du Communisme*, First Quarter, 1944, New Series, No. 1, p. 4.
[74] Assemblée Consultative Provisoire, *JO, Débats*, July 25, 1944, p. 243.

izing their strength; ever more actively they are entering the struggle against the common enemy of all freedom-loving peoples.[75]

As it turned out, the Communists' fears had some substance. There was at least one attempt by American diplomatic representatives to get in touch with representatives of the Vichy regime, and the administration in Washington was not convinced until the very last moment that De Gaulle represented the majority of French public opinion.[76]

Marshal Pétain was trying to preserve his "French state" and to prevent the "national insurrection" from taking power. He had remained in constant contact with the American government through the United States naval attaché in Bern, and the latter had encouraged the Marshal's belief that the Americans sought to deal directly with him.[77] Having learned from General von Neubronn that the Germans did not intend to defend Paris, Pétain hoped to convoke a National Assembly there in the short space of time between the German retreat and the Allied occupation.[78] At this time Pétain appointed Admiral Auphan "to make contact on my behalf with General de Gaulle or his qualified representatives for the purpose of finding in the movement of the liberation of the country a solution to the problem of French policy which will forestall civil war and reconcile all Frenchmen of good faith." [79] Pétain also sent an envoy to the Commissar of the Republic at Clermont-Ferrand (Henri Ingrand), proposing a declaration to unite all Frenchmen behind De Gaulle and thereby assure the legitimate continuity of power.[80] De Gaulle declined to enter into any negotiations with Pétain.

[75] L. Volynskii, "Bor'ba za osvobozhdenie Frantsii" [The Struggle for France's Liberation]," *Pravda*, August 18, 1944.

[76] Hull, *Memoirs*, II, 1431. Stettinius reported that the British actually feared that the Americans were looking for another Darlan to ease their way into France. The United States government was uninformed as to the true nature of De Gaulle's strength in the country. Hull wrote as late as April or May, 1944, that "we did not feel that Eisenhower should be forced to maintain the Committee in France with American bayonets, should the French people refuse to accept it." *Ibid.*, II, 1430.

[77] Dansette, *Histoire*, p. 98.

[78] Robert Aron, *Histoire de Vichy*, p. 629.

[79] Letter from Pétain to Auphan, quoted in De Gaulle, *Mémoires*, II, 319.

[80] Telegram from the Delegation in the southern zone to De Gaulle, dated August 14, 1944, as quoted in De Gaulle, *Mémoires*, II, 701.

On the other hand, Pierre Laval also wanted to convoke the national assembly, but in order to reestablish the Third Republic. His plan was supported by the councillors and mayors of Paris. He approached several parliamentarians, then elements of the Marshal's entourage, and finally Edouard Herriot, whose agreement and participation was of great importance to Leval. Herriot agreed to accompany Laval to Paris, and news of this reached the Resistance leaders.[81]

In these last days of the German occupation the Communists could be certain of nothing. Rumors, piled upon scant but suggestive facts, could lead to a conclusion that the "class enemies" were plotting to betray the Resistance. The Americans' hesitations were well known; Laval's machinations had been at least partially disclosed; the secret services of De Gaulle and the Delegation were also objects of suspicion, especially when they tried to slow up the guerrilla war. There was one way for the Communists to prevent any last-minute agreement and frustrate any behind-the-scenes negotiations, and that was to fight and to urge all Frenchmen to fight against Vichy and against the Germans. Rol-Tanguy explained this frankly to his subordinates:

All our plans of attack, of defense, and of mobilization were to be rapidly established because it was important that France, and particularly Paris, prove to the world that our unanimous movement represented the nation and that the nation had participated with all its strength and with all its soul in the liberation. It was . . . the only way to show definitely the legitimacy of the government of General de Gaulle and to recover our prestige.[82]

The Party was convinced that the truce in the Paris insurrection was an important and perhaps decisive phase in one of these intrigues. "It was a desperate attempt of the agents of the trusts, who have no country, to try to fasten their mortgage upon the future independence of the nation." The Communists denounced it as "trea-

---

[81] Robert Aron, *Histoire de Vichy*, pp. 635–38, and Dansette, *Histoire*, pp. 107–8. Herriot explained that Laval "wanted to convoke the National Assembly in order to hand back his mandate and thus permit me to replace him at the head of the government according to the desires of the Americans." Herriot, *Episodes*, pp. 198–99.

[82] Massiet, *La Préparation*, p. 61.

son to the Allies and to the people of Paris." [83] The Party maintained that it had frustrated this attempt by "patient stubborn efforts of organization, of an invincible faith in the destiny of the country." Comparing the events in Paris and Warsaw, the Party emphasized that the insurrection

could not be unleashed until the moment when the ratio of forces would be favorable to it, since it was . . . not a battle of desperation but a victory to be won. It seems that these are very simple truths, but if one goes back to the tragic example of the Warsaw insurrection, willed by political adventurers, one will better measure the terrible danger which Paris escaped. And Paris will better measure what a debt of gratitude *it has contracted toward this Party*, which, on the night of August 18–19, through the voices of its elected *members, issued in the loudest voice the call for insurrection.*[84]

According to the Communists, the key to the success of the Paris insurrection was the Party's acceptance of temporary "unity of action" with the other Resistance forces and with the government of General de Gaulle. Had that cooperation not existed, had the Communists followed a line of political adventurism, then the rising would have been crushed and an anti-Communist regime might have been built on the ruins of Paris. The Home Army in Warsaw had not accepted "unity of action" with the Polish Communists, and, therefore, it had been destroyed. The French Communists praised their military leaders for choosing the more judicious path to victory.

Rol was not only chief of the FTP; he became a chief of the FFI. He knew the price of unity, which was necessary for all the forces of the Resistance. He knew that this union is the first condition of victory, and he clung to it with all his strength, as he had clung to Paris. . . . *It is the pride of the National Military Committee of the FTP* to have known how, under the direction of *Charles Tillon*, organizer and chief of this innumerable army, to lead these men to victory. It is the merit of the Communist Party and of its chiefs . . . to have given the best fighters to the great army of national unity.[85]

The Communist suspicions of De Gaulle were unfounded. The General was opposed to a restoration of the Third Republic, and

[83] Duclos, *L'Insurrection de Paris*, pp. 41, 43.
[84] *Ibid.*, pp. 44, 46; emphasis as in original.
[85] *Ibid.*, emphasis as in original.

he, too, realized that "the street fighting was beginning which evidently made the illusions of the parliamentarians vanish." As we have seen, De Gaulle was also determined to avoid any agreement with Marshal Pétain. On the the other hand, he believed that the Communists and other elements in the Conseil planned to turn the insurrection into a sort of Commune "dominated by the Third International." [86]

Thus, while De Gaulle feared a Communist seizure of power, the Party feared the intrigues and betrayals which might recognize Vichy and thereby cast a shadow on the role of the Resistance and on themselves as the "first" and "best " resisters. Parisians of both opinions fought together in the streets against the German and Vichy forces. One side accused the other of fighting too vigorously —that is, of trying to seize power. The other blamed its critics for not fighting vigorously enough—that is, for hoping to arrange something with Vichy or to allow the Americans to take all the credit for the liberation. In retrospect, it appears that each side exaggerated the motives of the other.

Communist activities in the south and southwest portions of France do not fall into the same pattern as those in the center, north, and east. Especially in Toulouse, Montpellier, Bordeaux, and Marseilles, some Communist leaders and the rank and file of the FTP took matters more into their own hands. However, not enough information is available to clarify fully what actually happened in these major provincial centers.

After the liberation the commissars' authority in these areas was often challenged and the government's orders were ignored. Sometimes the commissars did not have control of the paramilitary groups in the cities, and occasionally, as in Toulouse and Bordeaux, certain elements of the FTP refused to obey their own chiefs. In Montpellier, where the Vichy militia had earned a notorious reputation, and in Marseilles the Francs-Tireurs occupied public buildings and printing establishments.[87] In the main cities of the south and southwest a tense and disturbed atmosphere prevailed, especially

[86] De Gaulle, *Mémoires*, II, 291–92.

[87] *Ibid.*, III, 298–99, Report to General de Gaulle from a high official making a tour of the Midi; Robert Aron, *Histoire de la Libération*, pp. 510, 583–97, 602, 614–16.

among the well-to-do people. Revolutionary slogans, occasional executions by *ad hoc* courts-martial, and the appearance of bands of armed men contributed to the belief held by many that the Communists were engaging in a "test of strength" with the new public authorities.[88]

A number of commentators on the history of the liberation have quoted unpublished documents as evidence that the Communists intended to seize power in France. Judging by the style and content of these excerpts, the documents are in most cases obvious forgeries. In other cases the quoted material appears to come from documents which are genuine but of local origin. The extremists, whose work this was, were defying Party orders by printing and circulating such revolutionary propaganda. Even the most meticulous scholars and the most partisan anti-Communist writers have quoted only one or two such documents.[89]

[88] Robert Aron is most careful not to interpret all these manifestations of disorder as signs of revolutionary Communist activities, but he does maintain that the Party was in many cases challenging governmental power. He believes that "De Gaulle and his men prevented a Communist insurrection." *Ibid.*, p. 632. According to one American commentator, there were many disorders and summary executions in Marseilles, Nîmes, Perpignon, and Toulouse; he claimed that the situation had become so serious in the winter of 1944–45 that Eisenhower sent a secret order alerting all Allied armies in France to the imminence of an uprising. Robinson, "Blood Bath in France," *American Mercury*, LXII (April, 1946), 391–98. A non-Communist member of the Resistance in the southern zone maintained that after Nîmes had been liberated by the Communists there were demonstrations with cries of "*Thorez au pouvoir*," and that arms were buried for later use. Lacipieras, *Au Carrefour de la trahison FTP*, pp. 121–22. Leaflets and tracts of the FN and the FTP from Nice are outspoken in their demands for purges and monster demonstrations, but there is no evidence of Communist intent to displace the legally constituted authorities. See tracts undated (September?) from the collection of the Bibliothèque de Documentation Internationale Contemporaine, *Documents,* (Nice) Alpes Maritimes, "La Libération en province." The Communists in Marseilles were a minority in the armed Resistance, and, once Raymond Aubrac had arrived, the transfer of power from the departmental committee to the Commissar of the Republic was accomplished smoothly. Negis, *Marseille*, pp. 237, 260. In Toulouse, non-Communist Spanish Republicans told me that the Communists had terrorized the population, but they were not certain what the immediate purpose of the Communist action was.

[89] An example of a specious document is the alleged letter of Maurice Thorez to Jacques Duclos quoted in Michel Prostoi, *Tempête d'Asie* (Paris, 1948), p. 277. "The Party has only a brief period of time between the departure of the Germans and the arrival of the Allies to seize power. If it does not succeed, its mission will be set back for years." The document is not reproduced, and its origin is not given. Another example of a purported secret instruction to Com-

One fact is clear. There were so-called Left-deviationists in the Communist Party who wanted to take advantage of the military strength of the Communists and the chaotic conditions in France in order to advance the power of the Communists at a more rapid rate than the Party wished. Eight years later the Central Committee of the Party accused Charles Tillon and André Marty of planning to seize power in France in September and October of 1944. Marty denied the charge and claimed that the Party had not properly exploited the favorable conditions to destroy the power of Fascist remnants in France.[90] Whatever the truth of these claims and counterclaims, it is significant that there were elements within the Political Bureau of the Party who believed that the French Communist policy was too moderate during the period of the liberation. In attacking Marty and Tillon, Thorez defended the Party's policy of not having attempted to seize power. He blamed the two deviationists for having tried to separate the FTP from the Party despite the fact that, "from their formation to the liberation, the FTP had always been directed by Party leadership." [91] This in turn had led, according to Thorez, to a desire to take power through the FTP, "as if the [armed] action could be separated from the general political action or even exist without it." [92]

---

munist militants to make use of the period of liberation to eliminate "class enemies" and thus prepare the way for a seizure of power is given in Mutter, *Pourquoi faut-il dissoudre le parti communiste?* p. 4. M. Mutter does not give the source of his information. The attempt to imitate Communist jargon by inserting a few revolutionary phrases in the document is clumsy. The instructions contradict the prevailing Party line in several instances. Finally, Robert Aron, *Histoire de la Libération,* p. 583, cites the following unsigned, undated document addressed to the FTP in Dordogne: "Standby order to seize Toulouse and Limoges to proclaim a Republic of Soviets in the South of France." The owner of the document is Colonel Druilhe, an anti-Communist commander of the FFI of Bordeaux, who took possession of the public buildings in the city to forestall what he claimed was a Communist seizure of power. A. Rossi (Tasca), who made a meticulous study of the "papillons," the Communist Party leaflets and throwaways of the period 1941–44, did not include any such documents in his *La Guerre des papillons,* plates I–XLVIII.

[90] Marty argues that he "never called for a Socialist revolution, but for backing the Communist members of the government by having the program of the CNR applied." He further explained that he wanted (1) to seize the property of the traitors—that is, most of the banks and industry; (2) to use the departmental committees to encourage the workers to seize these properties; and (3) to form a united-front government with the Socialists. Marty, *L'Affaire Marty,* p. 241.

[91] *L'Humanité,* September 17, 1952.

[92] *Ibid.,* October 4, 1952.

What was the political situation at the time of the liberation? Soon after the liberation Pierre Hervé, then a high-ranking Party member, defined it:

To guarantee our independence and the conduct of the war, it was necessary to avoid a conflict which would have provoked Anglo-American intervention and diminished our role in the destruction of Germany. . . . Who can say what the repercussions of a rupture between General de Gaulle and the Resistance would have led to? [93]

In 1952 the Central Committee still defined its aims of 1944 in terms of the demands of Soviet foreign policy:

Some excellent comrades may have believed, on the basis of an inexact understanding of the forces of that moment, that the working class should have seized power at the liberation. . . . After the liberation of France, thanks to the all-out sacrifices of the people of the Soviet Union, of the Soviet Army, of the Army of Stalin without which Hitler would not have been vanquished, what was our duty . . . ? To make war. . . . In taking another course the PCF would have betrayed the working class and the nation. In August, 1944, the war was not yet over. A reversal of alliances creating a coalition of capitalist powers against the Soviet Union was possible. If a pretext had been given to them, the Americans, having arrived in France at the eleventh hour out of fear of seeing the Soviet Union advance too far toward the west, would not have hesitated to ally themselves with Hitler in Europe and with Japan in Asia, to array all the international capitalist forces against the country of socialism.

Even in France, in spite of the considerable progress of its influence, the Party would have been quickly isolated if it had embarked on a course other than that of continuing the war against Hitler, and [such a course] could have resulted only in a bloody reverse. A pretext would have been furnished to De Gaulle to call upon Anglo-American arms to crush the working class, to make an arrangement with Pétain, and to pursue the sinister work of the Gestapo.

The wise and far-seeing policy of the Party did not allow that; the Communists are revolutionaries, not adventurers. It was in conformity with the interests of the working class and of the country to consider that the essential task was to end the war rapidly with complete victory over Hitlerite Germany, to create the conditions for the economic and political independence of France, to isolate De Gaulle from the broad masses in order to prevent him from imposing a Fascist dictatorship. The decisions of the Party taken at this moment under the compulsion

[93] Hervé, *La Libération trahie*, p. 105.

of M. Thorez, including the dissolution of the patriotic militia and the giving up of all arms for the fighters at the front, have shown themselves to be, in essence, absolutely correct.[94]

According to the Central Committee of the Party, any attempt by the Communists to seize power in 1944 would have failed because of the preponderance of Anglo-American arms. This opinion was, as we have seen, shared by Stalin, and Soviet propagandists explained this to the Red Army early in 1945:

> If politics sets up for strategy unreal adventurist goals which do not conform to the means available, it places strategy on shaky, unreal, and adventurist ground. . . . There have been occasions when tactical successes, outstanding in their immediate effects but ineffective in the long run created "unexpected" situations for the entire campaign. (Stalin, *Pravda*, March 14, 1923) Entirely different results are guaranteed by a sensible, realistic policy. The greater the accord between politics and strategy, the greater the chance of guaranteeing the successful outcome of a military campaign.[95]

The absence of the Red Army was one important reason for the French Communist tactics. The French Communists also exercised restraint in order to avoid alienating the Western powers. This too has its parallel in Yugoslavia, where Stalin wanted to avoid a head-on clash with British interests. The Central Committee declared that the short-term goals of the French Communists were to end the war, to establish the economic and social independence of France, and to forestall a Fascist dictatorship. This did not mean that the Party had renounced violence as a means of attaining power. "We are revolutionaries," they wrote, and they implied that it was advisable to build up their power on a short-term basis and wait until the international situation offered better opportunities for revolutionary action.

Though the Central Committee's analysis was written long after the events and was designed to the Party's past policy to its critics, there is no reason to believe that this declaration is not an accurate reflection of the thought of the Communist leaders at the time of

[94] *L'Humanité*, October 4, 1952. See also Garaudy, "Le Néo-Blanquisme," *Cahiers du Communisme*, No. 1 (January 1953), pp. 44–45.
[95] Leonov, "Lenin o voine . . . ," *Agitator i Propagandist Krasnoi Armii*, No. 6 (March, 1945), p. 24.

the liberation. As such, it is the first piece of substantial evidence that the Communist tactic of unity of action in liberating France was also aimed at strengthening the position of the Party for launching a subsequent revolutionary movement. There is no clearer indication than a comparison of this document with the statement of the Soviet Political Bureau to the Yugoslav Party in 1948 that the long-range goal of the French Communists, and of the Soviet leaders for France, was the seizure of power, and that only the unfavorable military situation had forced them to postpone their plans until a more advantageous moment. This was not, however, entirely clear in 1944. It was perfectly clear that the Communists had gone far toward what they considered the sum of their short-range goals.

The First Phase of Liberation:
Balance Sheet of Communist Achievements

During the liberation the main themes of Communist propaganda were: all-out attack on the German Army and the Vichy militia; bringing the entire population of France into the struggle; and establishment of the provisional government of the French Republic as the sovereign civilian authority in France. The Party showed a remarkable ability to transform these slogans into direct action. Though the attacks were not as well coordinated as the propaganda—a natural result of the greater difficulty of discipline in the underground and of variations in local conditions—they were extremely effective. By and large, they were carried out in accordance with the military requirements of the Allied command. This was especially true in the destruction of bridges, railway and telegraph lines, and rolling stock. In these activities the Communists cooperated closely with, and even accepted orders from, non-Communist groups and commands. However, they always maintained their separate organization until the conflict had passed its decisive stage. At the same time they tried, when possible, to have their members or supporters control the lines of command within the internal Resistance.

There were, it is true, some differences between the attitudes and activities of various FTP groups. Sometimes units within the same department appeared to be working at cross-purposes, and it is not clear in every case why these variations existed. Some general conditions were partly responsible. Communication with scattered bands was always difficult and often impossible. The lack of a clearcut functioning chain of command was evident everywhere, and certain leaders disobeyed or ignored the instructions that did reach them. Contradictory orders were sent out by the Communists, by COMAC and by the FFI headquarters in London. Finally, not all FTP groups were led by Communists.

The most significant difference between the FTP and the other Resistance groups arose over the premature liberation of certain towns and areas. In some crises, such as the liberation of Paris, the non-Communist armed groups were often in accord with the Party on the necessity of fighting. In others, such as the liberation of Toulouse and Montpellier, there was a lack of cooperation. General agreement existed on the need for creating the patriotic militias in order to brigade the civilian population into armed groups capable of occupying and protecting liberated territory as well as fighting the enemy. Likewise, representatives of both the external and the internal Resistance acted quickly to remove Vichy officials from administrative posts. Therefore, in a great many cases the Communists and the non-Communists were acting together. Concerning the rights and prerogatives of the internal Resistance, they both stood firm in the face of pressure from the external Resistance to compel them to relinquish part of their power. It is true that sometimes these similar opinions were held for different reasons, but a certain amount of thinking was always common to all or most of the Resistance, Communist and non-Communist alike.

With a few local exceptions, the Communist leaders had succeeded in carrying through their program of "unity of action" and cooperation with the Republican and Resistance elements of France. They consistently adhered to their plan to hasten the victory over Germany, to block a restoration of the Third Republic, and to prevent France from being dependent exclusively upon Allied military power. At the same time, the Communists tried to increase their prestige through their military exploits and to develop their power by organizing and leading the population.

Was this policy effective in advancing the interests of the Party and of the Soviet Union? To a very great extent it was. It would have been sheer madness for the Communists to attempt to seize power during the liberation of France. Such an action would have meant division and disunity in the internal Resistance. It would have prevented the underground from playing an effective role in the liberation. It would have destroyed all the prestige that the Party had been cultivating so assiduously among the middle classes, the peasantry, and the intellectuals. It would have resulted in civil war, intervention by the Allied armies, disruption of the Allied offensive against Hitler, and, conceivably, the collapse of the western front.[96] By such action the Communists would have brought about the very intervention by the United States in French internal affairs that the Party was so anxious to avoid. Furthermore, the insurrection could not possibly have succeeded. Even by Communist estimates, the FFI, let alone the FTP, was a

[96] The French and Soviet Communists were well aware that the Americans had the dominant military power, and it was obvious that no army could have tolerated a civil war in its rear. The United States government was determined to secure the supply lines for the army. As early as April 11, 1944, Garreau complained to Soviet diplomats that "too much, if not all, power will be exercised by the [Allied] supreme commander in the affairs of organizing the civil authority on the spot. . . . [Furthermore] the Czech government is in a more favorable position than the others, including France, since Czechoslovakia will be liberated by the Red Army and therefore, without doubt, the civil administration will be organized on a more democratic basis." SFO, p. 527, note 43. In a letter to General Koenig, General Dwight D. Eisenhower stated: "Supreme Commander Allied Expeditionary Force must possess whatever authority he may need for the unimpeded conduct of military operations." An agreement between the United States and France dated August 25, 1944, which entered into force the same day, stated that (1) in the forward zone (active military operations as the Supreme Commander defines it) the Supreme Commander possesses the authority "to ensure that all measures are taken which in his judgment are essential for the successful conduct of his operations"; (2) in the interior zone, under French administration, "special arrangement will be made between the competent French authorities and the Supreme Allied Commander at the latter's request in order that all measures may be taken which the latter considers necessary for the conduct of military operations." The memo adds that certain portions of the interior military zone may be subjected, on the request of the Supreme Commander, to a special regime. Department of State, *Civil Administration and Jurisdiction in Liberated French Territory*, pp. 1–3.

small, poorly armed force, ill-coordinated and insufficiently disciplined.[97] It would have been unable to seize a country from forces that had just organized and carried out the most brilliant amphibious attack in history against a powerful and well-armed enemy. In sum, any revolutionary attempt by the Communists in 1944 would not only have been doomed to failure, but would have created conditions opposite to those desired by both the Party and the Soviet Union.

[97] Recent Soviet figures estimate the total number of armed men in Paris to be 1,500; few of these had automatic weapons and only a third had rifles. Tsyrul'nikov, "Parizhskoe vooruzhennoe vosstanie" [The Paris Armed Uprising], *Novaia i Noveishaia Istoriia* [Modern and Recent History], No. 1 (January, 1959), p. 86.

CHAPTER VII

Order and Stability

BY THE END of September, 1944, most of France had been cleared of German troops and the heroic period of the Resistance was over. Since the French Communist Party had decided to eschew violent methods at least for the time being, it now faced the problem of making the transition from a clandestine fighting force to a legal mass party. This was not a simple task, but by the time of the Yalta Conference the Party had achieved most of its immediate goals.

The first challenge that the Communists faced was to reorganize their own party and make it as effective a weapon in the political arena as it had been in the armed struggle. The Party had, likewise, to develop its five-point program for the reconstruction and renascence of France. In the third place, the Communists were deeply involved in working out the relations between the provisional government and the Resistance groups, and hence were forced to seek answers to many new questions. How were decisions to be made in liberated France? What were to be the relations between the departmental committees and the reconstituted municipal councils, between the patriotic militias and the police, between the FFI and the regular army, and between the Conseil National de la Résistance and De Gaulle's cabinet?

The Party wanted to maintain the "unity of action" of all Frenchmen and, at the same time, to protect and advance the interests of communism. Sometimes these aims appeared to be incompatible. For example, General de Gaulle opposed the continued existence of Resistance groups that might be potential rivals to his government's authority. Yet the Communists, who were and wished to remain a governmental party, drew their main strength from re-

sistance. What would the Communists do in the event of a showdown between De Gaulle and the Resistance? Would they sacrifice the Resistance groups to the shibboleth of unity? Or would
they stand their ground against De Gaulle's demands, even at the
risk of being forced out of the government? Would the attitude
of the French Communist Party on these questions once again
answer the needs of Soviet foreign policy?

"A Party Counted by the Millions"

In many ways the basic decision by the Communist leaders to
create a mass party determined the course of the Party's action in
every field. During the occupation the Party organization had been
based on three-man cells; after the liberation the leaders decided
that new conditions required an overhauling of this structure:
"Today this organization no longer has a reason for existing," and
it must be replaced by a more flexible one. The long period of
quasi-military discipline, they warned, had "left traces that will
require an effort to eradicate. What was excellent yesterday could
rapidly become sectarian and hamper our development. . . . But
it is necessary to open the doors wide to the hundreds of thousands
of men and women who have followed [the Party] with sympathy
in its illegal existence and who have often been valuable auxiliaries
to it." The Party leadership further explained that the Communists
were faced with an "urgent duty" to recruit new members. "In
the present period the real support of the Party is in the masses.
The policy of the Party is not a policy for Communists, it is a policy
for the masses, and it is each primary organization, each Communist, who is charged with translating this policy to the masses." [1]

After his return from Moscow in November, 1944, Maurice
Thorez took the greatest interest in the formation of a mass party.
He demanded that the Communists become the leaders of a great
workers' party of France, surmount narrow sectarianism, and re-
turn to the tradition of "democratic centralism" in the Party.
"The task seems less heroic [than clandestine work]," he declared,

[1] *La Vie du Parti* (Dijon), September, 1944, pp. 16–17.

"it demands no less courage and political sense."[2] Thorez's slogan became the Communist battle cry, "A party ought to be counted by the millions."

The Party's propaganda and recruiting activities extended to every class and group in French society, but especially to the peasantry. The Party praised the peasants when they did not always deserve it, and it tried to organize them as it had organized the workers.[3] The Communists were instrumental in creating the Comités de Défense et d'Action Paysanne (CDAP), which were to be used to supply food, to collect patriotic levies, and to perform other temporary administrative duties. According to the Party, the formation of these groups corresponded "to the most profound aspirations of the peasants, since the committees organized all the peasants without distinction." The Party added that "they are growing stronger every day and benefit from this patriotic spirit which is rising up everywhere in the countryside."[4]

The Communist leaders believed that it was important for the militants to control these committees.

It is the duty of each Communist peasant or sympathizer to adhere without reservation to the CDAP. . . . Because when the peasants take up again the threads of their former existence, they will organize for their own interests. At their head they will choose those who proved themselves to be the best in the patriotic struggles, those who never deserted in the face of the enemy, those who always had confidence in the destiny of our country. The PCF [French Communist Party], which

[2] Thorez, *S'Unir pour vaincre le fascisme*, pp. 22–24.

[3] An example of the extravagant praise which the Communists heaped upon the peasantry was an article in the Communist monthly periodical for the peasants, *La Terre*, which read, in part: "With the patriots of the FFI maquis they [the peasants] occupied villages and inhabited areas; everywhere they fought like lions, and if they were obliged to abandon some important points, it was only from lack of arms and munitions and in the face of an enemy who was provided with armor. . . . Tomorrow when we will draw up the patriotic balance sheet of these historic days of June, we shall see that the French peasants have not been miserly with their generous blood to liberate the country. . . . No! The generous blood has not flowed in vain. The example has been given. The number of active patriots has increased and increases in considerable proportions." "Les Paysans et l'insurrection nationale," *La Terre* (Limoges), July, 1944.

[4] *Ibid.*

is honored through its militants who organized the first clandestine committees of peasant defense, asks its adherents to be the best workers in the core of the CDAP for the realization of the great peasant unity in liberated France.[5]

Aside from this propaganda and organizational work, the Party intended to help the peasant in every way possible. As Jacques Duclos said, "For us Communists the task is to work with enthusiasm among the peasants, to defend them, to demand remunerative prices for them, to consolidate the bonds which exist between the workers and peasants." [6]

The peasant program, as finally elaborated by the Party, was a very comprehensive one. Whatever the attitude of the authorities and the other Resistance movements might be, the Communists declared, "we ought to undertake effective action to improve agricultural prices at the production level." The Party condemned as inadequate the government plan to replace the regional corporate unions of the "French state" by provincial committees of agricultural action, which would be composed of property-owning peasants named by the prefect. The Communists wanted to add the sharecroppers and the wage-earning agricultural workers to the committee, and they endorsed the proposal that the peasant committees be confirmed by the departmental committees of liberation.

The Party proposed a seven-point program for the reform of the agricultural system: (1) the setting up of separate unions for farm workers; (2) the quick return of the prisoners of war and assistance to them in settling on the land; (3) long-term loans without interest for young married couples; (4) the return of rents that had been collected by speculators; (5) the expropriation of the property of traitors and agents of the Vichy regime and its transfer to poor peasants or agricultural laborers; (6) the establishment of more effective social security for the peasants; and (7) the creation of a national fund for agricultural disasters. The Party leaders presented this program in the form of instructions to Communist militants and exhorted them to launch a determined drive to increase

[5] *Ibid.* (Paris?), August, 1944.
[6] *L'Humanité*, September 2, 1944.

peasant membership in the Communist Party.[7] It was clear that the prime object of this drive was to attract the independent farmer, as well as the landless laborer, into the Party ranks. The Party foresaw that conditions after the liberation would be ideal for the introduction of large-scale reforms, and it appealed to those elements in the countryside which would be most anxious for a change.[8]

Despite their appeals to the peasantry, the French Communists continued to rely on the urban workers for their main support. The Party proclaimed that the basis for the reconstruction and economic renascence of France would be the Party and the working class. Immediately after the liberation of Paris the Communists developed their new economic program: "The battle of the barricades is won, but the battle for the economic renascence has begun." [9] Jacques Duclos turned it into a Party watchword by declaring that the Communists should be "the great Party of the

[7] La Vie du Parti, September, 1944, pp. 21–22. See also the elaborate program for the peasantry in Rochet, "Les Problèmes de la rénovation de l'agriculture française," Cahiers du Communisme, No. 3 (January, 1945), pp. 52–82. His plans included creation of an agricultural-machine industry, increased peasant credits, rural electrification, construction of rural roads, and a moral revitalization of the peasantry. Ibid., p. 65.

[8] At this time the Party also developed a similarly ambitious program for the returning prisoners of war. First of all, the Communists were to be in the forefront of those welcoming the more than two million men back to France. Militants were instructed to form committees for this purpose. "There ought not to be a Communist municipality," the Party stated, "without its center of welcome, without its chateau, its hotel where the repatriates can take life up again in the calm of a nation regained." If necessary, the Party added, places of this type were to be requisitioned. The militants were to organize the POW's and the forced-labor returnees into welcoming groups for the later arrivals. The Communist program for the troops, and civilians was also comprehensive: (1) The government should raise military allowances for the wives and other female relatives of the POW's, and all deportees' families should be given allowances; (2) the daily pay of the soldiers should be raised; (3) pensions should be awarded to all sick deportees; (4) a time limit of one year, instead of six months, should be established to determine whether a sickness had been caused by German imprisonment; (5) a decent suit of clothes should be given to each deportee upon his return; (6) all back debts were to be canceled; (7) a three-month paid leave was to be granted to all; (8) long-term loans were to be issued to artisans; and (9) food cards with extra rations should be given immediately to the deportees. Rochet, "Les Problèmes de la rénovation de l'agriculture française," Cahiers du Communisme, No. 3 (January, 1945), pp. 26–27.

[9] L'Humanité, August 28, 1944.

French Renascence. . . . Each region, each section of the Party, should actively tackle the problems of reconstruction." [10]

The Communists identified the production drive with the rest of their program. The need for weapons was uppermost in their minds. "We can and we must make cannon, tanks, and planes for the French Army," asserted Thorez.[11] Later he urged adoption of Soviet mass-production techniques and conversion of auto workers into tank specialists. Thorez also wanted greater output of coal, iron, and aircraft, and maintained that experts had proved that the Renault and Berliot plants could produce more.[12] The Communists demanded that "the government . . . publicize all the patriotic innovations being launched in the battle for the return to work so as to create a great wave of enthusiasm from one end of the country to the other and to contribute forcefully to the mobilizing of all French energies." [13]

The Party appealed to the worker to lead the new battle for production. Bénoît Frachon, the new Communist secretary-general of the CGT, declared that the reconstruction of France would be based on the very same "working masses [who] organized the struggle for national liberation" and whose role in the insurrection had been "preponderant and decisive." In the period of reconstruction they were the men most capable "of accepting responsibility with honor." [14] The Communists were already concerned over a tendency "in high places" to seek an answer to France's economic problems in help from abroad and thus to "transform France into a semicolonial country." [15] In the battle for production the working class and the Communist Party were the main guarantees for French independence, as well as for the rapid reconstruction of the country.

In its appeals to peasants, workers, and other elements in the

---

[10] Duclos, *La Lutte*, p. 21.

[11] Thorez, *Travailler*, speech of November 30, 1944, p. 12. This theme had been widely treated before in *L'Humanité*; see, for example, the issue of September 6, 1944.

[12] Thorez, *S'unir, combattre, travailler*, pp. 9, 18.

[13] Duclos, *Batailles*, p. 26.

[14] Bénoît Frachon, "Le Rôle de la classe ouvrière dans la renaissance de la France," *Cahiers du Communisme*, No. 2 (December, 1944), p. 23.

[15] Marty, "Les Conditions de la réconstruction," *ibid.*, p. 28.

population the Communist Party placed great emphasis on its patriotism. In a hitherto unparalleled propaganda campaign the Communists attempted to justify all their actions as best calculated to defend and glorify the nation. As part of its patriotic propaganda the Party attempted to prove that it had issued the call for resistance on June 6, 1940, almost two weeks before General de Gaulle made his radio appeal from England.[16] Also, Jacques Duclos reprinted what he claimed was an appeal by himself and Thorez to all Frenchmen in July, 1940, to take up arms against the enemy.[17] However, the declaration as published was carefully edited to delete all the anti-British and anti-Gaullist references in the original. This Communist attempt to rewrite the history of the period was aimed at proving to the French people that the Party had responded to the needs of France in 1940, not just to those of the USSR in 1941.[18]

The Party also presented its demands for a new army and a greater war effort in the name of the heroes of the French Revolution. For example, after alluding to the slowness of the French mobilization, Marty remarked that "Saint-Just was able to get the Army of the Rhine on the road in twelve hours by threatening to make the heads of a few traitors roll." [19] An important aim of this campaign was to minimize in the popular mind the influence of Soviet policy on the French Communist Party.

Thus, "in the present period" the Communist leaders wanted to submerge the hard core of the Party in the mass, to break up the insurrectional structure of the Party organization, and to develop a program which would help them to recruit new Party members from every class of the population. This so-called "Rightist line" ran parallel to that pursued by other Communist parties in Europe at the time. In France this plan had the immediate effect

[16] For a complete and devastating critique of this "patriotic fraud," see Rossi (Tasca), *Les Communistes français*, pp. 309–15.

[17] Duclos, *Les Communistes dans la bataille*, p. 2.

[18] For an equally complete analysis of this hoax see Rossi (Tasca), *La Physiologie*, pp. 395–402. A copy of *L'Humanité*, July 10, 1940, which carried the original appeal, is in the collection of the clandestine papers in the Bibliothèque Nationale.

[19] Marty, "Notre Avenir dépend de nous," *Cahiers du Communisme*, No. 3 (January, 1945), p. 29.

of discouraging any thought of a revolutionary seizure of power. It was the beginning of a short-range program to build up the influence of the Party in preparation for the first postliberation elections.

The great membership drive inaugurated by the Party leaders brought startling results.[20] Between January, 1945, and April, 1945, Communist Party membership increased from 400,000 to 600,000. Despite the Party's own admission that the cells were becoming too large and that there were insufficient numbers of new recruits from the working classes, the slogan remained "Recruit! Recruit! Recruit!" [21]

Discord within the Party

The concept of the mass party did not go unchallenged in the higher echelons of the Party. André Marty assailed the Party leadership from within for having adopted "a social democratic position aiming at the transition from capitalism to socialism without a struggle." [22] Auguste Lecoeur wrote later that at the time he considered the new policy contrary to Leninst doctrine and to the feelings of the working class. He maintained that it had not been discussed in the Central Committee either before its promulgation or after its obvious failure.[23] Marty, Lecoeur, and others were suspicious of those leaders who had not remained in France during the occupation and who did not share the underground's *esprit de corps*. At one meeting of the Political Bureau of the Party, when

[20] The Party militants were encouraged to issue special bulletins on new members, to conduct special promotion drives commemorating the anniversaries of members killed by the Germans, and to circulate membership applications at rallies. The Party leaders praised their comrades at Rennes, who had signed up 1,200 new members within a few days after the liberation. They pointed with pride to the alert recruiters in the second *Arrondissement* in Paris, who followed *L'Humanité's* newsboy in order to convert the buyers of the paper. *La Vie du Parti*, September, 1944, pp. 28–29. In many areas the Party offered prizes to stimulate recruitment. In one department the Party member who enrolled the most new members received an autographed copy of a book with a preface by Maurice Thorez. In the same department the Party cell which recruited the most members was awarded a colored picture of Stalin, sixty inches by forty, and a bust of the Soviet leader. *Affiches CBN*, "Fédération du Haut Rhin," October, 1945.

[21] Mauvais, *Le Parti*, p. 4, and Mauvais, *Le PCF*, pp. 4–5, 10.

[22] Marty, *L'Affaire Marty*, p. 248.

[23] Lecoeur, *L'Autocritique attendue*, pp. 17–18.

Jeanette Vermeersch, Thorez's wife, was speaking authoritatively on the role of women in the Resistance, Charles Tillon interrupted her to remark, in essence, that she did not know what she was talking about because she had not been in France during the occupation.[24] On another occasion the report of the Central Control Commission of the Party stated: "It is necessary to place at the head of the men, first of all, those who have passed the test in practical work during the underground period. . . . These men who ran all the risks have earned the right to be at the highest level and to take their place among the most advanced cadres of the Party."[25] For the most part these internal critics of the Party's policy were the same "Left-deviationists" who had demanded more radical action by the FTP during the period of liberation. They were the "hards," the veterans of the Spanish Civil War, of the mutiny in the Black Sea fleet, and of the active struggle against Vichy and the German occupation forces. There were men like them in every Communist party in Europe. Though they had done their work well in the past, the "present period" required more respectable methods. Thorez and Duclos, who had the ear of Moscow, successfully resisted the pressure from these elements, and the Party opened wide its doors to all.

The French Communists and the Provisional Government

At the same time that the Communists were preparing the Party for a greater role in the government, they tried to exploit the prestige of the Resistance organizations as auxiliary pressure groups. The purpose of the Party was to mobilize public opinion in favor of the rapid implementation of its original five-point program, which corresponded closely to the program of the CNR.[26] How-

[24] *Ibid.*, pp. 26–27.
[25] Chaumeil, *Le Problème des cadres*, p. 8.
[26] The CNR program drawn up in March, 1944, demanded the reestablishment of a Republic; the purge of traitors; confiscation of their property; restoration of universal suffrage and civil rights; establishment of true economic democracy; nationalization of the great monopolies of production, big banks, etc.; development of producers' cooperatives; the right to work and to rest; guarantee of wage levels to ensure dignity and security; plans for social security;

ever, the Communists' plan to work through the Conseil and its
subsidiaries, the departmental committees of liberation, as well
as through official government channels, was frustrated by General
de Gaulle's attitude. For all intents and purposes the Conseil had
ceased to be a force in French politics as soon as Paris was liberated. Its members, Communist and non-Communist alike, wanted
De Gaulle to proclaim the Fourth Republic from the balcony of
the Hôtel de Ville in the traditional revolutionary fashion. Not
only did the General refuse, but at a brief and formal reception
he told them that there was no further justification for the existence
of the Conseil as an active organization.[27] De Gaulle invited only
one of its members, Georges Bidault, to join his government as
Commissar for Foreign Affairs.[28]

Despite these setbacks, the Conseil continued to meet and issue
proclamations and, more often, protests against the government's
policy. The Communists, and sometimes the Socialists, supported
these proposals, and for some Frenchmen the Conseil continued
to embody the hope of a new way of life in postwar France,
based on the unity of the Resistance. However, the Conseil had
no power, and it soon became little more than a debating society.
The realignment and recovery of the political parties doomed it to
ultimate oblivion. Though the Communists were partially responsible for this state of affairs, they tried to make the Conseil a respectable organ of public opinion, or at least to retain it as a symbol of unity.

Theoretically subordinated to the Conseil, the departmental committees of liberation were more successful in maintaining their
prestige and power in the French countryside. Again, the Communists encouraged the committees to take a large part in the
rebuilding of France, but not at the expense of keeping order in
the provinces. The non-Communist elements in the Resistance were
often more eager than was the Party's national leadership to preserve the power of the committees. Certainly the Communists did

---

reestablishment of independent trade-unionism; adequate old-age pensions; the
extension of political, social, and economic rights to the colonial peoples; and
the equal education of all to create an élite based on merit instead of on birth.

[27] De Gaulle, *Mémoires*, II, 317–18.

[28] Louis Saillant succeeded him as president of the Conseil.

not intend to turn the committees into local soviets or to create a dual-power structure in France. Broadcasting from Moscow in September, 1944, Thorez had urged the French to have faith in the reconstituted municipal councils and in the departmental committees. He emphasized the importance of the committees as a means of mobilizing the population for the reconstruction of France.[29] Similarly, Duclos maintained that "the local committees of liberation can do everything possible to mobilize the population politically in order to lead it." [30]

There was no change in the Party line after Thorez's return to Paris in November, 1944. The Secretary-General of the Party indicated that the committees should not attempt to replace the elected municipal and cantonal bodies, but should serve as "organs for mobilizing the masses." [31] In his famous report to the Central Committee of January 21–23, 1945, Thorez declared that the local and departmental committees of liberation should not strive to displace municipal and departmental administrations, just as the Conseil had not attempted to take the place of the government. "The task of the committees of liberation," he firmly asserted, "is not to administer, but to help those who administer." [32]

The Communist leaders were in accord with De Gaulle on the duties and functions of the committees. The Government's confidential instructions to the Commissars of the Republic carefully defined the place of the committees in the administrative structure of France:

The committees of liberation are consultative organs.

From the moment you take up your duties, the committees of liberation will no longer be more than consultative organs in relation to you. You will not allow deliberating councils because their power of decision will cause yours to disappear. There cannot be two leaders in these troubled times. You represent the government to the population, not the population to the government.

Nevertheless, you ought to rely heavily on them and take them into confidence in your actions. You and your prefects will take no serious

[29] Thorez, *Un grand français*, pp. 47–48.
[30] Duclos, "Notre Politique," *Cahiers du Communisme*, No. 3 (December, 1944), p. 31.
[31] Thorez, *S'Unir pour vaincre le fascisme*, p. 12.
[32] Thorez, *S'Unir, combattre, travailler*, p. 22.

action without consulting them; they ought to be your counselors, your most steady supports.[33]

On the local level the Communists reacted to the appeals of the Party leaders much as they had obeyed the instructions on the national insurrection. In general they concurred, but it was many months before the central government was able to assert its control over all of France. The government encountered the greatest difficulties in the very same areas where the national insurrection had been unusually long and severe, in the south and southwest. At times Communists in the same department or region responded differently to orders from the Central Committee.

According to the government officials on the spot, the Communists supported the central government in the north, center, and east of France. The Commissars of the Republic at Rouen and Angers, Henri Bourdeau de Fontenay and Michel Debré, have maintained that the Communists gave them no trouble from the moment they assumed their duties. M. Bourdeau de Fontenay declared that the Communists carried out his orders "blindly." [34] The Commissar of the Republic Clermont-Ferrand, Henri Ingrand, indicated that the Communist Party was a stanch defender of the central government, and the prefect of the department of Creuze reported that the Communist Party, "more than the SFIO, poses as the defender of the provisional government. . . . They do not even demand a structural reform." [35] According to another prefect, the Communists in the department of Eure-et-Loire manifested "a great patriotic discipline." [36] In fact, in some places the Party was so outspoken in its support of the provisional government

[33] *Instructions confidentielles aux Commissaires Régionaux de la République*, pp. 3–4. I am deeply indebted to M. Bourdeau de Fontenay for showing me his personal copy of this memorandum.

[34] Interviews with Henri Bourdeau de Fontenay and Michel Debré. According to the former, the departmental committees hoped to reduce the powers of the prefect in the future administrative structure of France. It should be noted that this was not a purely Communist desire.

[35] Ministère de l'Intérieur, *Service central des Commissariats de la République: Bulletin sur la situation dans les régions et les départements* (hereafter cited as *SCCR*), No. 49 (March 6, 1945), "Situation dans la région de Clermont-Ferrand," p. 9, and *ibid.*, No. 48 (March 3, 1945), "Situation dans la région de Limoges," p. 8. I am deeply indebted to M. Robert Aron for allowing me access to these documents and permitting me to quote from them.

[36] *Ibid.*, No. 57 (March 22, 1944), "Situation dans la région d'Orléans," p. 18.

that the population, which demanded more action from Paris, turned against it.[37]

The situation was confused in Toulouse. The Commissar of the Republic maintained that he had no trouble with the Communists. He even appointed a Party militant as chief of internal security in Toulouse.[38] However, the departmental committee resisted all efforts to reestablish the municipal council. The following declaration expressed an attitude typical of certain extremist groups in the Resistance:

The CDL of the region of Toulouse (etc.), considering that they are the emanation of the resisting people, decide to continue their insurrectional action for the application of the program of the Resistance. They desire that all their decisions, taken after a thorough study of the economic, military, and political fields, be rapidly applied by the representative of the executive power, who was assured of his post by the Resistance and who is in the service of the nation. . . . The CDL want to be not general councils but deliberative assemblies which desire to have the program of the CNR applied in its totality by the Commissar of the Republic and by the prefects.

The CDL of the region of Toulouse refuse unanimously to set up the general councils.

They decide, further, that all the differences which could arise between the CDL and the prefects should be settled by the regional council of liberation.

However, *L'Espoir*, the Socialist daily in Toulouse, attributed the criticism of the municipal council less to the Communists than to the "resistant" elements in the committee, who wanted a new, more dynamic order in France.[39]

There was a similar situation in the southeast. Eleven committees of liberation in the area signed a manifesto declaring that they "opposed being relegated to a consultative role" and "intended

[37] *Ibid.*, No. 64 (April 5, 1944), "Situation dans la région de Poitiers," p. 5, and *ibid.*, No. 69 (April 13, 1944), "Situation dans la région de Lyon," p. 3.
[38] Interview with Pierre Bertaux. The Communist, Colonel Georges, was the former departmental chief of the FFI in the Lot. In Toulouse he issued proclamations which support M. Bertaux's contention that he was determined to maintain order; see, for example, his proclamation to the population against arrests and illegal searches by those not carrying police warrants, *La Victoire* (Toulouse), September 13, 1944.
[39] *La Victoire*, September 25, 1944; *L'Espoir* (SFIO), September 28, 1944.

to retain their power of decision in all areas on the departmental level." A confidential report to De Gaulle from the southeast indicated that if the representatives of the government in the provinces did not receive strong support from Paris, local dictatorships would develop and might plunge France into a state of anarchy.[40]

Though the public authorities ran into trouble with departmental committees elsewhere in France, it is not always clear who led the opposition within the committees. In general, communication between Paris and the provinces was difficult until October, 1944. Up to September 10 the retreating Germans made all contact impossible between Paris, the Massif Central, and Aquitaine. In a circular dated September, 1944, the Minister of the Interior stated that the public authority could not be fully restored without "at least gravely endangering public order." [41] Other official reports expressed considerable anxiety because "French territory is still cut up into sections isolated from each other so that governmental action cannot be exercised with sufficient authority." Postal and rail communications remained precarious as late as October 7, 1944.[42]

Under such conditions it is not surprising that local elements of the Resistance had taken on many responsibilities which they were not anxious now to relinquish. The greatest disturbances were in west-central France. Pierre Boursicot, Commissar of the Republic at Limoges, reported that "during the liberation of the region of Limoges the CDL, under the simple pretext of abolishing the 'Vichyite' institutions and legislation, tried to suppress the different organs of the General Food Supply by establishing new taxes and by abolishing the rules of rationing everywhere." He added that "in Dordogne opinion is calm on the whole. For one who knew this department on the day of liberation and during the months of September and October and who saw it now, it would not seem to be the same department." In the department of Allier,

[40] De Gaulle, *Mémoires*, III, 316–18, Report to General de Gaulle from a high official on a tour of the southeast.

[41] *L'Année politique, 1945*, p. 14.

[42] Commissariat de l'Information de Lot et Garonne, ed., *Revue politique*, reports No. 1 (September 17–23, 1944), p. 6, and No. 3 (October 1–7, 1944), p. 5. A later report stated that the period of uncertainty was over by mid-October. No. 5 (October 14–21, 1944), p. 1.

as late as February, 1945, "a great number of mayors, especially in rural communes, were in difficulty with the local committees." In Ariège the committee "had been for a long time a center of opposition to governmental directives." [43]

Opposition to the installation of prefects often took a drastic form, and sometimes the representatives of the central government were unable to take office immediately—for example, in Saône-et-Loire, Landes, Lille, and Alpes Maritimes.[44] The situation was so serious that the Minister of the Interior, Adrien Tixier, admitted in December, 1944, that his directives on the reestablishment of the general councils were not being carried out because of the opposition of the departmental committees of liberation. In late January, 1944, he maintained that his instructions had been completely ignored in three fourths of the departments. In many departments a reconstitution of the general councils with the representation of 1939 was never carried out, and only the elections of October, 1945, regularized the situation.[45]

The Communist Party leadership strove to limit the functions of the committees and to reestablish order in the country. Disagreements between the Resistance and the government would weaken the Communist Party and perhaps divide it into pro-government and pro-Resistance factions. They would give the Allies an impression that France was unable to solve its own problems and therefore should not be allowed to participate in the solution of European problems. An internal struggle for power would weaken the war effort and prevent the rapid reconstruction of the country. Both the Soviet leaders and the French Communists wanted to avoid either disrupting the western front or weakening the Party in France. Therefore, the French Communists condemned interference with the normal restoration of the public

[43] SCCR, No. 48 (March 3, 1945), "Situation dans la région de Limoges," p. 3; this remark was followed by the observation that "the position of the government appears very strong." No. 49 (March 6, 1945), "Situation dans la région de Clermont-Ferrand," p. 3. No. 52 (March 13, 1945), "Situation dans la région de Toulouse," p. 5.

[44] Henry, Histoire, p. 345. It is maintained by people in the Alpes Maritimes that the Communist Virgile Barrel had established a virtual "dictatorship" in that department.

[45] Doueil, L'Administration locale, pp. 189, 192.

authorities. Not all the resistants agreed, but without national leadership they were forced to give way to the demands for unity and order. For the time being, the Communist leaders planned to base their bid for power on a mass party and electoral successes. They wanted to establish their democratic and social program for France through legally elected bodies on the national scale. In such a scheme the departmental committees could serve the Party only as propaganda and recruiting agencies.

The Communists Fail to Create a New Army

In their five-point program the Communists had demanded the creation of a popular army to be led by "patriotic officers." As the fighting ended in the liberated departments, the Party began to agitate for the incorporation of the FFI into the regular army. The Communists claimed that the 125,000 FTP were the shock troops of the FFI and that they wanted to continue to fight in a new "people's" army. The government had other plans, and De Gaulle issued a decree dissolving the FFI command in London and all the local organs of the FFI in France. Then he promised that elements of the FFI would be incorporated into the army "in order that those who are capable of it will participate in future operations." [46] COMAC immediately expressed its disapproval of this "premature decision, [which is] such as to slow up the war effort." It demanded the fulfillment of the agreement of August 17, despite the fact that General Koenig was now in Paris.[47] In response to the request for further details on the future of the FFI, De Gaulle indicated that individual members of the forces could be incorporated into the army by signing up for the duration of the war or for a specified period of time.[48]

The Communists now stepped up their attacks against both De Gaulle and his Commissar of War, André Diethelm. Duclos assailed the enlistment policy as "distrustful" of the masses and

[46] *Le Figaro* (Paris), August 29, 1944. See also De Gaulle, *Mémoires,* II, 318.
[47] Archives of COMAC, September 1, 4, and 12, 1944, cited in Hostache, *Le Conseil,* pp. 403–4.
[48] *Le Figaro,* August 30, 1944.

demanded the total integration of the FFI into the national army.[49] The Communist Commissar of Air, Charles Tillon, went so far as to attack Colonel Passy and the Gaullist secret services for having sabotaged arms shipments to the FTP. The same fifth column, Tillon charged, now aimed to continue its policy of hampering the war effort by dissolving the FFI.[50]

The Party denounced De Gaulle's plans to dissolve the FFI as "contrary to the country's most obvious interests." It proposed that the government issue a statute for the FFI which would require that there be

(1) No dislocation of FFI units. No dispersion of their effectives or dissolution of the organs of command of the FFI. These units should be maintained with their ranks. (2) The new army should not be abandoned to the officers' ranks, which were the ranks of defeat. (3) The new army should be created out of an amalgam of all the forces which fought for France after the defeat and refused to accept the defeat. Places ought to be made for those, men and leaders, who were the artisans of the victorious national insurrection. (4) An initial effort to organize the FFI should be undertaken in such a way as to verify exactly all soldiers constituting the units . . . to resolve very quickly the problems of billeting, provisioning, and rapid instruction of the units.[51]

To win public opinion to its side, the Communists tried to gloss over any distinction between their forces and the FFI.[52] After complaining that the Armée Secrète was making a distinction between the FFI and the FTP, one Communist commander remarked, "At present we are remedying this state of affairs by intensive propaganda."[53] Later, in trying to persuade his men to fuse with the FFI, he declared, "We have nothing to lose, but everything to gain." If the letters FTP must disappear, he continued, they will always remain as symbols. By a fusion with the FFI and then with the

---

[49] Duclos, *Les Communistes dans la bataille*, p. 13.

[50] *L'Humanité*, September 6, 1944.

[51] *La Vie du Parti*, September, 1944, p. 4.

[52] *Ibid.*, p. 11. COMAC had already dissolved all separate commands of the FTP in the FFI.

[53] *Documents, Collection de la Bibliothèque de Documentation Internationale Contemporaine* (hereafter cited as *BDIC*), Maquis B (Dordogne Nord), Report of Commandant Louis, Chief Subsection B, September 11, 1944.

army, he concluded, "we will be . . . best prepared to enter
schools where we will be taught the tactics of the new arms." [54]
The FTP commanders in the Alpes Maritimes were anxious to
prove that their forces were an integral part of the FFI. [55]

Only one month before, Mauvais had opposed the fusion of
Resistance units in the southern zone; by September this change
was demanded by the Party. The distinct and separate functioning
of the FTP was no longer of any use to the Party. In fact, it had
become a decided disadvantage, because the Communists now
wanted to incorporate their paramilitary forces into the regular
French Army through the channel of the FFI, in order to create
a new "people's" army.

The government was determined to block the Communists'
efforts to pack the army and infiltrate the officer corps. First it
forbade the FFI to carry out arrests, searches, and requisitions
without police warrants. [56] Then, on September 23, 1944, by a
decree defining the new status of the FFI, it provided that the
members of the FFI would be incorporated into the army, but it
left open the question of who would command the units and
whether the units would be integrated intact into the army. The
Communists were displeased with the decree. Valrimont complained that the decision had been made without consulting
COMAC and that this was not the way to form a great national
army. [57] The Party demanded a clarification of the moot points
in the decree and insisted that the FFI units be commanded by
their present officers. [58] However, the FFI statute was close enough
to the letter of the Communist proposals to blunt the edge of
further criticism. The Communists continued to complain that the
new units were not being used effectively and were poorly armed, [59]
but the Communist fight for a dominant role in the new army was

[54] *Ibid.*, Report dated September 28, 1944.

[55] *Documents, Collection BDIC,* Maquis R² (Alpes Maritimes), leaflet, n.d.,
signed by the Commandant FFI.

[56] See, for example, *Affiches CBN* (Provinces), No. 1, "Avis à la population
d'Angoulême," September 1, 1944; No. 43, "Le Droit d'arrestation" (Limoges),
n.d.; and *Le Figaro,* September 23, 1944.

[57] *Le Figaro,* September 24–25, 1944.

[58] *L'Humanité,* September 24–25, 1944.

[59] Duclos, *La Lutte,* p. 13.

lost. On October 16, 1944, by then at its last gasp, COMAC ordered the FFI to conform to the instructions of the ministry. It then accepted three new members, representing the Organisation Civile et Militaire, Libération-Nord, and the ORA.[60] Thus, COMAC signed its own death warrant as a policy-making body and faded into obscurity.

Public Purge and Private Vengeance

In their original five-point program the Communists had also demanded a thoroughgoing purge of the public administration. After the liberation France underwent a purge which extended into almost every area of political, economic, and social life. This nation-wide "purification" and the French Communists' role in it constitute one of the most obscure and controversial subjects of contemporary French politics. The Communists, it is true, spearheaded the propaganda campaign for a thorough "cleansing" of French life. The members of the Party who were in government posts made wholesale replacements in the bureaucracies under their control, and the Party declared its own private war of revenge, of which no strict account was ever rendered.

At the moment of liberation the Party published a long list of traitors, including Vichy ministers, journalists in the pay of the Germans, managers of collaborationist trust, those who had relations with German officials, former members of Fascist organizations, and some of the police and *gardes mobiles*. However, as Duclos and Thorez pointed out, "the traitors do not have to suffer loss of life or liberty, but could have their property confiscated for the benefit of the nation." [61]

The Communists were not satisfied with the government's measures against the traitors. They accused the unpunished "fifth columnists" of sabotaging production, weakening the army, and wrecking the recovery.[62] More in line with the Party's wishes were Tillon's efforts to purge the air force of "undesirables." The Com-

---

[60] Archives of COMAC, October 4, 13, and 16, 1944, cited in Hostache, *Le Conseil*, p. 404.

[61] Duclos, *Les Communistes dans la bataille*, p. 14.

[62] Duclos, *La Lutte*, p. 16.

missar of Air issued a decree that all officers who had remained on French soil after November 11, 1942, and had not joined the Resistance or the fighting forces by June 6, 1944, were to be placed on the inactive list and forbidden to wear their uniforms.[63] This eliminated the *attentistes* from the air force, including all officers who had served under Vichy and had not changed their allegiance before the invasion. It also opened the way for Tillon to pack the air force with his own men and intimidate the waverers.

The personal vendettas of the Communist Party are, of course, the most difficult to document.[64] No agreement exists as to the total number of summary or even legal executions in France after the liberation, let alone of those attributed to the Party.[65] However, the number purged by the Communists is not so important for an understanding of the Party's purpose as is an analysis of the positions and past political activities of those purged. First, there were former members who had "betrayed" the Party in one way or another. Then there were long-standing enemies of the Party. Finally, there were men who, consciously or not, stood in the way of the Communist drive for power.

Only a few typical examples can be cited here. The prewar Communist deputy from Gard and mayor of Alès, Fernand Valat, had resigned from the Communist Party after the famous Bonte-Ramette "peace letter" to Herriot in October, 1939; in July, 1943,

[63] *Le Figaro*, September 24–25, 1944. For later activities of Communist ministers in nationalized industries see below, p. 289.

[64] A substantial number of books and pamphlets have been written on this matter, as well as on the purge in general. Figures are notoriously inaccurate, and many of the writers are understandably biased because of their participation in the vendettas or their sympathy with one side or another. See, for example, apologies for the purge in Farge, *Rebelles*, and Werth, *France*, and hostile criticism in Mauloy, *Les Nouveaux Saigneurs*, and Huddleston, *France*.

[65] Some of the following figures illustrate the impossibility of arriving at any exact figure. In February, 1945, Tixier, Minister of the Interior, gave the figure of 105,000 killed. Assemblée Consultative Provisoire, *JO*, *Débats*, February 16, 1945. *Le Figaro* estimated one million arrests and 60,000 shot by April 6, 1946. Paul-Henri Teitgen, former Minister of Justice, maintained that not more than 3,000–4,000 were executed. Assemblée Nationale, *JO*, *Débats*, June 19, 1947. C. Brune, Minister of the Interior in 1952, stated that, on the basis of an inquiry among prefects in 1948, he estimated 10,000 summary executions. Bidault concurred. Assemblée Nationale, *JO*, *Débats*, October 28, 1952. Estimates based on the figures of the Direction de la Gendarmerie et de la Justice Militaire range from 30,000 to 40,000 summary executions; Robert Aron, *Histoire de la Libération*, p. 655.

the Germans arrested him. He was liberated by the Resistance from a Marseilles jail and returned to Alès, but he did not reenter the Party. In September, 1944, he was assassinated by an unknown band. Léon Piginier, a former Communist deputy and mayor of Malakoff, had resigned his parliamentary seat after the Nazi-Soviet Pact; he was arrested and deported by the Germans. After being repatriated, he was assassinated on August 23, 1945, in the fourteenth *arrondissement* of Paris. A similar fate overtook the former Communist mayor of Draveil, De Bru, and the former Communist chief of peasant work in the Paris region, Jean Desnots. A former Communist senator of the Seine department and mayor of Bobigny had survived four assassination attempts during the war; his son, who had fought with the Spanish Republicans but had not joined the Resistance, was machine-gunned to death during the liberation.[66] It is difficult to ascertain whether the Communists had a hand in the summary execution of Vichy prefects, but at least five "collaborationist" prefects were assassinated in 1944.[67]

The Communist terror within the CGT was widespread, though it has never been completely revealed. Charles Bourneton, former secretary of the CGT (*unitaire*) and of the departmental union of the Syndicat du Nord, had been interned, then kept under house surveillance during the war. After February, 1943, he was in contact with the Resistance in Clermont. In September, 1944, he was tortured and killed by an unknown group. Ambrogelly, former secretary of the Syndicat d'Alimentation of the Paris region, was arrested and shot in August, 1944.[68] Bidegarry, the former secretary of the Fédération des Cheminots, was killed after being freed from an internment camp in Basses-Pyrénées. Three miners'-union officials accused by the Communists of having supported the Vichy labor charter—Malthus in Sâone-et-Loire, Rossi in Nord, and Arnaud in Saint-Étienne—were summarily executed.[69]

After the liberation the operating management of the PTT syndicate of the Paris region was placed under the direction of Emman-

[66] Mauloy, *Les Nouveaux Saigneurs,* pp. 180–82. See also the list of former Communist victims of liberation revenge in Rossi, *La Physiologie,* p. 444.
[67] Henry, *Histoire,* p. 344.
[68] Mauloy, *Les Nouveaux Saigneurs,* p. 180.
[69] Lefranc, *Les Expériences,* p. 119, note 11.

uel Fleury, head of the Communist faction. He ordered the arrest of Edmond Fronty and Jean Mathé. Along with another official of the PTT, they were held in the Drancy concentration camp during the period of the reconstitution of the PTT in September and October, 1944, and their absence made it easier for the Communists to gain control of that syndicate.[70] Fronty, a key figure in the PTT and in the trade-union movement in general, died soon after his release from prison.[71] The pressure of the Communists upon the rank and file of the unions was so great that there was very little opportunity or willingness to oppose these condemnations within the CGT. The rehabilitation of many who were unjustly purged came only later. A former secretary of the Loire section of the Syndicat des Instituteurs was purged in 1944–45; in 1949 an extraordinary session of the Syndicat National des Instituteurs reopened the case and found him not guilty.[72]

The most famous case in the record of the CGT purges was that of the former representative of the CGT in London, Albert Guigui. Guigui had left France before the reunification of the trade-union movement, but he claims to have been given written authority by the *confédéré* leaders "to speak and negotiate in the name of the CGT."[73] He received instructions from the underground bureau to broadcast messages to the French workers encouraging them to join unions, even within the framework of the Vichy charter of labor, so as to perform valuable tasks of disruption and sabotage.[74] Meanwhile, in France, during the negotiations over the reunification of the CGT, the Communists demanded that either Guigui be replaced or a representative of their choosing also be sent to London. However, Saillant continued to support and encourage Guigui.[75]

Despite the fact that the reunified bureau formally condemned the labor charter in its unity declaration, Guigui was not directed

[70] *Ibid.*, p. 155.
[71] Chambelland, "Deux assassinés," *La Révolution Prolétarienne*, No. 303 (May, 1947), p. 6.
[72] *Ibid.*, No. 235 (March, 1949), p. 22.
[73] Guigui, "Epuration et syndicalisme," *ibid.*, No. 341 (July, 1950), p. 18.
[74] Instructions of May 18, July 25, and August 7, 1943, as cited *ibid.*, pp. 18–19.
[75] Letters of July 25 and late August 1943 as cited *ibid.*, p. 20.

to discontinue his broadcasts.[76] Therefore, he continued to urge "all workers everywhere to join their unions again," and praised them for following his instructions "in greater numbers every day without letting [themselves] be stopped by the 'official' leadership of the union."[77] The CGT appeared to have complete confidence in Guigui and named him, together with the Communist Ambroise Croizat, as Albert Gazier's assistant in the northern zone.[78]

Then the situation changed suddenly. Croizat never met Guigui, and when Guigui arrived in Paris in August his friends warned him of Communist hostility. Within the next year several key officials of the CGT were purged because they had joined the Vichy-organized unions.[79] In other words, union leaders who had obeyed the orders of the CGT bureau, as broadcast by Guigui, were now targets for blackmail and faced possible elimination from their posts. Association with Vichy was a double-edged weapon. After liberation it was used to cut down some genuine resisters regarded by the Communists as hostile to the Party. The inability or unwillingness of others to stop this procedure was costly to the non-Communist forces, who thereby lost many of their leaders.

The Communist purge of the CGT was sometimes even more direct in its methods. On August 23, 1944, three armed members of the Railroad Workers Syndicate of Paris (Left Bank) forced their way into the house of Lucien Cancouet, secretary-general of that federation. Invoking the necessities of the insurrectionary period, they demanded his immediate resignation. He refused, despite his ill health and his helpless condition. Several days later a mimeographed tract was distributed among the workers of the district informing them of the appointment of a new provisional bureau whose members were largely Communists. The workers refused to accept the list, and a compromise bureau was established, consist-

[76] *Ibid.* Guigui quotes Gazier as having explained that "each word and almost every comma had been the object of long discussions between our comrades and the Communists."

[77] BBC broadcasts of December 1, 30, 1943, and February 12, 1944, as cited *ibid.*, pp. 17–18.

[78] Report of A. Gazier on the return to France and the delegated representatives of the CGT, undated, as cited *ibid.*, p. 21.

[79] The introductory editorial comment, *ibid.*, mentions Gayté and André of the Union Départmentale de Seine-et-Marne as two who were purged. Both men were reinstated in 1950, partly on the basis of Guigui's testimony.

ing of five *unitaires* and five *confédérés*. Both the Communist and
the compromise bureaus included the three men who had threatened Cancouet.[80]

The Party tried to utilize the purge to eliminate those members of
the administration, the armed forces, and the labor movement who
either were pro-Vichy or were the main obstacles to Communist infiltration of certain organizations. The purge also paid off certain
personal grudges, especially against former Communists.[81] From the
Communist point of view, the purge was most effective in the CGT.
When the Communists were forced out of the government in 1947,
the men they had placed in the bureaucracy were the victims of an
administrative counterpurge which took on extensive proportions,
but their grip on the CGT remained almost unshaken.

Despite these activities, the Communists were, as we have seen,
anxious to avoid the label of "terrorists." They were by no means
willing or free to unleash a mass campaign of intimidation and
brutality. The purge was kept within limits as far as this was possible in the chaotic situation. The Party wished to avoid giving any
excuse or reason for the government to crack down on Resistance
groups or to suspend civil rights and democratic practices, or for
the Allied forces to intervene. The Party was in favor of rapidly
restoring order and legality, conditions which it needed for its continued success.[82] However, the Communists and De Gaulle had

[80] Letter of L. Cancouet, September 8, 1944. Document No. 1 in *Le Cheminot
Libéré*, January, 1948. I am grateful to M. Cancouet for this document and for
his accompanying explanation of the incident.

[81] After Guingouin had liberated Limoges, he admitted that "on entering this
town numerous arrests were made, and if the majority were justified, unfortunately some cases are attributable to personal grudges." Guingouin stated that
there were seventy-eight death sentences in Limoges. See Guingouin, *Libération*, p. 13. A non-Communist source in Limoges told me 150 had been shot in
the department. Included in this number were summary executions of the former
Socialist mayor and a counsellor-general of Limoges, allegedly shot at Saumon
by FTP Maquis Pressac. These figures do not seem exaggerated or contradictory.

[82] The Communists often took action against terrorist bands that roamed the
countryside even if these happened to be former FTP. For example, the Communist sympathizer and Commissar of the Republic at Lyon, Yves Farge, wrote
to the Conseil that "in the Vercors there exist certain terrorist bands which are
terrorizing the population. Some have been identified, and Marc Laurent (Mar-
tel), with unanimous accord of the FTP, members of the AS [Armée Secrète],
and of the CDL [Comité Départemental de la Libération], is setting up am-
bushes for them." Letter, Grégoire to CNR, undated, cited in Farge, *Rebelles*,
p. 120.

their most severe disagreement over this very issue of maintaining order in France.

The Affair of the Patriotic Militia

As part of their plan to develop a "democratic" political and social program for France, the Communists wanted to maintain the patriotic militia as a "people's" police force which would "guarantee the restoration of republican liberty." This Party policy challenged the authority of the government to keep order in the countryside. The patriotic militia was the last surviving armed force of the Resistance on which the Communists could count for support. The question of its continued existence resulted in a crisis which almost led to violence. However, once again in the name of order and "unity of action," the Communist Party submitted to the government's decision to dissolve the militia.

The Communists' defense of the militia was based on the grounds that the state of "democratic legality is still to be defined in all its forms," and therefore "it is important to defend the country and the organs of power in France—that is to say, the Resistance and the provisional government—against the counteroffensive of the remnants of the Fifth Column, or the men of the trusts, who continue to hope that they will be able to reestablish Fascist methods of government against the will of our people. The groups of the patriotic militia are the legal organs of the Resistance, and no one has the right to force their dissolution." [83] The Communists also asserted that the militia would help to supply Paris with food and would guarantee public order and civil liberties.[84] They insisted that the militia merely wanted to collaborate with the authorities. The Party encouraged the formation of new units of the patriotic militia and for this purpose established an information and recruiting center in the city hall of at least one Paris *arrondissement*.[85]

---

[83] *La Vie du Parti*, September, 1944, p. 13.

[84] *L'Humanité*, August 29, 1944.

[85] *Affiches CBN* (Paris), No. 21, "Défense des libertés républicaines contre la cinquième colonne," September 21, 1944. *L'Humanité*, September 5, 1944. It has been claimed by some that more units of the militia were formed after the liberation than before, and this is quite possible.

Meanwhile the authorities in Paris and the provinces were taking action against the militia, which, more than the FFI, was challenging the exercise of public authority. De Gaulle had already warned that the maintenance of republican order was the sole responsibility of the state.[86] Throughout France his representatives expressed similar views.[87]

The government had given the Commissars of the Republic broad police powers in order to maintain public order. These were defined in the instructions to the commissars:

The police powers in their totality . . . have been transmitted to you by a special ordinance of the CFLN of February 29, 1944. If the French military authorities have occasion to use them, they will do so under your responsibility and consequently under your control.[88]

Officially, the representatives of the provisional government were entrusted with full police powers, which, by definition, must include jurisdiction over all organizations constituted for the purpose of maintaining public order. The militia fell into this category. It is not clear to what extent the government used direct action against the militia, but *L'Humanité* protested that the *garde mobile* was searching the militiamen for arms.[89]

The efforts of the government to reduce the influence and activities of the militia encountered stiff opposition from many local Resistance groups. In Toulouse, for example, the departmental committee decided that "the militia would obey the executive organs of the Resistance: the CDL and the local committees.[90]

In October the Communists announced that the militia was taking the new name of Patriotic Guard, implying that the Party

---

[86] *Le Figaro*, August 30, 1944.

[87] *Affiches CBN* (Provinces), No. 8, "Proclamation aux citoyens de Charente," n.d.; No. 32, "Préfecture de la Côte d'Or," September 14, 1944; No. 5, Angoulême, September 22, 1944; and No. 109, Drôme, n.d.

[88] *Instructions confidentielles aux commissaires régionaux de la République,* p. 1.

[89] *L'Humanité,* September 9, 1944.

[90] *La Victoire,* September 11, 1944; report of the CDL. There is evidence of a split in the ranks of the Resistance. The Socialists insisted that "the members of the patriotic militia ought to go back immediately to their work of pre-August 19." They pointed out that the militia had neither ranks nor billeting and would be more useful as workers providing the FFI with arms for their coming battle against the Germans. *L'Espoir,* September 2, 1944.

wanted this force to be a permanent organization.[91] Some days later the Central Committee confirmed this implication and issued a statement on the functions of the guard: "The Patriotic Guard does not have to substitute itself for the regular police authorities, but it can easily exercise a close watch over all suspect elements, transmit all useful information to the police, protect public assemblies, and participate, if need be, in searches and in arrests of traitors." [92] At the meeting which passed this resolution, Duclos called for the maintenance of the guard and for enrolling "thousands of soldier-citizens" in this organization.

The Patriotic Guard, placed under the authority of the local committee of liberation and of the municipality, provided with permanent barracks, and furnished with a stock of arms and munitions, ought to constitute in each locality the element of safeguard of republican institutions. . . . It ought to assist the police in eliminating agents of the Fifth Column from harmful positions. . . . The Republic is menaced by sabotage.[93]

The guard was to be something different from the militia, more like a private army, perhaps even a class army, resembling in some ways the National Guard of the Communards. The day after Duclos's remarks, the French Council of Ministers announced the end of the period of insurrection and brusquely charged the armed bands with being responsible for the continuing chaos. The militia was all but dissolved, and its individual members were invited to join the army if they wanted to fight.[94]

The Communists were furious, the CNR was outraged, and both put pressure on the government to reverse or modify its decision. In an effort to be conciliatory and moderate, the Conseil asked for an exchange of views and pleaded that republican order was not incompatible with the participation of the people in the organ of state security and power; they proposed a statute for the patriotic Forces.[95] All to no avail. De Gaulle was unmoved.[96] Duclos roared his condemnation of the dissolution at a mass meeting in Douai.

[91] L'Humanité, October 22–23, 1944.
[92] Ibid., October 27, 1944.
[93] Duclos, La Lutte, pp. 25–26.
[94] L'Année politique, 1945, p. 45.
[95] The CNR declaration in Affiches CBN, October 29, 1944.
[96] L'Année politique, 1945, p. 46.

"We are in the presence of a plot against the Republic," he thundered. "They dare not pronounce the dissolution of the patriotic militia because they fear clashing with the feelings of the entire nation, and this is why the legal possibilities of reinforcing the militia or Patriotic Guard ought to be exploited to the maximum." [97] The Political Bureau considered that the government's action showed "a disturbing lack of trust in popular sovereignty and democratic forms." The Communists called for popular demonstrations of disapproval of the measures, which were, they asserted, similar to those they [had] "wanted to take against the FFI and which finally had to be withdrawn because they were contrary to the national interest." [98]

At this time the Soviet press commented briefly on the situation in France. *Pravda* quoted a Reuter's dispatch which pointed out, quite correctly, that most of the Paris newspapers except the conservative ones were critical of the dissolution. Stating that articles in *Franc-Tireur* "reflect the general opinion," *Pravda* quoted one of them: "Disarm the people? First disarm the Fifth Column." Then it printed without comment the declaration of the Conseil.[99] In the following days the Soviet press continued to quote critical comments from the Paris press, without editorial discussion. At this time the Soviet Union was keeping hands off the dispute.

It is difficult to ascertain whether any non-Communist mass support for the militias ever materialized. There were protests in the Paris press and from some provincial areas. The departmental committee of Toulouse, a center of radicalism, refused "in the most absolute fashion to accept the disarmament and dissolution of any organizations, whatever they may be, which have participated in the national insurrection, and, in particular, the patriotic militia." [100] However, the Socialist Party accepted the government measures, published on October 31, which applied the original decision on dissolution.[101]

[97] *L'Humanité*, October 31, 1944.
[98] Declaration of Political Bureau in *Affiches CBN* (Paris), November 2, 1944.
[99] *Pravda*, November 1, 1944.
[100] *L'Espoir*, No. 67 (November 1, 1944).
[101] These were: (1) agents of the public order will strictly enforce laws on the carrying of arms; (2) in case of infraction of the laws the arms will be seized; (3) people still in possession of weapons of war should turn them over to the

An unexpected event then thrust the issue into the realm of public passion. An ammunition train exploded at Vitry on November 1, killing twenty-seven and injuring ninety-five. The November 2 issue of *L'Humanité* carried a banner headline, "Fifth Column Blows Up Ammunition Train," and supplemented the story with a manifesto of intellectuals and writers which demanded popular forces to protect Frenchmen against such crimes.[102] Demonstrations at Lyon and Paris were harangued by Saillant (ever drifting leftward) and Frachon, who exalted the militia and demanded its reconstitution.[103] Communist pressure on the government reached considerable proportions before it dropped off suddenly.[104]

The resistance of the French Communist Party to the disarming of the patriotic militia was one aspect of the general opposition of European Communists to giving up their arms before the political future of their countries had been settled. However, it would have been both impractical and foolish for them to take up arms against the dissolution of the militia. Impractical, because the Communist paramilitary formations had been dissolved or incorporated into the regular army and because the patriotic militia had insufficient arms, little actual combat experience, and no national or regional organization or command. Foolish, because such fighting would have wrecked the Communist short-range program for the restoration of order and the rapid reconstruction of France.

The Communists had maintained their FTP as separate units during the liberation to help forestall any compromise with Vichy

---

nearest police; (4) Frenchmen who wish to put themselves at the disposition of the authorities for the defense of republican liberties should enroll at the town halls or with police commissioners; in case of need they will be summoned; (5) centers of military training for the army will be established in each military region, and priority for entrance will be given to the volunteers from the militia or the guards. *L'Année politique, 1945,* p. 46.

[102] *L'Humanité,* November 2, 1944. This "spontaneous" protest was so precipitously organized and printed that the Leftist Resistance paper *Combat* protested against the Communist haste in criticism, November 3, 1944.

[103] *L'Humanité,* November 4 and 5, 1944.

[104] André Marty later denounced the sudden reversal of Communist propaganda. At the time, he was in favor of carrying out the policy which Duclos set down on October 27, 1944, at the Assembly of Information of the Party in the Paris region. However, he indicated that this directive was "buried" in the first days of November. He offered no explanation for the action. Marty, *L'Affaire Marty,* pp. 244–46.

or a restoration of the Third Republic and to increase their own prestige and power. They now hoped to keep the patriotic militia in being so as to retain some bargaining power against the government, guarantee the restoration of republican order, help carry out the purges, and serve as a means of organizing the population before the trade unions and the agricultural committees had been reestablished. They may also have envisaged the possibility of using these forces at a later date, much as the Czechoslovak Communists relied on the workers' militia and "revolutionary guards" to guarantee their successful seizure of power in February, 1948. Apparently the French Communist leaders decided that the preservation of the militia as a legal security force was not worth a breach with De Gaulle during this early phase of liberation and reconstruction, at a time when American and British troops were still in France. However, when the French Communists accepted dissolution of the militia, they did not necessarily disband the local organizations. Again, the Czechoslovak parallel suggests itself; the workers' militia in Czechoslovakia had been generally abolished in 1946 and 1947 on paper, but it reappeared on the streets of Prague to help the Communists carry out their coup of February, 1948.[105]

In November, 1944, the dispute over the dissolution of the militia became more acute after a tremendous explosion wrecked the chateau of Timons in Vaucluse, killing thirty-four members of the Forces Républicaines de Sécurité who were billeted there. These men were regular police who had been former militiamen. The French Communists immediately accused the Fifth Column of terrorism, citing instances of similar activities which could only be forestalled, they insisted, by increased vigilance of the Patriotic Guard.[106] At the same time, the Belgian Communist Party was leading riots and strikes against its government's attempt to disarm the Resistance forces.

In the midst of this growing crisis Maurice Thorez flew in from

---

[105] Ducháček, "The Strategy of Communist Infiltration," *World Politics*, II, No. 3 (April, 1950), 357–58.

[106] *Le Figaro*, November 28, 1944; *L'Année politique, 1945*, p. 48; and *L'Humanité*, November 28, 1944. *Le Figaro* reported considerable excitement in Vaucluse and the sentencing of five saboteurs to death by the local committee of liberation.

Moscow, without the French Communists having been forewarned of his arrival.[107] It was immediately apparent that Thorez was not overly concerned about either the Patriotic Guard or the disarming of the Belgian Resistance. In his first speech on November 30 he did not mention the events in Brussels, remarking only that the French government should have confidence in the people who were the "police of the democracy." [108] Thorez did not encourage overt resistance to the government. It is not known whether his lukewarm attitude on the matter of disarming the Resistance had any effect on the Belgian situation, but on the next day the strikes in Brussels ended and the workers returned to their jobs. The French Communists continued to agitate for the maintenance of the guard, but there were no more terrorist incidents in France.[109] Within a month the issue was laid to rest by Thorez, who declared at the January meeting of the Central Committee:

These armed groups [the Patriotic Guard] had their *raison d'être* before and during the insurrection against the Hitlerite occupation and its Vichy accomplices. But now the situation is different. Public security is to be guaranteed by regular police forces constituted for this purpose. The civic guards and, in general, *all* irregular armed groups should not be maintained any longer.[110]

Though Thorez may conceivably have brought instructions from Moscow to end the dispute over the militia, his declaration was consistent with the avowed French Communist policy of cooperating with the provisional government. The Soviet leaders, who were about to negotiate a treaty of alliance with De Gaulle, refrained scrupulously from taking sides in an affair of French domestic politics. This is all the more significant because Moscow had vigorously criticized the disarming of the Resistance in Belgium.[111] Clearly, the Soviet leaders did not want to prejudice their important negotiations with De Gaulle for the sake of encouraging a relatively minor aim of the French Communists.

[107] *L'Humanité*, November 28, 1944.
[108] Thorez, *Travailler*, p. 13.
[109] See, for example, *Cahiers du Communisme*, December, 1944, p. 70.
[110] Thorez, *S'unir, combattre, travailler*, p. 18.
[111] "Mezhdunarodnoe obozrenie," *Pravda*, November 19, 1944, and P. Androvskii, "Chto proiskhodit v Bel'gii i Golandii," *ibid.*, November 30, 1944.

"Unite! Fight! Work!"

Three words of Maurice Thorez—"unite, fight, work"—became the watchwords of the new patriotic, mass Communist Party. The original five-point program of the Party, still the basis of its action and propaganda, had been elaborated but not changed fundamentally. Greater advantages for the peasantry, large-scale assistance to the returning prisoners of war, guarantees of private property, and increased benefits for the workers were all part of the same appeal. The program promised something to each class in the population and national independence to all. The Party promised much, but who was to pay for it? This problem had plagued every political group in France under the Third Republic. In the prewar days the Communist answer had always been "the class enemies." They could not say this in 1944, because now there were only two kinds of Frenchmen—the patriots and the traitors. According to the Communists, the traitors would pay for all through the confiscation of their lands and the breaking up of the trusts.

To put this program into effect, the Communists relied on their ability to create a huge party with millions of members which would reform France by peaceful parliamentary action. Despite continuing opposition to this concept within the Party, the great recruiting campaign went forward. Ultimately this choice forced the Communists to abandon the Resistance groups from which the Party had drawn much of its power and prestige. However, even in giving ground, it yielded to government pressure only after a series of long disputes.

It was important for the Party to have the FFI-FTP integrated intact into the army; yet it accepted a compromise solution. The Communists wanted the CNR and its departmental committees to play a major role in organizing and directing the masses; yet they rejected all attempts by certain of the committees to rule local areas of France. The Party demanded the maintenance of the patriotic militia to mobilize the population against the threat of a return of reaction and possibly as the basis of a private army at a later time. Again it was forced to submit to a government decision to dissolve the militia. Though the participation of the Communists in the government had disadvantages, it gave the Party many opportunities to increase its influence in France, especially during the period of administrative purges. The Party's prestige also benefited from the association of the Communist commissars with De Gaulle.

The short-range policy of the Communist Party did not change during the second phase of the liberation, from September to December, 1944. The Communist leaders tried to mobilize the energies of the country in order to hasten the victory. They wanted to maintain order in France so that there would be no excuse for General de Gaulle to delay the restoration of republican liberties or for the Allied army to intervene in the domestic affairs of France. The Party endorsed rapid reconstruction of the country because it did not want France to rely on external financial or economic aid for fear that it would succumb to political dependence upon the United States. The Communist Party continued to support De Gaulle because he, too, was determined to conduct an independent foreign policy, as his trip to Moscow had proved. Moreover, by their growing strength in political life the Communists hoped to increase their influence within the government in order to steer its foreign policy on a more easterly course.

CHAPTER VIII

The Shift in Soviet Policy

FROM the Yalta Conference in February, 1945, until the London Foreign Ministers' Conference in September, 1945, Moscow publicly and fervently reaffirmed its belief in the Marxist-Leninist revolutionary theory as a guide to action in world politics. At the same time Soviet foreign policy became increasingly more aggressive. Though scarcely noticed among the paean of tributes to wartime cooperation, a long-muted Communist dogma was revived: the sources of war will continue to exist as long as capitalism survives.

War arises from the phenomenon of antagonistic class contradictions; wars have accompanied the entire history of class struggle. The possibility of war will exist as long as the antagonistic contradictions exist. Only the fundamental reconstruction of the world on genuinely democratic bases can liquidate war completely—that is, [only] the liquidation of the social reasons which give rise to wars. And while these social causes exist, the freedom-loving people ought to be prepared to block the possible attacks of the aggressors and to do all they can to stave off aggression for the achievement of a firm and lasting peace.[1]

Thus, even before the end of the Second World War the Soviet leaders made it clear that world peace and security depended upon the destruction of capitalism and the establishment of a Communist, classless society. Until the achievement of that ultimate goal the Soviet Union would remain in a state of constant armed preparedness to repel "the threat of imperialist expansion." In the long run the Soviet leaders could be satisfied by nothing less than world conquest. In the short run they began to put their theories into practice in Eastern Europe, where the Red Army pursued its goals

[1] Chuvikov, "Uchenie Lenina-Stalina," *Bol'shevik*, Nos. 7–8 (April, 1945), pp. 25–26.

of establishing regimes sympathetic to the Soviet Union and showed little concern for the attitude of its "capitalist" allies.

This arbitrary trend in Soviet policy was brought about by the rapid advance of Soviet forces into Eastern Europe and by the unwillingness of the Allies to press for a more active role in the administration of the territories occupied by the Soviet Union. Nevertheless, Moscow still tried to gain Western endorsement of its actions in Eastern Europe and insisted on the agreement of the great powers in settling the German problem.

The return of France, in theory if not in practice, to great-power status meant that Paris played an increasingly important role in the settlement of European questions. Could the Soviet Union rely on the French to support its policies in the spirit of the Franco-Soviet Alliance of 1944? Could Stalin succeed in detaching France from its Western orientation? What concessions were the Soviet leaders willing to make in order to win French endorsement of their aims in Eastern Europe and Germany?

At Yalta Stalin was far more interested in gaining Allied support of Soviet policies in Poland than in strengthening the cause of Franco-Soviet friendship. In fact, Stalin maintained that there was no difference between Soviet policy in Poland, which the Western Allies were reluctant to follow, and Allied policy in France, which the Soviet Union had strongly endorsed.

He said he saw little difference between the position of De Gaulle and that of the Polish provisional government. Neither had been elected, and he could not say which one enjoyed the greatest degree of popularity—yet we all had dealt with De Gaulle, and the Soviet government concluded a treaty with him. Why should we be so different with regard to the Polish government, and why could we not deal with an enlarged Polish government? He added that De Gaulle had done nothing to arouse popular enthusiasm, whereas the Polish had carried out a number of land reforms that had been most popular.[2]

The Soviet Union finally obtained recognition from the Allies of the Communist-dominated Polish provisional government as the basis

[2] *Foreign Relations of the United States, Diplomatic Papers: The Conferences at Malta and Yalta, 1945*, p. 780. The Bohlen notes have been used throughout, except where noted. Molotov maintained this same line of reasoning in discussion with Anthony Eden and Edward Stettinius, *ibid.*, p. 869, Matthews notes.

of a new Polish government.[3] The Curzon line was also sanctioned as the official eastern frontier of Poland.

Although Stalin was interested in strengthening the Polish provisional government, he was opposed to any increase in French power and prestige. At Yalta several questions under discussion directly concerned the national interests of France, but Stalin either refused to acknowledge the right of the French to participate in their solution or conceded this right only with ill-disguised dissatisfaction, at the insistence of the United States and Great Britain. The questions of the greatest importance to France were the proposals concerning the occupation of Germany.

Churchill and Roosevelt argued that France should have an occupation zone in Germany, and Churchill, alone at first, also suggested that France be admitted as a fourth member of the Allied Control Commission for Germany. Stalin was strongly opposed to French participation in the control mechanism because, he said, it might serve as an unfortunate precedent. Furthermore, he added, France had contributed little to the war effort and had opened the gates to the enemy in 1940.[4]

In the end Stalin agreed to the creation of a fourth occupation zone for France, so long as it was carved from the American and British zones.[5] Molotov presented an official Soviet proposal which agreed to a separate zone of occupation for France but specified: "It has been decided that the French occupation authorities shall exercise control in their zone of occupation under the general guidance of the Control Commission."[6] When President Roosevelt changed his mind in regard to the question of French participation in the Control Commission and supported Churchill's view, Stalin said he had no objection and agreed to have the French on the commission.[7]

[3] This is the way Stalin interpreted it. In May, 1945, he said to Hopkins: "At Yalta it had been agreed that the existing government was to be reconstructed and that anyone with common sense could see that this meant that the present government was to form the basis of the new. He said no other understanding of the Yalta Agreement was possible." Sherwood, *Roosevelt and Hopkins*, p. 882.

[4] *The Conferences at Malta and Yalta, 1945*, pp. 616–17.

[5] *Ibid.*, p. 618.

[6] *Ibid.*, p. 707, "Soviet proposal on the French zone of Occupation in Germany," submitted by V. M. Molotov on February 7, 1945.

[7] *Ibid.*, pp. 899–900.

However, the problem of French participation in the occupation of Germany had not been completely clarified. In the European Advisory Commission the negotiators encountered Soviet opposition when they tried to define the French sector in the occupation of Berlin. The Americans and British argued that each of the Big Three should transfer one of its wards (Bezirke) to form the French sector. The Soviet delegation "reacted violently to this proposal," charging a violation of the Yalta agreements.[8] The Soviet position remained adamant, and for other reasons a solution was adopted which left the Soviet sector unchanged.

In contrast to these concessions, Stalin was firm in his refusal to admit the French to the proposed reparations commission. He insisted that the three powers which had made the most sacrifices and had been the organizers of victory should have first claim on the reparations. The Soviet leader made a comparison between the French and Polish contributions to the war. France had only eight divisions in action, in comparison with Poland's thirteen and Yugoslavia's twelve. "France could not expect reparations from the Allies," Stalin declared, especially since it had "suffered less than Belgium, Yugoslavia, or Poland." [9] The Soviet position remained the same until the Potsdam Conference. Molotov told the French Ambassador, Catroux, that the French sacrifices in the war were hardly comparable to those of Poland and Yugoslavia. These two countries were worthy of sitting on the commission, Molotov added, and the Soviet Union would be disposed to allow France to be admitted if the Western powers agreed to seat Poland and Yugoslavia also.[10]

The Soviet leaders also opposed French membership on the Commission on Dismemberment. At Yalta it had been decided, at Stalin's suggestion, to add the word "dismemberment" to the Allied instrument of unconditional surrender. To negotiate the details of the proposal, the Commission on Dismemberment was created. The

---

[8] The demarcation of the three occupation zones in Germany had been signed in the European Advisory Commission a scant two weeks before the French representative joined it in November, 1944. The agreement was confirmed just prior to Yalta. The French zone was delimited in the Commission in June, 1945. See Mosely, "The Occupation of Germany," *Foreign Affairs*, XXVIII, No. 4 (July, 1950), 597–601.

[9] *The Conferences at Malta and Yalta, 1945*, p. 623.

[10] Catroux, *J'ai vu tomber le rideau de fer*, p. 50.

Anglo-Americans were concerned that France was not to be represented on this commission, but Molotov explained that the commission itself would decide on the participation of France.[11] Despite
the fact that Stalin had accepted the admission of France to the
Control Commission, he did not want it to have a seat on the dismemberment commission. The Soviet attitude remained unchanged
until the dismemberment commission ceased its meetings in April.[12]

As a minor Soviet concession to the West, Stalin agreed that
France was to be asked to sponsor invitations jointly with the
United States, Great Britain, and the Soviet Union to the international
conference at San Francisco to establish the United Nations Organization. Subsequently the French government refused to become a
sponsor unless two conditions were fulfilled: (1) the Dumbarton
Oaks proposals were to be taken as a basis for discussion rather
than as a basis for the charter; and (2) the French provisional government was to be permitted to introduce modifications of these
proposals.[13] The Soviet government did not "consider it possible to
agree to these conditions, in so far as acceptance of them would
mean an actual revision of the decisions of the Crimean Conference
. . . and would lead to a weakening of these decisions." [14] It thereby
withdrew its concession.

Five problems at Yalta involved a discussion and a decision on
the role of France in postwar Europe. The Soviet Union conceded
to the Western Allies on three of these—assigning a German occupation zone to France, giving France a place on the Control
Commission, and inviting France to become a sponsoring power of
the San Francisco Conference. Only the second was a real concession, because the Soviet government refused to relinquish any of
its occupation zone to help form a French zone, and it also denied
to France the right to propose changes in the Dumbarton Oaks
draft of the United Nations charter. On the other hand, Soviet opposition blocked French participation in two important commissions
which were to decide the future of Germany.

[11] *The Conferences at Malta and Yalta, 1945*, p. 701, Page minutes.
[12] See Mosely, "Dismemberment of Germany," *Foreign Affairs*, XXVIII, No. 3
(April, 1950), 494–98.
[13] *Le Monde* (Paris), March 6 and 9, 1945.
[14] *Izvestiia*, March 8, 1944.

For Stalin, the military cooperation of the Allies against Germany continued to be the single most important short-range goal of his policy. The Soviet press remarked that the Crimean Conference "demonstrated the durability of the military unity of the Allies." The Soviet people would learn with pleasure, it continued, that plans were laid for the destruction of Germany by the "closest co-ordination of the military forces of the three powers." [15] The fear of a separate peace had largely been dispelled, and, as a result, the Soviet Union declared, "the doors are completely closed in the face of the dying Hitlerite maneuvers of provocation." [16]

According to the Soviet Union, the Yalta Conference also "confirmed that the anti-Hitlerite coalition is not an accidental or short-term political combination." In fact, "the solidarity and agreement to action on all basic, vital questions constitute the outstanding feature of the Crimean Conference." Aside from the significant political decisions concerning Europe, the Soviet Union stressed the "unity in the organization of peace as in the conduct of the war." [17] However, Stalin pressed insistently for recognition of Soviet aims in Eastern Europe. In this connection it was already evident at Yalta that the Soviet Union was not satisfied with the development of French foreign policy. Since that time Soviet historians have made it even clearer.

After the conclusion of the Franco-Soviet Alliance the French government continued to carry on a policy which hindered France from drawing any advantage from the alliance with the USSR. Though having dealings with the Polish Committee of National Liberation and exchanging representatives with it, the French government continued to maintain its relations with the London Polish émigré government and gave protection to its pro-Fascist activities on French territory.[18]

The Soviet government wanted French approval of its policy in Eastern Europe or, failing that, a simple demonstration of French

[15] "Krymskaia konferentsiia rukovoditelei trekh soiuznykh derzhav" [The Crimean Conference of Leaders of the Three Allied Powers], *ibid.*, February 13, 1945.
[16] "Na mezhdunarodnye temy" [On an International Theme], *ibid.*, February 15, 1945.
[17] "Krymskaia konferentsiia rukovoditelei trekh soiuznykh derzhav" [The Crimean Conference of Leaders of the Three Allied Powers], *ibid.*, February 13, 1945.
[18] Manusevich, *Bor'ba,* pp. 105–6.

determination to avoid taking sides with the West on international issues. According to the Soviet leaders, France should have recognized the provisional government of Poland before the San Francisco Conference. On the occasion of the signing of the Soviet-Polish Treaty in April, 1945, Stalin emphasized the "great international significance of the agreement." He explained that the common front against Teutonic imperialism would prevent the Germans from exploiting differences between Poland and the USSR as they had in the past. "Undoubtedly," Stalin concluded, "if this barrier to the east were supplemented by a barrier to the west, then it could be stated boldly that German aggression will be chained and it will not easily break loose again." [19]

Since the Soviet Union was already allied with France and Britain, the French assumed that this was an invitation for alliances between the two West European powers and Poland.[20] Moscow also wanted France to support the membership of Poland at the charter meeting of the United Nations in San Francisco.[21] It hoped to have France break the Western front on this issue and criticized France severely for its failure to champion the Polish claims at San Francisco. Vyshinskii constantly asked Catroux in their private talks, "When will France conclude a pact with Poland?" [22]

The solid Western opposition to the Soviet-sponsored motion to admit Poland to the San Francisco Conference gave the Soviet delegation a feeling of isolation and aroused Soviet suspicions of a Western voting bloc. When the proposal for the election of vice-presidents was brought up, Molotov put great pressure on Bidault to support the Soviet motion that there be four vice-presidents, representing the four inviting powers.

The Narkom said that the question of the four presidents had primary significance for the Soviet delegation and that it would insist on it and

[19] "Rech' tovarishcha I. V. Stalina pri podpisanii dogovora o druzhbe, vzaimnoi pomoshchi i poslevoennom sotrudnichestve mezhdu Sovetskim Soiuzom i Pol'skoi Respublikoi" [Comrade I. V. Stalin's Speech During the Signing of the Treaty of Friendship, Reciprocal Aid and Post-War Collaboration Between the Soviet Union and the Polish Republic], *Bol'shevik*, Nos. 7–8 (April, 1945), pp. 1–2.

[20] Catroux, *J'ai vu tomber le rideau de fer*, p. 62.

[21] Manusevich, *Bor'ba*, p. 106.

[22] Catroux, *J'ai vu tomber le rideau de fer*, p. 63.

fight for it. . . . If the Soviet proposal was not accepted, then let there be one president and two vice-presidents without the participation of the Soviet Union. If the French did not support the proposal of the Soviet delegation, it would indicate that they were in a different camp from the Soviet delegation.[23]

The Soviet Union was also concerned with the revival of Pétainist, or Fascist, elements in France. It deplored the failure of the French to learn their lesson from the war, allegedly because they insisted upon discussing whether the admirers of Pétain were really accomplices of the Germans.[24] The Soviet Union indicated that though France "has resolved not to turn to the past, to the old bankrupt order, but to undergo a thorough reconstruction of its political-governmental structure," there were strong forces which sought to block this trend. There were economic groups which sabotaged French production; there were disquieting signs of a general reconciliation between the Pétainists and the government; and there was the "sinister" activity of Catholic circles in France. The Soviet Union urged the French to resist these tendencies, which in the prewar period had led to Rightist policies, and these, "as is well known, cost France and its people very dearly." The USSR advised the French to remember the "decisive role of the USSR and the Red Army in the task of rescuing the people, including the French, from the German-Fascist bondage. That is why the leaders of liberated France believed it necessary to sign an agreement of alliance and military assistance with the Soviet Union, to lay a firm foundation for French foreign policy."[25]

According to the USSR, these admonitions had gone unheeded because the French continued to pursue the will-o'-the-wisp of a Western bloc. Though there was a great deal of discussion in the British and French press about the possibility of a Western bloc, the Soviet Union exaggerated its influence by attributing every criticism of its own policies in Eastern Europe to the instigators of such a bloc. The Soviet leaders considered France the center of this dangerous agitation. "These stories about the 'Western bloc'

[23] SFO, No. 243, Notes on the conversation of V. M. Molotov and G. Bidault, April 25, 1945, p. 438.
[24] "Na mezhdunarodnye temy," Izvestiia, March 8, 1944.
[25] Ivanov, "O sovremennom polozhenii vo Frantsii," Bol'shevik, No. 6 (March, 1945), pp. 62, 70, 73.

are accompanied," they declared, "by a stream of sweet words about the defense of the interests of Western democracy, etc." However, Moscow charged, it had been admitted by some French journals that behind these euphemisms lurked real anti-Soviet motivations. The USSR insisted that "such a stupid and reactionary policy, of course, fundamentally contradicts the interests of the French people, who disapprove of it completely." [26] Despite this reassuring conclusion, the Soviet Union continued to condemn the idea.

Several minor incidents in the course of Franco-Soviet relations gave further evidence that the USSR wanted France to support its policy but did not intend to reciprocate. In June, 1945, when British and French troops clashed in Syria over French treatment of local nationalists, the immediate Soviet reaction was to send a note to the other permanent members demanding that the case be presented to the Security Council of the United Nations. Since this body had neither convened for the first time nor established its procedure, the proposal was ignored. The French ambassador in Moscow was instructed to sound out the Soviet government on the possibility of a joint Franco-Russian effort to solve the problem; in accordance with its custom, the USSR made no effort to interfere. Catroux commented bitterly that Moscow enjoyed seeing France and Britain settle the question themselves in a manner which did not enhance the friendship of the two Western European Allies.[27]

Another unpleasant incident was the Franco-Soviet dispute over the repatriation of French prisoners of war who had been liberated by the Red Army. The French protested that, though they allowed Soviet representatives freely to visit Russian prisoners of war and displaced-persons camps in France, no reciprocal facilities had been extended by the Soviet government in Poland. Molotov replied brusquely:

How can your prisoners complain of the Red Army, which in liberating them from the Germans rendered them an inestimable service? How can their feelings toward the Soviet command be unfriendly? How can

[26] "Na mezhdunarodnye temy," *Izvestiia*, August 30, 1945.
[27] Catroux, *J'ai vu tomber le rideau de fer*, p. 100.

they let themselves come to this, unmindful of the facts, scarcely a few days after the victory? [28]

East-West Hostility and Franco-Soviet Disagreements

Despite statements in the Soviet press about friendship and cooperation with the West, Stalin began to take unilateral action in several of the countries of Eastern Europe which had been liberated by the Red Army. When these actions were criticized in the Anglo-American press, the Soviet Union accused the West of fostering disunity in the anti-Hitlerite camp. The USSR apparently acted on the assumption that the "sphere of influence" agreement of October, 1944, and the Yalta declaration gave it the right to determine the terms of "unity of action" in Eastern Europe.

By May, 1945, the Soviet press was denouncing the "outburst of insane anti-Soviet pretensions" in American and British "reactionary circles." It insisted that certain groups in the West were trying to reverse the late President Roosevelt's foreign policy. There were people, the Soviet Union charged, "who do not welcome victory, but fear it." They were the reactionary circles in the United States and Great Britain, who talked about a war between the United States and the USSR or about an anti-Soviet coalition. The USSR further accused the British Conservative Party of conducting its election campaign on the theme of the approaching crisis with the Soviet Union.[29] The tributes to Soviet-American friendship were interspersed with expressions of doubt. Soviet reporters in the United States deplored "the strength of the anti-Soviet propaganda." [30] Though the results of the Potsdam Conference were hailed as new evidence of the mutual interests of the Big Three, the former enthusiasm over unity was gone.[31] Replacing

[28] *Ibid.*, p. 101. A repatriation agreement was signed a month later. About a hundred Soviet wives were not allowed to leave with their French husbands; after a year and an investigation of each case, about one half of these wives were permitted to leave.

[29] "Na mezhdunarodnye temy," *Izvestiia*, May 24, 1945, May 31, 1945.

[30] E. Zhukov, "O Sovetsko-Amerikanskoi druzhbe" [On Soviet-American Friendship], *ibid.*, June 6, 1945.

[31] "Berlinskaia Konferentsiia trekh derzhav" [The Berlin Conference of Three Powers], *ibid.*, August 3, 1945.

it was ideological suspicion of the West and a heightened emphasis on the unique role of the Soviet Union as the center of Marxist-Leninist truth and the champion of world revolution. Just before the end of the war the Soviet theorist E. Iaroslavskii had asserted that "the study of revolutionary theory, work on the heightening of its ideological and political level, should be demanded of every Communist from the first days of his enrollment in the ranks of the Party." He admitted that wartime conditions had created serious obstacles to the necessary and profound study of the life of the Party.

But each Party member is duty-bound to make use of every minute of the day in order to master revolutionary theory, by means of the revolutionary teachings of Marxism-Leninism. Lenin and Stalin always emphasized the very important concept of Marx and Engels: "Without revolutionary theory there can be no revolutionary movement. . . . The role of an advanced struggle can only be fulfilled by a Party directed by an advanced theory." [32]

Other Soviet commentators stressed the importance of revolutionary theory in defining the long-range goals of Soviet foreign policy. After the war, they maintained, the problem of the basic hostility between the Soviet Union and the capitalist world had not been solved, but rather had been intensified.

In the slave-owning society, under feudalism and capitalism, the ruling classes tried, by means of war, to attain the realization of their class goals, the strengthening of the state. Comrade Stalin showed that one of the functions of the state in the exploiting society is the extension of the territory of its ruling class at the expense of the territory of another state or the defense of its state from the attacks of another state.

The challenge to the Soviet Union from the predatory capitalist powers had to be met, they concluded, with determination and strength.

Marxism-Leninism teaches that the development of society will be completed on the basis of the struggle of the progressive forces against the obsolescent reactionary forces. The Bolsheviks are the most active supporters of such a struggle for the progress of society. The Bolsheviks not only acknowledge the legal struggle [and] the armed struggle of the

---

[32] Iaroslavskii, *Chego trebuet partiia ot kommunistov* [What the Party Expects of Communists], p. 8.

most advanced elements against the reaction, but they support that struggle by every possible means.[33]

One means by which the Soviet Union hoped to win "the struggle for the progress of society" in Europe was to isolate France from the Western Allies. Moscow was disappointed at the failure of its policy. "The Franco-Soviet agreement of 1944 could have been one of the basic guarantees of peace in Europe. However, it was constantly violated and in the long run was destroyed . . . by the ruling circles of France." [34] In the opinion of the Soviet leaders, France had not acted in the spirit of the Franco-Soviet alliance. Not only had France refused to endorse Soviet policy in Eastern Europe, but it had criticized that policy and had seemed inclined to associate itself with other Western countries in an anti-Soviet bloc. The Soviet Union did not intend to reward this attitude by welcoming France to participate in the deliberations of the Big Three, and at the Potsdam Conference the Soviet leaders continued to manifest their displeasure with the French stand.

There Stalin resisted efforts to give France a voice equal to those of the Big Three in the proposed Council of Foreign Ministers. The council had been suggested by the American delegation as an organ to consider and draft the peace treaties for Germany, Italy, and their satellites. Molotov insisted that France should participate in the drafting of only the Italian and German treaties, and Stalin indicated that "the three powers would represent the interests of all." [35] The Soviet representatives maintained this view during the discussions of the agenda for the first meeting of the council. Also, Molotov rejected the French plea to participate in the drafting of the treaties with Germany's former satellites.[36]

Also at Potsdam Stalin agreed to French membership on the Reparations Commission only after the most important decisions on reparations had been made. The serious disagreement over this complex issue was resolved on the last day of the conference, when

[33] Feodoseev, "Marksizm-Leninizm ob istokakh i kharaktere voin," *Bol'shevik*, No. 16 (August, 1945), pp. 31, 35.

[34] Ivanov, *Ocherki mezhdunarodnykh otnoshenii* [Outlines of International Relations], p. 222.

[35] Byrnes, *Speaking Frankly*, p. 72.

[36] Catroux, *J'ai vu tomber le rideau de fer*, p. 107.

it was decided that a certain percentage of reparations for the USSR would be taken from all the Western zones in Germany. Then Stalin finally consented, "after some grumbling," to have a French representative on the Reparations Commission.[37] With the percentages established, it merely remained for the commission to determine what equipment would be removed. Thus, the French were given the right to join the other powers in deciding what, not how much, to send to the USSR as reparations deliveries.

Thirdly, at Potsdam the Soviet Union came out very strongly for a solution to the Ruhr problem which was different from the French plan. In the light of the importance which both France and the Soviet Union attached to Germany and its war potential, the discussion of the future of the Ruhr ultimately became the most serious disagreement between the two powers in the immediate postwar period. The Soviet leaders wanted to establish a separate Ruhr region under three-power control with a veto, assuring them a high degree of bargaining power.[38] They held to that proposal throughout all subsequent negotiations.

The French position had been defined as early as October, 1944, when General de Gaulle asserted that France would not be satisfied until its security was guaranteed by a Rhine frontier.[39] A month later he declared that he had been asking for "the elementary security that nature itself has provided on the banks of the Rhine." [40] There was further information from Stalin that De Gaulle wanted to annex the Rhineland.[41] It was apparent, then, that France favored the annexation of the Rhineland and inter-Allied control of the Ruhr.[42] In April, 1945, the French presented their

[37] Leahy, *I Was There*, p. 423.
[38] Mosely, "Soviet-American Relations Since the War," *The Annals of the American Academy of Political and Social Science*, CCLXIII (May, 1949), 208.
[39] De Gaulle, *Discours*, p. 496.
[40] Assemblée Consultative Provisoire, *JO, Débats*, November 22, 1944, p. 331.
[41] *The Conferences at Malta and Yalta, 1945*, p. 616.
[42] This was the American assumption at Yalta; see "Briefing Book Paper, French Views on the Treatment of Germany," *ibid.*, p. 308, which stated: "Latest information indicates that De Gaulle prefers outright annexation rather than French control of an autonomous state. He is believed to favor the establishment of an international control for the Ruhr." See also De Gaulle, *Discours*, press conferences of January 25, 1945, and August 24, 1945. At the latter De Gaulle called the left bank of the Rhine "an old Franco-German affair," while referring to the Ruhr as "an inter-Allied affair." *Ibid.*, p. 657. De Gaulle com-

case to the Soviet Union. The French asked about possible Soviet support for the occupation of the left bank of the Rhine. Stalin's answer was noncommittal but tantalizing: "I repeat to you that the Soviet government is in no way bound as far as the Rhineland problem is concerned." Catroux told Stalin that the French had no objections to the Ruhr being under inter-Allied control, but "they could not share with others the responsibility and the control of the right bank of the Rhine." [43] By inter-Allied control Catroux naturally assumed four-power control. The French could neither obtain support for their Ruhr policy nor find out what the Soviet position was. In August, when Catroux asked Molotov about this area, the Soviet minister wanted to hear the French proposals. These had, of course, been known to him for months. After hearing them again he said. "You will have to convince the British." [44] The attitude of the French Communist Party on the future of Germany was even more vague at this time. Ignoring any territorial realignments in the West, the French Communists stressed the necessity of close cooperation with the USSR to prevent the rise of Germany. [45]

Moscow not only avoided taking a stand on the Ruhr problem, but refused to inform the French about the dismemberment negotiations which involved the future of the Rhineland. Before the surrender of Germany the French representative on the European Advisory Commission had learned of the Yalta decisions on this issue. He was privately informed of the Soviet opposition to French participation in the work of the commission, but he was unable to find out what decisions on dismemberment had been taken. [46]

Actually, Soviet policy on dismemberment had changed radically after the defeat of Germany. In his victory speech of May 8, 1945, Stalin stated that the USSR "does not intend to dismember or

---

mitted himself in Washington in August when he told Truman and Byrnes that France wanted administration of a separated Rhineland, annexation of the Saar, and international control of the Ruhr. Byrnes, *Speaking Frankly*, p. 170.

[43] Catroux, *J'ai vu tomber le rideau de fer*, pp. 65, 67.

[44] *Ibid.*, p. 108.

[45] See, for example, the major foreign policy address of Florimond Bonte in Assemblée Consultative Provisoire, *JO, Débats*, November 21, 1944; pp. 309–13.

[46] Mosely, "Dismemberment of Germany," *Foreign Affairs*, XXVIII, No. 3 (April, 1950), 495.

destroy Germany." [47] When Molotov finally told Catroux about the Yalta decisions on dismemberment and some of the work of the commission, he also explained that the whole question was no longer important because, on the proposal of the British delegation, it had been decided to abandon all consideration of dismemberment or the creation of a Rheno-Westphalian state.[48]

The Soviet Union strongly resisted French efforts to obtain an equal voice in deciding the future of Germany. Since France had not followed the Soviet lead in Eastern Europe, there was little likelihood that it would support the Soviet policy for Germany. Stalin was having enough difficulty over important issues with the United States and Great Britain without inviting further opposition from the French. Nevertheless, the Soviet leaders did not commit themselves on the subject of greatest interest to the French, the western frontier of Germany. They encouraged speculation that they would be willing to settle this issue with due respect to French interests if France would develop a foreign policy more favorable to the Soviet Union. It might be said that this was the "carrot" aspect of Soviet policy. At the same time the USSR assailed as dangerous and anti-Soviet the speculation that France might base its foreign policy on membership in a Western bloc. This might be called the "stick" aspect of Soviet policy. Moscow continued to dangle the carrot and wave the stick from afar, but it was still unwilling or unable to make full use of one or the other. France could not be trusted, and it was too far away to be coerced.

At the September Council of the Foreign Ministers in London the Soviet Union gave France another chance to show its willingness to back up its eastern ally. Molotov agreed that France (and China) could participate in the discussions of the peace treaties for Finland, Rumania, Bulgaria, and Hungary.[49] Though

[47] "Obrashchenie tov. I. V. Stalina k narodu," *Bol'shevik*, No. 9 (May, 1945), p. 4. This change was motivated by political, as well as economic, considerations. A dismembered Germany would not be in as strong a position to provide the requisite reparations for the USSR. It would be easier for the Soviet Union to control a centralized Germany than a dismembered one, the various sections of which would fall under the control of the occupying powers.

[48] Catroux, *J'ai vu tomber le rideau de fer*, p. 107.

[49] Byrnes, *Speaking Frankly*, p. 102; Catroux, *J'ai vu tomber le rideau de fer*, p. 113.

tactful in their remarks concerning the Balkans, the French delegates did not take a pro-Soviet stand. In discussions on the Italian treaty the French opposed some of the Soviet proposals. At the same time the Paris press was discussing the growing possibility of forming a Western bloc. For example, on the day before the conference opened, General de Gaulle had declared that an Anglo-French alliance, then under consideration, would lead to the formation of a West European economic unit.[50]

The Soviet Union reacted violently to these developments. On September 22 at the London conference Molotov demanded a reorganization of the Council of Foreign Ministers to exclude France and China from discussion of matters other than those concerning the peace treaties with Germany and Italy.[51] Molotov then blocked Bidault's attempt to discuss the question of the Ruhr and the Rhineland, insisting that the German problem be studied through diplomatic channels, and the conference then had no choice but to adopt his proposal.[52] Faced with what appeared to him a suspiciously united and determined opposition, Molotov fell back on his defense. He refused to consider the Italian or German treaty until concessions had been made to the Soviet view on Eastern Europe. Thus, France was prevented from discussing what it was most deeply interested in—the German problem.

Simultaneously the Soviet and French Communist press opened a new attack on the evils of the Western bloc. *Pravda* denounced the concept as a genealogical descendent of the *cordon sanitaire* and the Munich policy.[53] It further declared that the Western bloc had "received support from official figures" in France, as well as from the big banks and trusts. "In this persistent campaign for a Western commonwealth" at the time of the work of the London

[50] *Le Populaire*, September 11, 1945.
[51] Catroux, *J'ai vu tomber le rideau de fer*, p. 118. Byrnes, *Speaking Frankly*, p. 102. Molotov's attitude stiffened on all questions. He declared that American policy had changed since the death of Roosevelt; he demanded immediate recognition of the governments of Rumania, Bulgaria, and Hungary, and he wanted the establishment of an Allied Control Council for Japan. Finally, he insisted that discussion of the Italian peace treaty be postponed until the West agreed to his first two proposals. Byrnes, *Speaking Frankly*, p. 104.
[52] *Ibid.*, p. 122.
[53] "Mezhdunarodnoe obozrenie" [The International Review], *Pravda*, September 16, 23, 1945.

conference, *Izvestiia* charged, "there is undoubtedly a definite design directed not only toward undermining confidence in the Soviet Union but, as a special purpose, toward trying to sabotage the work of the Council of Foreign Ministers." [54] The French Communists were even more blunt. They declared that General de Gaulle "clearly advocated a Western bloc" and that this idea "torpedoed the conference." They supported all of Molotov's demands, especially the recognition of the three East European regimes, and they ridiculed Bidault for attempting to interfere in the discussion of the treaties for the Balkan countries. The Party also claimed that the Soviet representative, not the British, had enabled the French to present their memorandum on the Ruhr and the Rhineland.[55]

It became clear only later how completely the Soviet Union disapproved of the entire foreign policy of General de Gaulle at this time. A Soviet historian, Manusevich, has criticized De Gaulle sharply for his visit to the United States in August, 1945, in search of economic aid for France. Foreign economic aid, he declared, was not necessary for France's recovery; French industry needed a fresh capitalization of five to six billion gold francs, for which, more than sufficient funds lay in the vaults of the Bank of France and in the hands of individuals. "But laying the burden of reconstruction," the same commentator has asserted, "on the capitalist circles was alien to the policy of the De Gaulle government." Transfer of the burden to the working class would have been politically unwise and even dangerous. Therefore, he continued, "the provisional government preferred to embark on the path of accepting foreign credits and strengthening the dependence of France on American and English capital."

According to Manusevich, the failure of De Gaulle to secure anything for France in the United States led to the revival of the idea of a Western bloc centered on England. The Soviet historian accused the French Socialists of envisaging a West European Socialist federation: "Ignoring the alliance of France with the USSR and

[54] "Na mezhdunarodnye temy," *Izvestiia*, September 13, 20, 1945.
[55] Constant, "La Conférence de Londres," *Cahiers du Communisme*, No. 12 (October–November, 1945), pp. 66, 70.

all the unfortunate experiences of French prewar politics, *Le Populaire* stated: 'France will remain in isolation . . . as long as she does not conclude an agreement of alliance with England.' " [56] In his opinion, France was launched on the long, disastrous road which led to the Marshall Plan in 1947.

The Passing of an Illusion

Even while the cement of the wartime alliance was crumbling, Stalin continued to maneuver for Allied support in order to realize Soviet aspirations in Eastern and Central Europe and simultaneously to prevent the West from organizing a strong economic or political union. There was good reason for the Soviet Union to fear the widening breach in the Allied coalition over Soviet policy in Eastern Europe. American opposition to Soviet demands at Potsdam had encouraged the democratic elements in several countries under Soviet control.[57] Lack of unity could result in the breakdown of Allied control of Germany and the realignment of most of Germany with the West. At first through dismemberment and reparations, and then by inter-Allied control of Germany, the Soviet Union hoped to prevent a revival of German militarism and to obtain large-scale compensation from Germany for war damage. By proposing three-power control of the Ruhr, the Soviet leaders intended to secure an economic stranglehold on the industrial center of Germany, for political exploitation at a later time.

At bottom, however, the Soviet leaders were not concerned with reaching an immediate settlement of the German problem. Several factors appeared to operate in favor of postponing this issue. France had not yet held its first postliberation national election. After the election the French foreign minister might well be more amenable to Soviet policy; in fact, he might even be a Communist. Also, the United States was rapidly demobilizing its forces, and its power was diminishing rapidly in Europe and throughout the world. The Soviet leaders had good reason to expect that this trend would con-

---

[56] Manusevich, *Bor'ba*, pp. 116, 118.

[57] Mosely, "Hopes and Failures," in Kertesz, ed., *The Fate of East Central Europe*, pp. 69–71.

tinue and that the United States would soon withdraw most of its troops from the European Continent.[58] After the withdrawal of the United States from Europe, the USSR, with French support, would be in a strong position to overcome British resistance to Soviet domination of all of Germany.

The most serious obstacle to this ambition would be the creation of a "Western bloc." For several years Stalin had been wary of this possibility, and Roosevelt and Churchill had made special efforts to reassure him on this score. After the end of the war in Europe, Stalin's suspicions grew, and the threat of such a bloc supplanted the fear of a separate peace as one of the primary concerns of Soviet foreign policy. Obviously, France would be an important member of a Western coalition because it could serve, in the words of Pierre Hervé, as a continental "bridgehead" for the United States and Great Britain.

Since Germany, as well as France, could be the continental base for an anti-Soviet coalition, the Soviet Union was anxious to prevent both areas from falling under the influence of the United States and Great Britain. The Soviet Union's only means of persuading the French to follow its lead was to support their designs in the Ruhr and the Rhineland—that is, to give up the Soviet demand for three-power control of the Ruhr. However, Stalin never took this decisive step. He was not willing to jeopardize the possi-

---

[58] During the war the representatives of the United States, especially President Roosevelt, had expressed considerable doubt that the United States would be willing to shoulder heavy responsibilities in the postwar world. At the Teheran Conference Roosevelt had discussed with Stalin some of his plans for a postwar world security organization. He developed his idea of the Four Policemen—the United States, Great Britain, the USSR, and China—as guarantors of the peace. In reply to Stalin's questions, Roosevelt said that the United States would be able to furnish only sea and air forces for the maintenance of peace and that he did not envisage the sending of American troops abroad. He stated that the land armies would have to be furnished by Britain and the USSR. He further expressed doubts that Congress would favor American participation in a purely European defense system. Sherwood, *Roosevelt and Hopkins*, pp. 785–86. At Yalta Stalin asked Roosevelt for an opinion as to how long the United States would be willing to keep occupation forces in Germany. Roosevelt replied, "I can get the people and Congress to cooperate fully for peace, but not to keep an army in Europe a long time. Two years would be the limit." *The Conferences at Malta and Yalta, 1945*, p. 628, Matthews Minutes. The concern which Churchill expressed the next day over this estimate at a plenary meeting indicates that he scarcely regarded it as a casual remark. *Ibid.*, p. 660.

bility of controlling all of Germany on the assumption that France would support Soviet policy in Europe. Stalin was not a reckless gambler. Of no other period can it be said with more justice that he preferred one bird in hand to two in the bush. As a force which might change the course of French foreign policy without cost to Moscow, the USSR continued to look to the French Communists.

CHAPTER IX

The Communist Bid for a Popular Democracy

PARALLEL to the post-Yalta shift in Soviet policy, the French Communists reemphasized their allegiance to Marxist-Leninist-Stalinist revolutionary theory. The reconstruction of France should be based, they maintained, on the application of this theory to the practical problems of the nation. At the Tenth Party Congress in June, 1945, Etienne Fajon declared that

the Communists do not in any way renounce their Marxist views on the historical necessity of the socialist revolution and on the revolutionary role of the working class. But Marxism has never confused the socialist revolution, which will be the work of the united mass at a given stage, with "revolutionary" chatter and gestures, which can only divide the masses at the present stage.[1]

Duclos was equally frank:

It is true that we do not intend to establish communism in France in the next few weeks. . . . Our goals are more modest, but it is no less true that we are always Communists, and I will venture to say that in the light of what is happening in the world, we are [Communists] more than ever [but] in this period of history our policies are limited in their goals.[2]

According to Thorez, in his first speech after his return from Moscow, one of the most important of these "limited goals" was the merging of the Socialist and Communist parties into a single great workers' party.[3] On June 12, 1945, the Communists further

[1] Fajon, *Le Marxisme-Leninisme, notre boussole*, p. 12.
[2] Duclos, *La France devant son destin*, p. 31. As early as May Duclos had taken the American Communists to task for having advocated a lengthy truce between classes in the postwar era. *Daily Worker*, May 25, 1945.
[3] Thorez, *Travailler*, p. 13.

clarified their position on unity by publishing a Unity Charter. A few weeks later Jacques Duclos based his major address to the Tenth Party Congress on the theme of organic unity. Clearly, the new workers' party would be a revolutionary party "depending on and spreading the dialectical materialism of Marx and Engels, which has been enriched by Lenin and Stalin." The Party's ultimate aim would be

the conquest of power by the working class, the establishment of a state assuring the exercise of power by the working class in order to break the efforts of the reaction, with the aid of its natural allies in the towns (that is to say, the intellectuals and the middle classes) and in the countryside (that is to say, the peasants), and to prepare the progress toward a classless society which will allow full development of the individual.

Duclos quoted with approval Engels's words: "this [class] struggle has reached a stage when the exploited class (the proletariat) can no longer free itself from the class which exploits and oppresses it without at the same time freeing for all time all of society from exploitation, oppression, and class struggle." The revolutionary class which will carry out this task was, according to Duclos, the working class. "That is why," he continued, "we have proposed the name of French Workers' Party" for the fusion of the Left.

Despite the Communists' denial that the workers' party would submit to any external pressures, the Unity Charter stated: "The French Workers' Party, in order to show the superiority of the principles which it proclaims, will inform the masses of the tremendous victories of socialism which have been won by the Bolshevik Communist [sic] Party of the USSR under the leadership of Lenin and Stalin, the continuators of Marx and Engels."

The organization of the new party as proposed by the Unity Charter was modeled on that of the French Communist Party. The Parti Ouvrier Français was to be based on democratic centralism, tightly knit discipline, ideological unity. "To become a member of the party, it is not enough to express agreement with the ends and means of the party, it is necessary to work for the application of the party's decisions and to pay dues regularly." The program of the new party would aim at establishing a state-directed economy and a classless society.[4]

The Communists envisaged organic unity as a merger of the Socialist and Communist parties in a Bolshevik pattern of organization—in other words, a pure and simple absorption of the Socialists. As Duclos put it, this would be "a popular front not in the sense of a simple coalition of parties but in the sense of a mobilization of the masses. . . . it is not a question of remarking the Popular Front of 1935, but of creating something better." [5] In order to persuade the Socialist leaders to accept organic unity along these lines, the French Communists pointed to Soviet encouragement of such action and asserted that the only alternative was "the return of reaction" and the loss of France's economic independence.

The French Communist plans and tactics to absorb the SFIO closely paralleled those of the Polish Workers' Party (Communist) for destroying the Polish Socialists, but there were two important differences. The French Communists were not in power and could not use the political police as a weapon of persuasion, and they could not rely on Moscow to arbitrate between them and the French Socialists; otherwise, the pattern was the same, and the goal was the creation of a "popular democracy." [6] As Joszef Revai pointed out, the Hungarian experience showed that the "development into a dictatorship of the proletariat was crowned and definitively assured . . . by the destruction of the Right wing of the Socialist Party and the establishment of the unified Workers' Party." [7]

A few weeks after the Tenth Party Congress the French Communist appeal for organic unity was rejected by Léon Blum, who had just returned from imprisonment in Germany.[8] Reacting violently to Blum's criticism, the Communists set down the theoretical

---

[4] "Projet de charte d'unité de la classe ouvrière de France présenté par le parti communiste français" in Duclos, *Vive l'unité*, pp. 28, 36–40.

[5] Duclos, *Union des forces démocratiques*, pp. 25–27.

[6] Cf. "R," "The Fate of Polish Socialism," *Foreign Affairs*, XXVIII, No. 1 (October, 1949), 126–28.

[7] "The Character of a 'People's Democracy,'" *Foreign Affairs*, XXVIII, No. 1 (October, 1949), 146–47.

[8] Léon Blum, "Le Problème de l'unité," *Le Populaire*, July 5, 11, 1945. These were the first in a long series of articles which Blum devoted to this subject.

basis for the revolutionary seizure of power in a syllabus of social democratic errors. It was a mistake to believe with Daniel Mayer and Blum, they maintained, that "the proletariat cannot and ought not to take power if it does not constitute by itself the majority in the country." Equally fallacious was the concept that "the proletariat cannot secure power if it does not command in sufficient quantity the properly trained cadres and experienced administrators capable of running the country." Finally, it was incorrect to believe that "the Socialist state is conceivable only in a parliamentary form. It is clear that the October Revolution has overthrown these dogmas." [9] Though the Communists denounced Blum as a revisionist, they could not silence him. Their direct appeal to the Socialists for a monolithic revolutionary party had failed. But, again duplicating the tactics of the Polish Communists, they then tried to capture the organizations which linked the Socialist Party with the masses—the Resistance movements and the trade unions.

The Failure to Fuse the Resistance Movements

The Communist attempt to control the Resistance movement met with no greater success, primarily because the campaign to fuse the Mouvements de la Libération Nationale (the former MUR enlarged) and the Front National met with defeat. In November and December, 1944, Thorez had issued a call for unifying the Resistance organizations. He urged that the fifty groups represented in the Consultative Assembly be merged into one great movement "from Communists to Catholics." [10] The effect of his appeal was tested late in January, 1945, at the national congress of the MLN. The meeting had been preceded by a Communist propaganda campaign for unity, as part of the attempt to present the congress with a *fait accompli*. Its only spectacular result was a precongress fusion of the local organizations of the MLN with the FN in the Rhône-Alpes.[11] The decisive struggle began on the floor of the MLN congress. Led by Pierre Hervé, Pascal Copeau, and Emman-

[9] Alain Signor, "Déviation bolchévique?" *Cahiers du Communisme*, No. 4 (April, 1946), p. 444.
[10] Thorez, *Travailler*, p. 13, and *S'unir pour vaincre le fascisme*, p. 14.
[11] *Le Monde*, January 10, 1945.

uel d'Astier de la Vigerie, a minority of the delegates urged either a federal union with the FN or a great workers' union with the Socialist and Communist parties and the CGT. The "unity" faction was defeated 250–119 by the opponents of fusion, who supported unity of action with all Resistance movements.[12]

Within a few days the FN held its own congress, which, it had been hoped, would meet to accept the MLN offer of fusion; instead it welcomed a delegation of the defeated minority.[13] The speakers at the FN meeting deplored the attitude of the MLN and called for the "union of all Frenchmen." In fact, the way in which the FN delegates parroted the Communist line prompted Le Monde to dub the meeting "a congress of unanimity" at which "1,800 delegates applaud with order and discipline." [14] The spectacle impressed few, and, more important, the call for unity went unheeded.

In May, 1945, the Communist elements in the MLN forced a schism in the organization. After a departmental congress of the MLN at Lyon had voted to fuse with the FN, the national executive committee expelled those who had voted for the motion. At that time the MLN was engaged in negotiations to merge with other non-Communist groups, and the Communist minority in the national bureau of the MLN urged that the FN be added to the list of possible partners for merger. Blocked again on this issue, they appealed to all members of organizations of the Resistance to help create a united movement of the French patriotic forces. This new group would expose "all factional maneuvers for electoral purposes which are contrary to the will expressed by the unanimity of the assemblies of militants and sanctioned by universal suffrage." This act meant a secession of the minority from the MLN.

After negotiations that were hardly necessary, the MLN minority fused with the FN on June 21 to form the Mouvements Unifiés de la Résistance Française (MURF). It seems clear that the title was chosen to confuse former militants or sympathizers of the MUR, the predecessor of the MLN.[15] In the meantime the MLN

[12] Ibid., January 28–29, 1945; Le Populaire, January 25, 26, 27, 1945.
[13] Le Populaire, February 1, 1945.
[14] Le Monde, February 1, 1945.
[15] L'Année politique, 1945, pp. 228, 229.

itself fused with Libération-Nord and the Organisation Civile et Militaire to form the Union Démocratique et Sociale de la Résistance (UDSR).[16] These events spelled doom for the idea of the unity of the Resistance, and they also destroyed the Resistance as an independent force in French politics. The MURF was completely dominated by the Communist Party, and soon disappeared as a distinct movement. The UDSR, in turn, was closely identified with the Socialists of the SFIO. Any Communist successes with that group had to come, therefore, though direct discussion with the Socialists.

The Communist Appeal for Electoral Unity

In their appeals to the Socialists and the MLN for "unity of action" the Communists placed special emphasis on presenting a single list of Resistance candidates at the municipal elections to be held in the spring of 1945. When the government decided to hold municipal and cantonal elections in May, 1945, the Political Bureau of the Communist Party welcomed the decision with two qualifications. The elections should be merely provisional because, the Party said, there were still three million prisoners of war in Germany, and there should be a single list of candidates drawn exclusively from the Resistance.[17] The Party wanted "to make of the elections a great manifestation of national unity." [18] Duclos tried to justify the Communist position by asserting that it would be "harmful for the interests of France" to allow an electoral campaign which would "open old local quarrels, transforming our entire country into a sort of vast Clochemerle and offering our allies the painful spectacle of sordid disputes over municipal seats at a time when it is necessary, above all, to make war and to make war again!" [19] If the Communists did not want to distract attention from the war effort, neither did they want the elections to be held before they had had an opportunity to unite all the Leftist political groups in a monolithic organization.

[16] Le Populaire, June 12, 1945, for the MLN declaration.
[17] L'Humanité, October 13, 1944.
[18] Duclos, La Lutte, p. 27.
[19] Duclos, Batailles, pp. 32–33.

To stimulate the demand for electoral unity the Communists tried to appeal to the masses over the heads of the leaders of the political parties. In preparation for the elections to the National Assembly, the Communists called for a convocation of an Estates-General on July 14, 1945. They hoped to generate great enthusiasm and popular excitement in France which would result in a groundswell of mass support for a single list of Resistance candidates.[20] Reminiscent of its time-honored predecessor, the Estates-General would seek, according to the Party, to give widespread recognition to the wishes of the French people. They would draw up notebooks of grievances on the model of 1789, and these would be presented at the national meeting of the estates. The Communists wanted the local Estates-General to be organized by the departmental committees.[21] The purpose of this demonstration, according to Louis Saillant, was to unite the people "so that the flame that we have kindled . . . throughout the country is not extinguished." [22] That flame was the symbol of cooperation imposed by external oppression, and the Party was trying desperately to keep the blaze alive. However, once again the response to the appeals of the Party and the CNR was uninspiring.

The campaign in the provinces to draft the "notebooks" was characterized by two factors: there was no mass participation of the people in the work, and the FN and the Communist Party took the lead in trying to arouse the indifferent public.[23] As planned, the Estates-General met on the anniversary of its namesake, from July 10–14, 1945. The speeches and resolutions of the delegates were based on the "notebooks," which, it was reported, had been drawn up primarily by the departmental committees. The result

[20] Actually on December 17, 1944, the Conseil National de la Résistance proposed calling the Estates-General. At the time there was some support for the idea from certain Socialists. See L'Année politique, 1945, pp. 71–72.

[21] Marty, "Les Conditions de la réconstruction," Cahiers du Communisme, No. 2 (December, 1944), p. 31.

[22] L'Année politique, 1945, p. 71.

[23] SCCR, région de Bordeaux, June 27, 1945, p. 106; région de Clermont-Ferrand, June 29, 1945, p. 108; région de Toulouse, July 4, 1945, p. 111; région de Marseille, July 6, 1945, p. 112; région de Lille, June 26, 1945, p. 105; région de Poitiers, June 28, 1945, p. 107; région de Montpensier, June 30, 1945, p. 109; région de Limoges, July 3, 1945, p. 110; région de Nancy, July 17, 1945, p. 117. Only at Dijon was there a report of any serious interest in the Estates-General; région de Dijon, July 6, 1945, p. 113.

was a series of monotonously repetitious proposals. The important resolutions passed by the assembly were Communist-inspired.[24] The demonstration did not arouse enthusiasm among non-Communists.

Despite the Communist failure to join forces with all Leftist groups for the local elections, the Party tried to conceal its failure by entering the May, 1945, elections everywhere as the "Union Patriotique Républicaine Anti-Fasciste" (UPRA). The lists of this union varied according to the localities, but rarely grouped representatives of all parties or formations.[25] The Communists also tried to strengthen their position by proposing a modification of the electoral law for Paris; this would have favored them because of their large vote in Paris and their domination of the suburbs. It was rejected by the assembly.[26] Again the Party's action was blocked on the governmental level and frustrated on the Resistance level. The disadvantages of its position were beginning to show through.

This trend was obscured by the spectacular gains that the Communist Party chalked up in the first postliberation election. The Party increased its control of municipal councils from 310 (in 1935) to 1,413.[27] The Socialists and the Communists had cooperated in many instances on the second ballot, but the SFIO executive committee did not use party discipline to enforce joint lists, as the Communists had wished.[28] As soon as the results were known, the Communist Party declared that it was prepared to assume an important role in the direction of public affairs. It further demanded that the cabinet of the provisional government be reconstituted "in the image of the elections." [29] After De Gaulle had reshuffled a few posts in his cabinet (which did not affect the

[24] See *L'Année politique, 1945*, p. 246. The first resolution supported a sovereign constitutional assembly, and the second added eighteen new Communist members to the CNR and thus destroyed any vestige of independent action which remained in that organization.

[25] *Ibid.*, p. 185.

[26] Assemblée Consultative Provisoire, *JO, Débats*, March 1, 1945, pp. 234–38, 255.

[27] *L'Année politique, 1945*, p. 203.

[28] *L'Humanité*, May 3, 1945; *Le Populaire*, May 2, 3, 1945.

[29] "Notre Politique," *Cahiers du Communisme*, No. 7 (May, 1945), p. 4.

Communists), the Party criticized the action because it "did not bring the extensive changes that were rightfully expected." [30]

The elections had brought the Party great gains in the municipal councils, but the Communists could not exploit these victories fully in their struggle with De Gaulle. The elections, being purely local, could not be interpreted as giving a national mandate. Even if the local vote had been transferred to a national election, the Communists would have fallen short of one quarter of the total vote cast. The short-range tasks for the Party were clearly defined. It had to build its strength for the election of a Constituent Assembly and to make certain that this assembly would be sovereign and Leftist. To achieve these aims the Communists had to make every effort to persuade the Socialists to work with them.

The Communist Triumph in the Trade-Union Movement

Meanwhile the developments in the reunified CGT showed just how fusion with a strong Communist group would affect the future of any other organization. While the Communists moved swiftly to suppress any factional tendencies within the CGT, they also appealed to all working-class organizations in France for "total unity" of the trade-union movement and endorsed the creation of a new international trade-union organization. At all levels the Communists were striving for unity on their terms—in other words, for domination of the French labor movement and of the new International. Their goal was attained, curiously enough, first on the international level and then within the CGT.

When the reconstituted federal bureau of the CGT took up its functions immediately after the liberation of Paris, the Communist position on it was very strong. The six-to-three ratio of former *confédérés* to *unitaires* was diluted by the absence of Léon Jouhaux, a prisoner in Germany, and by Louis Saillant's Leftward drift. More often than not there was parity between the two orientations: Bothereau, Buisson, Neumayer, and Gazier against Frachon, Racamond, Raynaud, and Saillant. A further advantage to the Communists in their drive to take over the CGT was provided by the

[30] *L'Humanité*, May 31, 1945.

dynamism of their militants, who rapidly built up the Party's strength in the local unions. The purge of the CGT also helped them to increase their control over many federations.

Another factor contributing to the Communist success was the political inexperience of the mass of new workers who joined the reconstituted unions after liberation. The preservation by the Communists of their tightly knit cell organization during the occupation and their energetic recruiting policy likewise gave them substantial advantages in the race for votes. Finally, the Communists launched a vigorous propaganda drive, led by *La Vie Ouvrière*, to immortalize the martyrs of the *unitaire* faction and discredit those who had supported the split in 1939 or had accepted the Vichy charter.[31]

The Communists were especially insistent on "union democracy," which Frachon defined at the first information conference of the departmental union of the Paris region: "Union democracy would have made the split in 1939 impossible." [32] In other words, support of unity under any circumstances was the criterion for democracy.

The first public evidence that the Communists were moving closer to their goal was the reconstitution of the federal bureau, in March, 1945, by the newly elected Comité Central National. Though still in Germany, Jouhaux was retained as secretary-general. However, Saillant and Frachon were elected acting secretaries-general. The rest of the bureau was composed of ten secretaries, five from each former faction. The Communists had almost achieved official parity with the *confédérés*.[33]

The repatriation of Jouhaux in May, 1945, did not immediately modify the situation, partly because of his initial reluctance to take a vigorous stand against Communist infiltration. The former French ambassador to Germany and a fellow prisoner, André François-

---

[31] See *La Vie Ouvrière*, September 8 and 14, 1944. On one occasion Frachon wrote, "The charlatans of the Labor Charter boasted of having realized unity by obligatory enrollment in the Fascist unions. . . . Almost to a man the workers were absolutely opposed to these caricatures of labor organization." *Ibid.*, September 21, 1944. This was part of the offensive which helped discredit Guigui. See above, p. 180.

[32] *La Vie Ouvrière*, September 14, 1944. See also *ibid.*, September 8, 1944, and "Vive la CGT une et indivisible!" *Le Peuple*, September 16, 1944.

[33] *Le Peuple*, March 31, 1945.

Poncet, explains this attitude in a brief description of the trade-union leader:

He has good sense and good will and a highly estimable concern for the national interest. In the main he fought against the revolutionary demagogy of the Communists. There remains something of this in him. But at the present time he is afraid of looking like a moderate, a "soft." He defends himself vehemently against what he calls backsliding; he is anxious to acquire new conviction in his dislike of the privileged and rich, to persuade himself that he is not a bourgeois nor in danger of becoming one, [and] to conserve intact his class consciousness.[34]

There were, no doubt, many like Jouhaux who did not want to be accused of being soft or petty bourgeois at a moment when leaders of the working class were extolling their own heroism and "hardness" and the courage of those who had died for the cause. By the time Jouhaux and others took up the fight against the Communist infiltration, it was too late.[35]

A series of unforeseen events now gave the Communist control of the CGT executive bureau. In September, 1945, the Comité Central again reorganized the bureau, creating a second secretary-general and electing the Communist Bénoît Frachon to the post. The over-all ratio in the bureau remained the same, with the six *confédérés* (including Saillant) to five *unitaires*.[36] Within a year this had changed. Georges Buisson, one of the secretaries of the *confédéré* tendency, died, and in October, 1945, Albert Gazier, another secretary, was elected a deputy (SFIO) to the National Assembly; neither was replaced, and now the Communists had a clear majority in the bureau.[37]

The CGT national congress of April, 1946, confirmed the Com-

---

[34] François-Poncet, *Carnet d'un captif*, p. 49.

[35] *Résistance Ouvrière*, a non-Communist journal, expressed some divergence of views with the Communists in the CGT, but it was very prudent in its discussions. Only in September, 1945, a semiclandestine monthly, *Front Syndicaliste*, was first issued and began criticizing Communist views. It affirmed, for example, that the purge was a fraud. It was not until December, 1947, that Jouhaux and his friends created *Force Ouvrière*, which replaced *Résistance Ouvrière* and took on the task of fighting the Communists.

[36] Saillant voted against the Communist motion to create a second secretary-general, stating that only a national congress could change the statutes. He did, however, vote with the Communists on the proposal to have the CGT take a stand on the October referendum. See below, p. 224.

[37] Lefranc, *Les expériences*, p. 159.

munist conquest of the organization. By an overwhelming vote (21,238 to 4,862) the *unitaire* faction changed the statutes. To preserve the fiction of democracy, they elected only twenty of their own supporters to the administrative commission of thirty-five. Jouhaux and Frachon remained secretaries-general, and the Communist majority of six to five was retained in the bureau (with Saillant still listed among the *confédérés*).[38]

The enormous majority of Communist votes requires some comment. Besides the factors already mentioned—the purges, the dynamic Communist recruiting tactics, various pressures on the workers, and the deaths of some non-Communist leaders—the apathy of the non-Communist workers contributed heavily to the results. At a union congress on July 10, 1947, a report of the secretary-general of the Federation of Railroad Workers showed that only 4,217 out of 37,758 active members of fifty unions had been present at the general assemblies that prepared for the CGT congress. The report added that in the voting for the Union of Central Services a vote of 40 to 25 gave the Communists 2,025 mandates for the CGT congress; at Rennes a vote of 70 to 14 gave them 3,500 mandates! In the fifty cases cited by the secretary-general, the minority vote, which totaled 20 percent of those voting, was not represented at the congress.[39]

Along their path to the conquest of the CGT, the Communists and their sympathizers fought to give the organization a political orientation. Frachon moved cautiously at first in order to avoid making too rapid a break with the CGT's traditionally "independent" position on politics. At the March, 1945, meeting of the Comité Central, his proposals defining the attitude of the CGT toward the municipal elections were adopted with slight modification. The local and departmental unions were left free to participate in joint lists of the Resistance if this did not endanger unity of the labor movement.[40] Though the resolution stated that the decision did not constitute a precedent, it was considered a setback for the moderate position of maintaining union independence.[41] It was, in any

[38] *La Vie Ouvrière*, April 18, 1945.
[39] Lefranc, *Les Expériences*, pp. 156–57.
[40] *Le Peuple*, March 31, 1945.
[41] Lefranc, *Les Expériences*, p. 158.

case, a marked departure from the CGT's traditional aloofness from politics.[42]

Frachon soon took a more uncompromising stand and engaged in a verbal duel with Jouhaux over the issue. "The trade-union movement," Frachon declared, "cannot be neutral with regard to governmental action. Either it [governmental action] is quite contrary to the interests of the laboring masses, and it [the trade-union movement] fights it, or it conforms well with the popular aspirations, and the movement sustains it. In any case, it acts in order to effect an orientation favorable to the realization of its objectives."[43]

It was primarily on this point that Saillant solidified his alliance with the Communists. He asserted that the labor movement was responsible for a "dual collaboration." On the national level, he wrote, "it ought to accept a collaboration with other groups on specified points and objectives. In the international field it must promote and organize the collaboration of workers for the organization of peace, progress, and social security."[44] The Communist victory in the CGT assured a growing preoccupation of the trade unions with politics.

The second aspect of the Communist campaign for the unity of the working class was the drive to create a single CGT for all trade-union members. On September 19, 1944, the CGT bureau offered to discuss with the Confédération Française des Travailleurs Chrétiens (CFTC) the possibility of fusion "in such a way as to assure to all levels, to each tendency, a place proportionate to its real influence."[45] Frachon argued cautiously that there was no idea of imposing unity, but that unity was desirable and possible.[46] The CFTC bureau replied that it was not qualified to act and that consideration of the issue should be deferred until the meeting of a national congress.[47] The Communists continued to be insistent. Raynaud explained that the labor movement would be harmed if the

[42] Le Populaire, March 30, 1945. The decision, said one of the delegates, "cost us dearly."

[43] Le Peuple, July 28, 1945. For Jouhaux's arguments see ibid., July 21, 1945.

[44] Ibid., March 30, 1946. For an elaboration of Frachon's position on the participation of the WFTU in politics see below, p. 226.

[45] Le Peuple, September 23, 1944.

[46] La Vie Ouvrière, September 21, 1944.

[47] Le Peuple, September 30, 1944.

CGT and the CFTC campaigned against each other in the forth-coming elections for representation on the factory committees, and appealed for a single list of candidates.[48] At the same time another invitation for organic unity was extended to the CFTC.

As for the elections themselves, the CFTC set the precedent that the Socialist Party followed. It "recommended" that its militants establish common proportional lists "in places where the CGT has an organization and real influence." [49] The central executive bureau of the CFTC did not order any cooperation.

In 1945 the Communists made still further attempts to create a united labor front. By April they had become impatient and were criticizing the CFTC leaders for blocking unity.[50] The familiar tac-tic of attacking the leadership and appealing to the rank and file proved a failure. In September, 1945, the CFTC congress finally and decisively rejected the Communist proposals and reaffirmed its own conditions for unity.[51] The CFTC also refused to accept the new statutes voted by the Communist-dominated World Federation of Trade Unions (WFTU). The Catholic union then canceled its membership in that body and began negotiations with the Belgian Christian Democrats to form a Christian International.

Subsequently, the Communists in the CGT accused the CFTC of being priest-ridden and reactionary, and they spared no language in condemning the rival organization's close attachment to the Catholic Church.[52] The Communists then tried to force the CFTC to comply with their demands for unity. In April, 1946, Frachon told the CGT national congress: "There remains to us now only one way, for we continue to be determined partisans of unity within a single CGT. That is to fight tooth and nail to liquidate disunity at the workplace itself." [53] This could only mean CGT pressure for a closed shop and a resort to open labor warfare in order to break the resistance of the CFTC. Combining comradely appeals with bludgeons, the French Communists had narrowly missed bringing

[48] *La Vie Ouvrière,* December 7, 1944.
[49] *Ibid.*
[50] *Ibid.,* April 26, 1945.
[51] *Le Populaire,* September 18, 1945.
[52] *La Vie Ouvrière,* December 27, 1945.
[53] *Compte-rendu du congrès national du CGT, 8–12 avril, 1946,* as cited in Lorwin, *The French Labor Movement,* p. 101.

all organized labor under their control in a trade union of proletarian character, tightly organized and dominated by the Party—identical, in fact, with Lenin's definition of a trade-union movement under capitalism.[54]

The International Labor Front

The Communists' success in France assured the Soviet Union of strong support in the reestablishment of a world labor organization. In planning the World Federation of Trade Unions, the Soviet Union desired a new International having no links with the non-Communist Amsterdam group. The Soviet proposals were based on the assumption that Communists would dominate the new International and would be able to exploit its considerable power for the advancement of Soviet political aims.

On the initiative of the British Trade Union Congress, representatives of non-Fascist unions met at London in February, 1945. On the eve of this congress the Soviet Union emphasized that the success of the working-class struggle "will be more fruitful the more successfully it is able . . . to unite its forces and close its ranks." [55] Unity would serve three purposes: to destroy Hitler; to rally the workers against "all survivals of the Munich policy"; and to defend the economic rights of the working class. The Soviet Union charged the Amsterdam group, or International Federation of Trade Unions (IFTU), with failure to fulfill these tasks, and condemned the "pitiful attempts to revive the bankrupt Amsterdam International." [56]

At the world union congress in London both the Soviet delegation and Bénoît Frachon attacked the IFTU. Supported by other "Leftist" delegations, they established a commission to draw up a constitution for a new International. The congress also accepted the demand of the Soviet delegations that the unions of Rumania, Bulgaria,

---

[54] Hammond, *Lenin on Trade Unions*, pp. 13, 47, 63, 67–75.

[55] "K otkrytiiu mezhdunarodnoi profsoiuznoi konferentsii," *Voina i Rabochii Klass*, No. 3 (February 1, 1945), p. 1.

[56] Nazhenin, "O mezhdunarodnom edinstve profsoiuzov," *ibid.*, No. 1 (January 1, 1945), p. 6; "K otkrytiiu mezhdunarodnoi profsoiuznoi konferentsii," *ibid.*, No. 3 (February 1, 1945), p. 2.

Poland, and Italy be admitted to the congress. This time, led by Saillant, the CGT again voted with the USSR.[57]

Therefore, it was not surprising that the report of the constitutional commission, presented to the congress at Paris in September and October, 1945, reflected in many respects the position of the Communist group. Saillant again supported the majority view that the WFTU should participate in political activities, if necessary, to further its goals.[58] As a result of the demands of the Communist group, the preamble to the constitution stressed the need to create a new world order. The Communists obtained a very strong, but not majority, representation in the executive committee and in the bureau. Above all, their position was reinforced by the fact that Louis Saillant was elected secretary-general of the WFTU.[59] From this post he actively promoted the interests of the Soviet bloc—for example, in seeking representation for the WFTU in the United Nations.[60] At the same time the Soviet Union attempted to monopolize the contacts between the United Nations and world labor by gaining for the WFTU the exclusive right to speak for labor in the Economic and Social Council.[61] They also tried to obtain a regular seat for a WFTU representative on the council; again they failed.[62]

Undaunted by these defeats, Saillant attempted to secure representation for the WFTU on the International Bank for Reconstruction and Development, the Food and Agricultural Organization, the World Health Organization, UNESCO, and the International Labor Organization.[63] His last great propaganda campaign was

---

[57] *Le Peuple,* February 17, 1945. The other supporters of the move were the Italian, the Latin American, and the United States (CIO) delegations; the first two were Communist-dominated.

[58] *La Vie Ouvrière,* October 11, 1945.

[59] World Federation of Trade Unions, *Constitution* (1945), pp. 1–2.

[60] *Le Peuple,* May 19, 1946.

[61] *Report of Activity of the WFTU,* p. 236.

[62] For the development of these negotiations see *ibid.,* pp. 237–60, especially letter of Louis Saillant to Trygve Lie, July 3, 1947, pp. 254–57. In this letter Saillant requested the right to convoke the Council in a special session and the right to participate in the Council's deliberations on all questions, substantive and procedural.

[63] *Ibid.,* pp. 260–99.

aimed at persuading the Economic and Social Council to grant a special statute to his organization, which would guarantee the inviolability of unions, the recognition of the absolute right of unions to manage their internal affairs as they saw fit, the right of unions to interfere in the economic development of their country, and the creation of a special committee charged with directing the applications of these principles and arbitrating the conflicts which might arise between the unions and their respective governments.[64] By this time the tenor of the resolutions of the WFTU executive committee had begun to take on a decided anti-Western tone, and it was clear that the Communist domination of the movement was far-reaching.[65]

There are many parallels between the Communist attempts to take over the French and the international trade-union movements. In both cases the Communists sought to bring about a complete merger of all trade-union movements. Through the labor organizations under their control they tried to monopolize contacts with the policy-making bodies on the national and international levels. They also insisted that the labor organizations carry on vigorous political as well as economic activity against the antagonistic classes. Lastly, they attempted to mask their control of the CGT and the WFTU by keeping important non-Communists on the executive committees of both organizations, even after they had assured their own domination of the committees. However, there was an important difference in the results achieved by the Communists on the national level in France and on the international level. The French Communist control of the CGT was more important for the promotion of world communism than was the Soviet control of the WFTU, for whereas the CGT held the economic future of France in its hands, the WFTU had no similar power over the development of the world economy.

The French Communist Party had neither the internal strength nor the outside support necessary to carry out its program of monolithic unity of all republicans and resisters. The Socialists, the

<hr>

[64] *Ibid.*, p. 91. The date of the broadcast was March 8, 1947.

[65] See, for example, "Resolutions on the Activity of the WFTU since the Paris Congress," General Council (Prague, June 2–14, 1947), in *Report of Activity of the WFTU*, Appendix pp. 37–38.

MLN, and the Catholic trade unions refused to merge with the Party or its auxiliaries. The attempt of the Communists to rally the masses without their leaders through the Estates-General of the French Renaissance was an unmitigated failure. It was ironic that the Communists went on trying to preserve the spirit of the Resistance after they had done so much to destroy it as a political force by opposing the efforts of many Resistance groups to wrench concessions from De Gaulle during the early months of the liberation. Their one success was their colonization and conquest of the CGT. Again ironically, they used their newly acquired power to strengthen the government and restrain the legitimate demands of the French working class. By these tactics the Communists committed themselves for the time being to a bid for national power through parliamentary methods. As it turned out, the Communists merely succeeded in rebuilding France until the Fourth Republic was again strong enough to walk without its Communist crutch.

The French Communists and Economic Reform

The Party's attitude toward the catastrophic economic crisis which gripped France throughout 1945 clearly indicates its habit of using economic weapons to further its political purposes. After the liberation, inflation was rife; transportation facilities were badly disorganized and damaged; the food supply of the big cities was precarious; the black market was widespread and powerful; and industrial production had fallen off sharply. The workers were underfed and dispirited, and their working conditions were miserable. They faced hard toil in half-flooded mines or in factories with worn-out machinery and bombed-out roofs. The peasant either hoarded his food, waiting until there was more to buy in the cities, or sold it on the black market. War profiteers were making fortunes through speculation.

Faced with this critical situation, the government could either establish an austerity program, with rigid government controls, or let the economy take its own course in the hope that normalcy would return unaided. Even before the government acted, the Communists came out in favor of the politically more attractive alternative. The Party's answer to France's economic woes was to encourage the workers to produce more and to blame all the shortages, mismanagement, and technical difficulties on the "men of the trusts" and the remnants of the Vichy regime, while pressing for the nationalization of large monopolies.

The most serious challenge to the Communist program came not from the government, but from Pierre Mendès-France, Minister of National Economy. He was urging the government to carry out a thoroughgoing monetary reform, including the freezing of bank accounts and an exchange of notes, in order to check inflation and protect the value of the franc. Though he suggested other economic reforms, the Communists opposed only his monetary plan. In the Consultative Assembly Jacques Duclos asserted that to follow the Mendès plan

would be equivalent, in our opinion, to retreating behind a kind of inferiority complex, with the prospect of widespread apathy persisting in the field of production. We cannot approach the task of reconstructing France with such an attitude. We think that the search for the balance between the circulation of merchandise and banknotes is not a problem of restricting the circulation of paper money but, above all, a problem of production.

Duclos insisted that the attempt of the Belgian government to carry out a similar monetary reform "had not yielded conclusive results." Such an action "would cause considerable disturbance in the French economy and would hurt the peasants, the tradesmen, and the artisans—that is to say, the small and middle savers." It would not, he continued, force the speculators and profiteers to disgorge their ill-gotten gains. A better solution to the monetary problem, Duclos concluded, was to make a note-for-note exchange, which would provide an accurate and complete inventory of personal fortunes.[66]

Duclos's reasoning represented bad economics, but good politics.[67] The peasants were large-scale hoarders of notes, and the Com-

[66] Assemblée Consultative Provisoire, JO, Débats, March 30, 1945, first session, pp. 957–58.

[67] There were persistent rumors that the Communists also opposed the freezing of accounts and the delayed exchange of notes because they had enormous sums of "hot money" which they would then be unable to use; there is no documentary evidence to substantiate the rumors.

munists were making a special effort to win over the countryside to their Party. Considering that the municipal elections were to be held in one month, it would have been politically disastrous for the Party to support the freezing of accounts. Who was to pay for this Communist bid for the peasant vote? The worker was to pay in the form of producing more goods, and this involved little political risk because the majority of the proletariat could be counted upon at the polls.

The Communist leaders pressed their appeals to the workers to step up production, despite the accumulating evidence that the latter were not enthusiastic about the "battle of production." Reports from prefects and commissars to the Minister of the Interior revealed considerable anxiety over the "growing discontent of the working class with the government." [68] Undaunted, the Party redoubled its efforts. In July, 1945, Maurice Thorez, himself a former miner, went to the heart of the coal country in the department of the Nord. In a speech at Waziers he bluntly told his former comrades that "a worker who understands his duty multiplies his productive efforts." He further declared:

Now, dear comrades, I say it with full responsibility in the name of the Central Committee, in the name of the decision of the Party congress, I say it frankly: it is impossible to approve the smallest strike—above all, after it has broken out. . . . If we do not apply the decisions of our unions . . . we will fall into anarchy, we will facilitate provocations against the miners, against the working class, and against the Republic.

Thorez admitted that the lack of personnel, the physical exhaustion of the miners, and the poor state of equipment made the workers' task difficult. Moreover, he stated, two other factors were responsible for inadequate production—sabotage by the Fifth Column and an insufficient sense of responsibility on the part of the miners. It was the men's duty to eliminate the latter; it was the Party's duty to crush the former.[69]

The Party launched a propaganda offensive against political

[68] SCCR, région de Poitiers, April 5, 1945, région de Lyon, April 13, 1945, where "in a word, the working masses are not only separating themselves from the government but seem ready to fight it openly," p. 3.

[69] Thorez, *Produire*, speech of July 21, 1945, pp. 15, 18–19.

sabotage, blaming both the "men of the trusts" and former Vichy
officials still in office for France's failure to recover rapidly.[70] This
tactic sometimes led to ludicrous situations. The Party maintained
that the trusts "employ as their agents Trotskyite elements who,
under the pretext of returning to the anticapitalist struggle, provoke
the workers to strike." [71] Because the Party was against any inter-
ruption of work, it denounced all strikes as the result of provocation
rather than despair, and all strikers as "agents of the trusts."

In the agricultural sector the Communists stepped up their efforts
to win the peasants as allies in the revolutionary struggle. "The
masters of socialism show us that even if the working class is called
upon more and more to play the leading role, it cannot alone claim
victory; and the most powerful ally of the industrial proletariat is
the peasantry." What better authority could be quoted than Stalin?
"The revolution can prevail only if the proletariat, as its leader, is
assured of the alliance of the peasantry." Therefore, according to
the Communists, their program for the countryside should correspond "to the needs of the peasant groups whom we should win
over—the agricultural workers, the sharecroppers, the small and
medium proprietors." The Communists favored a series of reforms
which would give the landless peasants more security, standardize
wheat prices, and establish sections for sharecroppers in the agricultural workers' unions. "In the Socialist revolution only the poor
peasants can be resolute allies, because the middle peasants hesitate,
and consequently it is necessary to limit ourselves to obtaining
their benevolent neutrality." [72]

Another basic demand of the Communists was the nationalization
of the trusts and large monopolies. Though the Party had opposed
nationalization during the Resistance, at the liberation it endorsed
the charter of the CNR, which included a section on nationalization.
When, in early 1945, the Communists developed their own nationalization program, Etienne Fajon explained that nationalization

[70] Assemblée Consultative Provisoire, *JO, Débats*, February 15, 1945, pp.
100–1; February 27, 1945, pp. 204–6; and March 21, 1945, second session, p.
642.

[71] Monmousseau, "Une Nouvelle Étape de la lutte des classes," *Cahiers du
Communisme*, Nos. 8–9 (June-July, 1945), p. 15.

[72] Chervet, "La Conquête de la paysannerie," *ibid.*, No. 4 (April, 1946), pp.
379–82, 384.

of the large monopolies would not be socialistic, since France was not a Socialist state. He insisted that "the problem of socialism is the problem of the future. In the present historical period it is a question not of the struggle for socialism but of the war for the independence of France and for the destruction of fascism." The Communists, he declared, intended to nationalize not small or medium enterprises but "conclusively . . . genuine monopolies." [73]

The Party favored the indemnification of the expropriated owners, except in cases of confiscation for treason, and it proposed management by boards representing workers, technicians, and consumers. As areas of the national economy to be nationalized Fajon listed banking, electricity, coal and iron mines, the bauxite industry, oil refining, cement production, all forms of transportation, the steel industry, heavy machine-tool production, and the large-scale chemical industry.[74] It is debatable whether all these industries were, in fact, genuine monopolies in 1945.

To offset any disturbing political effects of their nationalization program, the Communists stressed that they were not enemies of private property. Etienne Fajon pointed to the Soviet constitution, which guarantees the fruits of one's labor. In France, he declared, the question of new forms of property that would satisfy the demands of the tenant farmers was not a problem of the moment. The present task, he continued, was to confiscate the property of traitors. "To speak of socialism is to obscure the present task." [75]

At first glance the Communist plans for the economic rehabilitation of France did not seem radical, and they did not offer much that was new or imaginative. "Hard work, the punishment of traitors, concessions to the peasants, and the nationalization of monopolies" constituted a program unlikely to alienate any numerous group from the Party, which, at the same time, resisted the austerity program and the proposals for tight government control of the economy. Though favoring nationalization of some industries, it wanted the enterprises to be autonomous of government control.

The Party justified its program by stressing its short-term aims of

[73] Fajon, "Les Communistes et les nationalisations," *ibid.*, No. 4 (February, 1945), pp. 33, 35.
[74] *Ibid.*, pp. 66–68.
[75] Fajon, "Les Communistes et la propriété," *ibid.*, p. 15.

waging the war and maintaining national independence. Thorez insisted again and again that "to make war with resolution, with energy, with self-sacrifice, and to carry it on to the end, to Berlin, to victory . . . this is the single task of the moment." [76] Also emphasizing the political importance of an economically healthy France, he indicated that the place of France "in the postwar world will be measured in the coming battles." [77] During the final military campaigns and after the end of the fighting the Communists warned that a national renascence was necessary to prevent the loss of French independence. "The danger for the liberated but ravaged European countries will be that the trusts, in order to alleviate the situation [of demobilization and industrial reconversion in the United States] . . . will launch a vicious exploitation of these countries, dividing Europe and Africa into guarded preserves and thus subjecting these countries to financial and consequently political tutelage." [78]

The Communists were very sensitive to Western criticisms of the state of the French economy.[79] They believed these remarks were a prelude to Western actions which would keep France a second-rate power tied to American and British apron strings. They also accused people in high places of believing that the salvation of the disordered French economy could come only from enormous Allied aid. The adoption of this solution, the Party claimed, would "transform France into a semicolonial country." [80] The saboteurs of French recovery were counting on this outside assistance, which would mean, the Party asserted, submission to capitalist cartels and the disappearance of French independence in the strait jacket of a Western bloc.[81]

The French Communists feared that economic reliance on the West would foreclose any possibility of close cooperation between

[76] Thorez, *Travailler*, p. 10.

[77] Thorez, *S'unir pour vaincre le fascisme*, p. 7.

[78] *L'Humanité*, September 11, 1944.

[79] *Ibid.*, September 19, 1944. An analysis of the economic weakness of France by the London *Times* brought the Communist rejoinder that the example of the USSR proved how a country could rebuild after having been destroyed.

[80] Marty, "Les Conditions de la réconstruction," *Cahiers du Communisme*, No. 2 (December, 1944), p. 28.

[81] *L'Humanité*, September 19, 1944.

France and the Soviet Union. In accord with the USSR, the Party denounced the idea of a political or economic bloc of West European countries as an "evil project" which posed a threat to continuation of the wartime cooperation among the Big Three. Of course, the Party continued, the national dangers of such a bloc were just as great as the international ones. A preferential trade system for Western Europe—suggested in the French and British press—was, according to the Communists, "a menace to the independence of France." The proposed standardization of military equipment for Western Europe was, in the eyes of the Party, an even greater evil than the economic suggestions.[82] Thus the French Communists identified the internal economic problems of France with the international problems which faced the once Grand Alliance.

In addition to the short-term aims of winning the war and preventing the growth of American influence in the French economy, the Party's economic program gave evidence of long-range Communist aims in France. The Communist policy of winning over the peasants as "allies in the socialist revolution" is solid evidence of this. When Fajon drew the analogy between the French Communist and the Soviet guarantees of private property, he showed not only the French Communists' adherence to the Stalinist pattern of thinking but also the real aim of the nationalization program. By indicating that socialism was not the "present task" but the "problem of the future" he was saying, in effect, that socialism was the ultimate goal of the Party.

The Hungarian Communist Joszef Revai has explained the part that nationalization could play in transforming a bourgeois-democratic state into a "people's democracy."

The struggle for the transformation in Hungary along anticapitalist and socialist lines was initiated long before when . . . the left wing bloc, under the leadership of the Communist Party, succeeded in the fight for the nationalization of heavy industry . . . and [later] in initiating the struggle not only for the control but for the nationalization of the great banks.

This transformation was carried out under the watchword "We are constructing the country not for the capitalists but for the

[82] Fontenay, "La Funeste Thèse du bloc occidental," *Cahiers du Communisme*, No. 10 (August, 1945), pp. 47, 49.

people." Arguing along the same lines as the French Communists, Revai pointed out:

It was correct at that time [1945] to stress that the issue was not a choice between socialism or bourgeois private property, but rather the following: Should we compromise with the forces of the old system or should we liquidate them? It was correct that in the fight against big capital we stressed not that this was a transition into the struggle for socialism but that the measures initiated against big capital meant at the same time the protection of small private properties. It was correct not to show our cards.[83]

In the short run the French Communists supported organic unity of Leftist political parties, Resistance movements, and trade-union groups in order to forestall the strengthening of anticommunism in France. The Soviet Union and the French Communists sought to preserve the Big Three coalition in order to block the formation of an international anti-Communist alignment that would be controlled by "reactionary" elements. They interpreted any solidarity of interests or even opinions among the Western powers as evidence of a new bloc directed against the Soviet Union.

The Communist interpretation of the Western bloc as a well-defined economic or political grouping was totally erroneous. At this time the United States and British governments had not developed any long-range economic, let alone political, program for Europe or the world.[84] However, the inflexible and unimaginative Soviet foreign policy ultimately forced the Western powers along the road to closer economic and political cooperation, though even the Western bloc as later embodied in NATO did not correspond in scale to what the Soviet Union imagined already existed in 1945.

During the early postliberation period French Communist activities and attitudes ran parallel in many ways to those of the East European Communist parties. This strongly suggests that the long-range goal of French Communist tactics can be summed up in Joszef Revai's words: "In the first phase of our transformation, when we struggled directly and apparently only for a steadfast achieve-

[83] "The Character of a 'People's Democracy,' " *Foreign Affairs*, XXVIII, No. 1 (October, 1949), 146–48.
[84] See Penrose, *Economic Planning for the Peace*, especially Chapters XII, XIV, and XVII.

ment of bourgeois democratic tasks, we fought also for the establishment and assurance of the conditions which made possible the Socialistic transformation." [85] However, the Communists had failed in their first attempt to establish these conditions; in turn the future success or failure of the French Communists was to depend in large measure upon the developing international situation. Yet the more uncompromising Soviet policy became, the more frantically the French Communists defended it against the criticisms and interests of the West. As a result, it was less likely that the Communists would be entrusted with any of the ministries which influenced the direction of French foreign policy. After the London Conference and on the eve of the French national elections in October, 1945, it should have been clear to the French Communist leaders that they did not have much more time to develop their bid to share power at the top.

[85] "The Character of a 'People's Democracy,'" *Foreign Affairs*, XXVIII, No. 1 (October, 1949), 146.

CHAPTER X

The Reconstruction of Europe

AS RELATIONS WORSENED between the Western powers and the Soviet Union between September, 1945, and April, 1946, the Soviet leaders took a firm stand on two vital questions of their postwar foreign policy: Would the USSR extend the struggle for power from Europe to the world? Would Moscow interpret the disputes between East and West as regrettable but minor incidents in the realignment of the great powers or as a new phase in the all-or-nothing conflict between capitalism and communism? The future of France and the French Communist Party depended largely on the Soviet answers to these questions. Any evidence of growing ideological estrangement between the Soviet Union and the West would make it increasingly difficult for France to maintain good relations with both power blocs. This, in turn, would jeopardize the position of the French Communists within the government and would lead to a growing polarization in French politics between Communist and anti-Communist forces.

Among the great unsettled problems inherited from the European war were the peace settlements with Germany, Italy, and the former Axis satellites in Eastern Europe, and the future of the colonial areas of Asia and Africa. Since the interests of both France and the Soviet Union were involved in all these questions, the negotiation of the postwar settlement was the real test of Franco-Soviet relations.

The Peace Treaties

At the London conference the obstacle to negotiating peace treaties with Italy, Bulgaria, Hungary, and Rumania had been the deadlock between the USSR and the West over which states were to participate in the drafting process. In December, 1945, at the Moscow Conference of the Big Three foreign ministers a compromise was reached. The Soviet Union agreed to participate with twenty other Allied belligerents in a general peace conference, which would meet not later than May 1, 1946, to discuss the draft treaties drawn up by those powers which had been at war with the German satellites. In return the United States and Great Britain conceded that the preliminary and final drafts of the treaties would be elaborated and approved only by the signatories to the various armistices.[1] This gave the Soviet government a veto over any recommendations made at the peace conference; the smaller allies would have an opportunity to criticize and make suggestions but not to change the draft treaties. France was not to have an important voice in the Balkan-Danubian settlement, being invited merely to concur in the decisions of the Big Three.[2]

According to the Soviet press, "the decisions of the Moscow Conference testify that a new step has been taken on the path of developing the solidarity of the Allied powers." It added that "without the unity of the three great powers there will not be this steadfastness, this confidence in the strength of peace."[3] In general, whereas the Soviet Union was cautious in its endorsement of the Moscow decisions, the French Communist Party was enthusiastic in praising the "felicitous results of the Moscow Conference." It encouraged the French government to endorse the unanimous decision made there because, the Party stated, it was in "the national interest to do everything in order to favor the solidarity of the Big Three." The Party assured the French that it was also to their national interest not to demand an important role in drafting the peace treaties for Bulgaria, Rumania, and Hungary. To do otherwise, the Party insisted, would be

[1] Byrnes, *Speaking Frankly*, pp. 111, 115. These decisions were printed in *Pravda* and *Izvestiia*, December 25, 1945, "O podgotovke mirnykh dogovorov s Italiei, Rumyniei, Bolgariei, Vengriei i Finlandiei [About the Preparation of Peace Treaties with Italy, Rumania, Bulgaria, Hungary and Finland] *Izvestiia*, December 25, 1945.
[2] Byrnes, *Speaking Frankly*, p. 115.
[3] "K itogam Moskovskogo soveshchaniia trekh ministrov inostrannykh del" [From a Review of the Moscow Conference of the Three Foreign Affairs' Ministers], *Izvestiia*, December 28, 1945.

to fail to see that the best way to guarantee our interests and our prestige
in the Balkans and Danubian Europe would have been not to ask for a
formal right . . . but to take substantial and far-reaching measures;
we want to point out the necessity of sending back French diplomats
. . . to forge solidly a friendship with the young democracies.[4]

The French government had little choice but to accept the Moscow
formula, as it did in an exchange of letters between Bidault and
Byrnes. Thus, the French delegates to the Council of Foreign
Ministers' Deputies in London were to participate only in drafting
the Italian peace treaty.[5]

In what was apparently a new test of the willingness of the
French to work closely with Moscow, Molotov withdrew his objections to French participation in the discussion of the Balkan
treaties when the four foreign ministers met in Paris in April, 1946.
The concession did not, of course, bind the Soviet Union to accept
French views, and it did not involve any weakening of Soviet bargaining power. As a result of Molotov's decision France was better
able to play the role of a mediator at the council meetings. The
proposed French line of demarcation of the Italian-Yugoslav bound-
ary was accepted as representing "roughly a compromise between
the American line and the Soviet line" and the Trieste problem was
shelved by the adoption of a French plan to create an international
free territory.[6] The Soviet Union also benefited from French support
of its claim for $100 million in Italian reparations to be paid over
a six-year period. Though the Soviet press noted the action, it did
not praise the French stand.[7] It is noteworthy that these examples
of French mediation all refer to the Italian treaty, in the drafting
of which France had an equal status.

The USSR was not impressed with the French record because it
had expected support, and not mediation. Therefore, Molotov reversed himself again and proposed a new plan for the Paris Peace
Conference, which had been set for July, 1946. He insisted that the
details of the treaties be negotiated in five commissions, one for each

[4] Cogniot, "La Conférence des trois à Moscou et ses heureux résultats,"
Cahiers du Communisme No. 1 (January, 1946), pp. 71, 72.
[5] Mosely, "Peacemaking, 1946," *International Organization*, I (February,
1947), 25, 26.
[6] Byrnes, *Speaking Frankly*, pp. 124, 127, 136–37.
[7] *Pravda*, May 27, 1946.

former enemy state. The commissions would be composed solely of those powers which had "actively waged war" against the respective enemy states. The plenary session of the conference would, according to Molotov, merely comment on and approve the proposals.[8] The Soviet Foreign Minister wanted to prevent the smaller nations from pressing for any revision of the work of the great powers. It was not inconceivable, he feared, that the Western three might try to rally the small nations against the USSR and thus force changes in decisions which had already been made. The Molotov plan was not accepted, but it revealed Soviet suspicion of the Western powers, especially of France.

The German Problem: Centralization

The Soviet and French views on Germany were different and more irreconcilable than those on Eastern Europe. Their disagreement over the future of Germany was also a more serious practical matter, because both France and the USSR considered Central Europe vital to their security. Furthermore, both countries shared in the military occupation of Germany and would not relinquish this territory short of war. Each demanded concessions which the other opposed as inimical to its security. Germany was the one place where East and West faced each other on equal terms. Therefore, it was the one place where there had to be either a compromise decision or a complete split. The disputed issues between France and the Soviet Union were the creation of a central German administration, the future of the Rhineland, and the final transfer of the eastern territories to Poland.

In the letter accepting an invitation to the Foreign Ministers' Conference in London on September 1, the French indicated that they could not accept a reconstitution of a central German government, of all-German political parties, or of central administrative departments.[9] Accordingly, in September, 1945, the French delegate

[8] Mosely, "Peacemaking, 1946," *International Organization*, I (February, 1947), 29.

[9] Ministère des Affaires Etrangères, *Documents français relatifs à l'Allemagne*, p. 8, Letter from the French Foreign Minister to the Ambassadors of Great Britain, the United States, and the USSR, dated August 7, 1945.

to the Allied Control Commission refused to agree to the establishment of a central German transportation administration.[10] The American and Soviet delegates protested vigorously, but in vain. In October the French delegate demanded suspension of the study of a central administration.[11] For all intents and purposes this was a French veto on any future plan for a centralized administration in Germany. The French also refused to countenance the creation of an all-German trade-union movement.[12]

The French brought down upon themselves from all sides charges that they were disrupting Allied unity. In retrospect and from the Western point of view, this French action was a diplomatic error. It is now evident that the Soviet leaders, though theoretically in favor of German unity, envisaged a type of unity totally different from that conceived by the United States and Great Britain. However, the French move to block further negotiations on the centralization of Germany temporarily prevented the West from seeing clearly the Soviet motives in Germany.

There were several early indications that Soviet policy in Germany aimed at the complete and unilateral exploitation of the Eastern Zone by the USSR. For example, the University of Berlin was placed under exclusive Soviet control, and no Western consulates were permitted in the Soviet zone. When the United States suggested opening all zonal boundaries with no restrictions, the French objected. This was understandable, for it was consistent with their policy; the Soviet government, which was committed in principle to treating Germany as an entity, also objected because "practical implementation [of the suggestion] at the present moment is impossible." [13] It is doubtful that the Soviet leaders intended to surrender any of their advantages as an occupying power for the sake of a centralized Germany. What they were aiming at was greater influence in the other zones without extending equal benefits to the Western powers in their own zone.

The disagreements over frontiers and territorial transfers were more clearly defined. The French presented their position on the

[10] Clay, *Decision in Germany*, pp. 109–10.
[11] *Documents français relatifs à l'Allemagne*, p. 15.
[12] Clay, *Decision in Germany*, p. 110.
[13] *Ibid.*, pp. 111–12.

dismemberment of Germany to the other three powers during the Council of Foreign Ministers conference of September, 1945. They declared that

a division of Germany into several states . . . would be favored for the maintenance of security in Europe. It [France] considers that the definitive separation of this region [Rhineland], including the Ruhr, from Germany [is] indispensable to protect the French frontier, and constitutes moreover the essential condition of the security of Europe and the world. If centralized German administrations are to be established, it then considers it necessary to state at the same time that the Rhine-Westphalian region will not be placed under their control.[14]

Somewhat later the French clarified their position on the Saar. They demanded that the Saar be integrated into the economic and monetary system of France and that the frontiers of the Saar territory be drawn along the line of 1919. The French opposed placing the Saar under the Allied Control Council or under German central administration at any time. They wanted French military forces to be permanently stationed there to maintain order and to serve as frontier guards. In February, 1946, the French government announced that "it will henceforth take all necessary measures to detach fully public services, such as railroads and posts [of the Saar] from those of the Reich."[15] Having explained their position, the French then tried to gain Soviet support for it.

In December, 1945, the French government sent Hervé Alphand to Moscow to discuss the German problem with the Soviet leaders. Prior to Alphand's arrival Ambassador Catroux once again attempted to draw out Molotov on the Ruhr-Rhineland problem, without success.[16] Alphand's proposals called for a political detachment of the Ruhr and the exploitation of the area "for the benefit of all peoples." The Soviet Union was assured that application of the French plan would in no way modify the decisions of the Allied Control Council on the economic disarmament of Germany and consequently "would not reduce the levies that the Soviet Union could impose in the Ruhr as reparations, except by joint

---

[14] *Documents français relatifs à l'Allemagne*, pp. 13–14.
[15] *Ibid.*, pp. 17–18, Note of the French Foreign Minister to the Ambassadors of Great Britain, the United States, and the USSR, dated February 12, 1946.
[16] Catroux, *J'ai vu tomber le rideau de fer*, p. 138.

decision of the four powers." In reply to Molotov's query on the Rhineland, Alphand replied that the area should be "taken from Germany and occupied by Allied forces."

Molotov pressed the French for more details on the political regime for the Ruhr. Alphand explained that the French plan distinguished between guaranteeing and governing powers. The former would be responsible for controlling the application of the general principles set down by the statute of the international regime. The latter alone would have the right to maintain military forces in the Ruhr. They would be chosen by the four powers, with Belgium and Holland eventually being added.[17] The French plans were vague in this respect; possibly they aimed at excluding the USSR from a governing status and thereby from maintaining troops in the Ruhr.[18]

The French were still unable to get satisfaction. Molotov merely asked to study the plan. Later he brushed aside French concern over Soviet policies by declaring that the treaty of 1944 was "irrevocable proof" of Soviet intentions and that it retains "all its value." The Soviet government wished, Molotov explained, "that the treaty had the same value as far as the French government was concerned." He indicated that, though the Soviet Union was the only country to which France was linked by a treaty, in several cases the position adopted by the French government differed from that of the USSR. The Soviet Union hoped, he said, that "the respective attitudes will draw closer together in the future." [19]

Molotov implied that he expected French support on such matters as the Polish frontiers. In September, 1945, the French government had indicated that it had "no objection in principle" to Polish administration of the eastern provinces; "it assumes, however, that the problem of the frontiers of Germany will be treated as a whole and could only be solved after being examined in common by all the interested parties." [20]

[17] *Ibid.*, pp. 140–41.

[18] Catroux feared that the USSR would demand that the government be restricted to the four powers. *Ibid.* He was correct, as Stalin's comments at the Potsdam Conference had revealed. See above, p. 203.

[19] Catroux, *J'ai vu tomber le rideau de fer,* p. 150.

[20] *Documents français relatifs à l'Allemagne,* p. 11, Letter of the French Foreign Minister to the Ambassadors of Great Britain, the United States, and the USSR, dated August 7, 1945.

The Soviet leaders did not see the question in the same light. When in February, 1946, Catroux asked Dekanosov whether the French could count on support from the USSR for their proposals on the Ruhr, the Soviet diplomat replied that "cooperation should be mutual" and then asked about the French representative at Warsaw.[21] A few days later Molotov asked the same question and also wanted to know if the French view on the western frontier of Poland had undergone a change.[22] It had not.

The Soviet Union and France were unable to work out a common policy on the German frontiers, based on reciprocal guarantees, because a decision between them could not be final without agreement by the United States and Great Britain. Neither France nor the USSR was willing to take the risk that the Western powers would recognize only one part of a Franco-Soviet compromise, thus forcing one of them to give up a valuable bargaining point for nothing. France did not wish to concede something as real as recognition of the Polish territorial claims in return for something as ephemeral as a promise of Soviet support. Although the promise could be easily withdrawn, recognition could not be retracted. On the other hand, the Soviet leaders could not have endorsed the French proposals without giving up their plans for Germany. At bottom they did not think that French support of Soviet policies in Eastern Europe was worth the price.

Ignoring the German question at the Paris Council of Foreign Ministers conference in May 1946, Molotov did not present his government's position until July.

It has of late become fashionable to talk about dismembering Germany into several "autonomous" states, federalizing it, and separating the Ruhr from it. All such proposals stem from this . . . line of destroying and agrarianizing Germany, for it is easy to understand that without the Ruhr Germany cannot exist as an independent and viable state.

Molotov argued that the Ruhr "must be placed under inter-Allied control exercised by our four countries, with the object of preventing the revival of war industries in Germany."[23] To some this argu-

---

[21] Catroux, *J'ai vu tomber le rideau de fer*, p. 160.
[22] *Ibid.*, p. 162.
[23] Molotov, *Voprosy*, pp. 64, 66.

ment seemed to embody a contradiction,[24] but not to Molotov. Separation of the Ruhr would have meant exclusion of the Russians from any control over this key area. Inter-Allied control of the Ruhr meant a direct Soviet voice in the future of the area. At the same time a Soviet veto on the recovery of the Ruhr would be a powerful political weapon which could be used to blackmail the Germans at a later date. The Ruhr was of importance to Belgium, Holland, and France as well as to Germany, and the ability of the USSR to determine, through four-power control, at least what was not to be done in this great industrial basin could have enormous repercussions on the economic recovery of all Western Europe. If skillfully manipulated, such control could bolster the strength of the local Communist parties in the West.

The Soviet position on the Ruhr question also gave encouragement and political assistance to the German Communists. Though the Soviet Union had put pressure on the German Social Democrats to fuse with the Communist Party in order to form the Socialist Unity Party in April, 1946, the Soviet authorities did permit other "non-Fascist" parties to exist in the Eastern Zone. These parties were allowed to participate in the municipal and *Länder* elections set for September and October, 1946. During the campaign the Socialist Unity Party could point to the Soviet stand on the Ruhr as proof that the USSR was against separatism and, therefore, more than the other powers, had the interest of Germany at heart. In sum, from both the economic and the political viewpoints, the USSR was completely opposed to the French solution of the Ruhr question in particular and the German problem in general.

The French Communists and the Ruhr

Despite the importance of the control of Germany for the USSR, the French Communist Party did not support Soviet policy on the future disposition of the Ruhr or the Rhineland. In fact, it endorsed the official French government proposals on Germany which had been presented by Bidault to the London Foreign Ministers' Con-

[24] Byrnes, *Speaking Frankly*, p. 180.

ference.[25] During a debate on foreign policy in the French National Constituent Assembly, Florimond Bonte supported the plan to separate the Ruhr and the Rhineland from Germany and to occupy both areas permanently with Allied forces. He accused those who favored the revival of a strong Germany of being champions of a Western bloc![26] Thorez later expressed these same views more definitely. He spoke of a unanimous decision of the government to confirm the Party's demands for economic and political internationalization of the Ruhr, prolonged occupation of the Rhineland, and French ownership of the Saar mines, with attachment of the entire Saar to the French economic, customs, and monetary system.[27]

However, the newly created German Socialist Unity Party (Communist) in the East Zone took a different view of internationalization, and the French press taunted the Communists with the discrepancy. Thorez was obliged to answer by repeating the charges of

some papers which say, "But those Communists are no longer recognizable; the French Communists demand internationalization of the Ruhr and the German Communists are against internationalization. . . ." Truthfully, all this ultimately results in having the masses of our country better understand the national character of our party. We represent the interests of France. . . . Thus, on the external level, as well as on the internal, we stand, and we will stand, as the real defenders of French interests.[28]

The Party did not even waver when, in July, 1946, Molotov revealed the great difference between the Soviet and the French views. Repeating that "the most effective and sure means of breaking the power of German imperialism is to take the Ruhr away from it," the Party said boldly: "The official French position, which is also the position of the French Communists, envisages the internationalization of these territories and their political separation from the rest of Germany." Internationalization "would associate all nations in the management, the government, and the administration of the

[25] Constant, "La Conférence de Londres," *Cahiers du Communisme*, Nos. 10–11 (October-November, 1945), p. 70.
[26] Assemblée Nationale Constituante, *JO, Débats*, January 15, 1946, pp. 9, 10.
[27] Duclos, *En avant*, pp. 23–24.
[28] *Ibid.*, p. 25.

zone; this specifically implies the participation of the Soviet Union in the control." "It is quite true," the Communists admitted, "that the Soviet Union is opposed to political separation and that on this point the French position and the Soviet position are divergent." This was not embarrassing to the Party because "the French Communists have already replied that they are in no way accountable to the Soviet government on the positions taken on the international level." The Party affirmed its faithfulness to its position "even when Molotov appeared to take the opposite view."

The Party skillfully developed its argument to show that Soviet policy was, in any case, better than that of the Western powers. The object of the Soviet Union, it stated, was "democratization of all Germany," while the Allied policy was "unity of Germany against the Soviet Union." Therefore,

it was difficult for the Soviet Union under these conditions to disappoint the hopes of the German Communist Party, which, in adopting a strictly national position, took a stand for unity. France, which has not obtained in the West the guarantee which the Soviet Union had been able to secure in the East because of the opposition of the Anglo-Saxons, . . . cannot and should not consider the question from the same angle.

The French Communists concluded that "the Soviet Union, more-over, perfectly understood our national point of view." Actually, the Party argued, the two positions were not contradictory but "complementary." The French position was not something else, but something more. According to the Party, it would bring the Soviet Union into West Germany and prevent a separation of Europe into two blocs.[29]

The Party's commitment to the official French policy for the Ruhr-Rhineland was based on more than the new patriotism or on "tripartism." It was one of the foundations of French Communist domestic policy, the "renascence of France." France needed coal immediately to carry out the ambitious program of reconstruction envisaged by the Communists. In January, 1946, the newly appointed Communist Minister of Industrial Production, Marcel Paul, visited the Saar and the Rhineland in an attempt to increase the export

[29] Courtade, "Le Problème allemand," *Cahiers du Communisme*, No. 7 (July, 1946), pp. 594–96.

of coal and electricity to France. In his public address he praised the French, whose efforts, he stressed, had tripled coal production in the Saar in one year.[30]

However, the Party leaders were not satisfied with the French share of Ruhr coal delivered to France. The immediate obstacle to importing more Ruhr coal was the British control of the area. Therefore, the Party was able to train its guns on the "City" and other "capitalistic groups" for blocking and even reducing shipments to France. The Communists went so far as to state, "The Anglo-French alliance is an eminently desirable thing—we are profoundly convinced of that—but it ought not to be paid for by giving up the internationalization of the Ruhr [and] its administrative and political separation from Germany." What cannot be denied, they insisted, was the "truly vital importance of the mines of the Ruhr for our recovery." Upon his return Marcel Paul demanded one million tons of Ruhr coal for France.[31]

Because of their emphasis on the importance of Ruhr coal for France, the Communists were thrown badly off balance by Molotov's stand in July. Yet they managed to simulate optimism that the Soviet plan would also assure France of adequate coal. True to its precept of governmental solidarity, the French Communist Party joined the Socialist and MRP ministers, one day after Molotov's speech, in voting unanimously to support Bidault's position in the Council of Foreign Ministers.[32] For once the French Communists and the French government agreed completely, but they were caught between East and West.

At the Paris Conference Byrnes countered the Soviet demands by announcing on July 11, 1946, a United States offer to merge the zones of occupation "with or without the Soviet Union." Even if central administrative agencies were established in Germany, the United States would also agree to the continuation of French administration of the Saar until Germany's western boundaries had been determined.[33] Molotov refused to admit the right of the French

---

[30] *L'Humanité,* January 10, 1946.
[31] *Ibid.,* April 13, 14–15, 16, 1946.
[32] *Ibid.,* July 12, 1946.
[33] Byrnes, *Speaking Frankly,* p. 195.

to administer the Saar as a precondition for the creation of a central administration, and he refused to permit the economic integration of the Soviet zones with the others.[34] On July 18 Radio Moscow declared that there could be no federative settlement for Germany and that the Ruhr must be under the economic control of the four powers. This would place France on the same footing as the Allies, permitting it "to take hold solidly and effectively in the Ruhr and to defend its interests there on an equal footing." [35]

The French Communists were embarrassed by the Soviet stand. They did not comment on Molotov's refusal to link the Saar with the issue of central government. In defending the Soviet position Pierre Hervé was obliged to fall back on the cliché of the "fundamental entente" between the USSR and France which "limited differences could never obscure." [36] The French government was not yet willing to choose sides. On August 10, 1946, the French delegates to the Allied Control Council, Koenig and Alphand, officially refused the American offer. After the rejection of his own compromise plan Koenig announced the creation of a *Land* (region) in the French zone, with its capital at Mainz.[37] The Americans were disappointed by the French refusal, but Byrnes advised the French government in September that the United States would support French claims to the Saar at the peace settlement.[38] On the other hand, the Soviet Union criticized the unilateral French action as a hasty move toward the federalization of Germany.[39] The French Communists reacted to their government's action by reiterating their support of its plans for the Saar. However, they were obliged to reconsider their stand on the Rhineland. Duclos declared that "the constitution of a Rhenish *Land* would pave the way for federalism, which played into the hands of the old ruling classes." [40]

How could the French Communists hold an opinion that contradicted the Soviet view on such an important issue? From the in-

[34] Molotov, *Voprosy*, p. 78.
[35] *L'Année politique, 1946*, p. 405.
[36] *L'Humanité*, July 13, 1946.
[37] *L'Année politique, 1946*, p. 409.
[38] Byrnes, *Speaking Frankly*, p. 197.
[39] *L'Année politique, 1946*, p. 410.
[40] Duclos, "Notre Politique," *Cahiers du Communisme*, No. 8 (August, 1946), p. 622.

formation now available, it is not possible to give a definitive answer to this question. However, the discussions among the foreign ministers at Paris were a preliminary sparring for position. Even after the sharp exchange between Molotov and the other foreign ministers the Soviet Union was unwilling to give up all hope of negotiating a German settlement with the West. The door was left ajar for further bargaining, and the USSR expected to benefit from a further postponement of the peace treaty. The French constitution had not yet been ratified, and the Communist Party was steadily increasing its strength in France. It was still possible that the Party would gain enough power to bring its representatives into the foreign ministry or the defense ministry.

The United States forces in Germany had been reduced considerably in number and quality. Both the United States and Great Britain were going through a period of economic dislocation. With the passage of time the Western powers might be unwilling or unable to pour large sums of money into Germany. They might then be more amenable to negotiating a settlement of the sort the Soviet Union wanted. There was no agreement among Soviet theorists over whether the United States was going to suffer a postwar depression. If a depression occurred and the United States consequently reduced its commitments in Europe, the Soviet Union would then have a great advantage in negotiating a German settlement. As long as the United States refrained from committing itself to massive support of the West European economies, the Soviet Union could let the German problem wait.

Furthermore, for the time being the French position had the merit, in Soviet eyes, of being in conflict with that of the British and the Americans. If the French Communists could not bring the French government to support Soviet policy on Germany, they could at least do a great deal to avert a common front of the West against that policy.

While the Soviet Union was temporizing, it was not only possible but also desirable, from the Communist point of view, for the French Party to support its own government and pose as the defender of French national interests. Aside from propaganda value, the French Communist stand offered a real diplomatic advantage. The Party's stand strengthened those elements in France which hoped to prevent their country from choosing between East and West. However, Molotov's blustering tactics at Paris had given a severe jolt to the French Communists. They had already been forced to retreat from their position on the Rhineland, and they were unable to explain satisfactorily their endorsement of the Soviet Union as the champion of French interests. The Soviet Union was simply not willing to wait quietly until developments in the West became more favorable to a solution on its own terms. Instead it took the offensive against the West. In so doing, it aroused its enemies and embarrassed its friends.

As long as there was no showdown on the German question, the French Communist Party could maintain its patriotic stand and the French government could hold firmly to its position. However, if the differences between East and West led to a split over Germany, then France would be forced ultimately to abandon its own views and adopt the views of one of the great powers. At that time the Communists and the government would part company. In retrospect, it is clear that by July, 1946, the moment of the dénouement was not far off. The United States was taking a more active role in European affairs, and the Soviet Union was determined to stand fast on its German policy, even at the expense of dividing the world into two blocs and forcing the Communist parties outside the Soviet bloc into opposition to their governments. For the French Communists the new Soviet stand meant that the firm control of one part of Germany was more important to Moscow than the uncertain promise of winning all of France. The cold "revolution" was being carried out successfully in East Germany under Soviet pressure. A consistent rule of Soviet foreign policy has been not to abandon a successful limited revolution for the lure of an anticipated but possibly illusory general revolution.

CHAPTER XI

Stalin on the Postwar Development of Capitalism

THROUGHOUT most of the Second World War the Soviet leaders had muffled their revolutionary oratory. There had been no recantation or modification of Marxist-Leninist-Stalinist principles, but neither had there been any special emphasis on the doctrine. Until the post-Yalta shift, Soviet propagandists had played down the so-called basic antagonism between the capitalism and the Communist system. The French Communist Party and other European Communist Parties had adopted the same attitude of reserve. There was much speculation in Washington and in the French underground as to the significance of this development. Some observers in Washington and many in France believed that constant and close contact with the Communists in a common war effort might do much to allay Communist suspicions of the capitalist West. Though there was little reason to believe that the Communists would suddenly abandon their philosophy, there was hope that the give and take of wartime cooperation might gradually bring the Soviet Union to accept the traditional role of one nation in a community of nations. This belief was encouraged by Moscow's public praise of the West during the war. It became more difficult to nurture these hopes when the Soviet government began, especially after the Yalta Conference, to disregard and to violate some of its own recent agreements. At the same time the Soviet propagandists implied that the wartime arrangements had indeed been merely temporary expedients useful in achieving the short-term goal of a military victory over Hitlerism; rather than stating this revived orthodoxy bluntly, they simply reasserted more and more frequently the Communist belief in the fundamental struggle which must inevitably go on between the two rival systems until one or the other had achieved world domination.

It was not until February 9, 1946, however, that Stalin publicly reaffirmed his belief in the inevitability of wars as long as capitalism survived.

As a matter of fact, the war broke out as the inevitable result of the development of world economic and political forces on the basis of present-day monopolistic capitalism. Marxists have more than once stated that the capitalist system of the world economy contains the elements of a general crisis and military conflicts, that because of this the development of world capitalism in our times proceeds not smoothly and evenly but through crises and catastrophic wars. The point is that the uneven development of capitalist countries usually leads, in the course of time, to a sharp disturbance of the equilibrium within the world system of capitalism, and the group of capitalist countries which regards itself as being less securely provided with raw materials and markets usually attempts to change the situation and to redistribute "spheres of influence" in its own favor, by employing armed force. As a result of this, the capitalist world is split into two camps, and war breaks out between them.

Perhaps catastrophic wars could be avoided if it were possible periodically to redistribute raw materials and markets among the respective countries in conformity with their economic needs by means of concerted and peaceful decision. But this is impossible under the present capitalistic condition of world economic development.[1]

Though Stalin emphasized the danger of war between the capitalist nations, he implied that such a conflict could, like the Second World War, involve the Soviet Union. This important speech was received with dismay by observers in the Western capitals who had not attached equal significance to similar statements in the Soviet press during the previous year. There had been disagreements among the leaders of the coalition, but this was the first time since the German invasion of the Soviet Union that Stalin himself had publicly asserted the inevitability of conflict between his regime and the West.

Stalin's speech had, in fact, come as a dramatic climax to a series of statements by Soviet leaders on the need for renewed vigilance

[1] "Rech' tovarishcha I. V. Stalina na predvybornom sobranii izbiratelei Stalinskogo izbiratel'nogo okruga," *Bol'shevik*, No. 3 (February, 1946), pp. 1–2.

against imperialist threats from abroad. These statements were partly aimed to prevent the war-weary Soviet population from slowing up its drive toward reconstruction and industrial expansion, partly to forewarn the Communist parties abroad against "illusions" of continued cooperation with the Western democracies. Speaking before a group of Party militants in Leningrad, M. I. Kalinin had declared, in August, 1945:

But even now, after the greatest victory known in history, we cannot for one minute forget that our country remains the one Socialist state in the world. You will speak freely about this to the collective farmers. The victory achieved does not mean that all dangers to our state structure and social order have disappeared. Only the most concrete, most immediate danger, which threatened us from Hitlerite Germany, has disappeared. In order that the danger of war may really disappear for a long time, it is necessary to consolidate our victory.[2]

Soon after this declaration the Central Committee of the Communist Party announced the decision to establish a postwar Five-Year Plan from 1946 to 1950 in order to restore completely the damage caused by the German invasion and to raise significantly the level of production above that of the prewar period.[3] What better way was there to urge the Russian people toward greater productive efforts than to invoke the foreign threat? V. M. Molotov was the first Soviet leader to link the international situation with the industrial needs of the USSR. On the twenty-eighth anniversary of the October Revolution he pointed out the new dangers that faced the Soviet Union from abroad.

There is not a little noise arising around the creation of blocs and groups of powers, as a means of guarding definite external interests. The Soviet Union never has participated in groups of powers directed against peace-loving governments. In the West such attempts have been made more than once, as is well known. The anti-Soviet character of a number of such groups in the past is also well known. In each case the history of the blocs and groups of Western powers illuminated the fact that they were not so much restraining aggression as inciting aggression—

---

[2] *Propaganda i Agitatsiia* (Leningrad), No. 18 (August, 1945), p. 3; cited by Barghoorn, "The Soviet Union between War and Cold War," *Annals of the American Academy of Political and Social Science*, CCXXXVI (May, 1949), 4.

[3] "Piatiletnii plan poslevoennogo razvitiia" [The Five-Year Plan of Postwar Development], *Izvestiia*, August 30, 1945.

above all, with the support of Germany. This is why vigilance . . . in these matters must not weaken on the part of the Soviet Union and other peace-loving governments.[4]

Molotov went on to explain that the needs of both reconstruction and the defense of the Socialist Motherland required the implementation of the new Five-Year Plan. He further emphasized the seriousness of the international situation by concluding that "while we live in a 'state system' and roots of fascist and imperialist aggression have not yet finally been pulled out of the earth, our vigilance in relation to possible new victories of peace should not weaken."[5] The exhausted Russian people were being exhorted by their leaders in the same way that the French people had been encouraged by the French Communists to shoulder the burden of reconstruction alone in the face of predatory capitalist threats. When the new Five-Year Plan was presented to the Supreme Soviet in March, 1946, the Soviet press emphasized that it

will demand great efforts from all our people. . . . The Soviet people will remember that in the world there are still reactionary forces which are trying to sow hatred and enmity between peoples. . . . It is necessary to raise still higher the economic and military strength of the country, to strengthen the Red Army, which guarantees the peaceful labor of our people.[6]

After his election speech in February, 1946, Stalin pointed more and more strongly and frequently to the "imperialist threat." For example, later in February, 1946, Stalin denounced Churchill's famous speech at Fulton, Missouri, as "a dangerous act, calculated to sow seeds of dissension between the Allied governments and to impede their cooperation."[7] He attacked Churchill as a "fomenter of war" [who] "is not alone here—he has friends not only in England but also in the U.S.A." He went on to condemn the British leader for his "racist" theories and his "thirst for war."[8]

---

[4] Molotov, "28-aia godovshchina velikoi oktiabr'skoi sotsialisticheskoi revoliutsii," Bol'shevik, No. 21 (November, 1945), p. 6.

[5] Ibid., pp. 12, 13.

[6] "Budem neustanno krepit' moshch' nashei sotsialisticheskoi derzhavy" [We Shall Strengthen the Might of Our Socialist State Tirelessly], Pravda, March 13, 1946.

[7] "Interv'iu tov. I. V. Stalina s korrespondentom Pravdy otnositel'no rechi g. Cherchillia," Bol'shevik, No. 5 (March, 1946), p. 1.

[8] Ibid., pp. 1–2.

In his May Day speech of 1946 the Soviet leader again warned the Russian people that

In developing peaceful socialist construction, we ought not to forget for a minute the intrigues of the international reaction, which is hatching plans for a new war. It is necessary to remember the statement of the great Lenin that, in making the transition to a peaceful economy, it is necessary to be on guard constantly, to care for the armed strength and defensive capacity of our country as for the apple of our eye.[9]

In his analysis of the postwar crisis of capitalism Stalin did not state clearly whether he thought the contradictions in the system would lead first to a war between rival capitalist nations or between a capitalist coalition and the Soviet Union. Because of this ambiguity there was an unusual difference in interpretation of Stalin's position by Soviet political and economic experts. One school stressed the Western threat and, by implication, justified putting an end to co-operation. Another stressed the imperialist rivalries and, by implication, advocated continuing, if limited, cooperation with some of the rivals within "the Western camp."

The "Western Threat" Interpretation

Reviewing the events of the year 1945, one Soviet political analyst, I. Lemin, warned that the American departure from a policy of isolation did not mean the establishment of "democratic, peace-loving principles in foreign policy and diplomacy." Rather, he asserted, "America emerged from the war with barefaced, imperialist, predatory ideas, a doctrine of uncontrolled militarism, [and] the pretensions of the United States to a leading role in world affairs." He criticized the pressure of certain reactionary circles in the United States government. "In this connection," he continued, "there is the characteristically energetic campaign for the acquisition by America of bases on almost all seas and continents, inspired by the naval interests of the United States, and the campaign to preserve great permanent armed strength for America in peacetime . . . by strengthening its naval and air power in the world." Lemin also

---

[9] "Prikaz ministra vooruzhennykh sil Soiuza SSR" [Order of the Minister of Armed Forces of the USSR], *Pravda*, May 1, 1946.

charged that the extension of the sphere of active American diplomacy created a new situation in Soviet-American relations. Formerly, he explained, there had been but few points of contact between the two nations. Now there were many contacts, and every other nation in the world had become "a potential ally or potential enemy." Though he referred to the need for continued cooperation among the three powers, he concluded that the campaign for the creation of a Western bloc was being revived "with redoubled strength" and was leading to an anti-Soviet campaign in the Western press.[10]

When writing for *Pravda*, on the other hand, Lemin stressed the economic rivalries between the United States and Great Britain. According to him, the lend-lease agreement, signed in January, 1946, "reflects like a drop of water the form of the economic interrelations between the two countries on the new postwar level." The relative strength of the United States had increased, that of Britain had declined. "England by no means intends to surrender without a battle. The economic contradictions between the interests of both countries are being intensified, and the spheres of these interests are expanding." Lemin conceded that the two countries sought to avoid a clash. But, he added, the agreement signed in Washington "does not at all change the sharp, competitive struggle for markets, for spheres of economic interest and political influence." [11]

Direct attacks against the United States government and emphasis on the American threat to the USSR became more frequent with the postwar expansion of American economic activity in the world. Throughout 1946 negotiations were completed and ratifications of previous agreements were exchanged between the United States and Great Britain, France, India, Australia, New Zealand, Belgium, and Turkey. In June the International Bank for Reconstruction and Development began to organize its work. It was calculated that by the end of the year the Export-Import Bank had extended almost $3.5 billion of credit to many countries.[12]

[10] Lemin, "Mezhdunarodnye otnosheniia v 1945 godu," *Mirovoe Khoziaistvo i Mirovaia Politika*, Nos. 1–2 (January-February, 1946), pp. 28, 34.
[11] I. Lemin "Anglo-amerikanskoe ekonomicheskoe soglashenie" [Anglo-American Economic Agreement], *Pravda*, January 17, 1946.
[12] Goodrich and Carroll, eds., *Documents on American Foreign Relations, 1945–1946*, pp. 638–39.

The Soviet attacks on American aid placed the French Communists in a quandary. They saw the need for an American loan, but they did not approve of the terms. According to the Washington Agreement, the Export-Import Bank was to extend a loan of $650 million to France in exchange for a reduction in French tariffs and other trade concessions. The Party defined the American insistence upon more liberal trade as characteristic of the expansionism of a nation with a stronger economy.[13] In the debate in the National Assembly, Communist spokesmen deplored the tearing down of some tariff walls in order "to follow American economic policy." Fernand Grenier charged that the agreement to accept imports of American films constituted a "very serious menace to the French film industry." Finally, Duclos concluded that it was more than a coincidence that the agreement providing such desperately needed funds had been signed only four days before the French national election. However, true to their role as a government party, the Communists voted for ratification as "an arrangement to which the two partners were carried by unavoidable circumstances." [14] Such a severe setback for the French Communists could not have gone unnoticed in Moscow. American economic pressure was beginning to have serious political repercussions.

Molotov continued to lead the Soviet offensive against the United States as the main threat to peace:

In some American circles there exists the hope of pushing aside the Soviet Union from its rightfully honored place in international affairs and causing damage to the international prestige of the USSR. But only shortsighted reactionary circles, doomed to failure. can so act. They do not remember that the Soviet Union, having borne the main weight of the struggle for the salvation of humanity from the tyranny of fascism, now occupies a position in international relations which corresponds to the interests of the large and small countries in their aspirations for hope and security.[15]

[13] Duclos, "Notre Politique," *Cahiers du Communisme,* No. 7 (July, 1946), p. 545.

[14] Assemblée Nationale Constituante, *JO, Débats,* August 1, 1946, second session, pp. 2893, 2894, 2896, 2903.

[15] "Zaiavlenie V. M. Molotova ob itogakh parizhskogo soveshchaniia soveta ministrov inostrannykh del predstaviteliam sovetskoi pechati" [V. M. Molotov's Declaration about the Result of the Paris Conference of the Council of Ministers of Foreign Affairs], *Pravda,* May 27, 1946.

Molotov indicated that in the light of American actions it was difficult to draw the line between requirements for security and hopes for expansion. "For example," he asked, "what security interests of the United States of America dictate the need for military bases on the island of Iceland?" According to Molotov, the world press had revealed that certain groups in the United States and Great Britain "aspire to create naval and air bases in all parts of the Eastern Hemisphere." The Soviet Foreign Minister warned that the "aspirations of several strong countries to impose their will on other people . . . are doomed to failure as far as the Soviet Union is concerned." [16]

By mid-1946 the theme of the Western capitalist bloc as a primary and immediate threat to Soviet security was being expanded upon by the Party's theoretical journal, *Bol'shevik*. The Second World War had destroyed, it wrote, only German and Japanese imperialism. "However, monopoly capitalism continues to exist, and, consequently, the sources and forces which engender new imperialist aggression, leading to new conflict and to world war, continue to exist." As the editors explained the new dangers, "side by side with the growth and strengthening of democracy and progress as a result of the destruction of the main center of fascism, the position of the monopolist groups in the leading capitalist countries, England and the United States, was strengthened in the course of the Second World War. The postwar program of the reactionary monopolist clique is a program of attack against the democratic achievements of the working class and the popular masses; within their countries [it is] an adventurist program of new imperialist expansion, a program of world supremacy of Anglo-Saxon imperialism." [17] The Soviet editors accused the United States government of using its economic power to secure a preponderant position in the Far East, the Near and Middle East, South America, Northern Europe, Italy, and Spain.[18] "The pretension of the imperialist circles of the United States to world supremacy," they complained, "has found its clearest expression in the struggle for the

[16] *Ibid.*

[17] "Opasnye tendentsii v mezhdunarodnoi politike," *Bol'shevik*, Nos. 11–12 (June, 1946), pp. 2, 3.

[18] *Ibid.*, p. 2.

retention of old, and the acquisition of new, naval and air bases."
Great Britain, they continued, was guilty of similar activities, especially in the colonial areas and in Southern Europe.

But what of the actual or potential imperialist rivalry between
the two powers? The editors asserted that, "though the interests of
English and American imperialism clash at many points on the
globe and Anglo-American rivalry has a tendency to grow more
intense, nonetheless, for the sake of the triumph of reaction, the
English fomenters of a new war are ready to accept for England
the role of 'junior partner' to the United States in the Anglo-American bloc." Thus, they concluded, the Anglo-Americans sought to
bury their differences and to turn to a "policy of forcing their wills
on other powers, in particular on the Soviet Union." [19]

The "Imperialist Rivalry" Interpretation

The opposite point of view—that the Western nations would
turn on one another in a new imperialist war—was maintained by
the well-known Marxist theorist Eugene Varga. As editor of *World
Economics and World Politics* he devoted special attention to the
postwar phase of the general crisis of capitalism. "After the end
of the Second World War the struggle for the preservation of the
capitalist structure again became the chief political problem for
the capitalist countries." In some countries capitalism had not been
shaken by the war. On the contrary, victory had saved the bourgeoisie from being discredited. However, this momentary arrest of
an inevitable decline had been accomplished at the cost of strengthening the power of the army. Varga therefore concluded that "one
of the characteristic features of postwar politics is the strengthening
of militarism in the Anglo-Saxon [*sic*] countries and especially in the
United States." [20]

Such was not the case in the countries of continental Europe,
where the bourgeoisie, according to Varga, was completely discredited. War and famine inevitably drove the workers into radical

---

[19] *Ibid.*, pp. 5–8.
[20] Varga, "Osobennosti vnutrennei i vneshnei politiki kapitalisticheskikh
stran," *Mirovoe Khoziaistvo i Mirovaia Politika*, No. 6 (June, 1946), pp. 11, 12.

paths. The petty bourgeoisie was being proletarianized, and the result was a polarization of society. This antagonism was sharpened in the occupied countries by the identification of the big bourgeoisie with collaborationism and of the workers with the Resistance. Finally, both the increased activity of the Communist parties in Europe and the enormous strength of the revolutionary Socialist motherland were decisive in overwhelming capitalism in parts of Europe.[21]

However, the Anglo-American capitalist countries were strong enough to attempt to restore the bourgeois *émigré* governments in Europe. Despite some reactionary successes, "it had been necessary almost everywhere to introduce broad reforms of the capitalist structure, from the hope for a planned economy to the introduction of social insurance." Varga drew a distinction between nationalization with compensation in Britain and France and outright nationalization in Eastern Europe. The former did not alter the distribution of wealth and constituted merely a desperate attempt to save the capitalist structure. The bourgeois reform method involved persuading the Social Democratic parties to support the capitalist regime in return for economic and political concessions. Varga maintained that the struggle for control of the Social Democrats was "the main content of internal politics of capitalist countries."

There is also, he continued, a struggle within the Social Democratic Party between the mass and the reformists. To illustrate his point, he chose the situation in East Germany, where the unity of Socialists and Communists had been established. Incidentally, to strengthen his argument, he might well have taken the French situation as an example of the failure of unity and its causes. Varga mentioned Anglo-American opposition to the fusion of the German workers' movements, which led him to believe that "the rise of a single party of the working class in Germany is a serious blow to the reformist movement. It is therefore natural for all the reactionary elements to take up arms against the new party." [22]

A second means for the defense of capitalism, as Varga saw it, was the strengthening of religious influences, Catholic, Protestant,

[21] *Ibid.*, pp. 12–13.
[22] *Ibid.*, pp. 13–14.

and Moslem. The revival of fascism was a third method. This last development was an outgrowth of the crisis stage of capitalism.

Having established the theory that capitalism remained strong in some countries and was trying to increase its strength in others, Varga went on to explain how this phenomenon affected the USSR. The attempt to bolster capitalism at home means a similar attempt on the international scene. Since the USSR is the sworn enemy of capitalism, "the reactionary powers of the various countries are conducting an intense campaign to isolate the Soviet Union and to scrape together an anti-Soviet bloc."

However, despite these machinations of the West, the struggle of the two systems of communism and capitalism was not, to Varga, the logical or inevitable upshot of the policies of the capitalist countries. On the contrary, he saw the primary factor in the growing rivalries between the major imperialist countries, even though they might form a common diplomatic bloc in some international questions. "American policy now aspires," Varga declared, "above all, to crush the English colonial empire in order to seize for American capital equal conditions in a real struggle for the whole world." Developing this interpretation, he arrived at a remarkable conclusion: "With the colonial question is linked also the plan of the Western bloc. The Western bloc . . . is directed, above all, against the Soviet Union and is an attempt to revive the *cordon sanitaire.*" However, he asserted, this bloc, from which Varga excluded the United States, had 95 percent of all the colonies in the world. Therefore, its formation could equally be "an attempt to defend the colonies against United States hopes for destroying the old colonial regime." [23]

Other economists writing in *World Economics and World Politics* also tended to stress the primacy of imperialist rivalry in shaping postwar international politics. Academician I. A. Trakhtenberg noted that the Second World War, as a war of liberation, had resulted in toning down the class struggle in capitalist countries. However, "the transition from war to peace has changed the situation." Trakhtenberg discussed the various problems that were involved, including inflation, reallocation of resources, and unemployment.

[23] *Ibid.,* pp. 16–17.

The result, he declared, would be increased suffering of the proletariat and a "period of the unmasking of the great illusion of
reformism." He concluded that "the period of transition will be
characterized by the aggravation of class contradictions and the
strengthening of the class struggle by the aggravation of imperialist
contradictions and the struggles of various governments for a place
in the world economy." [24]

Comparing the two Soviet positions on the future development
of capitalism, we find that both accepted the fact of a hostile West
united, or in process of uniting, against the Soviet Union. Both
stated that there were contradictions between those same capitalist
nations. They differed as to whether or not the bonds of anticommunism would hold the West together in the face of growing imperialist rivalries.

The two interpretations coexisted uneasily until early 1947. By
that time Varga's view had been almost totally discarded, and in
May, 1947, his book on *Changes in the Economy of Capitalism
Resulting from the Second World War* was severely criticized.
Varga's opponents sought now to show that the struggle between
the socialist and capitalist systems had not been suspended during
the wartime coalition. The attacks upon Varga for his "optimistic"
view of the international role of capitalism steadily mounted, reaching a high point early in 1948.[25] The increasingly critical attitude
of the Soviet leaders toward Varga's views foreshadowed and
measured the changes in their view of the West.

Increased Attacks on the West

During the summer of 1946 the idea of an emerging truce among
the imperialists gained vogue in the Soviet press. It asserted, for
example, "that the United States and Great Britain, as though by
tacit agreement, are allowing one another freedom of action in

---

[24] *Ibid.*, pp. 31, 32, 8.
[25] For an incisive analysis of the Varga discussion and its implications, see
Barghoorn, "The Varga Discussion and Its Significance," *The American
Slavic and East European Review*, VII, No. 3 (October, 1948).

various parts of the globe. A similar tendency may be observed clearly in the conduct of the American and British representatives in the organizations which have been set up to promote international cooperation." It was admitted that "the interests of the two Anglo-Saxon powers are by no means in harmony. Moreover, on many major issues they clash." Also, "the economic and financial power of the American concerns makes possible a colonial policy different from the British." However, Soviet political analysts insisted, the bonds of unity were stronger than the divisive tendencies.

The real meaning of the Anglo-American bloc . . . lies in a desire for world domination. It is a plan for the establishment of the world supremacy of the Anglo-Saxon countries that forms the basis of the understanding that so often determines the actions of their representatives in the international arena, notwithstanding the undoubted rivalry and deep-seated divergencies between American and British interests in various parts of the globe. That compact is based on the principle which always guides the imperialist powers when they seek for agreement on the division of spheres of influence—the principle of *do ut des* (I give that you may give in return).

Though denying that the bloc could be "stable," the Soviet government concluded that "it creates international tension and is a cause of legitimate alarm." [26]

The Soviet Union also charged that the two imperialist nations were cooperating in the military sphere by supporting "large contingents of troops on the territory of a number of sovereign states, members of the United Nations, who had fought actively against the Fascist aggressors." They further maintained that "the embassies of the United States and England in these countries, wittingly or not, have become the central point of all reactionary forces, the 'embassy opposition,' as the progressive elements so well nicknamed them." [27]

The theme of "capitalist encirclement" underwent a strong revival. The Soviet leaders accused the United States of building bases "supposedly for defense" but actually in preparation "for

[26] Sergeeva, "K voprosu ob anglo-amerikanskikh otnosheniiakh," *Novoe Vremia,* No. 15 (August 1, 1946), pp. 6, 7, 8, 9.
[27] Kharlamov, "Ekspansionizm v poslevoennoi politike SShA i Anglii," *Bol'shevik,* Nos. 17–18 (September, 1946), p. 37.

offensive action." [28] The proof of the claim, they declared, was the location of bases in Saudi Arabia and Iceland, much closer to the USSR than to the United States. These bases not only "build up distrust between states, creating anxiety and uncertainty among peoples . . . but they lead to the infringement of sovereignty and create a threat to independence." Finally, the Soviet Union maintained that "the American and English bases and garrisons on the territory of other countries serve as a means of alien pressure on the internal affairs of these governments and in several cases are used to create external fears in relations with their neighbors." [29]

At the very time that these ominous pronouncements were filling the pages of the Soviet press Stalin appeared to follow a more moderate attitude. As in his March and June pronouncements, he stressed the distinction between the real danger of a war and the noise made by fomenters of a new war.[30] He denied that world tension had increased, and stated his unconditional belief in peaceful cooperation. In fact, he added, this cooperation "can even increase." [31]

What did Stalin mean by these conciliatory words? Since the Soviet Union was actively negotiating on many problems, Stalin probably considered it better not to appear irreconcilably hostile. Furthermore, a policy of unrelieved tension might have had deleterious effects upon the morale of the Soviet people, especially since the war had evoked a widespread pro-Western feeling among them. Alternation of relaxation and tension is a standard Communist technique of negotiation and rule, offering a better chance of obtaining some concessions than implacable opposition.

The Soviet press fastened on one implication of Stalin's October interview—that cooperation with the USSR meant acceptance of its views. "It has been repeatedly declared in Soviet quarters," the journal *New Times* stated,

[28] Cheprakov, "Strategicheskie bazy SShA i Velikobritanii," *Mirovoe Khoziaistvo i Mirovaia Politika*, Nos. 10–11 (October-November, 1946), p. 33. See also Lemin, "Poslevoennye tendentsii vneshnei politiki SShA," *Bol'shevik*, No. 22 (November, 1946), especially pp. 60–64.

[29] Cheprakov, "Strategicheskie bazy SShA i Velikobritanii," *Mirovoe Khoziaistvo i Mirovaia Politika*, Nos. 10–11 (October-November, 1946), pp. 34, 41.

[30] Interviews with Alexander Werth and Hugh Baille, *The New York Times*, September 24, October 29, 1946.

[31] *Ibid.*, September 24, 1946.

that differences of social system and ideology constitute no obstacle to effective cooperation between the Soviet Union and other countries. . . . But it is deeds, not words, that count. And when it comes to deeds, we find that the instigators of a reactionary line of international policy, who are striving for a free hand in order to pursue an imperialistic policy, a policy of expansion and aggression, are doing their utmost to poison relations and to put an end to cooperation between the powers that won the war together.[32]

In other words, the "deeds" or concessions were to come from the West.

What did the Soviet Union expect from the West? How did Moscow define the "deeds" which were to ensure international cooperation with the West?

One indication in 1945 and 1946 was provided by Soviet comparisons of the course of events in Eastern and Western Europe after the defeat of Nazi Germany. According to Moscow, there was a fundamental difference in the political and socioeconomic institutions of Eastern and Western Europe, based on the differing implementation of the Yalta decision to eliminate the last vestiges of nazism and fascism and create democratic institutions in the liberated areas by free elections. "In the countries of Eastern and Southeastern Europe the Red Army and the occupying Soviet forces created, in the full spirit of the decisions of the Crimean Conference, all the conditions necessary for the successful struggle of the peoples of these countries against the reactionary Fascist and pro-Fascist elements." The "absolute conditions for crushing fascism" were, according to the Soviet Union, "elimination of the reactionary regimes created by fascism in the European states, punishment of the criminals and culprits of war, undermining of the economic base of the Fascist elements, and giving the people themselves the right to determine their form of government [and] the need for political and economic reforms." Because these conditions had been fulfilled in Eastern Europe under the aegis of the Red Army, "new forms of democracy sprang up." The Soviet Union claimed that its policy in Eastern Europe was "in full accord with the decisions that had been taken . . . at the con-

[32] "Politika mezhdunarodnogo sotrudnichestva i ego vragi," *Novoe Vremia* [New Times], No. 22 (November 15, 1946), p. 2.

ferences at Teheran, Crimea, and Berlin. According to these decisions, the necessity for democratizing the sociopolitical life in the liberated states of Europe was strongly emphasized."

However, the Soviet leaders did not feel that the wartime decisions of the great powers, and hence Soviet aims, had been realized in Western Europe. They praised the "broad popular movements" in Western Europe, which, "as in Eastern Europe, had their roots in the common struggle of all patriotic elements against fascism. . . . However," they significantly added, "differently from the governments of Eastern and Southeastern Europe, the democratic movements in the West did not develop broadly enough to achieve a democratic reconstruction of government life [and] a change in the domestic and foreign policies to accord with the genuine interests of the people: the democratic movement was not crowned with the creation of a new democracy."

The Soviet Union attributed the failure of its policy in Western Europe to "the occupation policies of our allies [who] permitted deviations from these principles" of Teheran, Crimea, and Berlin. Thus "despite the growth of broad democratic movements in these countries, all the urgent demands of the popular masses remain unsatisfied" and "the great influence of the reaction [remains entrenched] in the state apparatus of these countries." The Soviet Union singled out France in particular as an example of the failure of the "democratic movements" to attain power. It charged that Fascist elements remained in the government, that the armed forces of the Resistance had been unjustly dissolved and the army isolated from the people, that economic reforms had not been implemented, that France had become the center of agitation for the Western bloc, and that its attitude toward Franco Spain and Monarchist Greece was antidemocratic.[33]

The long-range goals of Soviet foreign policy included the establishment of regimes in Western Europe similar to those it had imposed in Eastern Europe. Moscow wanted the "democratic movements"—which it identified with the Communist parties—to set up "popular democracies" in Western Europe. The "obstacle" to

[33] Oleshuk, "Razvitie demokratii v osvobozhdennykh stranakh Evropy," Bol'shevik, Nos. 19–20 (October, 1945), pp. 52–56.

achievement of this goal had been the "unwillingness" of the United States and Great Britain to carry out the decisions of the wartime conferences in the same way as the Soviet Union.

According to the Soviet view, the presence of American and British forces in Western Europe had prevented the Communist parties from taking power there after the war and thus from fulfilling the aims of Soviet foreign policy. As the prospects of Communist success receded, the USSR increased its direct attacks on the Western democracies, charging them with imperialist designs. The only way the West could have satisfied Soviet demands in 1946 would have been to agree with and carry out the wartime decisions according to the Soviet interpretation. This would have meant their taking the initiative to establish Communist control throughout Europe. These were the "deeds" that the Soviet Union demanded as proof of Western desire for peaceful cooperation among the great powers.

The Soviet analysis of the new situation, as it emerged from ideological verbiage, took on great significance for the French Communist Party. Its role as a government party, even the extent of its electoral success and the possibility of achieving fusion with the Socialists, depended upon the continuation of great-power cooperation. Yet Moscow was steadily increasing its attacks on the West for alleged failure to cooperate on Soviet terms, and more and more Moscow interpreted this more or less normal political struggle as a prelude to a decisive struggle for world domination, not only between two power blocs but also between two irreconcilable ideologies. If the French Communist Party was to remain loyal in its allegiance to Marxism-Leninism-Stalinism, it would be obliged, in the event of a break between East and West, to renounce its policy of cooperation with republican elements in France. When that day came, how would the inflated, largely newly recruited French Party stand the test of its "Bolshevik tempering"? Had the French Communists really remained loyal to the Leninist revolutionary tradition? Or had the experiences of working with other Frenchmen to fight the Germans and to rebuild and govern France modified their views of the means and aims of attaining power?

CHAPTER XII

A Marxist Constitution

BETWEEN October, 1945, and November, 1946, in addition to increasingly tense international relations, the French Communists were confronted by several crucial domestic problems. During this period a new constitution was fought out, the first postwar National Assembly was elected, and important social and economic reforms were threshed out. Immediate economic and political crises complicated the making of long-range decisions. Food shortages and inflationary trends persisted. In January, 1946, the unexpected resignation of General de Gaulle provoked a major crisis. In this situation could the Party both hold on to its position as a governmental party and retain the loyalty of its members and voters?

The future of the overseas territories also presented many difficult questions. The bonds between France and its empire had been strained or broken during six years of war and occupation. French prestige was shaken by postwar revolts and other disturbances in North Africa, the Near East, and Asia. How could the French Communists uphold the national prestige of France and yet support the aspirations of the colonial peoples? The Party appeared undaunted as it tackled these various problems. Its primary short-term aim was, as before, to absorb the Socialists in a workers' party, but at the same time the Communists were prepared to work with the SFIO to draft a Marxist-style constitution for the Fourth Republic.

Solidarity of the Left and the Elections

Ever since the liberation the Communists had been campaigning actively for new elections. However, they had not paid much attention to the constitutional issue since early 1944. At that time the Party had expressed its views on the future constitution in its theoretical organ *Cahiers du Communisme* and also in its comments on the draft of a common program prepared by the Socialists.[1]

In general, the Communists favored the drafting of a constitution by the elected representatives of the people rather than by a committee of experts. They feared that De Gaulle might hand-pick a group of his collaborators to draw up a constitution, which he would then submit to the people for approval and which, they assumed, would subordinate the elected assembly to a strong executive. This type of plebiscite, the Communists argued, had had several dangerous precedents in the nineteenth century.[2] The avowed goal of the constitution, the Communists asserted, should be "government by assembly"—that is, complete sovereignty of a unicameral legislature.[3]

In the late spring of 1945 General de Gaulle considered asking the people through a referendum whether they wanted to keep the constitution of 1875 or elect a constitutional assembly to draft a new constitution. Though he favored the latter solution, he was not anxious to see his government at the mercy of an all-powerful legislature. Before De Gaulle had taken a firm stand on the matter, the Communists vigorously opposed him on the matter of restricting the powers of the assembly. Marcel Cachin opened the campaign for a sovereign constitutional assembly in *L'Humanité*.[4] By mid-June, 1945, the Political Bureau had fully defined the Communist attitude:

The Political Bureau has decided to pursue the campaign for the election of a sovereign constituent assembly to which the government will be responsible. It stands against all plebiscites (whether covered or not by the term referendum) prior to the elections to the constituent assembly [and] against any constitution of a presidential character.[5]

Other political groups also expressed concern over De Gaulle's

[1] For an analysis of the former, see Wright, *The Reshaping of French Democracy*, pp. 38–40.

[2] Michel and Guetzévitch, *Les Idées politiques*, p. 221.

[3] *Cahiers du Communisme*, No. 1 (January, 1944), as cited in Wright, *The Reshaping of French Democracy*, p. 39.

[4] *L'Humanité*, June 1, 5, 1945.

[5] *Ibid.*, June 15, 1945.

tactics. Despite growing opposition to his plans, in the second week of July De Gaulle submitted a draft referendum to the Council of Ministers. The Political Bureau attacked the referendum as "anti-democratic and unacceptable." [6] It criticized De Gaulle for having given a "personal character to the plebiscite" which "smacked of Bonapartism." [7] Georges Cogniot, the Communist constitutional expert, deplored the fact that General de Gaulle had failed to await the recommendations of the Estates-General. [8]

The Communist campaign was successful in mobilizing public opinion against De Gaulle on this issue. The Socialists, the CGT, the CNR, the UDSR, and the League of the Rights of Man agreed that the people should also be offered the choice of a constitutional assembly with complete powers. De Gaulle yielded to this pressure and added a third choice to the referendum, that of a sovereign constituent assembly. This was the first and last time that this Communist tactic was successful, because it was the only time that the Socialists supported the Communists against a governmental decree.

The debate on constitutional questions was now carried to the floor of the Consultative Assembly. There Georges Cogniot argued persuasively for ministerial responsibility. He maintained that limitations on the power of the assembly would lead to rule by decree and consequently to the type of policy conducted by the French government in 1938 and 1939. [9] The Communist proposals won a majority all along the line. The Consultative Assembly voted for a sovereign constituent assembly and for absolute ministerial responsibility. The governmental project was buried by a vote of 210 to 19; even a Socialist compromise proposal was defeated by the curious alliance of the French Communists with the Radicals and the extreme Right. [10]

However, this was the Resistance Assembly, which did not accurately reflect the mood of the people. With its dissolution the

[6] *Ibid.*, July 12, 1945.

[7] Duclos, "Notre Politique," *Cahiers du Communisme*, Nos. 8–9 (June-July, 1945), p. 6.

[8] *L'Humanité*, July 11, 1945.

[9] Assemblée Consultative Provisoire, *JO, Débats*, July 28, 1945, first session, pp. 1569, 1572.

[10] *Ibid.*, July 29, 1945, second session, p. 1636.

Communists lost their strong support. Of course, the government was not obliged to accept the recommendations of the Assembly. However, De Gaulle now discarded his own previous project and accepted the Socialist compromise. Significantly, he selected the only proposal besides his own which was opposed by the Communists, and the only one which split the Left. According to its provisions, the nation was to be consulted in a double referendum. Should the national assembly be a constituent assembly? If so, should the government have the right to determine the functions of the legislative and executive powers until the assembly had completed its work? While vigorously criticizing De Gaulle's decision, the Communists declared that their answer to the questions would be "yes" and "no," respectively—that is, in favor of a constituent assembly unlimited by any previous ordinance or law.[11]

The Party moved quickly to secure endorsement of its position by the CGT. At a special meeting of the Comité Central National of the CGT, Frachon, Marcel Paul, and Ambroise Croizat urged the CGT to adopt a more active political role; they demanded that it instruct the militants to vote "yes—no" on the referendum. Despite small but vociferous opposition, the motion was passed.[12] The CGT had completely abandoned its independent course in politics. Pressing forward in their attempts to mobilize public opinion, the Communists joined with the Délégation des Gauches in submitting another memorandum to De Gaulle criticizing what they called the violation of rights in the new election law. Upon receipt of a brusque reply, the Party issued a call for common election lists in order to defend "republican legality." [13] Then it jammed through the executive bureau of the MURF and the FN a motion to vote "yes—no" on the referendum. Riding roughshod over the minorities in these organizations was a mistake, because the intellectuals, unlike the workers, refused to go along with the Communists. Most of the moderate members of the front organizations resigned.[14]

[11] L'Humanité, August 9, 1945.
[12] Le Populaire, September 7, 1945. Frachon was elected second secretary-general at this meeting. See above, p. 222.
[13] L'Humanité, September 13, 1945.
[14] L'Année politique, 1945, p. 294. These included François Mauriac, Max André, Jacques Debrû-Bridel, and Monseigneur Chevrot.

The Socialists again rejected the Communist appeal for unity and joint lists in the local and national elections.

As a result, despite some signs of cooperation with other groups on the Left, the Communists campaigned virtually alone in the cantonal elections of September and the national elections of October.[15] They promised to work for a unicameral legislature to be elected by direct, universal, and equal suffrage from the age of eighteen, for national lists, and for pure proportional representation with the full use of the unassigned remainders on a national scale. The assembly would have complete power over the police, the diplomatic corps, the armed services, and the Council of State. Judges were to be elected. The Communists wanted to abolish prefects and subprefects and delegate all administrative powers to the departmental councils elected by universal suffrage. The president of the council would act as the executive. They promised to guarantee the right to work, in addition to the usual civil rights. They also campaigned for separation of church and state. Most unusual was their proposal to introduce the principle of recall by decision of the majority of electors.[16]

The Communist electoral campaign was active and aggressive. Duclos argued that "the people want something to change, and we must reply to this profound desire for change which exists in the masses by presenting our party to the electors as the only party which has not even begun to show what it is capable of doing in the posts of command in the state." This was a Communist appeal for at least one of the key ministerial portfolios. Duclos further insisted that "it is necessary to develop in the masses the idea that

[15] The fellow-traveling MURF was allied to the Communist Party. Despite the fact that since their debate on the referendum in July the Radical Socialists had been carrying on a mild flirtation with the Communists, the two parties were unable to effect an electoral alliance. According to Wright, only one joint ticket was worked out, but a truce between them was in effect during the elections. Wright, *The Reshaping of French Democracy*, p. 92.

[16] Marty, "Idées sur la nouvelle constitution de la République française," *Cahiers du Communisme*, No. 7 (May, 1945), pp. 29–31. The Communists later dropped the recall principle, which was not only impracticable under a system of proportional representation but also potentially dangerous to the Party. An anti-Communist coalition could have demanded the recall of many Communist deputies who had won only a plurality of votes in a given department.

nothing serious can be done without the Communists."[17] In other words, Duclos asserted that, even if the Party was not getting its due, it must continue in the government. During the electoral campaign the Party, realizing the necessity of keeping the lines open to De Gaulle, restricted itself to attacks on his ministers.[18]

The Party made a special effort to provoke dissension in the Socialist ranks, since the leaders of the SFIO had decided to avoid common lists and to vote "yes—yes." Stressing the need for unity, Duclos quoted Pietro Nenni with approval: "All policy not based on the unity of the working class would be an opportunist policy, and consequently our party would progressively slip from a revolutionary position to a reformist one." The only correct policy, Duclos explained, was a "pact of unity of action between the Socialist Party and the Communist Party." Nevertheless, Duclos added, men such as the notorious "revisionist" Léon Blum were responsible for blocking this important development.[19]

Therefore, in the campaign the Party opened fire on the Socialist leadership while attempting to cajole or confuse the militants into voting "no" on the second question.[20] From the second week in October, half the pages of *L'Humanité* were often devoted to an onslaught against the Socialists. Cogniot, Marty, and Cachin exhausted their imagination in attacking their compatriots of the Left. They revived and distorted incidents of the Spanish Civil War, the "phony war," and the Vichy regime in order to discredit the Socialist leaders.[21] The Socialists charged that along with these propaganda attacks the French Communists had begun a "systematic sabotage" of their ballots and posters. A Communist mayor in Aisne was caught red-handed posting an unsigned notice over a Socialist proclamation.

The Party also assailed Socialist views on foreign policy. Supplemented by articles in the Soviet press, the French Communists denounced advocates of a "Western bloc" and critics of Molotov's

[17] Duclos, *Union des forces démocratiques*, p. 13.
[18] *L'Année politique, 1945*, p. 313.
[19] Duclos, *Union des forces démocratiques*, pp. 27–28, 25.
[20] Cf. *L'Humanité*, September 20, 1945, and *Le Populaire*, September 28, 1945.
[21] See, for example, *L'Humanité*, October 11, 14, 15, 17, 18, 1945.

conduct at the Foreign Ministers' Conference. *L'Humanité* attacked the editor of *Le Populaire* for "repeating the lie that the USSR wishes to eliminate France [as a great power]. It is known that this is said in order to drag our country into a catastrophic association with the 'Western family' desired by the trusts, the forces of reaction." [22]

Pravda concentrated its attention on the disturbing signs of anticommunism which it discerned in the attitude of many French Socialists. By way of contrast, it praised the efforts of those Socialists who had actually joined with the PCF in the electoral struggle.[23] The Soviet press also attacked *Le Populaire* for its domestic views, charging that it "had not once assumed the role of defender of Socialist or French ideas." [24]

It is difficult to determine the effectiveness of the Communist campaign to split the ranks of the Socialists. The Socialist federation in the department of Bouches-du-Rhône was so badly disrupted that it had to be dissolved by the national council,[25] but this appears to be the only instance of a serious split within the Socialist Party.

The election returns of October, 1945, give some indication of how much appeal the Communist program had for the French people. The Communist candidates for the Constituent Assembly received 5,004,121 out of 19,661,515 votes. Together with its ally, the MURF, the Communist Party held 159 seats in the assembly. However, only 5,381,106 Frenchmen voted "no" to the second question. Election analysts in France calculated that in certain districts a number of Communist voters had turned against the Party on the second question.[26] Thus, the Communist referendum campaign propaganda had failed to persuade a significant group of voters from other parties to support a sovereign assembly.

After the election the Communists quickly changed their tactics and renewed their appeal to the Socialists for unity of action and a

[22] *L'Humanité*, October 10, 1945.

[23] "Mezhdunarodnoe obozrenie" [The International Review], *Pravda*, October 10, 1945.

[24] "Na mezhdunarodnye temy" [On an International Theme], *Izvestiia*, October 14, 1945.

[25] *Le Populaire*, October 8–9, 1945.

[26] *L'Année politique, 1945*, p. 318.

popular-front government.[27] It is useful to consider briefly the reasoning behind this brusque reversal of the Party's tactical line. The Communist ability to zigzag is proverbial, but it never ceases to startle and irritate non-Communists. The tactical shift can best be explained as a part of the process of harassing and wearing down the political opposition. It often consists of sudden changes in Communist attitudes toward the views of other groups. Such actions have been labeled opportunistic. If opportunism is defined as sacrifice of principle for circumstances, then this explanation fails to measure up. The Communist goal or principle remains constant. In the case of the French Communists, this goal before and after the election was the creation of a popular-front government. The Communists changed their methods only because they believed that the election returns had modified the "objective situation." In other words, before the election the Socialists had rejected the idea of unity; therefore, the Communists had tried to bludgeon them into changing their minds. After the election the Communists still needed Socialist support to form a government. Since they could no longer bring any electoral pressure to bear on the SFIO, they now appealed for "unity of action" in the name of proletarian solidarity.

Solidarity of the Left and the Government

The first step in the Communists' revised plan for consolidating the Left under their control was to work out with the Socialists and other groups a common declaration of aims and policy. This was done in early November, in meetings of the Délégation des Gauches. The program, largely a detailed commentary on the CNR program, was moderate in tone. The foreign-policy plank stressed the need for France to support collective security rather than to help constitute a bloc antagonistic to other blocs.[28]

The second step for the Communists was to seek support for a Socialist-Communist government which would exclude the Catholic-

[27] *L'Humanité,* October 16, 1945.
[28] *L'Année politique, 1945,* p. 485. The entire text of the program can be found *ibid.,* pp. 470–86.

oriented Mouvement Républicain Populaire. In this government the Communists demanded "important posts . . . which, to reflect the image of the country and of the Constituent Assembly, ought naturally to be Communist in its majority." [29] At this moment the Socialists held the destiny of France in their hands. If they agreed to work only with the Communists, the latter would attain several of their major short-term goals: the control of key ministries, the isolation of the MRP, and a serious check on De Gaulle's power. They would have been on the threshold of creating a "popular democracy." On the other hand, if the Socialists insisted upon a tripartite basis for the government, then the Communists would be trapped. The Party leaders could not reject this proposal; in their words, it was "unthinkable" for the Communists to exclude themselves from the government.[30] They were still committed to remain a governmental party in order to prevent the return of "reaction" and preserve their own position. Yet acceptance of tripartism would be a great defeat. In large measure, the Party had surrendered its bargaining power because it refused to threaten to quit the government.

When the Socialists rejected the united-front idea, the embittered Communists were forced to accept a compromise program in conjunction with the MRP and the Socialists. To ensure cooperation with the other two large parties, the Communists had to vote for De Gaulle as president. Duclos rationalized the Communist position in a letter to the Socialist executive committee: Despite its position as the leading party, the French Communists had been defeated in the referendum. Consequently, they "would not block a manifestation of national unanimity around a candidacy which derives quite naturally from the results of the referendum." [31] Later Duclos asserted more frankly that, in voting for De Gaulle, the Communists "showed that it is necessary to sacrifice something in order not to lose everything." [32]

The next Communist retreat also followed "quite naturally."

[29] L'Humanité, November 6, 11, 1945.
[30] Duclos, Union des forces démocratiques, p. 11. See also Manusevich, Bor'ba, p. 135.
[31] L'Humanité, November 13, 1945.
[32] Duclos, En Avant, p. 7.

After the unanimous election of De Gaulle as president, the preliminary consultations began for the formation of a cabinet. Thorez demanded one of the three most important ministries—War, Foreign Affairs, or Interior. He suggested General Mallaret-Joinville, Florimond Bonte, and Laurent Casanova, respectively, for these posts.[33] In two subsequent letters Thorez reiterated his demand for a "fair distribution in number and in importance of the various ministerial departments and the assignment [to the Party] of one of the following great ministries—Interior, Foreign Affairs, and War." [34] De Gaulle refused to give the Communists any one of these posts, and he even backed up his decision by submitting his own resignation to the Constituent Assembly. Actually, he was thereby asking the assembly to reelect him as president and to ratify his refusal. In a radio broadcast to the people he explained that it was impossible to give the Communists any post which controlled foreign policy, for this would endanger the French policy of equilibrium between the two great powers.[35] The Party, outraged, accused De Gaulle of entering on the path of "dictatorship." [36] In this dispute the Socialists again held the balance, and again they were successful in working out a compromise.

De Gaulle's resignation called for immediate conversations among the three largest parties to choose his successor or decide on his reelection. The Communists formally proposed the election of one of their members as president. The SFIO agreed to support this candidacy if the MRP acquiesced,[37] whereupon the MRP refused and suggested another endorsement of De Gaulle. The Communists made one final, desperate attempt to avoid that alternative by offering the Socialists a two-party coalition with Félix Gouin as president and Maurice Thorez as premier.[38] When the Socialists rejected on principle any bipartite government, the stalemate appeared to be final.

On November 19, 1945, the National Assembly was the center of

[33] Manusevich, *Bor'ba*, p. 143. This is the only source in which I found the names of the proposed Communist ministers.
[34] *L'Humanité*, November 6, 1945.
[35] *Le Populaire*, November 18, 1945.
[36] *L'Humanité*, November 18, 1945.
[37] *Le Populaire*, November 18, 1945.
[38] *L'Humanité*, November 18, 1945.

unusual excitement. The *gardes mobiles* and police forces surrounded the building. The ambassadors of the United States, Great Britain, and the Soviet Union were seated in the galleries.[39] The spokesmen of each party merely restated their well-known positions. Duclos was adamant. "We do not accept being second-class citizens." He accused De Gaulle or his followers of pro-Pétainist sentiments, of besmirching the national honor of the Party, and of autocratic tendencies.[40] However, he did not nominate Thorez for president. Finally, a UDSR-Socialist motion was passed requesting General de Gaulle to try once more to form a government. The Party voted against the resolution, but did not offer any alternative. The Communists had been defeated by the same combination: De Gaulle's prestige, their own fear of a prolonged crisis, and the attitude of the Socialists.

The Communists capitulated within two days when a compromise formula enabled them to save face. The functions of the War Ministry were divided between a Minister of Armaments and a Minister of Armies. Charles Tillon received the Armaments portfolio, but there were no armed forces under his control. In addition, Thorez was made Minister of State (in charge of the reform of the administration), supposedly a compromise with the Communist demand for the premiership. Finally, François Billoux, Marcel Paul, and Ambroise Croizat were given the important economic ministries of National Economy, Industrial Production, and Labor, and the Communists received two undersecretaryships, including the department of coal production, which went to Auguste Lecoeur. This decision, a Soviet historian later claimed, "averted the establishment of a regime of personal dictatorship." [41]

Whether the outcome of this struggle with De Gaulle could be considered a partial victory for the Communists was to be decided by future events.[42] The compromise was worth while if the Party could persuade the Socialists to work closely with them in the making of a constitution or if the Communists could create strong-

[39] *L'Année politique, 1945*, p. 350.
[40] Assemblée Nationale Constituante, *JO, Débats,* November 19, 1945, pp. 73–74.
[41] Manusevich, *Bor'ba,* p. 145.
[42] Cf. Wright, *The Reshaping of French Democracy,* p. 118.

holds of Party power in the ministries assigned to them. Nevertheless, in estimating the general significance of the Party's action for
the future of its program, it must be remembered that the Communists were engaged in a race with time. They could not afford to
relax their pressure to secure more power within the government.
International cooperation between East and West was disintegrat-
ing, and if France should be forced to choose between East and
West before the Party had increased its power substantially, the
Communists would be isolated and their chances of gaining power
would be dashed. Furthermore, the domestic situation was changing
rapidly. The prewar pattern of life was returning.[43] The recent wartime unity, whether real or illusory, was fading. The non-Communist
Resistance groups, no less than the Party, were left dismayed and
disconcerted by this development.

The failure of the Left to revolutionize France after 1944 has a
parallel with the failure of the Right to do the same thing after
1940. The "national revolution" of the men of Vichy and the "national insurrection" of the Resistance did not have much time to
experiment. In both cases the would-be reformers were divided,
harassed, and finally overwhelmed by the demands of a world conflict from which France could not escape. At the same time they
were hampered by the great staying power of their country's
historic traditions.[44]

Solidarity of the Left and the Constitution

In terms of Communist strategy, the drafting of the constitution
set the stage for the Party's second attempt to unify the Left and at
the same time to clear the way of legal obstacles to its march toward power. Since the Communists and the Socialists controlled a
majority of votes in the forty-two-man constitutional commission,
the Party saw a splendid opportunity to lead a working alliance of

[43] "The second striking characteristic of the years following the occupation
is the rapidity with which French life appeared, superficially, to return to its
familiar pre-war pattern. The nature of the French economic organization,
with its peasant basis and thousands of small villages, constituted an important element of stability and no doubt encouraged political movements
to fall back into well-worn channels. It was certainly a powerful positive
force for economic conservatism." Pickles, *French Politics*, p. 2.

[44] Cf. Farmer, *Vichy, passim.*

the Left toward a radical change in the political structure of France.

However, almost from the beginning the Communists were forced on the defensive by a growing collaboration between the Socialists and the MRP. Defeated on a number of important proposals, the Party fought back by carrying on the debates in *L'Humanité*, thereby violating the unwritten rule of secrecy. Led by Pierre Hervé, the Communists publicly assailed the Socialist leaders for their "consistent and deliberate alliance with the Catholics." [45] *Izvestiia* also raised its voice against specific Socialist proposals.[46] Stung by accusations of clericalism, Left-wing Socialists stepped up pressure on their party's executive committee to cut short its co-operation with the MRP.[47] The Communists then suggested to the Socialists that together they should revive the then dormant *comité d'entente* in order to draft a Marxian constitution which could be pushed through the commission by their combined votes. When the Socialists finally accepted a modified view of this plan, it was decided that a few leaders of both parties would meet regularly to consider each issue as it arose in the commission.[48]

While this phase of the constitutional drama was unfolding, the Communists were making strenuous efforts in the Assembly to vote with the Socialists on all major issues. In the face of the initial opposition of Charles Tillon, the Communist Minister of Air, the Communist Party backed a Socialist motion to cut the national defense appropriation by 20 percent. Defending this *volte-face*, Jacques Duclos claimed that, though the Party retained its confidence in the provisional government, any split between Socialists and Communists would wreck the "union of the republican forces of this country." [49] On the other hand, the Soviet press recognized that the French Communists had been forced into a corner and

---

[45] *L'Humanité*, December 8, 22, 1945.

[46] *Izvestiia*, December 16, 22, 1945.

[47] Wright, *The Reshaping of French Democracy*, p. 124.

[48] *Ibid.*, p. 125; *L'Humanité*, January 4, 19, 20–21, 1946. It was this Communist pressure on the Socialist leaders that brought about the resignation of the then strongly anti-Communist Daniel Mayer as secretary-general of the SFIO and the election of Guy Mollet, who was more willing to work with the Communists, *L'Année politque, 1946*, p. 28.

[49] Assemblée Nationale Constituante, *JO, Débats*, December 31, 1945, second session, pp. 716–17, 730.

denounced the Socialist stand on the budget as a maneuver calculated to "clear [the SFIO] in the eyes of the electors." [50]

The incipient *rapprochement* of Socialists and Communists was upset in January, 1946, when General de Gaulle suddenly resigned as president of the provisional government. The Communists immediately proposed that Thorez be made premier of a Socialist-Communist coalition government. The reaction of the other parties was sharp and negative. The MRP refused to vote for Thorez, and the Socialists rejected the Communist proposal for a two-party government. They declared that Thorez himself had already committed the Communists to a tripartite agreement in his conversations with Socialist leaders.[51]

The Party did not insist. Instead it concluded that the only solution was to choose a candidate above the parties and suggested the Socialist deputy Félix Gouin. The Socialist group nominated Vincent Auriol, but the Communists, fearing another strong personality at the head of the government, would have no part of him. Having no basis for disagreeing with the Communist endorsement of Gouin, the Socialists finally agreed to his election as President of the Republic.

For reasons that are not entirely clear, this time the Communists made no great difficulties over the redistribution of ministerial posts. They did not request any of the key ministries and received no additional portfolios. One explanation that the Communists have given for their apparent failure to exploit the crisis was that a new political upheaval "could have been used by the reaction to attack the republican institutions." The difficulties in forming a new government, they maintained, had been easily straightened out "because our party, acting as a great party of government, as a great courageous party, conscious of its responsibilities, decided to oppose any threat to democracy, and created the conditions for the formation of a new government." In reviewing their policy the Communists put great emphasis on stabilizing the country and ending the uncertain, provisional situation in political life.[52]

[50] *Pravda,* January 14, 1946.
[51] *L'Humanité,* January 22, 1946, and *Le Populaire,* January 22, 23, 1946.
[52] "Notre Politique," *Cahiers du Communisme,* No. 1 (January, 1946), pp. 6, 16.

The Party appeared to view the crisis in terms of a threat to the gains they had made rather than as an opportunity to broaden them. How could they know whether De Gaulle planned to appeal again to the nation for support? Their working alliance with the Socialists was just beginning to pay dividends in the work of the constitutional commission. If the Communist demands had been stiffly resisted by the Socialists or the MRP, the Party might have found itself isolated. Occurring at the moment of De Gaulle's resignation, a rupture between the Communists and the other two major parties would have looked like a victory for the outgoing President. De Gaulle's scornful treatment of the Communists would have been vindicated, and his prestige would have been increased at the expense of the Party. Furthermore, the Communists could not but fear a prolonged crisis, which would have been an invitation to De Gaulle to intervene with force. As they saw it, their time had not yet come.

The Party leaders quickly reestablished their working relationship with the Socialists in the constitutional commission. The Communists concentrated on persuading the SFIO to reverse its stand on several important issues which had presumably already been decided by a Socialist-MRP majority, and in this they were largely successful. What emerged from the commission and the delegates on the floor of the Assembly was largely a Communist-Socialist-inspired document.

From the outset of the discussions in the commission it was clear that the Communists strongly favored a unicameral legislature with almost unlimited powers. The frail structure of the constitution would offer no check on the power of any group which controlled a majority of the Assembly, if only for a brief period. Thus, though the Communists worked hard to end the provisional government dominated by a strong executive, they intended to establish an equally provisional government dominated by an all-powerful assembly.

Together with the Socialists, the Communists resisted the attempts of the MRP and the Right to create a second chamber which, though restricted in powers, might at a later time be able to expand its political prerogatives in the fashion of the old Senate.[53] The Party even went so far as to oppose public sessions of the Council of the French Union and publication of the stenographic record of its debates because, in the words of Hervé, "we do not want the council to become a second chamber." Under pressure to accept a compromise formula, Etienne Fajon grudgingly agreed to have a summary of the council debates published, but only in a publication separate from the *Journal Officiel.*[54]

The Communists fought as rigorously to prevent the principle of constitutionality of laws from being written into the constitution. According to Fajon, no institution offered a better guarantee of constitutionality than the Assembly. So strongly did the Communists feel on this matter that they provoked a breach in the tripartite coalition rather than compromise. As a result of their unyielding stand, François de Menthon of the MRP resigned as reporter-general.

According to the Communists, verification of disputed electoral contests should be made by the Assembly and not—as the MRP and, at first, the Socialist wanted—by a special electoral committee. Hervé explained that the principle of the sovereign assembly ought not to be impaired by any judicial authority.[55]

The Communists further showed their opposition to a strong executive by abstaining from a vote endorsing the principle of a president of the Republic, and then went on to lead the fight to deprive the chief executive of all but ceremonial functions. Together with the Socialists, they beat down a proposal of the MRP and the Right to have the president elected by the Assembly and the Council of the French Union. They denied the president the right to pardon and to preside over either the Council of National Defense or the Council of Ministers.[56]

Claiming that the problem of governmental stability rested solely on the loyalty of the individual deputy to his electoral promises,

[53] Assemblée Nationale Constituante Elue Octobre 1945, *Séances de la Commission de la Constitution: Comptes rendus analytiques*, pp. 31, 40.

[54] *Ibid.,* pp. 593–95, 626, 778.

[55] *Ibid.,* pp. 47, 433.

[56] *Ibid.,* pp. 82, 120–27, 731.

the Communists opposed in principle the dissolution of the Assembly at any time before the expiration of its term. Whether dissolution was automatic or decided by the premier, the government could, the Party claimed, put strong pressure on the deputies to support its program. The Communists maintained that the constitution should say nothing on the question of dissolution.[57]

Another sharp controversy developed between the Communists and their opponents over the issue of whether the principle of obligatory vote and a statute of political parties should be included in the constitution. In both cases the Communists opposed measures which would strengthen the powers of the executive branch over the actions of political parties which made up the Assembly. To Pierre Hervé the obligatory vote was a political maneuver directed against the extremist parties. But he was even more sharply critical of the Socialist proposal that every party should enjoy the free and equal use of public facilities, such as the radio and the press, to conduct its election campaign. What about the creation of new parties or a split in an old one? asked Hervé. Was this a device to maintain the political *status quo*? In view of their recent success in raising funds, the Communists charged that the idea of equality would hurt the party whose members are "willing to make great personal sacrifices."

Fajon attacked with equal vigor the proposal to make enrollment in a party obligatory for every deputy. In his eyes neither the constitution nor the governmental authorities should have any control over political life in the Assembly. A deputy should be responsible to the electorate, not to his party. Otherwise, Fajon added, a Socialist deputy who had broken ranks to vote against the Munich agreement could have been thrown out of the chamber because he had violated party discipline.[58] Clearly, the Communists feared that the advantages of a well-disciplined and wealthy party such as theirs

[57] *Ibid.*, pp. 87–88. Defeated on this proposal, the Communists finally accepted a weak Socialist compromise, which made dissolution difficult, if not impossible. See *ibid.*, pp. 731–32.

[58] The only alternative to Party discipline which Fajon could offer was the idea of recall by the electorate, which, as the MRP pointed out, was impracticable in a system of proportional representation. *Ibid.*, pp. 67–68.

had become would be swept away by the principles of party equality and obligatory enrollment.

To regulate more closely the political life of the new Republic, the non-Communist delegates wanted to draw up a statute of parties which would have required every group to make public the source of its funds, to organize in a democratic fashion with effective control of its leaders by the rank and file, and to repudiate the idea of a one-party state. Strongly opposed to outside intervention in Party affairs, the Communists were forced ironically to take up the defense of liberty of association against what they called the threats of a "totalitarian state." [59]

In the field of local administration the Communists argued for strict limitations on the power of the central government. The functions of the prefect, they declared, should be transferred to the municipal and departmental council. Communist spokesmen rejected both regionalism and centralization as "authoritarian or cooperative tendencies," and demanded the immediate abolition of the Commissars of the Republic.[60] The reasoning behind their stand was that the strong grass-roots organization under Communist control which the Party had recently developed through the committees of liberation and the patriotic militia could bring greater pressure to bear on local elective units than upon a representative of the central government.

Why were the Communists so determined to turn out a vaguely worded constitution with some new rights, but few specific safeguards? A fellow-traveling delegate in the commission, Pascal Copeau, let slip the real reason.

The commission has little time. Let us not deceive ourselves that its role is to draft a provisional constitution. It would do well to restrict its pretensions and not to waste its efforts on questions which will not be solved by moralizing. The commission ought to avoid any effort to try to solve political questions by strict regulation. That has already been done in order to achieve governmental stability. Now you want to settle the party system. But you can do nothing to prevent change.[61]

[59] *Ibid.*, pp. 58–62, 424, 426.
[60] *Ibid.*, pp. 147, 150–54, 164.
[61] *Ibid.*, p. 61.

At another point Hervé pointed out that the "declaration [of rights] ought to proclaim principles which are above any constitution. To include in the declaration the concept of workers' control would make this a permanent innovation [thus] failing to take into consideration [the possibility of] future changes." Fajon expressed much the same sentiment.

There is no question, for the moment, of making a Socialist or Communist constitution; this can only be done when the conditions of socialism are ripe. The Communists do not mistake the constitution for their party program. For us [the constitution] ought to reflect the present state of society.[62]

True to their revolutionary Marxist aims, the French Communists set their sights on the maximum goals attainable in the "present historical period." At the same time they looked forward to the future when they would be in a position to solve in a decisive fashion what Copeau called "the political question."

The Communist delegates sought to mask their intentions by deleting from the constitutional draft Marxist phraseology which might frighten the moderate groups in France. Pierre Hervé suggested eliminating Article 36, which declared that "the rights set down in the present declaration mark a stage in the establishment of an economic and social system organized and established for the common good in which work will cease to be a commodity and the exploitation of man by man will be completely abolished." "If the commission seeks to win support for the constitution of the largest number of republicans in the country," he explained, "such an expression might be untimely." [63]

Though the Communists were not able to jam all their proposals through the commission, they were satisfied with the final draft and resisted last-minute efforts by Vincent Auriol to arrange a compromise with the MRP in the interests of rallying tripartite support of the constitution. Superbly confident of victory in the referendum, Jacques Duclos proclaimed that France would adopt the new "democratic constitution." "It is not Communist," he declared, "it is not

[62] *Ibid.*, pp. 169–71.
[63] *Ibid.*, p. 393.

at all Socialist, but it proclaims new rights." [64] What Duclos did not say was that, because of the all-powerful Assembly it created, the constitution offered a promising opportunity for the Party to make a bold advance along the road to socialism by peaceful parliamentary means.

The Fruits of Coalition Government:
Communist Infiltration

Although the Party had cooperated with the Socialists in drawing up the new constitution, it was pursuing an independent course within the executive branch of the government. Taking advantage of its strength within the cabinet, the Communist Party tried to infiltrate and control branches of industry and units of the armed forces. It expected its efforts in the industrial area to be facilitated by the nationalization laws which it supported. Contrary to its former proposals, the Party now endorsed a highly centralized structure for nationalized industries, since the administrative boards would be under the supervision of Communist-dominated economic ministries.[65] The Communist plans met with considerable success in the organization and control of the nationalized coal industry. The board of the central national corporation consisted of eighteen representatives, including six workers, six governmental representatives, and six consumers, all of whom were to be appointed by the various interests concerned. Most of the workers' representatives were Communists, chosen by the CGT. Since the Minister of Industrial Production, Marcel Paul, was responsible for naming the government's representatives, they too were Communists. To confirm his control of the board, Paul also appointed a Communist representative of the nationalized railroads (SNCF) as a consumer representative—the secretary-general of the Federation of Railroad Workers likewise sat on the railroad board as a representative of labor.[66] Though

---

[64] Duclos, "Notre Politique," *Cahiers du Communisme*, No. 4 (April, 1946), p. 318.

[65] See, for example, the project of Marcel Paul on the nationalization of gas and electricity. Assemblée Nationale Constituante, *JO, Débats*, March 27, 1946, first session, pp. 1108–9.

[66] Moch, *Confrontations*, p. 240.

this was an irregular, if not illegal, action, it went unchallenged at the time.

The Communists also gained control of the central committee of social work for the nationalized gas and electric industries. Marcel Paul, who became head of the committee, hired 300 more men than was necessary to participate in the work. Most of these came from the CGT, and they remained entrenched in the central committee of social work until 1951.[67]

A similar situation prevailed in the aircraft industry. The Gnôme-et-Rhône Company had been nationalized and placed under the direction of the Ministry of Air. While he was Minister of Air, Charles Tillon appointed a Communist, Marcel Weil, to be director-general of the company. From this powerful position Weil carefully packed the bureaucracy with Communists and, according to a parliamentary report, overcentralized the administration.[68]

The Communist control of the Ministry of Air also had its effect upon the labor force in the nationalized factories. Job openings in aircraft factories were advertised only in *L'Humanité*, *Franc-Tireur*, *Paris-Liberté*, and *Ce Soir*, all Communist or sympathizer papers. Without a special card issued by the hiring services of the ministry, no one could obtain a position. Consequently, there was such a heavy infiltration by Communists that a reported 80 to 90 percent of the workers in the aircraft factories were of "the same tendency." [69] Even when the director of the SNECMA was replaced, his non-

---

[67] *Le Monde*, February 20, 1951.

[68] René Pleven, "Rapport fait au nom de la commission des finances sur le projet de la loi plaçant la Société nationale d'études et de construction de moteurs d'aviation (SNECMA) sous un statut provisoire en vue de sa réorganisation," pp. 10–12, JO, *Documents parlementaires* (Assemblée Nationale), Première Session Legislative (Paris, 1951), Session de 1948, No. 4629. See also M. Pellenc, "Rapport annuel fait au nom de la sous commission chargée de suivre et d'apprécier la question des entreprises industrielles nationalisées et des societés d'économie mixte; Seconde partie, la SNACA," JO, *Documents parlementaires* (Conseil de la République), Première Session Legislative (Paris, 1949), Session de 1949, No. 505.

[69] Pleven, "Rapport," *Documents parlementaires* (Assemblée Nationale), pp. 15, 16. The information was elicited by a commission of inquiry interviewing non-Communist labor-union miltants. At the Argenteuil factory the personnel chief and the heads of social, administrative, manufacturing, bargaining services, etc., were Communists.

Communist successor was unable to reverse the trend because Communist labor inspectors refused to sanction dismissals.[70]

Another case of Communist infiltration occurred in the army. While the Party controlled the Ministry of Armaments, a certain Commandant Teulery (known in the Resistance as De Viguier) was the chief of the security services. According to the Ministry of the Interior, in 1946–47 he handed over to the Yugoslav military attaché "numerous documents which he had been able to gather in the course of his functions in the cabinet of the Ministers of Armaments and of National Defense." The accused had been an officer in the FTP, later integrated into the regular army, and a member of the French Communist Party.[71]

Communist officials in executive posts were also active at the local level. For example, the Communist prefect of the Loire was partially responsible for replacing 80 percent of the effectiveness of about a dozen companies of Republican Security with his own men.[72] Despite these and other infiltrations at the local and regional level, the French Communists were steadfastly opposed to a return to a local or departmental police. With a possible eye to the future, Thorez asserted: "We wish to maintain the concept of state control of the police." [73]

The reason for this Communist attitude became clear when Thorez tried to secure the adoption of a new statute for public officials. Its most important section provided for creating a secretary-general of public administration who would be responsible for all officials formerly under the control of personnel services, of various ministries, or of other state agencies. His powers would include the regulation of bounties and the exercise of official discipline, including warnings of dismissal without pension.[74] Some elements of

[70] Ibid., pp. 21–22. There was even allegedly a misappropriation of funds by M. Weil in his capacity of director-general. The controller made a formal protest to the Ministry of Air concerning this. Ibid., p. 39.

[71] Communiqué of the Minister of the Interior, quoted in Le Monde, February 28, 1949.

[72] Moch, "La politique des prix et le renforcement de l'autorité," Bulletin Intérieur du Parti Socialist SFIO, No. 39 (February, 1949), p. 67.

[73] Assemblée Nationale Constituante, JO, Débats, March 22, 1946, first session, p. 992.

[74] Le Figaro, April 9, 1946.

the police would naturally fall under his control. There can be no doubt that Thorez, who as Minister of State was concerned with a reform of the public administration, foresaw a Communist, perhaps himself, in the enormously powerful post of secretary-general.

These examples give some idea of what the Communists might have done had they controlled one of the key ministries, such as Foreign Affairs, Interior, or Defense. The infiltration by the Party was usually carried out legally, or at least without violence, but this did not exclude the possibility that the Communists might use their newly won positions at a later date in the struggle for power, even in a violent struggle.

Solidarity of the Left Endangered:
The Second Constitution

The draft constitution, so largely molded by the Socialist-Communist coalition, was to be submitted to the people for approval in May, 1946. The Party hoped, of course, to conduct the campaign for ratification jointly with the SFIO, and it appealed to the Socialists to combine forces in the referendum.[75] Despite their common interest in the constitution, the Socialists refused to campaign jointly with the Communists. Undaunted, the Communists conducted another confident and vigorous campaign. If anything, it erred in being too enthusiastic.

The Communists associated the adoption of the constitution with a change in the government. Duclos began to beat the drums for a Communist-led cabinet. With unconscious irony he asserted, "It is we who appear as the great Party of order. Those who vote against the constitution, those who wish to maintain the provisional conditions, to drive France to anarchy and adventure . . . appear as the enemies of the country, as the people of disorder." [76] Carried away by their own enthusiasm, the Communist militants thundered forth at mass meetings the long-muted battle cry of *"Thorez au pouvoir!"* [77]

[75] *L'Humanité*, April 20, 1946.
[76] Duclos, *En avant*, pp. 30, 31.
[77] Wright, *The Reshaping of French Democracy*, p. 178.

The Soviet press also campaigned for the ratification of the draft constitution and for organic unity of the Left. The "democratic parties," it announced, "are repulsing the maneuvers of the Right and want to put an end to the transitional period and strengthen the democratic base in France." [78] The reactionary forces, it continued, were strong in the officer corps, the general staff, the diplomatic service, and the high administrative posts. From these positions they were trying to split the Socialists from the Communists. "It is that danger," Moscow declared, "against which [the Communists] direct all their strength. That is why the reactionaries of the most varied types are trying to hinder the formation of a bloc of Communists and Socialists." According to the Soviet Union, these varied types of reactionary included "allies in the Socialist Party" who were especially "easy to find in the leadership." As for the MRP, the Soviet press did not "find it difficult to discern the leading role which the Vatican plays in the mobilization of the strength of the reaction." [79] Soviet and French Communist propaganda was identical in the campaign for the ratification of the new French constitution.[80]

The result of the balloting was defeat for the draft constitution and hence for the Communists. It showed once again that the Party could not rally a majority of Frenchmen. The Left had been defeated on the constitutional issue even though the Communists and the SFIO had taken the same stand. When the two parties campaigned separately for an election, they commanded a majority. Thus, we can only conclude that there were many Socialists who refused to follow their party when it was allied with the French Communists.

The Communist Party came to the same conclusion, but it blamed the Socialist leaders for not having enforced discipline within their party. George Cogniot wrote, "One of the lessons that follows naturally from the vote [on the constitution] is the regrettable fact

[78] "Mezhdunarodnoe obozrenie," *Pravda*, April 28, 1946.

[79] E. Vladimirov, "Frantsuzskaia reaktsiia pered referendumom," [French Reaction Before the Referendum], *ibid.*, April 29, 1946.

[80] In March, 1946, the Soviet government agreed to send France 400,000 tons of wheat, to be paid for in dollars. The arrival of the first Soviet transport at Marseilles was the occasion for a symbolic ceremony of Franco-Soviet friendship attended by Ambassador Bogomolov. The non-Communist press treated the incident as an electoral maneuver. *L'Année politique, 1946*, p. 119.

that the unity of forces grouped in the 'yes' camp was not more complete." [81] In general, the Communists were very bitter about the Socialists' refusal to conduct the referendum struggle in common.[82]

The Soviet Union was also disappointed by the results. "The reaction achieved a success," commented *Pravda*, and this was due to the strength of the church and of international provocation. The French people were threatened, Moscow charged, with the alienation of the Western Allies if they voted "yes." Of course, the lack of unity on the Left also contributed to the defeat. The Soviet press reiterated that "the people know that their strength lies only in unity." [83]

Some of the Socialists, however, concluded that they had been too closely associated with the Communists. It was not surprising that they now reversed their position and conducted their campaign for the election of a new Constituent Assembly in an atmosphere of outspoken anticommunism.[84] The stunned Communists deplored this "provocation" and the "division" of the working class.[85] Once again the Soviet Union came to the defense of the French Communists, praising them for their "broad and striking" advance in industrial production despite the obstacles placed in their path by the reaction.[86] It denounced the "vicious anti-Communist" campaign by Daniel Mayer and Le Troquer and the equally "pernicious provocation" of Walter Lippmann, who had written in *Le Figaro* that "if the Communists take power in the West, they will collide with the American and British armies." [87]

Until the last moment the French Communists did not offer anything new in their appeals to the electorate. Then, several days

[81] *L'Humanité*, May 6, 1944.

[82] Duclos, "Notre Politique," *Cahiers du Communisme*, Nos. 5–6 (May-June, 1946), p. 395.

[83] Iurii Zhukov, "Posle referenduma vo Frantsii" [After the Referendum in France], *Pravda*, May 9, 1946.

[84] See the speech of André le Troquer, *Le Figaro*, May 24, in which he revived the desertion charge against Thorez.

[85] *L'Humanité*, May 24, 1946.

[86] Iurii Zhukov, "Bor'ba frantsuzskikh rabochikh za vosstanovlenie proizvodstva" [The Struggle of French Workers for the Restoration of Production], *Pravda*, May 29, 1946.

[87] *Ibid.*, May 27, June 9, 1946.

before the election, the CGT suddenly demanded an across-the-board wage increase of 25 percent. Up to this time the Party had been the most outspoken advocate of holding the line on wages, but on May 31, 1946, it publicly supported the demands of the CGT.[88]

This was clearly an electoral maneuver, aimed not only at winning more adherents to the Party, but also at holding the allegiance of those workers who already supported the Communists. There was evidence that the pressure for higher wages was increasing enormously among working-class elements.[89] To continue to ignore it might have been politically suicidal. However, for the Party to yield to that pressure in the face of the government's policy of holding the line would endanger the Communist position within the coalition. The Party managed to avoid a crisis over this issue until after the elections; even then it did not resolve the dilemma.

The election results were a disappointment for the Communists. They lost two seats, although their popular vote increased by 200,000 votes to a total of over 5,199,000. The Socialists lost fifteen seats, with the result that the former majority of the Left in the Assembly now disappeared. Even with the support of the Socialists, the Communist Party could not dictate a new constitution. This new situation was to influence the Communist point of view both on forming a government and on negotiating a draft constitution.

For the third time within a year the Communists were in a position to demand control of one of the three most powerful ministries. Yet they were unwilling to do so. As in November, 1945, and in January, 1946, the shadow of De Gaulle and the fear of being excluded from the government continued to influence the Party. The preliminary interparty negotiations showed how vacillating Communist Party policy was.

When the MRP proposed Bidault as head of the new government, there was a difference of opinion in the Central Committee on the

[88] *L'Humanité*, May 31, 1946. For a discussion of the wage problem see below, p. 310.
[89] See, for example, Duclos, "Notre Politique," *Cahiers du Communisme*, No. 2 (February, 1946), p. 4. Duclos quoted the Socialist paper *L'Avenir du Nord* as having labeled Thorez's speeches "Stakhanovism which scarcely has aroused the sympathy of the miners."

policy to be followed. Most of the speakers, including Vermeersch, Hervé, and Guyot, were opposed to an MRP candidate for premier. A few, such as Berlioz, saw no objections to it. Thorez stressed the need for the reconstitution of the former government. His compromise view was finally accepted.

The Central Committee . . . believes that all partisan preoccupations should be obliterated before the higher interests of the country. It considers that the best solution of the governmental problem in the present circumstances is the renewal of the present government with its president.[90]

The Communist suggestion was rejected by the Socialists, who decided to support Bidault.[91] Though it is not clear whether the Party would have voted against Bidault under these circumstances, an unexpected event assured at least their abstention. Speaking at Bayeux, General de Gaulle explained for the first time his ideas on the constitution. What he said boldly challenged the Communists.[92]

For the Communists, participation in the government now seemed more necessary than ever. The Party could not risk voting against Bidault, even as a gesture, for fear he would exclude them from his cabinet. They did, however, abstain from voting, and Bidault was chosen premier. Duclos explained that certain Fascist threats "which recalled those of 1934 . . . underlined the necessity of giving France a government quickly." [93]

The Communists then agreed to participate in the government without insisting on receiving a key ministry. Instead they made it a condition of their cooperation that the government would adapt the 25-percent wage increase.[94] When offered 15 percent, they accepted. Again Duclos explained that "it is necessary to put an end quickly to the provisional situation in order that France may be able to play a most important role on the international scene." He assured the assembly that the Communists would cooperate in the work of the constitutional commission "in such a way as to endow

[90] *L'Humanité,* June 18, 1946.
[91] *Le Populaire,* June 18, 1946.
[92] For the speech see *Le Figaro,* June 18, 1946.
[93] Assemblée Nationale Constituante, *JO, Débats,* June 19, 1946, p. 2546.
[94] Letter from Thorez and Duclos to Bidault in *L'Humanité,* June 23, 1946.

France with a constitution . . . which will discourage any tendency to slide toward dictatorship." [95]

The Communists held to these stated policies, although it required another threat from the Right to convince them that their line had been correct. During the next three months of constitution-making the Communists were pushed back on the defensive. The MRP-Socialist coalition revived much of the work of their earlier cooperation. A second house, the Council of the Republic, was added to the draft; the president was to be elected by both houses and was given back many of his prewar powers. The judiciary was granted a greater degree of independence of the assembly. Despite strong Communist objections, the proposal favoring a referendum on the constitutionality of laws was passed.[96]

However, the future structure of the French Union was the most hotly debated issue in the commission. The Communists argued that the rights given to the overseas natives in the first draft, including representation in the French National Assembly, should be guaranteed until a constituent assembly of the French Union could meet to draw up its own constitution. At first they were joined by the Socialists and Ferhat Abbas to defeat a series of MRP proposals to strengthen the hand of the *colons* in the assembly of the French Union and to write into the draft a strongly worded anticolonialist statement. But pressure from Bidault and the Socialist Minister of Overseas Territories, Marius Moutet, broke up the Communist-led coalition. Enraged by the acceptance of a government-sponsored proposal to create a system of double representation of *colons* and natives in the assembly of the Union, the native African delegates, including members of the Socialist group, stormed out of the commission. Fajon warned that sections in the constitution dealing with the French Union would lose all their significance if they were not supported by representatives of Overseas France in the commission. "If we have remained here," he added, "it is because it is our tactic to try to cut our losses when we are beaten on one point. Neverthe-

[95] Assemblée Nationale Constituante, *JO, Débats*, June 26, 1946, p. 2564.
[96] Assemblée Nationale Constituante Elue Juin 1946, *Séances de la Commission de la Constitution: Comptes rendues analytiques*, pp. 66–73, 92, 103–5.

less, this attitude has scarcely been rewarded, since we have not gained any concessions." [97]

As the demolition of their previous work proceeded, the Communists' attitude stiffened. By the time the new draft was brought up for discussion on the floor of the assembly, Fajon was ready to declare his open opposition to it.

"We are hostile to this draft of the commission, as it is presented. The project ends up by ranging a series of barriers against the sovereignty of the assembly. . . . We demand that barriers be raised against dictatorship." [98]

According to Pierre Cot, the Communists had made all the concessions in the new draft. Unless reciprocal concessions were made on the floor of the Assembly, he declared, the struggle for revision would be carried to the people.[99]

The Communist threat vanished when General de Gaulle publicly launched a detailed criticism of the constitution. The Party at once shut off its propaganda attack and reconsidered its position. On the surface it appeared that De Gaulle was preparing to return to the political scene. The hitherto dormant Gaullist Union took on a new life.[100] The Communists now faced the unpleasant prospect that their opposition to the second draft, combined with that of De Gaulle, would mean certain defeat for the project, and this would require the election of a third Constituent Assembly. There was no doubt that Gaullist leaders were counting on this eventuality in order to enter the elections at the head of an anti-Communist bloc. In an interview with the Associated Press, René Capitant spoke of the period of uncertainty which would follow the rejection of the second draft constitution; it would then be possible, he said, to proceed to a solution based on the Bayeux constitution.

Immediately the Communists charged that the reaction was on the march. "The danger is outlined with inescapable clarity." [101]

[97] *Ibid.*, 522, 531, 566, 599–600, 609.

[98] Assemblée Nationale Constituante, *JO, Débats*, August 20, 1946, p. 3200.

[99] *Ibid.*, August 22, 1946, third session, p. 3252.

[100] See Wright, *The Reshaping of French Democracy*, pp. 210–11.

[101] *L'Humanité*, September 10, 1946. The Soviet commentators contended that the violent manifestations of anticommunism in some of the Paris press would lead one to think that the Hitlerites were back in power. "But Hitler is no more," Moscow added, "and those who counted on him have now changed

A third election would undoubtedly doom the moderates and would provoke a deep split in French political life. The Party might well have been isolated, to the benefit of the "forces of reaction." The dilemma had never been posed so clearly. This realization and a month of compromise were sufficient to swing the Party back to a positive stand in the referendum. In his final speech favoring adoption of the constitution Jacques Duclos reiterated the reasons for the Communist vote and set the tone for the Communist propaganda campaign to follow. The constitution was a series of compromises on the basis of tripartism, a condition, Duclos insisted, which was "the expression of a certain balance of political forces in our country in a given situation." He warned against allowing the reaction to undermine the constitution once it was adopted. On the other hand, the constitution could be modified later "from a democratic point of view." [102]

The Communists decided that, from two points of view, the new constitution was the best they could expect. It still protected them from the threat of a strong executive (who was most likely to be anti-Communist). Furthermore, under the second draft constitution the legislative assembly conserved enough of its powers to satisfy the Communists. If they could gain control of the Assembly, they would still be able to dominate the country. The Communists were not enthusiastic about this revision of their earlier work, but at least it preserved tripartite unity. The endorsement of the constitution by the Communists was one of the last major concessions they were to make to republican solidarity.

In campaigning for ratification of the constitution the Party adopted a more moderate position than it had in May, 1946. Its main argument was a negative one: The reaction "wants a continuation of the provisional status because it calculates that the provisional [regime] will signify disorder, and, taking advantage of disorder, the plotters could succeed in their evil assault upon the

---

their orientation. The admiration for certain American circles in certain strata of France has taken on a simply shameful character." Thus the Soviet Union linked the return of reaction with United States foreign policy. B. Izakov, "Osen' vo Frantsii," *Pravda*, September 23, 1946.

[102] Assemblée Nationale Constituante, *JO, Débats*, September 28, 1946, second session, p. 4239.

Republic." [103] Despite Communist restraint and the endorsement
of the draft by the Socialists and the MRP, the new constitution
was barely approved by a vote of 10.6 million to 9.5 million votes,
and five million Frenchmen abstained. Nevertheless, the Party rejoiced that "the efforts of factionalists to unleash this civil war with
which Mr. René Capitant has menaced us" had been defeated.[104]
Though the Soviet press welcomed the results as a "victory for the
democratic forces in France," it insisted that the struggle for French
democracy had not ended. According to *Pravda*, "this struggle urgently demands the cooperation and unity of all the genuine democratic forces of France.[105] The French Communists appealed again
to republicans of every stripe to work together. Thus, in high spirits
the Party prepared for the election of the first National Assembly
of the Fourth Republic.

In the autumn of 1946 the Communists entered the new electoral
campaign for the last time as as a government party. The election and
the process of forming a new government showed how isolated and
ineffective the Communists had become. The Communists chose
to base their campaign upon two moderate and well-worn demands:
the fight against rising prices, and unity of the working class to
prevent exclusion of the Party from the government.

The joint Communist-CGT fight against rising prices was obviously not so attractive to the workers as one for a wage increase,
but it was dictated by political necessity. The Socialists opposed a
wage increase, and the Communists could not afford to break with
them on this major issue. On the other hand, the restive workers
demanded something. Thus, the weak compromise was devised.[106]

The appeal for the cooperation of all workers and republicans
was dubbed by Thorez "the essential idea" of the election. The new
constitution, he argued, must be implemented by a large majority

---

[103] *L'Humanité*, October 13, 1946.

[104] *Ibid.*, October 16, 1946.

[105] Ia. Viktorov, "Pobeda demokraticheskikh sil Frantsii" [The Victory of
Democratic Forces in France], *Pravda*, October 16, 1946.

[106] For the Communist view see *L'Humanité*, October 19, 24, 28, 30, 1946.
The object of Communist vituperation on this issue was the MRP Minister of
National Economy, François de Menthon, who favored certain price increases.
See *ibid.*, November 7, 1946.

of the Left.[107] This appeal took on new urgency when the MRP assailed the French Communists. Maurice Schumann, militant anti-Communist, launched the battle cry: "Allow France to be governed by Bidault without Thorez!"[108] The French Communists denounced this "plot to eliminate the PCF from the government" as "a shameful policy."[109] They also put increased pressure on the Socialists to join them and gleefully reported desertions of Socialist militants to their ranks.[110]

The Soviet Union stepped up its criticism of the Socialists for ignoring the mating calls of the Communists, and reaffirmed its belief in the unity of the Left on Communist terms as the basis for a revolutionary change in Western Europe. A Soviet political analyst, S. Ivanov, outlined the failure of the SFIO to take into account the new factor in the struggle for power, the factor represented by the mass movement organized into popular committees or front movements. "In the countries of Eastern and Southeastern Europe liberated by the Red Army," he explained, "these committees rallied around them all the healthy popular forces and became the base and the lever of a state with a new structure." The result was no mere coalition of parties, but "the powerful alliance of workers, peasants, artisans, and intellectuals" fused by a common struggle in the resistance to the Germans. Admittedly, the author stated, such developments were impossible elsewhere because "in the countries of Western Europe and for different reasons (in particular, the presence there of the English and American armies) the organization of the Resistance movement was driven out of the political arena." However, despite these different objective conditions, the French Socialists were guilty of a "negative attitude with regard to the united front [which] leads objectively to the denial of the necessity of isolating the reaction and, consequently, helps the reaction."[111]

Like the French Communists, Ivanov criticized Léon Blum for

---

[107] *Ibid.*, October 18, 1946.
[108] *Le Monde*, October 22, 1946, speech at the Vélodrôme d'Hiver.
[109] *L'Humanité*, October 22, 23, 1946.
[110] *Ibid.*, November 9, 1946.
[111] S. Ivanov, "O roli sotsialisticheskikh partii posle vtoroi mirovoi voiny," *Bol'shevik*, Nos. 17–18 (September, 1946), pp. 52, 53.

having accused the Communists of serving the interests of the
USSR, and complained that in international disputes the Socialists
always chose to support the capitalist states against the socialist
state. In fact, he added, "their solidarity with regard to the foreign
policy of the labor government takes such forms that one is forced
to treat [them] as voluntary or involuntary servants of the British
Labour Party." Ivanov argued that the Socialists should mend their
ways and, in the face of the rising reaction, should join the Communists in a common effort.[112]

Before the election the French Communist Party had not drawn
any public parallels between its plans and the activities of the
Communist parties in Eastern Europe.[113] However, their great
success in the November, 1946, elections, and possibly the encouragement given by the Soviet press, modified the situation and
encouraged them to launch a political offensive.

In the elections the Party gained twenty seats and over 500,000
additional votes. It was again the largest party in France. The
Socialists again lost heavily. Swept along on a wave of enthusiasm,
the Communist leadership taunted the Socialists, demanded the
position of premier, and appealed to the republican elements to
rally to its leadership.[114] Again the USSR joined the attack against
the Socialists, denouncing their "opportunistic and schismatic tactics" and the "anti-Communist and anti-Soviet policy of some of
the leaders, the chief reason for the party's losses." The Soviet press
charged that the Right was extending a "clear invitation to the
Socialists to enter the other bloc, the bloc of the Right camp."
For Moscow this bloc was the chief threat to the success of the
Communists in France. "Do not forget," one Soviet commentator
warned, "that one of the leading slogans of the reaction in the
preelection campaign was the unity of all anti-Communist forces.
The exclusion of the Communists from the government coalition
became the problem of the whole French reaction." Moscow further
argued that the most dangerous weapon of the Right in this campaign was its threat to the electorate that "France will lose Amer-

[112] *Ibid.*, pp. 54, 56.
[113] Ivanov's criticism of the Socialist Party was reprinted in the December
issue of *Cahiers du Communisme.*
[114] *L'Humanité*, November 14, 1946.

ican support and financial aid if it votes for the Left parties." [115] Still the embattled Socialists held firm. They demanded to know what the Communist program was, who would constitute the governing majority, and whether other parties would be asked to approve the agreement.[116]

A week later in the elections to the Council of the Republic the Socialists again lost votes and seats. They were under heavy pressure to reverse their policy. Cachin asked, "How many defeats of this importance does it take for the Socialist leaders to renounce their anti-Communist polemics and finally decide to accept our loyal proposals of unity?" [117]

Solidarity of the Left Is Sterile:
The New Government

Despite Socialist vacillations the Central Committee of the Communist Party "decided to present the candidacy of Maurice Thorez" as head of the cabinet.[118] The committee then proceeded to outline in advance its governmental program. There was nothing new or Communist about it.[119] The Communist leaders again insisted that the prerequisite for the success of their plans was an agreement between the Communists and the SFIO. They again appealed to the national council of the Socialist Party to form a two-party government.[120] The very moderation of their program made it difficult for the Socialists to criticize it.

---

[115] B. Leont'ev, "K itogam vyborov v natsional'noe sobranie Frantsii," [The Results of Elections in the National Assembly of France], *Pravda*, November 15, 1946.

[116] *Le Populaire*, November 19, 1946.

[117] *L'Humanité*, November 26, 1946.

[118] "Résolution du Comité Central à Puteaux, 27 novembre, 1946," *Cahiers du Communisme*, No. 11 (November, 1946), p. 1011.

[119] *Ibid.*, p. 1012. Nine points were enumerated. Briefly they were (1) to accelerate the recovery of the French economy; (2) to assure stability of the franc by reversing the trend to higher prices, etc.; (3) to organize food delivery; (4) to guarantee the purchasing power of wages; (5) to give social benefits to mothers, older workers, etc.; (6) to renovate democracy; (7) to help the development of the well-being and liberty of all people in the French Union; (8) to secure reparations and guarantees of security for France and reinforce ties with the Allies; and (9) to break relations with Franco Spain.

[120] *Ibid.*, p. 1013.

The Party had never been so confident publicly. Candidate Thorez gave an interview to the London *Times* in which he appeared to be reassuring the English of his intentions. In the area of foreign policy Thorez strongly reiterated the "demand for the internationalization of the Ruhr and the attachment of the Saar to our economic system." [121] He stressed the need for Big Three unity and rejected any policy which would involve "formation of a bloc or an exclusive orientation toward any one of our allies, our gratitude extending equally to all." The alliance with England was important and desirable, but Thorez cautiously questioned the British refusal to deliver more Ruhr coal to France. Finally, he tried to dispel fears of a Bolshevik France. "The progress of democracy across the world, in spite of the rare exceptions that confirm the rule, enables one to consider other roads to socialism than that followed by the Russian Communists. In any case, the road is necessarily different for each country."

Thorez then alluded to the French way. "The union of the laboring and republican forces is the sure foundation of democracy. The French Workers' Party that we propose to constitute by fusing the Communists and the Socialists would be the guide to our new and popular democracy. It would open wide its ranks to Catholic workers, to whom we have extended . . . a fraternal hand that many have seized." [122]

In this interview Thorez gave more important evidence of the real Communist goal in postwar France: The French government would be led by a Communist; it would be controlled by a single party of the Left; its foreign policy would aim at making France a bridge between East and West; and its major domestic policy would be the attainment of socialism. Clearly, the Party proposed a form of government for France which already existed in Czechoslovakia, a government which was still one step from a "people's democracy." The French Communists had been working toward this solution for many years. Their policy of rapid restoration of political and economic stability in France was justified by this November gesture.

[121] *Ibid.*, "Interview de Maurice Thorez au *Times*," p. 1014.
[122] *Ibid.*, pp. 1015, 1016.

On the basis of Thorez's speech, Raymond Guyot, a member of the Party's Political bureau, made one of the most revealing analyses of the long-range Communist aims in France. Guyot was primarily concerned with defining the French "road to socialism." He asserted that the Russian Communists had solved the question of socialism through revolution "in a situation which cannot be repeated exactly, as Lenin remarked," and that the people's democracies had resolved the question with the aid of the Soviet Union by inflicting "a decisive military and political defeat on fascism." What, then, of the French way? Guyot maintained that "the movement along the road to socialism is necessarily different in each country," but, whatever the way "there is no progress without struggle. It is not possible," he continued, "to define [this way] exactly, and there is no ready-made formula. It is the struggle which will decide." [123] As to the type of socialist state which would emerge from the struggle, Guyot had in mind the popular democracies of Eastern Europe. "In such countries as Yugoslavia and Bulgaria basic reforms have been pushed forward much farther than in France in so far as the sovereignty of the people and the real control by the popular masses of the government of the country are concerned." [124]

Guyot concluded that, although the French Communists intended to establish socialism on the Soviet model, they did not expect to achieve their goal in the same way as the Russian or East European parties. However, indispensable characteristics of the movement on the road to socialism were struggle, violence, revolution.

How was the struggle to be conducted, and how would this campaign lead to the final battle for the establishment of socialism in France? As Guyot stated frankly, "It is incontestable that democracy is the most favorable form, in the capitalist system, for the development of the workers' movement," and that "the democracy which now exists in France no longer resembles the democracy which existed in the years between the two wars." The "profound changes" in French politics were of great significance for the triumph of socialism because "the balance of forces has changed."

[123] Guyot, "La Démocratie et les voies du Socialisme," *Questions du Moment*, pp. 25–33, 40. A speech of February 12, 1947.
[124] Guyot, "Les Chemins du Socialisme," *Cahiers du Communisme*, No. 1 (January, 1947), p. 17.

The role of the working class "tends to grow uninterruptedly, while that of the trusts tends to diminish." Furthermore, it was very important that the intellectuals were joining the Party in droves because, "as the *Communist Manifesto* pointed out, at the moment when the class struggle approaches the decisive hour, the process of dissolution of the ruling class, of the entire old society, takes on so violent and so bitter a character that a small fraction of the ruling class detaches itself and rallies to the revolutionary class, to the class which carries aloft the banner of the future." According to Guyot, other "progressive characteristics" of French democracy were the nationalizations, the *comités d'entreprises*, the revisions in the social-security plan, and the new constitution. Guyot urged that these features be made the basis of the "daily struggle against the forces of reaction." [125]

The Communist leaders had waited to publicize their plans for the "French road to socialism" until France was endowed with permanent political institutions, and the Communist electoral success in November, 1946, had merely added weight to Thorez's words. It cannot be denied that the ground had been well prepared for this statement of aims. However, the simple truth remains that every aspect of this dramatic Communist political gamble was ill-judged. France was not the place for it, and the time—November, 1946—was too late for its success.

Thorez's proposals were followed by a short period of intense political maneuvering. The MRP supported continuation of the existing government, but the Socialists agreed to meet with the Communists and to discuss the Communist program and the Thorez candidacy. During the talks Duclos proposed the principle of interdependence of the four presidencies, meaning that the presidencies of the Republic, the Council of Ministers, the National Assembly, and the Council of the Republic should be shared among the parties according to a prearranged plan.[126]

The Socialists decided to postpone the meeting of their national council until after the election of the president of the Assembly.

[125] Guyot, "La Démocratie et les voies du Socialisme," *Questions du Moment,* pp. 34–38.
[126] *L'Humanité,* November 27, 29, 1946. Félix Gouin was the only Socialist leader who favored this concept. *Ibid.,* December 3, 1946.

They then presented Vincent Auriol as their candidate for that post. In this way they blocked Communist efforts to link the election of the president of the Assembly with the choice of the premier. Thereby they trapped the Communists. If the latter did not vote for Auriol, the Socialists could scarcely be expected to vote for Thorez. If the Communists did vote for him, he would probably be elected unanimously, and the Socialists might then demand a unanimous election of the other three presidents to follow the precedent. Acceptance of this idea would mean defeat for Thorez.[127] Faced with this predicament, the Communists abstained, and Auriol was elected on the first ballot by the votes of the SFIO, the MRP, and the Right (Parti Républicain de la Liberté, or PRL). A non-Communist coalition was in the making.

The same day the Socialist council met and decided without enthusiasm to vote for Thorez as premier.[128] This was another skillful move to disarm Left-wing Socialists, who were in favor of some sort of common action with the Communists. It also blunted the edge of Communist criticism of Socialist leaders. Thus, on December 5, 1946, Maurice Thorez stood as the only avowed candidate for premier of France. He needed 310 votes, but received only 259. Some Socialists violated party discipline by not voting for him. This scarcely mattered, since the Left had already lost its absolute majority in the Assembly. The Socialists had observed the forms of Left-wing solidarity. They did not enthusiastically accept the Communist nine-point program, or interdependence plan, or even Thorez. Even if they had, it is unlikely, contrary to Communist propaganda, that a score or so other republicans would have joined the two Marxist parties to elect Thorez.

After this defeat there was a danger that the Communists might be excluded altogether from the new government. The Socialists could have voted with the MRP and the Right to elect Georges Bidault premier. It was only by the smallest of margins that this did not come about. The Socialists' national council voted 2,242 to 2,145 not to participate in any government without the Communists.

[127] For the Communist attack on the unanimity principle as a precedent, see *ibid.*, December 4, 1946.
[128] *Le Populaire*, December 5, 1946.

The immediate result was a defeat for Bidault and a political stalemate. Interparty bargaining began again. The time had not yet come to bury tripartism, though it was rapidly becoming moribund.

The conversations broke down on two points. The MRP insisted upon a government of national union. The Communists refused to participate in a government which included representatives of the PRL. The Center and the Right objected to the Communist demand for control of one of the key ministries, and there was no sign that the government crisis would soon end.[129]

The Communists wanted to avoid a prolonged stalemate. They feared that under such conditions a non-Communist majority might coalesce in the Assembly and force them out of the government. Yet they could not bring themselves to allow the "black reaction," the PRL, to join the government. Therefore, they made the startling proposal that a homogeneous Socialist cabinet be elected, to "preserve a government of the Left." [130] The Assembly concurred.

The Communists were in headlong retreat. Their optimism of November had vanished. They were obliged to count themselves out of the new government in order to hang on to their chances of again becoming a governmental party in the future. They had now voted into power the party which they had hoped to absorb, thus giving that party enormous prestige and justifying the stand of the Socialist leaders against fusion with the Communists. The crisis showed that, though the Party had gained an impressive electoral victory, it had suffered what proved to be an irreparable political defeat. Its presence in the government could no longer be considered either inevitable or indispensable.

[129] *L'Année politique, 1946*, pp. 284, 285.
[130] *L'Humanité,* December 17, 1946.

CHAPTER XIII

The Dilemma of French Communism

THE COMMUNISTS found it much more difficult to support the solidarity of the Left on the wage and colonial issues than on the constitutional problem. Higher wages for the workers and the fate of the overseas territories were and have remained two difficult questions in postwar France. By 1946 the Communists, by insisting on political solidarity of the Left, were standing out against the tide of popular demands among the French working class and the native populations of the colonies. The emphasis of the Soviet Union on strengthening political cooperation between itself and France hampered the French Communists in working actively toward greater economic and social equality at home and throughout the French territories. This contradiction became more sharply defined as the other elements in the French coalition tended to postpone or ignore the problems of the workers and the overseas territories.

The French Communists in 1946, like the Bolsheviks in 1917, found a ready-made set of grievances to exploit for their own ends. However, unlike their Russian counterparts, the French Communists were not masters of their own destinies; more important, they were not acting in a revolutionary situation. The government was strong and commanded the allegiance of the police and the army. The international situation was, as the Communists themselves admitted, unfavorable to a revolutionary seizure of power. The result was reflected in the helplessness of the Party and its surrender to, rather than its conquest of, the difficulties which faced it.

The Communists and the Working Class

Soon after the end of hostilities the Party had been forced to acknowledge the growing seriousness of wage and labor problems in France. Yet its reaction to the crisis was deeply disappointing to the workers. Ever since the liberation the Communist leaders had maintained that the "policy of stepping up production rests on a deep feeling of the masses." [1] The moratorium on strikes was necessary and even desirable, given the objective circumstances. Monmousseau defended the Communist policy:

The strike is a redoubtable weapon when it answers a need, when it is used with deliberation, and when one knows how to make use of it. As on February 12, 1934, for example, or on August 19, 1944. But this is a weapon of the working class; the reaction can delegate its Trotskyite lackeys to wrench it away from the trade-union arsenal, to turn it against the workers, but [the reaction] will break its teeth on it. And we guard this weapon jealously, believe us, so that in case of need we can use it in the service of the country and of democracy.[2]

The Party thus put its great prestige and power within the labor movement at the service of the government. But it was doing this in the face of a runaway inflation which imposed great hardships on the poorer classes. The Communists had staked a great deal on their May, 1946, demand for a 25-percent wage increase. Theirs was a paradoxical position. They posed as the champions of the wage earners and at the same time as the only force capable of restraining the masses. The Party took up the demands of the workers only when the satisfaction of these demands was politically valuable to the Communists. It fought them when the opposite was true.

One example of the Communist strategy was the Paris printers' and photographers' strike, in January, 1946. The workers demanded higher wages. Since salaries and wages were fixed by the state, the matter was taken up by the Council of Ministers. The ministers unanimously refused an increase in wages. The CGT disavowed the strike, and the strikers went over to the anarcho-syndicalist opposition. In a radio broadcast the Communist Minister of Labor,

[1] Duclos, *Union des forces démocratiques,* p. 10.
[2] *La Vie Ouvrière,* March 28, 1946.

Croizat, accused the strikers of having worked for collaborationist journals. He argued that they were better paid than workers in metallurgy or than government employees and reproached them for having chosen an unfortunate moment—the time of De Gaulle's resignation—to paralyze the press.[3] L'Humanité tried to print the radio broadcast with editorial comment. The strikers censored the text, and the Communist daily appeared with blank spaces.[4] The Communists then resorted to distributing antistrike leaflets until the irate workers stopped them.[5]

Non-Communist militants protested the Party's ruthless actions. At the CGT congress in April, Frachon's general report was brought under heavy fire by J. Capocci, a leader of the former confédéré faction, who condemned as "deception" the Communist emphasis on increasing output and accepting the wage freeze. He attacked the Communist "colonization" of various unions as a step toward suppressing minority opinion in the CGT leadership. Finally, he rejected the basic notion of trade-union interference in politics. His own counterproject demanded a currency reform and salary increases tied to increased production. The protest was of no avail, because the Communists, having the votes, buried Capocci's proposals by a vote of more than seven to one.[6] Warned by this display of opposition, the Communist faction strengthened its hold on the Confederal Committee by adopting a new system to increase the representation of federations having a larger number of members.[7] The federations were, of course, Communist strongholds.

In the summer of 1946, while negotiations were under way with the Bidault government, the Party encouraged its militants to participate in CGT-organized demonstrations, but they were unable to prevent a series of spontaneous strikes that followed. A great strike of the postal union (PTT) broke out on July 30 soon spread throughout France.[8] The Communist-controlled bureau of the PTT had originally ordered a ten-hour protest strike, but it

[3] L'Année politique, 1946, p. 23.
[4] L'Humanité, February 1, 1946.
[5] Lefranc, Les Expériences, p. 173.
[6] Le Peuple, April 12, 13, 1946.
[7] L'Humanité, April 13, 1946.
[8] Ibid., July 26, 1946; Le Monde, July 30, 31, 1946.

proved far from easy to get the workers back on the job. The strikers defied their union executive bureau and established their own strike committee independent of the bureau. The Minister of Finance felt obliged to deal with this latter group, since it had the workers' support. Socialist deputies urged the government "to make contact with the new chiefs of the postal, telegraph, and telephone union," whereupon the Communists snapped back, "You will bear before the working class the responsibility of sowing dissension." [9] Duclos asserted that certain elements "want to exploit this strike for nonunion ends whose anti-Communist character appears even here." [10]

The dissidents in the postal union were part of the strong non-Communist minority that had resisted Communist colonization of the organization at the Limoges Congress in 1945.[11] By bringing their opposition into the open, they shook the internal unity of the CGT. The strike committee demanded the calling of an extraordinary congress of the PTT. The Socialists cheered this development and encouraged the idea of union autonomy.[12] The Communists protested that the Socialists were encouraging the "split in the working class." [13] At a meeting of the Comité Central National of the CGT, the split was along the same lines. Racamond's motion, jammed through the committee with vigorous support by Frachon, insisted that "all efforts to bypass the decisions of the regular organs can be profitable only to the enemies of the working class for their own reactionary ends." [14] The PTT insurgents refused to accept this verdict and accused the bureau of "multiplying its political maneuvers without regard to the interests of the postal workers." [15] After a running battle between the two factions, the active rebel minority ceded from the PTT.

In September the idea of monolithic trade-union unity was chal-

[9] Assemblée Nationale Constituante, *JO, Débats,* August 2, 1946, second session, p. 2975.
[10] *Ibid.,* p. 2977.
[11] *L'Année politique, 1946,* p. 216.
[12] See series of articles by Léon Blum in *Le Populaire,* beginning August 6, 1946.
[13] *L'Humanité,* August 6, 1946.
[14] *La Vie Ouvrière,* August 7, 1946.
[15] *Le Monde,* August 17, 1946.

lenged again by the Federation of Customs Officials. This time the strikers defied the orders of the Communist-controlled General Union of Officials to demand higher salaries. Once again the Socialists approved, and the Communists disapproved, this independent action. Duclos raged against the external political pressures which, he said, were being exerted on the Assembly at the culminating moment of its work. "They hope," he declared, "that we will be incapable of showing that democracy is a regime of order, a regime of tranquillity and of work. There are people who would perhaps like this country to fall into chaos, into disorder, and anarchy, to make the people desire a savior of France." [16] The Communists held fast again, isolating the strikers within the CGT and rejecting their demands in the government. The strike finally collapsed.

The wage crisis, like the constitutional crisis, showed that the great edifice of republican unity, tripartism, and Communist cooperation was being severely strained. The Party was subjected to great pressure from elements of the working class that were discontented with the government and the Communist wage policy. By going out on strike, these workers challenged the Communist control of the working class. On the other hand, non-Communists in the government encouraged the independent demonstrations of labor and gleefully reported strikes which challenged Communist leadership. However, they did not support the workers' specific demands. They were concerned solely with the political significance of the strikes. The Party could not be expected to maintain for long a policy which endangered its power base in the working class and was no longer appreciated in the government. The real tragedy of this situation was that the workers were being used as a political pawn by both sides. They were the mute victims of an international struggle which split France into two blocs.

The Colonial Question: Algeria

The colonial problem provided the third and perhaps most convincing proof of the growing inability of the French Communists to

[16] Assemblée Nationale Constituante, *JO, Débats,* September 20, 1946, p. 3884.

reconcile their presence in the government with the policy of that government. The Communist position on the colonial question in many ways ran parallel to their stand on the problems of the constitution and of wages.

One of the original five points of the Communist governmental program had been to complete the union of France and the overseas territories by satisfying the legitimate aspirations of the native populations. The Communists were concerned with increasing their electoral and Party strength in the French empire. In order to use that strength most profitably, they wanted to maintain the links between metropolitan France and the overseas territories. The native non-French Communists would gain ground through the support of the experienced, disciplined, and influential French Communist Party, a member of the government coalition. At the same time the increased Communist strength overseas would mean more support to the French Party through the votes of native deputies in the Assembly.

The Communists also regarded the empire as a vast source of economic wealth which could be exploited more efficiently to bolster the domestic economy and strengthen the independence of France. As Florimond Bonte explained to the Constituent Assembly, "France, guardian of the great interests of civilization and of a necessary balance in the eastern Mediterranean, may not without danger underestimate the importance of its role in the Mediterranean. It is and it ought to remain a great African power." Greater France had 110 million people and unlimited resources. "We need not feel crushed," he concluded, "by an inferiority complex which would oblige us to consider our country an appendage . . . of other states." [17]

To justify the preservation of a colonial system, the Communists resorted to an original variation on Stalin's interpretation of the nationality question. "Union of the colonial peoples with the people of France," said the Communists, offers two advantages. First, "the French nation wishes to install a real democracy by fighting the trusts which betrayed it at the same time that they pillaged the colonies." Secondly, "because the colonial territories are objects of

[17] Assemblée Consultative Provisoire, *JO, Débats*, November 21, 1944, p. 311.

powerful desires, they are not in a position to guarantee their own independence." Naturally, the argument continued, the Party supported the self-determination of peoples. Yet one must balance, paraphrasing the words of Stalin, "the right to separate against the usefulness of the separation." Consequently, "if the populations of Overseas France have the right to separate from the mother country, this separation at the present time would go against the interests of the population, for [the above] two reasons." [18] The Communist spokesman then drew an exact parallel between the Soviet post-revolutionary decision to retain non-Russian areas of the old empire and the postwar decision of the French to do the same.[19]

The Party therefore acted on the assumption that self-determination was not an absolute right. It could be justified only on the basis of mutual advantage for the colonial territory and for France.

As we have seen, Stalin's views on the future of the French empire as expressed at Teheran were very different from those which the French Communists supported in 1945. Soon after the end of the war, clear indications of this long-muted difference of opinion began to show up in the Soviet press.

The events of the last months in India, Syria, Egypt, Burma, the uprisings in the colonial possessions of Holland (Indonesia) and France (Indo-China) remind the world clearly enough that besides the governments of the great powers interested in the fate of the colonies, there are populations of many millions in these very colonies who are no less interested in the definition of their own future.

A Soviet commentator added that another new factor in the colonial question was "the participation of the USSR, a great and strong power [which] on the basis of principle and in full consistency stands for the right of all nations, large and small, to self-determina-

[18] Lozère, "La Question coloniale," *Cahiers du Communisme*, No. 6 (April, 1945), p. 74.
[19] *Ibid.*, p. 75. Stalin's article in *Pravda*, November 6–7, 1921, was quoted as applicable to the French colonial relationship. "These peripheral regions," Stalin had explained, "are, from the industrial and military point of view, less developed than central Russia (or not developed at all). This is why they are powerless to safeguard their independent existence without the military and economic aid of central Russia, just as the latter is not in a position to maintain its military and economic power without the aid of supplies, raw materials, and food products which the periphery furnishes to it."

tion, freedom, and independence." [20] Within a year Soviet demands for greater self-determination of the native populations in the French colonial areas had increased. As the colonial peoples resorted to direct action, the French Communist Party failed to influence either the French administration of overseas territories or the development and spread of indigenous liberation movements. The bankruptcy of the French Communists' colonial policy was reflected in the Levant, Algeria, and French Indo-China.

The Party's view of the events in Syria and Lebanon in 1945 was calculated on the Communist interpretation of French interests in the area. Pierre Hervé took the position that the most satisfactory solution in these troubled areas was to acknowledge Syrian and Lebanese independence. Once confidence was reestablished, the French could "obtain advantages in the cultural and economic spheres" through negotiation. Hervé was less concerned with the legitimate desires of the native peoples than with the assumed desire of the British and the Americans "to eliminate France from these territories." He rejected the idea of negotiating with Britain or the United States over strategic bases in the area, as this would mean "accepting our relative eviction and the Anglo-Saxon [sic] preeminence in these regions." Rather, "if bases are to be awarded to any nation, it is France which ought to have preeminence . . . but I think that in this area we can safeguard perfectly our necessary positions by giving proof of generosity . . . which is the only effective and realistic policy for the still weakened nation that we are." [21]

The Communists wanted to preserve as much French influence as possible in Syria and Lebanon, but they wished to avoid having to thank the "Anglo-Americans" for that position. In the summer of 1945 the French Communists still attacked "certain gestures" which "imperiled the traditional influence of France in the countries of the Levant." [22] However, the Soviet Union appeared unconcerned with the "traditional position of France" in the Levant:

[20] Korovin, "O mezhdunarodnoi opeke," Bol'shevik, No. 22 (November, 1945), pp. 39–40.
[21] Assemblée Nationale Constituante, JO, Débats, June 19, 1945, pp. 1146–47.
[22] Cahiers du Communisme, Nos. 8–9 (June, 1945), p. 79.

The efforts of the Arabs to release their countries from a state of dependence and to put an end to the various imperialist maneuvers that have impaired their national sovereignty and have artificially retarded their economic development have now taken concrete form in a struggle for the withdrawal of all foreign troops from the territories of Syria, Lebanon, and Egypt and for a revision of those treaties between the Arab countries and foreign states which palpably curtail Arab independence.[23]

More concretely, the Soviet Union supported the request of the Arab nations at the United Nations for the evacuation of foreign troops. "We must meet the demands," Andrei Vyshinskii asserted, "put forward by the governments of Syria and Lebanon. The demands are just and have the full support of the Soviet delegation. The Council must declare that there is no basis for the presence of these foreign troops on the soil of Syria and Lebanon." The Soviet spokesman condemned "as a violation of sovereignty" France's offer to evacuate its troops in return for guarantees of certain cultural, economic, and strategic concessions from Syria and Lebanon.[24]

In 1945 the fate of the French Empire hung in the balance. Soviet interests could be advanced by a Communist seizure of power in France or by successful "national liberation movements" directed against France. The state of flux which characterized so much of the world at this time tempted the Soviet leaders to keep open two lines of approach toward their goal of smashing the "imperialist grip" on the colonial territories.[25]

The French Communists regarded the colonial issue as a battleground for conflict between their own forces and those of the reactionaries, the latter in league with the West. They were convinced that Anglo-American intervention in French colonies was aided by French die-hards whose old-style colonialism merely excited native hostility to France. If any revolts which might follow could be suppressed only with Western aid, this would lead to greater dependence on the West and to the ultimate loss of French independence. On the other hand, it seems likely that the French Communists intended to maintain French influence in the colonial areas until they

[23] Serezhin, "Problemy arabskogo vostoka," Novoe Vremia, No. 3 (February 1, 1946), p. 12.
[24] Pravda, February 17, 1946.
[25] Interview with Pierre Hervé.

had attained their main goal, the taking of power in France. Fear of
the West and confidence in the Party's own destiny were equally
responsible for the "quasi-colonialist enthusiasm" of the French Communists down to 1947.

In the light of this interpretation, it is not surprising that the
Communists attributed native uprisings to Fascist plots and Vichy
remnants. When bloody riots broke out in the Constantine prefec-
ture of Algeria in May, 1945, the Communists denounced the local
French officials as high Vichy officials and extreme Rightist colo-
nials.[26] Fajon took exception to the government interpretation,
which condemned the nationalist movements. He attacked the
"handful of miserable laggards, traitors, and Fascists" who were
"resolved to provoke disorders which would array the Moham-
medans and the Europeans in two hostile blocs and which would
justify, according to them, the maintenance in Algeria of an anti-
democratic regime." [27] To strengthen French prestige and power in
the colonial areas, the Communists insisted on a broad program of
reform.

Fajon deplored the food shortage and the depressed state of
agriculture and industry in Algeria. He reiterated, "No one is more
convinced than we that the interest of the population of North
Africa lies in the union with the French people." [28] But he demanded a series of fundamental reforms to assure Algerian allegiance otherwise than by force.[29]

Ambroise Croizat was no less emphatic in his denunciation of
the reactionary elements in Tunisia who "carried on a policy which
is absolutely contrary to the interests of Tunisia as well as France." [30]
The joint electoral platform of the Délégation des Gauches for the
First Constituent Assembly, which the Communists helped draft,

---

[26] *L'Humanité,* May 7, 1945.
[27] Assemblée Nationale Constituante, *JO, Débats,* July 11, 1945, p. 1373.
[28] *Ibid.,* p. 1375.
[29] *Ibid.* The reforms were to (1) abolish the semifeudal agricultural system;
(2) lift the state of siege, to liberate all political prisoners and guarantee
democratic liberties to all Algerians; (3) end racial distinctions in salaries, pensions and social legislation; (4) eliminate literacy by immediate introduction
of an elementary school system.
[30] *Ibid.,* August 1, 1945, first session, p. 1718.

again stressed equality of rights, progressive liberation, and social reforms for colonial peoples.[31]

The results of the Communist bid for native votes were not immediately apparent. The Algerian delegation to the Constituent Assembly was largely made up of "tame" Arabs. The more radical groups had been decapitated by the arrest of their leaders in May, 1945, and the nationalists had declared a boycott of the elections. However, the Communists gained two seats, apparently through the support of nationalist voters who disregarded the boycott.[32] The Communists considered this a moderate success and tried to exploit it. In so doing, they miscalculated seriously.

Theoretically, the Communists agreed with the Algerian nationalists that a policy of assimilating the native population was a fraud. Yet they had welcomed the March 7, 1944, ordinance which broadened the Moslem electoral college and extended French citizenship to a small group of Moslems.[33] Obviously motivated by electoral considerations in supporting this essentially assimilationist decree, the Party did nothing to resolve the contradiction. For example, the two Algerian Communist deputies in Paris continued to attack the assimilationist policy on the floor of the Constituent Assembly.[34] The Party also came out strongly against the assimilationist policy as "contrary to the customs, history, and aspirations" of the Algerian people.[35] However, the Third Congress of the Algerian Communist Party (PCA), although reiterating its antipathy toward the assimilationist policy, supported an extension of the March 7 ordinance.[36]

The Communists' bid to enjoy the best of both worlds backfired. Their tactics appeared to strengthen the suspicion of the Moslem population that the Algerian Communist Party was essentially a French party whose policy was determined in Paris. In the election for the second Constituent Assembly the Algerian Communist Party

[31] *Cahiers du Communisme*, No. 12 (October-November, 1945), pp. 100–104.
[32] Julien, *L'Afrique du nord en marche*, p. 309.
[33] *Ibid.*, p. 298.
[34] See, for example, the speech of Amar Ouzegane, Assemblée Nationale Constituante, *JO, Débats*, February 26, 1946, p. 467.
[35] Barbe, "La Politique du parti et les thèses colonialistes," *Cahiers du Communisme*, No. 7 (July, 1946), p. 577.
[36] Julien, *L'Afrique du nord en marche*, p. 312.

was overwhelmed. André Marty claimed that the débâcle had been due to the Party's retreat from its stand against assimilation.[37] At his urging, an enlarged Central Committee of the Algerian Party rejected the electoral maneuver, called for a policy looking toward "*la nation Algérienne en formation,*" and reasserted the necessity of "federative links, freely decided by the people of France and the other peoples federated in the French Union." [38] Marty insisted on developing a program for an autonomous Algeria within the French Union, based on the assumption that

The national movement is . . . a progressive factor, in Algeria as in all the colonies. It is one of the essential forces of all real social improvement. On condition, of course, that the independence of the popular movement be preserved. That requires that the workers, the peasants, the intellectuals have the opportunity to organize freely in their own groups.[39]

In order to guarantee this "progressive orientation," Marty proposed, first, the immediate creation of an Algerian assembly and government to manage all internal affairs; second, the suppression of the post of governor-general and the colonial administration; third, the sending of a representative of the French Republic to collaborate with the Algerian government on military and foreign affairs. To fight for this program, the Party asked for the "formation of a broad National Algerian Democratic Front, with the people of France as an ally." [40]

Despite this emphasis on internal autonomy, Marty's concluding remarks to the Central Committee revealed that what he really envisaged for Algeria was the kind of relationship that existed between Kazakhstan and the USSR.[41] Perhaps we should define this as "national in spirit but assimilationist in content."

Though the Algerian Communists had been routed in the elections of June, 1946, the Algerian delegation in the Constituent Assembly brought added strength to the Left. The amnestied nationalist

[37] Marty, "La Question algérienne," *Cahiers du Communisme,* No. 8 (August, 1946), p. 680.
[38] *Ibid.,* p. 690.
[39] *Ibid.,* p. 686.
[40] *Ibid.,* pp. 691, 692.
[41] *Ibid.,* p. 697.

leaders, who had captured eleven of the thirteen Algerian seats, were committed to "a free Algeria joined to a free France." [42] Forming a tight group called "Friends of the Manifesto" under the leadership of Ferhat Abbas, they insisted upon being assigned seats next to the Communists. This group held the balance of power between Left and Right in the new Assembly. If their eleven votes were cast with the Communists and Socialists, the Left would have 293 votes, exactly one half of the Assembly. In fact, so important was the Algerian group that its leader, Ferhat Abbas, was conceded a seat on the constitutional commission, where once again his vote could control the balance. [43] As a result of Abbas's strong position, the second constitutional commission accepted his draft for the government of the overseas territories, now called the French Union. The project took as its base the Communist-Socialist idea of "progressive federalism"—i.e., a union to be built up gradually from the bottom. As we have seen it was only through the personal intervention of Bidault that the Left was forced to back down on this issue.

On other important issues the Communists also benefited from the votes of the Friends of the Manifesto, even with the help of these deputies a final effort of the MRP and the Right wing to introduce freedom of instruction or equality of status between state and church schools was barely defeated by a vote of 274 to 272. [44]

The Communists sealed their alliance with the Abbas group when the now embittered native leader spoke for the last time to the Assembly. A near-riot broke out as the Algerian leader assailed France's inability to protect its colonies. The Communists alone defended Abbas, who was verbally and physically besieged by hotheads from the Right and the Center. [45] In the elections to the National Assembly in October, 1946, the Communists maintained their working alliance with Abbas. The return to the Algerian scene of the ultra-nationalist Hadj Messali blocked the plan for a com-

[42] Wright, *The Reshaping of French Democracy*, p. 189.
[43] *Ibid.*, pp. 189–91, 192.
[44] *Ibid.*, pp. 213–15.
[45] Assemblée Nationale Constituante, *JO, Débats*, September 28, 1946, second session, pp. 4230–31. For a more colorful rendering see Wright, *The Reshaping of French Democracy*, p. 215.

mon electoral front which would have included the Communists. Abbas deserted his rival Messali and supported the Algerian Communists, who were thereby able to secure two seats in the Assembly.[46]

While the Communists were moving closer to the Arab position on North Africa, the government was under increasing pressure from the European *colons* to resist the native demands. Though the Socialists agreed with the Communists, they were, as later events would show, more willing to compromise. On the Algerian question there was evidence that the Communists would eventually have to make a choice between further compromising to hold tripartism together and leaving the government. This problem, always present, was greatly aggravated with the passage of every postwar month.

The Colonial Question: Indo-China

In early 1945 the Communist attitude toward Indo-China coincided with that of the provisional government. The Party underlined "the urgent necessity for the provisional government to proclaim solemnly that the highly developed populations of Indo-China shall benefit from substantial democratic liberties" in order to strengthen the fight against the Japanese.[47] The Communists believed their demands had been met by the government declaration of March 23, 1945, which defined Viet-Nam as "a free state, with its own government, parliament, army, and finances" which was "part of the Indo-Chinese Federation and the French Union." [48] A sign of coming difficulty for the French Communists was the lack of enthusiasm shown in the USSR for the March declaration. Moscow considered it an offer of "artificial autonomy." [49]

---

[46] Julien, *L'Afrique du nord en marche,* p. 315.

[47] *Cahiers du Communisme,* No. 6 (April, 1945), p. 93.

[48] Services Français d'Information, *Notes Documentaires et Etudes,* No. 548 (February 15, 1947), Série France d'outre-mer, "Documents relatifs aux problèmes indochinois, accords entre la France et le Viet-Nam," XIX, 4.

[49] Guber, "Chto proiskhodit v Indonezii i Indokitae?" *Novoe Vremia,* No. 11 (November 1, 1945), p. 13. The Soviet press did not devote much space to the Indo-Chinese problem. However, in a book published after the exclusion of the French Communists from the government, a Soviet commentator accused France of having "intended fully to conserve its sovereignty over Indo-China. Such a decision could not satisfy in any measure the aspira-

More serious in the short run for the French Communists was the decision taken in March, 1945 by the Central Committee of the Indo-Chinese Communist Party to unleash a "general insurrection" against the Japanese aimed at creating a "Popular Revolutionary Committee of Viet-Nam which will take the form of a provisional revolutionary government of Viet-Nam." "French imperialism, having lost its sovereignty over Indo-China, is not for the present time our immediate enemy," the resolution continued, "though we must remain on guard against the machinations of the Gaullists who wish to reestablish French domination in Indo-China." With the collapse of Japanese resistance in the Far East, the Indo-Chinese Communists moved rapidly "to arouse the popular masses in order to disarm the Japanese before the arrival of the Allies in Indo-China, to wrench power away from the Japanese and their phantom lackeys and finally, in proportion to their control, to greet the Allies who will come to disarm the Japanese troops stationed in Indo-China." Subsequently, the rapid disintegration of all authority in the colony encouraged the Communists on the spot to declare that "a very favorable opportunity to gain independence is at hand. . . . The goal of our struggle at the present time is to win complete independence." [50]

The debarkation of strong French units in Saigon and the evacuation of the northern part of the country by the Kuomintang armies prompted some of the Communist leaders to open secret negotiations with the French and then to sign the preliminary agreement of March 6 which recognized the formula of "a free state in the Indo-Chinese Federation and the French Union." Justifying this compromise to the aroused Viet-Minh, Vo Nguyen Giap declared that the unfavorable international situation and the hopeless prospects for a fighting victory over the French made the agreement necessary. But, he added, the struggle for complete independence would be renewed with success under the conditions of internal

tions of the Indo-Chinese people [who are] moving rapidly toward achievement of independent for their country. Later events fully underlined this." Vasileva, *Indo-Kitai*, p. 253. It appears likely that the Soviets were skeptical of attempts to hold Indo-China within the French Union. Sufficient evidence is lacking to warrant a more conclusive judgment.

[50] Fourniau, "La Révolution d'août 1945 au Viet-Nam," *Cahiers du Communisme*, No. 9 (September, 1961), pp. 1426–27, 1431.

autonomy granted by the agreement. Ho Chi Minh then urged his followers to accept the compromise which would guarantee the goals they all cherished by means of negotiations over the next five years.[51]

In their conversations with various Indo-Chinese delegations to Paris during the spring of 1946 the French Communists strongly supported the maintenance of some ties between Indo-China and France. The head of the Cochin Chinese delegation was so surprised by the attitude of the Communists that he declared,

But it is M. Thorez, the first [political figure] with whom I could make contact, who expressed to me the most remarkable opinion: The Vice-Premier has affirmed to me that the Communist Party under no circumstances wished to be considered as the eventual liquidator of the French position in Indo-China and that he ardently wished to see the French flag fly over all corners of the French Union.[52]

However, it appears that the French Communists were acting on a different set of assumptions than was Ho about the future of Indo-China. To them the prospect of their victory in France seemed much more likely to bring the revolution to the former colony than a Viet-Minh victory on the spot. Therefore, when in June, 1946 Ho Chi Minh arrived in Paris to begin negotiations for a permanent settlement, the Party took an active interest in the negotiations, but refrained from supporting Ho right down the line. According to one report, the French Communists "tended to advise the Viet-Namese to yield to the French position on various issues." [53] There is some evidence that Ho believed in, or was persuaded to adopt, a moderate attitude in his relations with the French government.[54]

Ho's public statements at home and abroad concerning French–

[51] Devillers, Philippe. *Histoire du Viet-Nam de 1940 à 1952.* Paris, 1952, p. 231.

[52] *Paris-Saigon,* Saigon, No. 19 (May 29, 1946), as cited in Fall, "Tribulations of a Party Line," *Foreign Affairs,* XXXIII, No. 3 (April, 1955), 500.

[53] Hammer, *The Struggle for Indochina,* p. 170. The opinion of a non-Communist Viet-Namese delegate to the Fontainebleau Conference in a conversation with the author.

[54] See Sainteny, *Histoire d'une paix manquée,* pp. 186, 195, 209, 213, and 218, for a reproduction of a telegram, September 2, 1946, which read: "From President Ho Chi Minh to the Viet-Nam at Hanoi. I know that the commemoration of independence day is now taking place in the country. I want the ceremonies to be stripped of all character inimical to France, thus permitting its representative to be associated with it."

Viet-Namese relations were conciliatory in tone. *L'Humanité* quoted with approval the words of Ho at a Paris press conference on July 13, 1946. The Viet Minh leader,

insisting on "the sincere and lasting friendship" which should unite our two countries, emphasized that the statute of Viet-Nam in the French Union ought to conform to the right of self-determination of peoples.

According to President Ho Chi Minh, France and Viet-Nam can be associated on the economic as well as the cultural level.[55]

Even after the failure of the Fontainebleau talks Ho assured the French of his "firm will to conclude partial accords on the spot with the representatives of the French authorities . . . and to prove our good will and cooperation with France.[56]

When the negotiations between Ho and the French broke down in August, 1946, the Communists accused the government representative, Max André, of being a tool of colonial financial interests and of thereby wrecking the conference.[57] *L'Humanité* warned of the necessity for concluding an agreement because "British imperialism and American imperialism are stalking the prey." The Party also attacked the subsequent activities of French officials in Indo-China and called the high commissioner, Admiral Thierry d'Argenlieu, "a veritable dictator."[58]

Yet, lest anyone think the Party line had changed, André Marty reviewed Communist policy on colonial areas. He indicated that the Communists "stood for the right of self-determination in principle." However, he added,

that does not mean to say that they are always and everywhere for the right of separation. The question of the recognition of the right of separation should not be confused with the usefulness of separation in such-and-such a condition.

[55] *L'Humanité*, July 13, 1946. He added that French interests would be safeguarded and French technicians would be favored in the development of the national economy.

[56] *Le Monde*, September 14, 1946.

[57] *L'Humanité*, August 2, 1946. Actually, a *modus vivendi* was signed on September 14, but it was mainly a recognition by both sides of the *status quo*. For the document, see Services Français d'Information, *Notes, Documentaires et Etudes*, February 15, 1946, pp. 7–8.

[58] *Ibid.*, August 15, 1946.

Only an agreement between Viet-Nam and France would preserve in Indo-China [French] industrial, commercial, and intellectual positions." [59]

The Communists not only failed to launch a propaganda campaign in favor of Viet-Nam, but were reticent about discussing the matter at all. Some native Communists in Indo-China resented this attitude. One of them told an American observer that the French Communists were "Frenchmen and colonialists first and Communists after." [60] As tension grew in Saigon, the local French Communist group did not support the demands of its Annamite comrades. Rather, it appealed to the native Communists

to be sure before they acted too rashly that their struggle "meets the requirements of Soviet policy." It warned that any "premature adventures" in Annamite independence "might not be in line with Soviet perspectives." These perspectives might well include France as a firm ally of the USSR in Europe, in which case the Annamite independence movement would be an embarrassment. Therefore, it urged upon the Annamite comrades a policy of "patience." It advised them in particular to wait for the results of the French elections coming up the following month, October, when additional Communist strength might assure the Annamites a better settlement. In the meantime it boldly proposed that an emissary be sent to contact not only the French Communist Party, but also the Russians, in order "to acquaint yourselves with the perspectives of coming events." [61]

So far as this goes, it is self-explanatory. In addition, it must be remembered that the French Communists, themselves in no position to control events, were urging a militant group of comrades, in a highly explosive situation, to exercise self-restraint. The French Communists chose to invoke the needs of Soviet policy and French promises of a better settlement in the future, rather than admit that a Communist insurrection in Indo-China at any time would be embarrassing to the Party's policy of participating in the French government. Ignoring these appeals, the more aggressive Viet-Minh leaders organized a series of raids to smash the francophile non-

[59] *Ibid.*, August 18–19, 1946; emphasis in the original.
[60] Isaacs, *No Peace for Asia*, p. 173.
[61] *Ibid.*, pp. 173–74. The author was handed this leaflet dated September 25, 1946, and took notes from it, which he later expanded.

Communist nationalist groups and began a military build-up to engage the French army in open fighting.[62]

The French Communists were desperately trying to walk the tight-rope of conciliation in a situation which tended to feed the two extreme positions. The outbreak of serious fighting in November and December, 1946, placed the Communists in an almost untenable position. As part of the government, they were obligated to come to the defense of French citizens. On the other hand, they were committed to support the aspirations of colonial peoples. Their response to the challenge was to temporize vigorously.

To meet the emergency of November, Bidault called a meeting of the interministerial committee for Indo-China. Charles Tillon, the only Communist member, was missing. The committee decided to take military precautions. The Communist ministers demanded that the government send directly to Ho Chi Minh a telegram of sympathy over the outbreak of fighting. A threat by the UDSR to open a debate on Indo-China forced the chastened Communists to withdraw their proposal.[63] Meanwhile in their press the Communists practically ignored the incident.[64]

Though the struggle had become very serious by December, the Party still tended to minimize the affair. It accused the Right of provocation and of dividing the French people for its own political purposes.[65] The USSR also denounced the "generals and admirals whose activities are reminiscent . . . of the colonial wars," and it accused the French Right of seeking to exploit the situation in order to restore the former colonial rule backed by the French armed forces.[66] The French Communists warned that native extremists were reproaching Ho Chi Minh for his French sympathies. The Party implied that if France did not support Ho, his rivals, by virtue of their excesses, would provoke Sino-American intervention.

[62] Lancaster, *The Emancipation of French Indochina*, pp. 166–67.

[63] *L'Année politique, 1946*, p. 289.

[64] *L'Humanité*, November 23, 1946, carried a very short article on page 3 concerning the incident. After the election returns were in, the Communist daily gave more details, but scarcely made an issue of the fighting. See, for example, *ibid.*, November 27, 1946.

[65] *Ibid.*, December 20, 1946.

[66] P. Efimov, "K sformirovaniiu novogo pravitel'stva vo Frantsii," [Concerning the Formation of the New Government in France], *Pravda*, December 23, 1946.

The Communists urged that negotiations be continued in order to keep the affair "purely French." [67] In January, 1947, they finally opened a great campaign to stop a war which they knew would endanger their entire position.

By the end of 1946 the French Communists were in serious difficulties. Their position in the government was no longer secure. The Party had failed either to unite the Left under its control or to revolutionize the political institutions of postwar France. The constitution was a compromise which had barely been accepted by a skeptical French nation. The Party had failed to have Thorez elected premier; it had been unable to secure even one of the key ministries, although its participation in the government had been essential to France's economic reconstruction. The decision of the Socialists not to unite with the Communists had been influenced in part by the growing estrangement of East and West. Politically, the French Communists had attained neither their short-range goal of uniting the Left and securing control of important posts in the government, nor their long-range goal of modifying French foreign policy and setting the stage for a seizure of power from within the government. In fact, a non-Communist government coalition was rapidly taking shape within the National Assembly.

Though the Communists had fought the battle of production well, they had not succeeded in enabling France to rebuild its economy without aid from the United States. Though they had held the workers in check, endorsed only one wage increase, and prevented all strikes but wildcat ones, they did not receive what they considered was their just reward in terms of ministerial posts, and the workers were becoming more restive. Thus, in the economic field the Communists had done much for France, but they were unable to reap the political fruits of their labor.

The Communists conducted a moderate colonial policy, one which aimed at keeping the French Union intact and at the same time extending new rights to the colonial peoples. Yet at home they were blocked by the more conservative elements, and abroad they were outdistanced by more radical Communists. The role of the Soviet Union in encouraging the aspirations of the nationalists made

[67] *L'Humanité*, December 25, 26, 1946.

the Communist task impossibly difficult. In the colonial field, as in the political and economic fields, the dilemma of whether to remain in the government was sharply posed. "Unity of action" was bringing fewer and fewer advantages to the Communists.

Until the Indo-Chinese crisis exploded in all its fury, the Communists remained in an outwardly strong position within the government. The Socialists were unwilling to break with them because it was not yet necessary for them to choose between East and West. In fact, the SFIO continued to believe that a complete split with the Communists must be avoided. Possibly the Communists could even have won some concessions in 1946, such as the control of a key ministry, if they had then threatened to leave the government. Even if their collective resignation had been accepted by the Socialists and the MRP, the Party would, as a result, have gone into opposition of its own accord instead of being expelled, and it would doubtless have carried with it substantial support from many non-Communist Leftist elements. If the Communists had chosen to leave the government in 1946 on a purely domestic issue, they might have split the Socialists or at least have thrown discredit on the Socialist leaders. The latter could not have appealed effectively to their rank and file to hold firm against the Communists under the old slogan of "the Republic in danger," as they did when the break finally came in the spring of 1947.

Why did the Communists not try to exploit their strength before it was too late? For one thing, they feared the return of the "reaction," possibly with General de Gaulle at its head. In foreign affairs the return of the "reaction" meant to the Communists a rupture between France and the Soviet Union and the creation of a Western bloc. In domestic affairs it meant personal dictatorship, persecution of the Communists, and a resurgence of Vichyite elements. The Communists had also used their position in the government to infiltrate the army and the bureaucracy. They had tried to ride into power on the basis of their electoral victories and fusion with the Socialists. It was difficult for them to understand that this path to power was now blocked. The fear of the "reaction" and the hope of power reduced them to a state of political paralysis which immobilized the Party as crisis after crisis shook its position.

What was Moscow's attitude toward the French Communist decision to remain in the government? The Soviet leaders have never criticized the French Communists for this particular policy. At the founding session of the Cominform in October, 1947, A. A. Zhdanov berated the French Party for lack of initiative in fighting the Marshall Plan, but made no mention of its recent participation in the government. The implication is that Moscow favored Communist presence in the government and its support of "unity of action" until the beginning of the Marshall Plan, which required more active countermeasures. Though the Soviet leaders had expressed doubts over the immediate possibility of setting up a "people's democracy" in France, it is likely that they saw no harm in supporting the French Communists' attempts to move along a parliamentary path toward that goal. In the short run, at least, the Soviet Union may have hoped to benefit from the activities of the Communist ministers. Whether the decision to endorse a coalition government in France was made in Moscow or in Paris, the result was that the Communists frittered away their last few months in political office with what appears in retrospect a remarkable lack of initiative and imagination.

CHAPTER XIV

The Last Gamble

DURING 1947 a series of dramatic events was to demonstrate conclusively that the Soviet Union had abandoned its policy of limited cooperation with the Western powers. The stalemate at the Moscow Conference in April, the Soviet rejection of the Marshall Plan in June, the proclaiming of the Cominform in October, 1947, were so many hammer blows against the fragile edifice of East-West collaboration. Under cover of the policy of wartime cooperation with the capitalist powers the Soviet Union had attained two of its short-term aims—the defeat of Nazi Germany and the reshaping of Eastern Europe in the Soviet image. But the Communist revolution had not spread to any area in Europe beyond the limit reached by the Soviet occupation forces. In its negotiations with the West, Moscow had failed to advance its aims and was violently abusing the Western powers for the diplomatic stalemate. Despite its avowed revolutionary aims for Europe, was the USSR willing to compromise on some issues in order to maintain the illusion of cooperation with the Western democracies? Was there any further advantage for Moscow in avoiding a break with the West at this time? The answers to these questions were of great importance to the French Communists because there was little chance that the French Communist Party could pursue a policy of "unity of action" and at the same time support an intransigent Soviet policy.

The Soviet Union as "Defender of Europe"

The chief obstacle to the achievement of Soviet aims in postwar Europe was the influence of the United States and Great Britain, but

more especially the United States, on the Continent. The Western
powers continually protested against Soviet methods in Eastern
Europe and, in the opinion of the Soviet leaders, harbored dangerous *émigré* groups, potential nuclei of counterrevolutionary anti-
Soviet forces. Although neither the United States nor the British
government had worked out a long-range policy for strengthening
Western Europe against communism, the Soviet Union continued
to regard any evidence of Anglo-American cooperation as evidence
of an anti-Soviet Western bloc. Therefore, through its propaganda
the Soviet Union strove to discredit the United States and Great
Britain in the eyes of the rest of Europe and through negotiation it
sought to exclude the West from Central Europe by bringing about
a unification of Germany on Soviet terms.

A lengthy article in *Pravda* by Otto Kuusinen in February, 1947,
was typical of the broadside attack by Soviet propagandists against
the Western powers. The expansionist tendencies of the Anglo-
Saxon countries were "directed against the sovereignty of the
countries on the European Continent." The Western powers had
encroached on the sovereignty of the East European governments,
had launched an offensive against the economic independence of
all European countries, and planned to establish either a "Western
bloc" or a United States of Europe in order to limit the sovereignty
of the West European states. Reactionary circles in the Anglo-
American governments had tried to interfere in the internal affairs
of the democratic governments of Eastern Europe, "not only the
former German satellites, but allies like Poland and Yugoslavia."
As examples Kuusinen cited the Anglo-American attempt to dictate
the conditions of elections and to supervise voting procedures. He
condemned the British for using the reserves of Polish gold as a
means of blackmailing Warsaw into holding "unfettered elections."
These tactics were aimed at encouraging the local "reactionary opposition, acting in the interests of the foreign imperialistic circles
in the name of the national interests of the country." [1]

"As is well known, the Americans are working out a broad plan,"

---

[1] O. Kuusinen, "O pretendentakh na opeku nad narodami Evropy" [Con-
cerning the Claimants to Guardianship of the European Nations], *Pravda*,
February 19, 1947.

Kuusinen charged, "for the creation of a world trade and currency system" in order to take "complete control of the economies of a majority of other countries." This plan would be facilitated by the need of war-ruined countries for financial credits; these could be provided by American banks and capital, which, having been spared the ravages of war, had been able to conserve "a surplus of free liquid capital." The banks could exploit these credits to force open the gates for the sale of American goods and for investment of American capital in the enterprises in which they were interested. The American tactic of breaking down trade barriers of other countries, Kuusinen claimed, proved how much more powerful American monopoly capital was than the British had been in the nineteenth century.[2]

Kuusinen was especially concerned with developments in France. He pointed out that the Franco-American trade agreement of May 28, 1946, created free and open competition in the French markets, "but, as is well known, in such competition it is always the big capitalists who win out." By returning the foreign trade of France to private hands, Kuusinen affirmed, the government

not only makes it difficult to solve the problems of nationalizing the French trusts and concerns but [endangers] the very success of a planned policy for the reconstruction and rehabilitation of the French economy. Even the interests of defense of the country, which under present conditions is closely linked . . . with the development of many important branches of the industry, remain unguarded from the caprices of an unregulated international market or, still worse, become dependent on the will of the world champion of such competition [which is] capable of putting into circulation the heaviest money bags.

Such an intolerable situation resulted, according to Kuusinen, in America's controlling France with dollars and wheat and in England's blackmailing France with Ruhr coal. He went on to charge that "at the same time the United States, by its cruel measures of limiting American food supplies to Europe, holds many European people on hunger rations in the literal sense of that word," and "such a cruel attitude of the Anglo-Saxon [sic] powers toward the peoples of continental Europe is dictated by political

[2] Ibid.

calculations arising from the fact that hungry nations are more pliant than satisfied ones." [3]

In his discussion of countries favoring a Western bloc Kuusinen emphasized that Great Britain was "the center of such agitation." He rejected protestations from the West that the bloc was peace-loving. "It is too evident," he commented, "that the English imperialists, trying to organize enthusiastically a special bloc of West European countries, wish to direct it against Eastern Europe and, in particular, against the Soviet Union . . . West Europeans know that the real plan is to rob them of their sovereignty." Kuusinen maintained that the French remembered Churchill's offer to fuse Great Britain and France in 1940 and that the Belgians recalled the British interference in their affairs in the fall of 1944. These were only two examples, added Kuusinen, of what a Western bloc would mean for the peoples of Europe.

As for "the United States of Europe," it too would be directed against the "democratic East." A broader concept than that held by the Western bloc, according to Kuusinen, would be the United States of Europe, which would include Germany, but also would involve limitations of sovereignty of West European countries. The European countries were interested, he insisted, in developing economic, cultural, and political cooperation among themselves and with non-European nations, but they wish to do so without losing their sovereignty. "The model for these relations is to be found," he significantly added, "in the treaties of friendship, mutual aid, and postwar cooperation concluded by the Soviet Union with Czecho-slovakia, Poland, and Yugoslavia." These agreements had rallied the democratic forces of Europe, whereas, Kuusinen concluded, "a sympathetic response to [Anglo-American] plans could be found only in the most reactionary circles of European countries, and in par-ticular in the ruling circles of Fascist Spain, Portugal, and Mon-archo-Fascist Greece." Being afraid of their peoples, such ruling groups had to rely on foreign imperialist circles and were "ready to buy this support at the price of . . . the independence of their

[3] *Ibid.* The same analysis was made of American activities in Italy, Denmark, Holland, and Belgium.

countries." [4] In this and similar denunciations the Soviet press laid down the new role of the Soviet Union as the defender of the sovereignty of the European states against the "predatory aims of the American imperialists."

Germany Remains the Basic Problem

Although the USSR continued to pay much attention to the question of American intervention in Europe, the Soviet press indicated that the German problem stood out as the main short-range consideration in the minds of the Soviet leaders. During the three months before the opening of the Foreign Ministers' Conference in Moscow the Soviet press carried on a drumfire of criticism against the activities of the Western powers in Germany on such matters as denazification and demilitarization, the merger of the British and American zones, and the refusal to pay reparations.

The Soviet Union charged that the three Western powers had not carried out the Potsdam agreements. Moscow was especially critical of the bizonal agreement between the United States and Great Britain.

At the base of this agreement is the long-term credit to German industry from the English and American banks and the new, powerful, mainly American capitalists in Germany. Thus, it is not strange that the questions of carrying out the denazification and the demilitarization of Germany, of guaranteeing the payment of reparations, as well as the problem of setting up a democratic structure in Germany, have not received attention from the Anglo-American occupation authorities.[5]

What did the Soviet Union mean by demilitarization and denazification of Germany? How did the Soviet leaders plan to democratize the fallen enemy? Their plans were illustrated by the role of the Soviet High Command in bringing about the fusion of the

[4] *Ibid.*

[5] "Mezhdunarodnoe obozrenie" [The International Review], *Pravda,* January 12, 1947. See also Iu. Korol'kov, "O denatsifikatsii v zapadnykh zonakh okkupatsii Germanii" [About the de-Nazification in the Western Occupation Zones of Germany], *ibid.,* March 30, 1947, and Iu. Zhukov, "O demilitarizatsii Germanii" [Concerning the Demilitarization of Germany], *ibid.,* March 13, 1947.

German Communist Party and the Socialist Party in the East Zone.

> The creation of a single party of the working class of Germany became possible only thanks to the great victory of the Soviet Army. . . . The wise Stalinist policy of the USSR in the German question created the conditions in which the vanguard of the German working class could achieve the creation of a single workers' party.

Despite this fusion under pressure, "there was not yet actual ideological unity" due to the survival of opportunist elements within the party. Therefore, "in its struggle to turn the Socialist Unity Party into a party of the new type, the revolutionary vanguard elements of the party were guided by the great example of the Bolshevik Party." [6]

The Soviet High Command and its ward, the Socialist Unity Party, then undertook a massive economic reconstruction of East Germany under the watchwords "demilitarization and denazification." According to Moscow, "of enormous significance for the business of democratizing the East Zone . . . was the sequestration of war industries owned by criminals and important Fascists and the nationalization of these industries." This meant that by 1948 40 percent of the industrial capacity of the East Zone had been nationalized. A sweeping purge of the industrial administration brought in former workers to occupy almost 40 percent of the directorships of German industry. Under a Soviet-sponsored agrarian reform all estates of over 100 hectares were confiscated and distributed to "poor peasants." This made possible, in turn, the formation of a peasants' party which "followed the policy of strengthening the union between the peasants and the working class . . . to democratize the German countryside." These policies were supplemented by Sovietization of the press and education, and by unification of the trade unions on the Soviet model.[7] Clearly, in Moscow's opinion "denazification and demilitarization" meant Sovietization. When the Western powers refused to accept the Soviet views on "denazification and demilitarization," Moscow accused

---

[6] Mel'nikov, *Bor'ba*, pp. 71–72.
[7] *Ibid.*, pp. 51–52, 61, 65, 77.

them of using "the powerful industrial resources of West Germany in the interests of Anglo-American capital." [8]

During the Moscow conference in March the Soviet press reflected the opposition of the Soviet leaders to a partition of Germany between East and West and displayed an even stronger aversion to the unity of Germany on any terms but its own. The French-sponsored plan of German federalism was severely criticized.[9]

The Soviet leaders were, however, unwilling to negotiate on the basis of their demands for the "democratic reconstruction of Germany"; they simply demanded that the Western powers accept them. This was clearly revealed even before the conference by the refusal of the USSR to bargain with France over the future of Germany. Molotov tried to lead the French to believe that concessions to the Soviet point of view might be recompensed. In November, 1946, he had told Couve de Murville that, although the Soviet Union was opposed to treating separately the different aspects of the German settlement, this position "could be revised if France showed itself ready to support the Soviet Union in its demands for reparations."

When French Ambassador Catroux tried to pin Molotov down on an agreement which would involve French endorsement of the Soviet reparations demands in return for Soviet support of the French plan for the Saar, the Soviet Foreign Minister balked. He stated that the Americans had changed their position on the reparations question (which was not true), and he implied that French help in the matter was no longer very important. Catroux then proposed a bargain on the basis of French support of the Oder-Neisse line as the permanent frontier between Germany and Poland in return for Soviet endorsement of the Saar plan. Molotov replied that Bidault had already accepted the delimitation of the western frontier of Poland; therefore, the French had nothing new to offer on this question.[10]

[8] B. Leont'ev, "Politicheskoe i ekonomicheskoe razchlenenie Germanii" [The Political and Economic Dismemberment of Germany], *Pravda*, January 29, 1947.

[9] A. Leont'ev, "K voprosu o gosudarstvennom ustroistve poslevoennoi Germanii" [From the Question of the Organization of Postwar Germany], *ibid.*, March 31, 1947.

[10] Catroux, *J'ai vu tomber le rideau de fer*, pp. 211, 216, 218.

The Soviet Union not only refused to negotiate seriously with France, but was increasingly suspicious of the motives of the French government. At this time a serious blunder on the part of the French further irritated the Soviet leaders. In January, 1947, Léon Blum, visiting London in his capacity as premier and foreign minister, cabled Catroux that his discussions with the British would be solely of an economic nature and that the Soviet leaders should be informed of this fact. Several days after Catroux had given these assurances to Stalin and Molotov, the conclusion of an Anglo-French alliance was announced! It is not surprising that Molotov was extremely skeptical of Catroux's explanation that the political agreement was entirely unexpected.[11] Although the incident did not have any direct bearing on the refusal of the Soviet leaders to negotiate, it can only have reinforced their view of the French Socialists as "servants" of a Western bloc.

The Soviet decisions on the German problem determined in advance the disastrous outcome of the Moscow Conference and the complete break between the USSR and France over the issue of Central Europe. Throughout the conference Molotov insisted especially on settling the reparations question; if the Soviet Union received satisfaction on this point, the solution of other problems would be "greatly facilitated." If the Soviet view were rejected, Molotov indicated, then "nothing could be decided." [12]

According to Molotov, the reparations problem was closely linked with that of Germany's economic unity, and therefore, "the Soviet government is fully prepared to help promote Germany's economic unity and the elimination of interzonal barriers of any sort." The Soviet Union proposed to establish central German administrative departments for industry, finance, and other areas of economic importance in order to raise the level of German industry to ten or twelve million tons of steel; to increase German exports; to confiscate cartels; and, most important, to rescind the agreement for the economic fusion of the British and American zones and place the Ruhr under four-power control. These steps, Molotov indicated, would permit Germany to pay reparations of ten billion

[11] *Ibid.*, pp. 214, 215.
[12] *Ibid.*, p. 231.

dollars to the Soviet Union over a period of twenty years. To guarantee German payment, Molotov proposed the creation of a provisional political organization which would "assume responsibility for the fulfillment of Germany's obligations to the Allied states," and he was very insistent that the central German government have enough authority to ensure the payment of reparations.[13]

Though the Soviet Union placed great emphasis on the economic importance of reparations, it also intended to use this commitment as a political weapon. Moscow would have limitless possibilities for bringing pressure to bear upon a centralized German government saddled with a twenty-year, ten-billion-dollar debt to the USSR. Acceptance of these provisions, combined with a Soviet veto over the production of the Ruhr, would ensure Soviet domination of the German economy and ultimately of the German government.

Appealing to the French to support him, Molotov remarked that the Soviet Union "understands the feelings of the French, who demand compensation for the losses caused by the occupation and who insist that German coal be delivered to France for the rehabilitation of its economy. We consider that this is a legitimate demand of France which can be satisfied through reparations." [14]

The French were willing to support the Soviet demands for reparations out of current production despite Anglo-American opposition, and after some hesitation the French also agreed to support an increase in German steel production to ten million tons.[15] However, they were unyielding on the disposition of the Ruhr and the Rhineland. Bidault proposed a special statute for the Ruhr; mines and furnaces would be placed under United Nations control, with actual management of industry in the hands of the Big Four, Belgium, The Netherlands, and Luxembourg. According to Bidault, the Rhineland must be separated, politically and economically, from Germany. It should enjoy internal autonomy, but should be permanently occupied. Bidault wanted the Saar to be attached economically to France.[16]

When the United States and Great Britain again rejected the

[13] *Pravda*, March 18, April 3, 1947.
[14] *Ibid.*, April 1, 1947.
[15] Catroux, *J'ai vu tomber le rideau de fer*, pp. 232–33.
[16] *L'Année politique*, 1947, p. 74.

Soviet proposals on the Ruhr and on reparations, the French government faced a serious problem. Having failed to secure a general settlement through its policy of compromising between East and West, France could only hope for an agreement on the Saar and for additional deliveries of much-needed coal from the Ruhr. A partial settlement of the German problem which involved only the Western powers and dealt only with these two issues posed a momentous choice for the French government. Already relying on the good will of the West for its economic survival, France would become even more dependent on London and Washington once it had negotiated an agreement on Germany which excluded the USSR. In other words, France would have to abandon its persistent attempt to be a mediator between East and West, and its diplomacy would lose what measure of independence it still had. A dispute with the Soviet Union on this matter would also have repercussions on the domestic scene, perhaps endangering the government coalition. The French Communists could scarcely endorse the exclusion of the USSR from the settlement of such a vital issue. The resignation of the Communists could in turn cause great internal difficulties, followed by large-scale, violent labor disturbances and the division of France into two warring camps.

Balancing the disadvantages of a partial German settlement were several important advantages. France needed German coal quickly, and there was no sign that a general settlement of the German problem was in sight. French concessions to the Soviet point of view would not mean more coal for France, but only a prolongation of the stalemate. By itself the Soviet Union was unable or unwilling to provide coal for France, and therefore Franco-Soviet cooperation would not provide the answer to French needs. Furthermore, Moscow could not prevent a partial agreement between France and the West because it had no way of bringing direct pressure on Paris. Both the Soviet and the French Communist leaders were intent upon holding the coalition government together in France, and the Communists did not wish to threaten the other parties with resignation for fear the offer might be accepted. An agreement with the Anglo-Americans was not only necessary but also possible under the existing conditions.

Though France would thereby surrender its position as mediator between East and West, that action would no longer be of great significance. The illusion of cooperation had vanished, and the era of one-sided concessions was over. France was not powerful enough to force East and West to compromise after it had failed to persuade them to do so. In the immediate postwar world France had to follow one of the superpowers in order to gain any advantages in Europe. Signing a separate agreement with the West meant, not that France was signing away its diplomatic initiative, but that it was recognizing a situation which had existed at least since 1940.

Even if the French Communists did go into opposition, the domestic situation would be less serious than it would have been in 1945 or 1946. By mid-1947 there had been almost three years of reconstruction, and the presence of the Communists in the government was no longer so vital. In fact, it did not appear that the Communists could much longer fulfill their function of restraining the workers' demands.

Because of the pressure of its economic needs, the clarification of the international alignment between East and West, and the relative stability of the domestic situation, the French government now chose to press for a solution of part of the German problem in the face of Soviet opposition. At Moscow Bidault asked for support of his plan for the economic attachment of the Saar to France. After having obtained Anglo-American support, Bidault pressed Molotov again and again for his concurrence. The most that the latter would reply was that "the Soviet government recognizes that this problem merits attention and that it will have to be settled." [17] Perhaps the Political Bureau overestimated the ability of the French Communists to deter their government from a break on this issue, or its own ability to extort French support for its demands by withholding assent to French claims on the Saar. This was a decisive moment in Franco-Soviet relations. The French turned to the West to negotiate an agreement on coal. According to its terms, the amount of coal exported to France from Germany would depend on the level of production in the Ruhr. When the Saar was attached

[17] *Pravda*, April 12, 1947.

to the French economy, all coal from that region would be under French control, and the percentage of Ruhr coal sent to France would be revised.[18]

The agreement was attacked in chorus by both the French Communists and the Soviet Union. The Party declared that it "makes France the dupe of the Western bloc." Thorez asserted that the Soviet position at the Moscow Conference had been closest to the French position on all the essential points.[19] Jacques Duclos accused the United States of having exploited the Saar issue in order to separate the Soviet Union and France and "create the basis of a Western bloc." He denounced Bidault for having fallen into this trap and declared that the French delegation should have "emphasized the Ruhr" and should not have been tricked into separating one German problem from another. Besides this, he asserted, the Saar would not supply France with enough coal. It was through reparations that France stood to gain the most, Duclos concluded, but the French delegation had given those up "for a mess of pottage." [20]

The Soviet leaders took much the same line in denouncing the accords. The production of Ruhr coal, they stated, would permit France to receive only 270,000 tons a month for some time. *Pravda* maintained that, since the Monnet Plan of reconstruction required first 500,000 and then a million tons a month, "the new agreement in no way resolves the problem of Ruhr coal for France." Moreover, "the political character of the agreement is obvious," because the arrangement facilitated the formation of a Western bloc.[21] Despite the opposition of the French Communists and the Soviet Union to the coal accords, the Party did not threaten to leave the government over this issue. When the cabinet decided to ratify the Marshall-Bevin-Bidault agreement, the Communist ministers abstained, with a denial that this involved a rupture of the coalition.[22] The French

[18] The text of the treaty in *Le Monde*, April 23, 1947. An explanatory commentary can be found in *L'Année politique, 1947*, pp. 83–84.

[19] *L'Humanité*, April 22, 1947.

[20] Duclos, "Notre Politique," *Cahiers du Communisme*, Nos. 3–4 (March-April, 1947), pp. 180, 181, 183, 185.

[21] Ia. Viktorov, "Mezhdunarodnoe obozrenie," *Pravda*, April 29, 1947.

[22] *Le Monde*, May 3, 1947.

Communists had failed to make their views on foreign policy prevail in the inner councils of the French government. The attempted alignment with the Soviet Union was discarded by the French, and the alignment with the West was confirmed.

Violence in the French Union

The two great issues which continued to plague the French Communists were the Indo-China problem and the wage problem. The only way the Party could forestall a showdown in the government over one or both questions was to gain control of one of the ministries, which would enable it to influence policy-making either in the overseas empire or in the domestic economy. Therefore, the Party insisted that the homogeneous Socialist government, l'expérience Blum, should not continue beyond the election of the first president of the Fourth Republic. It claimed that the reaction was interested in prolonging the exclusion of the Communists from the government and that nothing positive could be accomplished without the Party's approval.[23]

The Communists hoped to facilitate their reentry into the government by supporting a candidate of the Left for the presidency of the Republic. They warned against the candidacy of General de Gaulle. "It is hardly necessary to underline how serious the situation would be for France if a determined adversary of the constitution were elected president of the Republic." The Party concluded that "it is the rally of all republicans which is required at this moment, and when we speak of all republicans, we mean Communists, Socialists, members of the RGR, and members of the MRP." [24] They therefore rallied behind Auriol and greeted his election as "a great republican victory." [25] The Soviet press also considered the election of Auriol a "victory for the democratic camp and a defeat for the reaction." It praised the Communist Party, which, "true to its postwar tactics of consolidating the democratic strength,

[23] L'Humanité, January 7, 8, 1947.
[24] "Notre Politique," Cahiers du Communisme, No. 12 (December, 1946), p. 1112.
[25] L'Humanité, January 17, 1946.

. . . did not present its own candidate and decided to support the candidate of the Socialist Party." [26]

However, the Communists then declared their absolute opposition to the reconstitution of the all-Socialist Blum government.[27] Represented this time by Paul Ramadier, the SFIO took the lead in forming a new government. Again there was trouble over the Communist demand for the Ministry of National Defense. Finally, a variation of the Blum compromise was accepted which virtually stripped that ministry of its major powers. The ministries of War, Navy, and Air were retained and assigned to non-Communists. The functions of the Minister of National Defense and his relations with the other ministers were to be fixed by decree. The Communists were also given the ministries of State (Thorez), Labor (Croizat), Reconstruction (Tillon), and Public Health (Georges Marrane). When François Billoux was named Minister of National Defense and the new decree was published, it became evident that the powers of the Minister of National Defense had been curtailed more sharply than those of the Minister of Armaments. The president of the council retained control of the general staff and the various important committees of national defense. He was also responsible for countersigning the ministerial nominations of new officers.[28] By accepting this face-saving device, the Communists remained in the government, but they were unable to control or greatly influence the course of events in Indo-China, which were soon to sweep them perilously close to the brink of political isolation.

The continued fighting in Indo-China demanded the immediate attention of the new government. In late December, 1946, Marius Moutet, Socialist Minister of Overseas Territories, had arrived in Hanoi to investigate conditions there. Meanwhile, the French Communist press was demanding negotiations "with the only organization that represents something, the Viet-Namese government" under Ho Chi Minh. The Party argued that the Viet-Namese did

---

[26] "Mezhdunarodnoe obozrenie," *Pravda*, January 19, 1947.
[27] *Ibid.*, January 18, 1946.
[28] Assemblée Nationale, *JO, Débats*, February 8, 1947, pp. 1294–95.

not deny that France had cultural rights in a free Viet-Nam within
the French Union. It supported Ho's conviction that "a just peace
can still be obtained." [29] The Party leaders warned the rank and
file that "elements of provocation have intervened in Indo-China,
and its is indispensable that our militants display the greatest
vigilance to unmask the maneuvers and provocations of the enemies
of democracy." [30]

When the Indo-Chinese question came up for debate in the
Assembly, Pierre Cot delivered the major Communist speech,
offering a moderate program that was consistent with the Party's
efforts to negotiate a settlement. First, he upheld the French presence in Southeast Asia. "France has a job to do and, without wishing
to use high-sounding words, a mission to fulfill." He added, "It
is necessary to say this in order to discourage certain Viet-Namese
extremists and, above all, foreign intrigues." [31] Cot admitted there
had been atrocities on both sides. "We are not a court," he pleaded;
"we are politicians who are trying to understand." He did not deny
that the Viet-Namese government shared the blame for the conflict,
but he skillfully exculpated it. The government, he stated, "was
born in circumstances like ours . . . at the moment of the liberation.
It has all the faults of youth. Can we seriously suppose that all
the wrongs, all the political errors, are on one side?" Not in the
least, Cot replied, because the French military on the spot were
guilty of "terrorism" and "madness." [32]

Then he painted a terrible picture of the consequences of war in
the rice paddies and mountains, of the losses to France, of the ruin
of Indo-China, and of world opinion becoming ever more hostile
to France. Cot insisted that France must negotiate in the face of
these alternatives. These negotiations, he stated, must be with the
Viet-Nam government, which was the most representative, the
most powerful, and the most respectful of future ties with France.[33]

[29] *L'Humanité*, January 4, 12, 1947.
[30] "Notre Politique," *Cahiers du Communisme*, No. 12 (December, 1946), p.
1113.
[31] Assemblée Nationale, *JO, Débats*, March 18, 1947, p. 869.
[32] *Ibid.*, pp. 870, 871, 872.
[33] *Ibid.*, p. 874.

It was a masterful speech designed to appeal to reason and justice, but it convinced no one. The Communists were obviously alone in their desire for negotiation.

Therefore, when faced with the problem of endorsing the government's military actions or challenging them, the Communists abstained.[34] In this way the Party avoided a governmental crisis, at least for the moment. What would the Communists do when the government submitted the budget, which included a demand for military credits for the war in Indo-China?

On March 20, 1947, soon after the budget debate began, the Communists declared that they would not vote for the credits, and their only concession to republican unity would be to abstain.[35] Duclos explained that "if we followed the logic of our reasoning, we would have to vote against [the credits], but we care too much for the interests of the country, we are all too conscious of the seriousness of the situation . . . to go that far." What, then, of ministerial solidarity? Duclos assured the Assembly that the Communist ministers would vote for the budget to avoid breaking this solidarity. He gave two reasons for this unusual action. France could scarcely be governed without the existing coalition, and unity at home was absolutely necessary to support the French delegates at the Moscow Conference, who were trying to obtain more coal for France.[36] Thus, except for their ministers, the Communists abstained from the motion of confidence in the government over the issue of credits. The Party could not long sustain itself in such an awkward posture. Yet it did not want to break with the coalition on the Indo-Chinese issue. To leave the government on an issue which appeared to most Frenchmen to involve the national interest in opposition to a native rebellion would be a grave political error. It would expose the Communists to charges of foreign influence and lack of patriotism, if not outright treason.

[34] *Ibid.*, p. 906.
[35] *Ibid.*, March 20, 1947, first session, p. 952.
[36] *Ibid.*, March 22, 1947, p. 1023.

The Final Problem: The Wage Crisis

In the spring of 1947 the long-suppressed demands of the workers for higher wages came out into the open with a vehemence which destroyed tripartism. The wage crisis developed simultaneously with the colonial and German problems, reaching a climax just as the Ruhr coal agreement was signed and a new rebellion broke out in Madagascar.

When the Blum government came to power in December, 1946, the CGT demanded a firm price-fixing policy and a downward revision of the latest price rises approved by the state. It also began agitating for a minimum living wage of 7,000 francs a month to be paid from January 1, 1947.[37] As the government took action to lower prices, the CGT gave its enthusiastic approval, but Frachon insisted that this was not enough. Under his leadership the Communist-controlled Commission Centrale of the CGT continued pressing for increased wages, retroactive to January 1, 1947.[38] Despite these protests against the government policy, and a few discussions between the government and representatives of the CGT, the latter maintained its strict no-strike policy. The Communist agitation appeared as a sop to working-class opinion and failed to answer the needs of the proletariat.

The workers were beginning to take matters into their own hands. In February, spontaneous agitation broke out among workers in the nationalized Régie Renault; demanding a wage increase of ten francs an hour, they elected a strike committee and stopped work. Under pressure from the CGT, work was resumed quickly, but the men remained discontented. A month later the smoldering opposition to the wage-freeze policy erupted when one of the shops at Renault voted to go on strike despite the disapproval of the CGT delegates. This shop appealed to others, and by April 28 the strike had spread throughout the Renault plant.[39]

As with the Indo-Chinese crisis in December, the Communists tried to ignore the incident, whereas the rest of the Paris press gave

[37] *Le Peuple,* December 31, 1946.
[38] *L'Humanité,* January 7, 16, 1947
[39] Bois, "La Grève des usines Renault," *La Révolution Prolétarienne,* No. 304 (June, 1947), p. 10. The author was president of the strike committee.

it a wide coverage. In a small article on page three, *L'Humanité* denounced the "reactionary press" which "yesterday tried to give considerable importance to the movement . . . at Régie Renault led by a handful of Trotskyites who succeeded in involving 1,500 out of 30,000 workers."[40] Within twenty-four hours the CGT had taken active measures to crush this breach of trade-union discipline. It also denounced the movement as a provocation calculated to wreck the fruitful negotiations between its own delegation and the government.[41] At the factories the strike committee accused the CGT of behind-the-scenes intrigues with the directors to force the strikers back to work. Incidents between the workers and the CGT representatives multiplied. At mass meetings outside the plants some pro-CGT workers were forcibly barred from the microphones, and in one workshop the CGT stalwarts barricaded themselves behind locked doors to avoid contact with the rest of the plant.[42]

Meanwhile, representatives of the CGT and the directors of the Régie Renault were meeting in the office of Ambroise Croizat to try to reach a settlement. Under pressure from the Communist Minister of Labor, a three-franc increase was granted by the directors.[43] Thus, the Communists tried to settle the strike quickly without allowing the radical elements in the factory to bargain directly with the management. However, the representative of the CGT delegation, Eugène Hénaff, met with little sympathy when he tried to persuade the strikers to accept the compromise.[44] Firmly in the hands of Trotskyite (Parti Communiste International) and Anarchist (Confédération Nationale du Travail) elements, the strike leadership was supported in a secret ballot by 80 percent of the workers in its rejection of the three-franc raise.[45]

Suddenly the Communists shifted the center of attention to a new crisis. On the day their appeal went unheeded by the Renault

[40] *L'Humanité*, April 27–28, 1947.

[41] *Ibid.*, April 29, 1947.

[42] Bois, "La Grève des usines Renault," *La Révolution Prolétarienne*, No. 304 (June, 1947), p. 11.

[43] *Le Monde*, May 1–2, 1947.

[44] *Ibid.* The non-Communist papers of the Right and Left asserted that Hénaff had been hooted down and spat upon by the workers. *Le Figaro*, *L'Aube*, and even *Combat*, May 1–2, 1947.

[45] *Le Monde*, May 1–2, 1947.

workers, they came out in vigorous support of a number of wage-
and-hour demands by the Union of Metallurgy Workers of Paris.
Soon after, the Political Bureau "decided . . . to give its support
unreservedly to the legitimate demands of the confederal unions,
such as those presented by the union of metallurgists of the Paris
region." At the same time the Communist members of the Council
of Ministers declared their support of a general increase in wages;
price-fixing had failed, they argued, and increased production now
made a wage increase possible.[46] This constituted a challenge to
government policy, and the rest of the ministers refused to accept
the Communist reasoning.

On the afternoon of May 2 Premier Ramadier informed the Assembly of the breach in the ranks of the cabinet. He vigorously defended the price-and-wage policy and appealed for its support in
the name of economic and political stability. In the debate the
Communist deputies refused to support the government policy.
Duclos protested that the working class was being asked to shoulder
the entire burden of reconstruction. This was, he continued, a sign
of the revival of French reaction and its shameless alliance with the
anti-Communist, racist circles in the United States. He warned that
"it would be most dangerous to demoralize the working class." The
Communist Party chose, he concluded, to base its policy on "confidence in the workers." [47]

Ramadier put the question of confidence, and after the interval
specified by the constitution the National Assembly met to take a
historic vote. Holding firm to their new course, the Communists
voted against the government, which was backed by a majority.
The Party then stubbornly refused to order its ministers to resign.
After a period of hesitation and some confusion the Communist
ministers were dismissed by decree of the Premier, countersigned
by the President of the Republic.[48] Three years and one month after
becoming a governmental party the Communists were forced to relinquish their posts and return to their more familiar and comfort-
able role of permanent opposition.

[46] L'Humanité, April 30, May 2, 1947.
[47] Assemblée Nationale, JO, Débats, May 2, 1947, second session, pp. 1426–
28, 1434.
[48] L'Année politique, 1947, p. 326, complete text.

Why did the Communists choose to break with the majority over this issue and at this time? There had been strikes before, and there had been other issues, such as Indo-China and the coal agreement, over which the Party had opposed the government. Yet until May, 1947, it had gone to great lengths to avoid a rupture with the majority, especially with the Socialists. In May it refused even to consider bargaining on the wage issue. There were no dramatic Communist-Socialist conferences. The Communist ultimatum was simply presented and rejected. Why this sudden haste and arbitrariness?

The timing of the Communists' withdrawal from the government was determined largely by the international situation, though elements of internal politics also played a role. It was obvious to the Communist leaders that the "international reaction" had forced them into a desperate position. As Jacques Duclos admitted, "in the course of the recent period the events of internal policy appear to be closely linked to problems of foreign policy." There had been several anti-Communist demonstrations throughout the world, he continued, particularly President Truman's declaration on American aid to Greece and Turkey, the results of the Moscow Conference, events in the French Union, and the reappearance of General de Gaulle on the political stage. Duclos denounced American policy. "Its primary goals are to isolate the USSR and drag France into an Anglo-American policy for Germany." [49] He denounced the "reactionary maneuver" of extending aid to the present regimes in Greece and Turkey. These two examples of "aggressive" American intentions were giving hope and strength, Duclos stated, to reactionary elements in France. "No serious man can deny that there are close links between the development of certain reactionary campaigns in the United States and the reentrance of General de Gaulle on the political scene." [50]

[49] Duclos, "Notre Politique," *Cahiers du Communisme*, No. 3–4 (March-April, 1947), pp. 177, 183.

[50] *Ibid.*, p. 188. On March 30, at Bruneval, De Gaulle launched his first appeal for a "Rally of the French People" against the politicians and the misshapen constitutional structure. This speech was followed by another at Strasbourg which was even more political in character. De Gaulle demanded "a profound reform of the state." The Communists reacted quickly. Thorez denounced the General as the "handyman of the reaction." *L'Humanité*, April

Duclos accused De Gaulle of being a protégé of American re-action and denounced the "Rally of the French People" as an in-trigue which recalled the days of General Boulanger or even of Louis Napoleon Bonaparte. De Gaulle's Rally was an extension of the international reaction into France, the Communist leader as-serted, and it was combatted by the committees of republican vigi-lance "which are being formed almost everywhere . . . on the initiative of the departmental committees of liberation." Duclos also attributed the situation in Indo-China to provocations of the same international reaction; there could be no quick solution to the prob-lem, and the only way to solve it was through negotiation.[51]

It was clear to the Communists that the international situation could easily provoke a major crisis within France over either the German question or the colonial question. How could the Party best prepare for a test of strength between the "forces of democracy and the forces of reaction"? In general terms, the Party had to persuade or force other republican elements to accept its program, or it would have to resign and take up the battle outside the government. The Party could demand an immediate debate on colonial or foreign policy, making the crisis in Indo-China or Germany the issue; it could try to avoid a showdown as long as possible while vigorously campaigning for public support of its program; or, third, it could precipitate a government crisis on an issue offering the most advantages to the Communists. Although the available evidence does not provide a conclusive answer, the pre-sumption is strong that the Communists chose the wage problem in preference to any other issue in their struggle to remain in the government on their terms.

There were obvious advantages in fastening on the issue of wages. This would be a popular move among the workers and would strengthen their allegiance to the Party. If the Communists had any real hope of challenging the government and winning, they would

---

3, 1947. The Party encouraged and sponsored the formation of committees of vigilance for the defense of the Republic. Symbolically, the first committee was formed in Ajaccio in Corsica by the reconstituted Front National. *Ibid.*, April 12, 1947.

[51] Duclos, "Notre Politique," *Cahiers du Communisme*, No. 3–4 (March-April, 1947), pp. 189–90, 192, 194.

have to rely on the loyalty of the rank and file. Furthermore, they needed working-class backing in order to bring pressure to bear upon the rank and file of the Socialist Party. Pressure from the working-class base of the SFIO had often proved a useful method of intimidating its leadership. Yet there were signs that the Communists had been losing support among the workers, as demonstrated by CGT losses in the recent elections to the social-security boards.[52] The danger was growing that the workers would no longer respond readily to Communist slogans that were not in their direct interest; higher wages meant much more to them than the Ruhr coal or the future of the French Union.

This appraisal of the Party's tactics is confirmed indirectly by the efforts that it made on May 3 to avoid a decisive clash with the government over two other explosive issues, the coal accords and the Madagascar crisis. In April anti-French demonstrations had broken out in Madagascar, followed by fighting between native and French troops. When the French Minister of Overseas Territories accused two native deputies to the French National Assembly of being involved in the rebellion and ordered their arrest,[53] the Communists protested immediately against the waiving of parliamentary immunity.[54] When the Communists clashed in the cabinet with the other ministers and were overruled, they withdrew abruptly,[55] but denied that this step constituted a collective resignation.

These tactics would succeed only so long as the national Assembly was in recess, which lasted until April 29. Even after the Assembly urged an immediate discussion, the majority, including the Communists, agreed to put off the Madagascar question for several days.[56] Thus, on this question, as on the ratification of the Ruhr coal agreement, the Communists tried desperately to avert or post-

[52] *Le Monde*, April 30, 1947. Though the CGT gained a slight majority of seats on the boards, it had been expected to win by a far greater margin. The CFTC and other groups showed unexpected strength.

[53] Assemblée Nationale, *JO, Débats*, April 29, 1947, p. 1332, "Communications de M. le ministre de la France d'outre-mer, 5 avril, 1947."

[54] *L'Humanité*, April 18, 1947.

[55] *Le Monde*, April 18, 1947.

[56] Assemblée Nationale, *JO, Débats*, April 29, 1947, pp. 1335, 1339. Waldeck-Rochet was hooted down by the Center and the Right for his suggestion.

pone a government crisis; they did not attempt to dodge the wage question once it had been clearly posed.[57]

Several other factors support the hypothesis that the Communists deliberately forced a showdown on the question of higher wages. For example, although Communist delegates of the CGT had just previously tried to bring the Renault strike to a halt, the Communist ministers now forced the showdown in the Council of Ministers without any hesitation. Was the Communist *volte-face* a sudden, almost spontaneous reaction to the fear of being "outflanked on the left"? This explanation glosses over several important points. First, other strikes, more widespread and more serious, had preceded the Renault strike, but apparently the Communists had not feared being outflanked then. Second, it is difficult to explain the rapid and decisive Communist response to this particular strike unless they had been preparing to put forward their own demands. The Renault strike did not become serious until April 26 or 27. Yet on April 30 the early-morning edition of *L'Humanité* carried the demands of the *metallos*, and two days later the Communist ministers demanded a general wage increase, thereby precipitating the crisis. After the Communists had taken their stand for higher wages, Charles Tillon remarked in the cabinet, "For three months I have been in disagreement with the government on everything." [58] This comment reflected a long-standing opposition in the Party to the Communist role in the government; it may also mean that the dispute over the wage issue was an occasion rather than a cause for the break with tripartism.[59]

One further question: Why did the Communists in the CGT first seek to end the Renault strike? This may have been due to the Communists' desire to keep in their own hands all initiative, and all credit, for demanding higher wages. The Renault workers could not be trusted to follow their policy docilely, but the *metallos* were more powerful in the French labor movement, and their postwar record of restraint entitled them to share in the rising national in-

---

[57] *Le Monde,* May 3, 1947.

[58] *Ibid.,* May 4–5, 1947.

[59] Cf. *Le Monde,* May 4–5, 1947, which otherwise accepts the thesis that the Party feared being outflanked.

come.[60] Through these tactics the Communists were largely successful in reasserting their control over the labor situation; when the Renault strike was finally settled on May 7, the workers accepted the three-franc increase originally suggested by the Communist Party, and the latter claimed to have won a great victory.[61]

In general, the international situation was forcing the Communists toward a choice sooner or later between breaking with the Soviet Union and breaking with the governing coalition in France. Hoping to win allies in its struggle to return to the government and to hold France at least neutral in international politics, the Party encouraged the strongest and most deserving of the unions to demand a revision of government policy. The move failed to shake the Socialists and led to the exclusion of the Communists from the government.

The French Communists Adrift

France was now divided, as the world was divided, into two camps—Communist and anti-Communist. The Party had not won "its battle of Prague." It had not even persuaded a majority of the Assembly to assume a temporarily neutral role in the continuing struggle between East and West. The solidarity of the non-Communist parties forestalled a government crisis and thus prevented the Communists from putting pressure on other political groups, particularly the Socialists, by unleashing mass strikes.

It may never be known how narrow was the margin by which a government crisis was avoided. After the exclusion of the Communists, the Socialist leadership was split over whether to resign. On May 5, 1947, the executive committee voted twelve to nine for resignation. A later vote reversed this position by a ten-to-nine vote, with one abstention. A few days later the Socialist national council voted on whether to continue in the government without the Communists. Since the last such vote in the winter of 1946 a slight shift in opinion had occurred, and the council now supported Ramadier's

[60] See, for example, Duclos, "Notre Politique," *Cahiers du Communisme,* No. 5 (May, 1947), pp. 250–51.
[61] *L'Humanité,* May 7, 1947.

policy by a majority of only 400 out of almost 4,700 ballots.[62] In these decisions the Soviet press detected "the activities of several overseas circles participating in the big game around France, but also outside France." [63] The Right-wing Socialists had attained their objective, *Pravda* maintained, and the government of France had been pulled sharply to the Right by excluding from the government the largest party in the National Assembly. In the face of the threats of American capital and General de Gaulle, the Socialists had split the democratic forces of France and had frustrated the solidarity of the Left. This was, according to Moscow, a serious failure of nerve in the face of a great challenge.[64]

Not accepting the decision of the Socialist council as final, the Communists tried to influence enough Socialist Party members to change the vote of the leaders, bringing to bear their most potent weapon, the political strike inspired by economic necessity. By May 8 strikes were breaking out all over France. In an interview Jacques Duclos aimed his words at the Socialists: "We intend to work with the government to take all measures in favor of the working class, even though we are outside the government for the time being. And note well that I say 'for the time being.' " [65] Despite these conciliatory remarks, the strike movement spread rapidly; as soon as the government settled one strike, another began. The bakers' strike led to bread lines and demonstrations. The Socialists accused the Communists of trying to intimidate the government.[66] Conservatives attributed the strikes to "scarcely disguised political operations." [67] The Communists struck back by attacking the anti-strike tactics. Fajon denounced as illegal the government's mobilization of strikers at gas and electricity plants. He warned, "No government can be strong today if it does not have the confidence and support of the working class." Ramadier condemned the strikes as an attempt, "by repetition and multiplication of attacks, to violate the authority of the government." [68] As the strikes reached their

[62] *Le Monde*, May 6, 9, 1947.
[63] B. Leont'ev, "Mezhdunarodnoe obozrenie," *Pravda*, May 13, 1947.
[64] Ia. Viktorov, "Mezhdunarodnoe obozrenie," *ibid.*, May 27, 1947.
[65] *L'Humanité*, May 8, 1947.
[66] *Le Populaire*, June 2, 1947.
[67] *Le Figaro*, June 3, 1947.
[68] Assemblée Nationale, *JO, Débats*, June 3, 1947, pp. 1874–75, 1877.

climax, Maurice Thorez declared: "Because the people approve of
us for having defended their interests and those of the Republic,
we will return to the government." He insisted that the Communists
would restore order and grant the demands of the workers.[69] The
promise or threat was not carried out. Even the railroad strike,
which paralyzed France from June 2 to 6 and a mass demonstration
organized by the Party against the government budget failed to
shake the determination of the Socialists. The Communists had
played their last card and had lost.

The rejection by the Soviet Union of European economic cooperation and the inauguration of the Marshall Plan merely confirmed
the isolation of the French Communists. However, the Party clung
to its new line. At its Eleventh Congress in June, 1947, Thorez reiterated his old position: "We are ready to accept our responsibilities
to the country . . . We cherish the same desire for unity with all
the workers and democratic forces. We have not changed and we
will not change."[70] Despite his denunciations of the Socialists,
Thorez once again appealed to them. "We—Socialists and Communists—can formulate a new policy together in the assemblies and
congresses of a single and great Party of the Working Class." He
invited the SFIO to reestablish a *comité d'entente* and to work
with the Communists toward building a new France.[71]

The Party's foreign policy also remained unchanged. While
criticizing "international reaction . . . constructed on the base of
English and, above all, American capitalism," he supported the cooperation of the Big Three. "We denounce those adventurers," he
declared, "who speculate on the inevitable divergences between the
great allies and those who consider the world irrevocably divided
into two great antagonistic camps doomed to clash in the near
future."[72] Thorez maintained this view literally until the eve of
the founding meeting of the Cominform in Poland, in September
and October, 1947. On October 2 in an election speech the Communist leader announced that "nothing can be done in France with-

---

[69] *L'Humanité*, May 20, 1947.

[70] Thorez, *Au Service du peuple de France: Rapport au XIIème congrès du
PCF, 25–28 juin 1947* (Paris, 1947), p. 37.

[71] *Ibid.*, pp. 64–65.

[72] *Ibid.*, pp. 58–59.

out the Communist Party, whose role is only beginning." [73] Several days later the French Communists printed the text of the Cominform declaration, and on October 30 the Central Committee adopted a resolution which rejected collaboration with the Socialists and cooperation among the great powers. Now Thorez heaped abuse upon himself and his party for having failed to recognize the gravity of the international situation. Henceforth, he promised, the Party would struggle actively against the external and internal forces of reaction.[74] The demands of Soviet foreign policy had changed, and the policy of the French Communist Party had now changed with them. The Party began a campaign to show France that it could not afford internal disunity and latent civil war as the price of anticommunism. A new period was opening in the evolution of French communism.

[73] *L'Humanité,* October 3, 1947.
[74] *Ibid.,* November 1, 1947.

CHAPTER XV

The Pattern of Soviet Foreign Policy

FROM 1941 to 1947 the French Communists and the Soviet Union planned and worked actively toward the ultimate establishment of a "people's democracy" in France. Neither Moscow nor the Party limited its aims to an acceptance of the *status quo* in Europe after the end of the Second World War. The Soviet leaders had only occasionally acknowledged their continued adherence to Leninist principles during the war against Hitler, but they never repudiated their long-avowed aim of world revolution. After the Yalta Conference they began to reemphasize the basic antagonism between the Soviet system and the 'capitalist West." By reasserting their belief in the inevitability of war as long as capitalism survived, they underlined clearly their unwavering allegiance to revolutionary Marxism-Leninism-Stalinism.

The pattern of Soviet foreign policy toward France offers further evidence of long-range Soviet goals. Moscow strove consistently to turn French foreign policy away from a Western orientation and toward complete identification with Soviet aims. Stalin's dealings with De Gaulle on Allied policy in North Africa and French participation in the settlement of the German problem illustrated the Soviet tactics of isolating France from the West without accepting the French ambition to "mediate" between West and East. The bilateral Franco-Soviet Treaty was another step in this direction. At the same time the Soviet Union put pressure on the French to recognize the Lublin regime even before it had been "reconstructed," and to endorse Soviet plans for Germany. Ultimately, Stalin wanted French foreign policy to be identical to Soviet foreign policy.

The Soviet leaders favored the establishment in France of a

radically altered social, economic, and political structure along the lines of the "people's democracies" in Eastern Europe. Stalin regretted even later that the unfavorable balance of military power in Western Europe had blocked this development and had prevented the Red Army from lending a hand to the French Communists.

Soviet policy in general and toward France in particular was vigorously endorsed by the French Communist Party. Even when there appeared to be important differences in policy, as over the future of the Ruhr and the French colonies, the French Communists either pleaded that the general advantages of a settlement with Moscow outweighed the particular and temporary disadvantages, or they remained silent, deferring action until the Soviet position became clearer.

Throughout the period 1941–47 French Communist leaders maintained their allegiance to the Soviet brand of revolutionary Marxism. After Yalta, Fajon, Duclos, and Guyot made it clear that they had never wavered in their loyalty to the Stalinist model. They drew exact parallels between their definition of private property and that of the Soviet constitution, between their concept of the status of a backward area and the Stalinist concept. Rationalizing their liberation policy, the French Communist leaders denounced any "adventurist line" first and foremost because it might lead to a reversal of alliances, creating a coalition of capitalist powers against the Soviet Union."

In general, the Party leaders stressed the importance of France achieving agreement with Moscow even at the expense of French national interests. They condemned any action which was not in accord with Soviet aims as reactionary, traitorous, antidemocratic, and Fascist. On the other hand, by virtue of their total adherence to Soviet policy the Communists considered themselves the only completely "democratic" and "patriotic" group in France. Therefore, they assumed that the interests of France and "democracy" required the Communist Party to become the ruling power in France.

The French Communist Party worked persistently to achieve the long-range Soviet aim in France—the establishment of Communist domination. Bénoît Frachon's interpretation of unity in the trade-union movement and the Party's ruthless methods of creating and enforcing that unity aimed at building a monolithic organization of all French workers on the model of Soviet trade unions. This Communist definition of unity was marked by the repeated elimination of opposing factions and the use of the strike as a political weapon. Similarly, Pierre Villon's offer of unity to the Resistance movements and the Party's skillful infiltration of non-Communist Resistance groups was designed to establish a tightly knit, monolithic underground organization under Communist leadership. When the non-Communist groups refused to surrender their independence, the Communists maintained their own separate chain of political and military command. In urging unity on the Socialists, the Communists supported Leninist-Stalinist principles of democratic centralism and ideological conformity.

As far as possible, the Communist ministers packed the bureaucracies under their control with their own men and, according to some evidence, even used their position for espionage. Their activities in the economics and armaments ministries give some idea of the way in which Communist ministers would have acted had the Party taken control of one of the key ministries, as it so ardently desired to do.

The Communists also demanded the creation of a "people's army" in which the Resistance forces would play an important role, the maintenance of the patriotic militia, and the perpetuation of the CNR and other Resistance organizations as consultative organs in the provisional government. They advocated a purge of "collaborationists," a group in which they included many of their political enemies. They sought to modify the administrative structure, first by substituting local elective committees for prefects, and then by making a unicameral legislature the omnipotent master of French society. All along the line the Communists entrenched themselves in positions of power from which to launch their final drive for control of France.

No conclusive evidence exists to show how the Soviet Union or the French Communist Party intended to carry out the final stage of the revolution. It remains a matter of speculation whether or not in

1944 the Soviet leaders considered the possibility that the Western Allies would not cross the Channel and that the Red Army alone would defeat Germany in the field and occupy France. After the British and American landings in France, Soviet spokesmen openly expressed doubts as to the likelihood of a quick victory for the Communists in France. Soviet leaders continued to consider the presence of Allied troops in France as the decisive factor.

Publicly, the French Communists were more optimistic about their chances for taking power, but they did not outline any particular "road to socialism." Though they denounced "revisionism" and emphasized their revolutionary traditions, they placed great emphasis on increasing their power and prestige by legal, parliamentary, and constitutional methods. The Party broke up its wartime insurrectional structure and recruited many new and untried members. It is not clear whether it hoped to take power without an armed struggle or whether it expected to organize a coup along the lines of the Czech Communists. Having carefully prepared their power positions in the government, the trade unions, and other organizations, the French Communists had several alternatives open to them. As Raymond Guyot put it, circumstances would determine their choice of the road to power.

It is difficult to define the exact nature of the relationship between the French Communist Party and the Soviet leadership. Clearly, they both followed the same general line of thought and action; they supported each other consistently and brushed aside their differences as minor and unimportant. Moscow kept in touch with the French Communists during the early part of the war by means of its embassy in Paris and Vichy. After November, 1942, occasional Soviet couriers reached France through Switzerland. However, according to Pierre Hervé, who knew of these contacts, detailed instructions from abroad were kept to a minimum for security and political reasons. The general line laid down by the Soviet press was, he maintained, a satisfactory guide to action.[1] This is why the French Communist Party often was not informed in advance of important shifts in Soviet policy—for example, in September, 1939, and the summer of 1947. The Soviet Union did

[1] Interview with Pierre Hervé.

not publicly make clear its own position on many matters of great interest to the French Communists, such as the future of the French colonies and the seizure of power in France. The Soviet position tended to embarrass the French Communist leadership and to disturb the Party rank and file.

This indifference of the Soviet leadership to the perplexities of its supporters suggests that Stalin's view of a successful Communist revolution stressed the Soviet contribution rather than that of the local party—in this case, the French Communist Party. During the postliberation period the Soviet leaders and, at times, the French Communists emphasized the importance of the Red Army in the revolutionary scheme of events. The French Communists did not try to "go it alone" in 1944 because of the absence of Soviet support, and they were berated in 1947 for having half forgotten this lesson in power politics.

The success of the Communist tactics in France depended largely on the ability of the Soviet Union to negotiate quick settlements of the outstanding questions resulting from the war and thus encourage the Western powers to withdraw their forces from the Continent. The USSR failed to do this; because of its aggressive and threatening conduct, it brought the power of the West back to Europe in force. The major error of Soviet foreign policy was due in no small measure to ideological blindness, as well as to considerations of immediate national interest. Because the Soviet leaders insisted on describing any opposition to their demands for more and more concessions in Europe as the "machinations of world capitalism," they were unable to take advantage of a rare opportunity to seize control of all of Europe. They warned the Russian people that foreign threats made it imperative to reconstruct the motherland rapidly without external aid. At the same time the Soviet leaders resisted efforts to solve the problem between East and West because they believed all Western proposals were motivated by "imperialist designs."

If the Soviet leaders had been pure opportunists, they could have contributed to a continuation of the spirit of wartime cooperation long enough to settle the German problem and thereby to hasten the evacuation of the American forces; they could have made concessions to the French on the German and colonial issues in order to bolster the prestige of the French Communist Party and increase its chances of electoral success. Their failure to do so shows up one of the basic weaknesses of Soviet foreign policy. Their faulty reasoning was due to a rigid adherence to Marxist-Leninist-Stalinist assumptions about "the capitalist West."

At the same time the Soviet leaders were genuinely concerned about the security of their state, which they identified with expansion of Soviet control in Central Europe and the Near East. Therefore, they also interpreted Western unwillingness to see Soviet gains in these areas as a struggle for power over territories which were of strategic and economic importance to the USSR. The West could not shake these assumptions, which were based on considerations of both power and ideology.

The French Communists were obliged to support Soviet policy despite the immediate, practical disadvantages to them of such action. When the Soviet Union insisted upon a policy of cooperation, the Party could not threaten to disrupt tripartism in order to win concessions from the Socialists. At the same time the Soviet Union carried on a policy which made it impossible for the French Communists to cooperate permanently with other parties. The result was that, although the French Communist Party had won a strong position within France by its sacrifices first in the Resistance and then in the national effort of reconstruction, the Party was unable to use its position to advance effectively either its own interests or those of the Soviet Union.

Bibliography

THE WRITING of contemporary or near-contemporary history always presents a serious problem of sources, especially when the subject of the study is, as in this instance, one of continuing political controversy. Some important official sources on the French side and many more on the Soviet side remain unavailable in unpublished archives which are closed to scholars as well as to the general public. Collections of documents, newspaper files, and posters of the Resistance and liberation periods in France are still widely scattered and incomplete. The best collection of these sources available to the public is in the Bibliothèque de Documentation Internationale Contemporaine. The Bibliothèque Nationale has a very complete file of clandestine newspapers and is beginning to organize its collection of posters and leaflets; though the latter sources have not been catalogued, I was fortunate in receiving access to them. At present the most ambitious effort to collect and catalogue materials on the Resistance period is being undertaken by the Comité d'Histoire de la Deuxième Guerre Mondiale, under the supervision of Professor Henri Michel. The Comité, which publishes the *Revue d'Histoire de la Deuxième Guerre Mondiale* (Paris, 1949–), has also edited one volume of documents and has published several monographs on the Resistance. Its archives were not open to me.

In my listing of newspapers, the dates following the names of certain papers signify that the issues have been thoroughly examined for that period. Other papers have been consulted for reports of certain events or for samplings of opinion on certain issues.

Interviews

Barton, Paul. May 24, 1956.
Bertaux, Pierre. July 20, 1956.
Bohlen, Charles. January 26, 1956.
Bourdeau de Fontenay, Henri. August 7, 1956.
Cancouet, Lucien. April 6, 1956.

Dauphin, Roger. July 23, 1956.
Debré, Michel. May 2, 1956.
Hervé, Pierre. June 29, 1959.
Laloy, Jean. January 30 and June 12, 1956.
Rebattet, Georges. September 4, 1956.
Renouvin, Pierre. May 25, 1956.
Rossi, A. (Pseudonym of A. Tasca). April 10 and June 6, 1956.

Documentary Sources

Affiches. "Provinces," "Paris." Collection de la Bibliothèque Nationale. Cited in footnotes as *Affiches CBN*.
Assemblèe Consultative Provisoire. Journal Officiel [Cited in footnotes as *JO*], Débats, 1944–45.
Assemblée Consultative Provisoire. Journal Officiel, Documents, 1943–45.
Assemblée Nationale. Journal Officiel, Débats, 1946–47.
Assemblée Nationale Constituante Elue Octobre 1945. Séances de la Commission de la Constitution: Comptes rendus analytiques. Paris, 1946.
Assemblée Nationale Constituante Elue Juin 1946. Séances de la Commission de la Constitution: Comptes rendus analytiques. Paris, 1946.
Assemblée Nationale Constituante. Débats, 1945–46. Paris, 1946.
Bibliothèque de Documentation Internationale Contemporaine, "La Libération en province," Cited in footnotes as *BDIC*.
Comité Departemental de Libération de Cher. Bulletin Officiel. Bourges, 1945.
Commissariat à l'Information de Lot et Garonne, ed. Revue politique. N.p., 1944.
Documents édités par le comité directeur de FN, June, 1944, No. 4, lettre de P. Villon, 4 avril 1944.
Documents Parlementaires: Journal Officiel. (Assemblée Nationale). 1946–47.
Documents Parlementaires: Journal Officiel. (Conseil de la République). 1946–47.
Ministère des Affaires Etrangères. Documents français relatifs à l'Allemagne (août, 1945–février, 1947). Paris, 1947.
Ministère de la France d'Outre-mer. Bulletin hebdomadaire. Paris, 1946–47.
Ministère de l'Information. Notes, Documentations et Etudes, LXVI, No. 225, série française. 'Esquise d'une histoire de la Résistance française," deuxième partie. Paris, January, 1946.
Ministère de l'Intérieur. Service Central des Commissariats de la République. Bulletin sur la situation dans les régions et les départements. Paris, 1945–46. Cited in footnotes as *SCCR*.
Ministerstvo Inostrannykh Del SSSR. Sovetsko-frantsuzskie otnosheniia

vo vremia velikoi otechestvennoi voiny, 1941–45: Dokumenty i materialy [Soviet–French Relations during the Great Patriotic War, 1941–45: Documents and Materials]. Moscow, 1959. Cited in footnotes as *SFO*.

Ministry of Foreign Affairs of the USSR. Correspondence between the Chairman of the Council of Ministers of the USSR and the Presidents of the U.S.A. and the Prime Ministers of Great Britain during the Great Patriotic War of 1941–45. 2 vols. Moscow, 1957. Vol. I, Correspondence with Winston S. Churchill and Clement R. Attlee (July, 1941–November, 1945). Vol. II, Correspondence with Franklin D. Roosevelt and Harry S. Truman (August, 1941–December, 1945). Cited in footnotes as *Correspondence*.

Report of Activity of the World Federation of Trade Unions Presented to the IInd Trade Union Congress, Milan, June 29–July 10, 1949. Paris [1949?].

Royal Institute of International Affairs. The Soviet–Yugoslav Dispute. London, 1948.

Service Français d'Information. Notes, Documentations et Etudes. Paris, 1946–47.

U.S. Department of State. Civil Administration and Jurisdiction in Liberated French Territory. Washington, 1952.

—— Foreign Relations of the United States, Diplomatic Papers: Conference of Berlin (Potsdam), 1945. Washington, 1960.

—— Foreign Relations of the United States, Diplomatic Papers: Conferences of Cairo and Teheran, 1943. Washington, 1961.

—— Foreign Relations of the United States, Diplomatic Papers: Conferences at Malta and Yalta, 1945. Washington, 1955.

Vneshniaia politika Sovetskogo Soiuza v period otechestvennoi voiny [The Foreign Policy of the Soviet Union in the Period of the Patriotic War]. 2 vols. Moscow, 1946.

World Federation of Trade Unions. Constitution Adopted by the World Trade Union Conference, October 3, 1945. Paris [1945?].

BOOKS, TREATISES, PAMPHLETS, AND ARTICLES

Abetz, Otto. Histoire d'une politique franco-allemande 1930–1950. Paris, 1953.

Adeline, General H. La Libération du sud-ouest. Algiers, 1948.

Anishev, D. "Pol'skii narod po puti k svobode i nezavisimosti" [The Polish People on the Road to Freedom and Independence], *Bol'shevik*, Nos. 13–14 (July, 1944), 48–64.

L'Année politique. Revue chronologique des principaux faits politiques, économiques, et sociaux de la France de la Libération de Paris au 31 décembre 1945, preface by André Siefried. Paris, 1946. Same for years 1946, 1947.

Armstrong, Hamilton Fish. Tito and Goliath. New York, 1951.

Aron, Raymond. De l'Armistice à l'insurrection nationale. Paris, 1945.

Aron, Robert. Histoire de la libération de la France, juin 1944–mai 1945. Paris, 1959.

—— Histoire de Vichy, 1940–1944. Paris, 1954.

Auphan, Admiral. Les Grimaces de l'histoire. Paris, 1951.

Barbe, Raymond. "La Politique du parti et les thèses colonialistes," *Cahiers du Communisme*, No. 7 (July, 1946), 566–77.

Barghoorn, Frederick C. "The Soviet Union between War and Cold War," *The Annals of the American Academy of Political and Social Sciences*, CCLXIII *The Soviet Union since World War II* (May, 1949), 1–8.

—— "The Varga Discussion and Its Significance," *The American Slavic and East European Review*, VII (October, 1948), 214–36.

Beloff, Max. The Foreign Policy of Soviet Russia 1929–1941, Vol. II, 1936–1941. London, 1949.

Blocq-Mascart, Maxime. Chroniques de la Résistance suivies d'études pour une nouvelle révolution française par les groupes de l'OCM. Paris, 1945.

Bois, Pierre. "La Grève des usines Renault," *La Révolution Prolétarienne*, No. 304 (June, 1947), 9–12.

Bonte, Florimond. Le Chemin de l'honneur. Paris, 1949.

Bor-Komorowski, T. The Secret Army. New York, 1951.

Bourdelle, J. L. Départs. n.d., n.p.

Bourdet, Claude. "La Politique intérieure de la Résistance," *Les Temps Modernes*, No. 112–113, special number, "La Gauche," pp. 1837–62.

Bourdet, Claude, ed. *Annuaire de la Résistance*. Paris, 1948.

Broz-Tito, Josip. "Bor'ba narodov poraboshchennoi Iugoslavii" [The Struggle of the Peoples of Enslaved Yugoslavia], *Bol'shevik*, Nos. 10–11 (May–June, 1944), 22–38.

Byrnes, James R. Speaking Frankly. New York, 1947.

Catroux, Georges. Dans la Bataille de Méditerranée: Egypte, Levante, Afrique du Nord, 1940–44. Paris, 1949.

—— J'ai vu tomber le rideau de fer. Paris, 1952.

Ceyrat, Maurice, La Politique russe et le parti communiste français, 1920–1945. Paris, 1946.

—— La Trahison permanente. Paris, 1948.

Chaintron, Jean. Discours prononcés à la radio par M. le préfet. Limoges, 1944–45.

Chambelland, M. "Deux assassinés," *La Révolution Prolétarienne*, No. 303 (May, 1947), 6.

"The Character of a 'People's Democracy,' " *Foreign Affairs*, XXVIII, No. 1 (October, 1949), 143–52.

Chaumeil, J. Le Problème des cadres: Rapport de la commission centrale des cadres du PCF; 7 octobre 1944 à Paris. Lyon, 1944.

Cheprakov, V. "Strategicheskie basy SShA i Velikobritanii" [The Strategic Bases of the U.S.A. and Great Britain], *Mirovoe Khoziaistvo i Mirovaia Politika* Nos. 10–11 (October–November, 1946), 33–41.

Chervet, Louis. "La Conquête de la paysannerie," *Cahiers du Communisme*, No. 4 (April, 1946), 379–86.

Churchill, Winston. The Second World War. Vols. III–V. Boston, 1950–54.

Chuvikov, P. "Uchenie Lenina–Stalina o voinakh spravedlivykh i nespravedlivykh" [The Teachings of Lenin and Stalin on Just and Unjust Wars], *Bol'shevik*, Nos. 7–8 (April, 1945), 14–26.

Clay, Lucius D. Decision in Germany. Garden City, 1950.

Cogniot, Georges. "La Conférence des trois à Moscou et ses heureux résultats," *Cahiers du Communisme*, No. 1 (January, 1946), 66–74.

Constant, Etienne, "La Conférence de Londres," *Cahiers du Communisme*, No. 12 (October–November, 1945), 63–72.

Courtade, Pierre. "Le Problème allemand," *Cahiers du Communisme*, No. 7 (July, 1946), 592–98.

Dallin, David J. Soviet Russia's Foreign Policy, 1939–1942. New Haven, 1942.

Dansette, Adrien. Histoire de la Libération de Paris. Paris, 1946.

D'Astier de la Vigerie, Emmanuel. Les Dieux et les hommes, 1943–1944. Paris, 1952.

Davydov, D. "Antigitlerovskoe dvizhenie v okkupirovannoi Frantsii—na pod"eme" [The Anti-Hitlerite Movement in Occupied France—on the Rise], *Bol'shevik*, Nos. 7–8. (April, 1943), 54–61.

Deane, John R. The Strange Alliance. New York, 1946.

Deborin, G. A. Mezhdunarodnye otnosheniia v gody velikoi otechestvennoi voiny, 1941–45 [International Relations in the Years of the Great Patriotic War, 1941–45]. Moscow and Leningrad, 1948.

Dedijer, Vladimir. Tito. New York, 1953.

De Gaulle, Charles. Discours aux français. Paris, 1948.

—— Discours et messages, 1940–1946. Paris, 1946.

—— Mémoires de guerre. 3 vols. Paris, 1954–59.

"Deistvennaia sila marksistsko–leninskoi teorii" [The Active Strength of Marxist–Leninist Theory], *Bol'shevik*, Nos. 23–24 (December, 1945), 1–7.

Doueil, Pierre. L'Administration locale à l'épreuve de la guerre, 1939–1949. Paris, 1950.

Dragnich, Alex N. "Yugoslavia," in Stephen D. Kertesz, ed., The Fate of East Central Europe: Hopes and Failures of American Policy. Notre Dame, Indiana, 1956. Pp. 358–76.

Duchaček, Ivo. "Czechoslovakia," in Stephen D. Kertesz, ed., The Fate of East Central Europe: Hopes and Failures of American Policy. Notre Dame, Indiana, 1956. Pp. 179–218.

Duchaček, Ivo. "The Strategy of Communist Infiltration: Czechoslovakia, 1944–48," *World Politics*, II, No. 3 (April, 1950), 343–72.

Duclos, Jacques. Batailles pour la République. Paris, 1947.

—— Les Communistes dans la bataille pour la Libération de la France: Rapport au comité central, 31 août, 1944. Paris, 1944.

—— En avant pour la victoire de la République: Rapport au comité central, 20–21 avril, 1946. Paris, 1946.

—— La France devant son destin. Paris, 1946.

—— (pref.). L'Insurrection parisienne, 19 août–26 août, 1944. Paris, 1944.

—— La Lutte des communistes pour gagner la guerre et reconstruire la France: Rapport à l'assemblée d'information des régions parisiennes du PCF. Paris, 1944.

—— "Notre Politique," *Cahiers du Communisme*. Statements of Party policy appearing monthly. Occasionally Duclos is not indicated as the author.

—— Union des Forces Démocratiques: Rapport au Comité Centrale, septembre, 1945. Paris, 1945.

—— Vive l'unité de la classe ouvrière de France. Paris, 1945.

Earle, Edward Mead, ed. Modern France. Princeton, 1951.

Ehrmann, Henry W. French Labor from Popular Front to Liberation. New York, 1947.

Evnina, E. M. Literatura frantsuzskogo soprotivleniia [Literature of the French Resistance]. Moscow, 1951.

Fajon, Etienne. "Les Communistes et les nationalisations," *Cahiers du Communisme*, No. 4 (February, 1945), 29–36.

—— "Les Communistes et la propriété," *Cahiers du Communisme*, No. 3 (January, 1945), 11–18.

—— Le Marxisme–Leninisme, notre boussole. Paris, 1945.

Fajon, Etienne, and Joanny Berlioz. La France en bataille. Algiers [1944?].

Fall, Bernard B. "Tribulations of a Party Line," *Foreign Affairs*, XXXIII, No. 3 (April, 1955), 499–510.

Farge, Yves. Rebelles, soldats et citoyens. Paris, 1946.

Farmer, Paul. Vichy, a Political Dilemma. New York, 1955.

Fédération communiste de l'Hérault. Communistes de l'Hérault dans la Résistance. Montpellier [1945?].

Feis, Herbert. Between War and Peace: The Potsdam Conference. Princeton, 1960.

—— Churchill, Roosevelt, Stalin. Princeton, 1957.

Feodoseev, P. "Marksizm–Leninizm ob istokakh i kharaktere voin" [Marxism–Leninism on the Sources and Character of Wars], *Bol'shevik*, No. 16 (August, 1945), 31–59.

Fontenay, Ferdinand. "La funeste Thèse du bloc occidental," *Cahiers du Communisme*, No. 10 (August, 1945), 47–53.

Fourniau, Charles. "La Révolution d'août 1945 au Viet–Nam," *Cahiers du Communisme*, No. 9 (September, 1961), 1424–1442.

Frachon, Bénoît. "La Rôle de la classe ouvrière dans la renaissance de la France," *Cahiers du Communisme*, No. 2 (December, 1944), 21–33.

François-Poncet, André. Carnet d'un captif. Paris, 1945.

Friedrich, Carl J., and others. American Experiences in Military Government in World War II. New York, 1948.

Fuller, C. Dale. "Soviet Policy in the United Nations," *The Annals of the American Academy of Political and Social Science*, CCLXIII, *The Soviet Union since World War II* (May, 1949), 141–51.

Garaudy, Roger. "Le néo-Blanquisme de contrebande et les positions antileninistes d'André Marty," *Cahiers du Communisme*, No. 1 (January, 1953), 38–50.

Giraud, General Henri. Un Seul But, la victoire, Alger, 1942–1944. Paris, 1949.

Godunov, N. I. Bor'ba frantsuzskogo naroda protiv gitlerovskikh okkupantov i ikh soobshchnikov, 1940–1942 gg. [The Struggle of the French People against the Hitlerite Occupiers and Their Accomplices]. Moscow, 1953.

Goodrich, Leland M., and Marie J. Carroll, eds. Documents on American Foreign Relations. Boston, 1945.

Granet, Marie. "Dessin général de maquis," *Revue d'Histoire de la Deuxième Guerre Mondiale*, No. 1 (November, 1950), 51–72.

Granet, Marie, and Henri Michel. Combat: Histoire d'un mouvement de Résistance de juillet 1940 à juillet 1943. Paris, 1957.

Grenier, Fernand. C'était ainsi. Paris, 1959.

Guber, A. "Chto proiskhodit v Indonezii i Indokitae?" [What is Happening in Indonesia and Indo-China?], *Novoe Vremia*, No. 11 (November 1, 1945), 10–13.

Guigui, Albert. "Epuration et syndicalisme," *La Révolution Prolétarienne*, No. 34 (July, 1950), 17–21.

Guillaume, Paul. La Sologne au temps de l'héroisme et de la trahison. Orléans, 1950.

Guingouin, Georges. Documents et récits sur la libération de la ville de Limoges. Limoges [1944?].

—— Nouvelle de prison. Limoges [1952?].

Guyot, Raymond. "Les Chemins du Socialisme," *Cahiers du Communisme*, No. 1 (January, 1947), 11–24.

Hammer, Ellen J. The Struggle for Indochina. Stanford, 1954.

Hammond, Thomas Taylor. Lenin on Trade Unions and Revolution, 1893–1917. New York, 1957.

Henry, Pierre. Histoire des préfets. Paris, 1950.

Herriot, Edouard. Episodes 1940–44. Paris, 1950.

Hervé, Pierre. La Libération trahie. Paris, 1945.

Hostache, René. Le Conseil national de la résistance: Les Institutions de la clandestinité. Paris, 1958.

Huddleston, S. France: The Tragic Years 1939–1947. New York, 1956.

Hull, Cordell. The Memoirs of Cordell Hull. 2 vols. New York, 1948.

Iaroslavskii, E. Chego trebuet partiia ot kommunistov v dni otechestvennoi voiny [What the Party Demands of the Communists during the Days of the Patriotic War]. Leningrad, 1945.

Institut Marksizma-Leninizma pri TsK KPSS. Istoriia velikoi otechestvennoi voiny Sovetskogo Soiuza, 1941–1945 [History of the Great Patriotic War of the Soviet Union, 1941–1945]. Vols. I–II Moscow, 1960–61.

"Interv'iu tov. I. V. Stalina s korrespondentom *Pravdy* otnositel'no rechi g. Cherchillia" [Interview of Comrade I. V. Stalin with a Correspondent of *Pravda* Concerning the Speech of Mr. Churchill], *Bol'shevik*, No. 5 (March, 1946), 1–5.

Isaacs, Harold R. No Peace for Asia. New York, 1947.

Israelian, B. L. Diplomaticheskaia istoriia velikoi otechestvennoi voiny [Diplomatic History of the Great Patriotic War]. Moscow, 1959.

Ivanov, L. N. Ocherki mezhdunarodnykh otnoshenii v period vtoroi mirovoi voiny, 1939–1945 gg. [Outline of International Relations in the Period of the Second World War). Moscow, 1951.

Ivanov, S. "O roli sotsialisticheskikh partii posle vtoroi mirovoi voiny" [Concerning the Role of Socialist Parties after the Second World War], *Bol'shevik*, Nos. 17–18 (September, 1946), 50–65.

—— "O sovremennom polozhenii vo Frantsii" [Concerning the Present Situation in France], *Bol'shevik*, No. 6 (March, 1945), 62–73.

Julien, Charles-André. L'Afrique du nord en marche. Paris, 1952.

Kardelj, E. "Put' novoi Iugoslavii" [The Way of the New Yugoslavia], *Bol'shevik*, No. 16 (August, 1944), 23–31.

Kertesz, Stephen D., ed. The Fate of East Central Europe: Hopes and Failures of American Policy. Notre Dame, Indiana, 1956.

Kharlamov, M. "Ekspansionizm v poslevoennoi politike SShA i Anglii" [Expansionism in the Postwar Policy of the U.S.A. and England], *Bol'shevik*, Nos. 17–18 (September, 1946), 37–49.

Khavison, Ia. "Na rubezhe dvukh let" [On the Border of Two Years], *Bol'shevik*, No. 1 (January, 1944), 47–56.

Kogan, Norman. Italy and the Allies. Cambridge, 1956.

Kokorin, M. A., and A. A. Struchkov. "O boevoi deiatel'nosti sovetskikh patriotov na territorii Frantsii v 1943–44 godakh" [Concerning the Military Activities of Soviet Patriots on French Territory in 1943–1941], *Voprosy Istorii*, No. 3 (March, 1960), 88–101.

Korovin, E. "O mezhdunarodnoi opeke" [Concerning International Trusteeship], *Bol'shevik*, No. 22 (November, 1945), 39–51.

"K otkrytiiu mezhdunarodnoi profsoiuznoi konferentsii" [On the Opening of the International Trade-Union Conference], *Voina i Rabochii Klass*, No. 3 (February 1, 1945), 1–2.

Kozlovskii, Iu. "Osvoboditel'naia bor'ba frantsuzskogo naroda" [The Liberation Struggle of the French People], *Bol'shevik*, No. 15 (August, 1944), 53–60.

Lacipieras, Jean. Au Carrefour de la trahison FTP. Paris, 1950.

Lancaster, Donald. *The Emancipation of French Indochina*. London, 1961.

Langer, William L. Our Vichy Gamble. New York, 1947.

Leahy, William D. I Was There. New York, 1950.

Lecoeur, Auguste. L'Autocritique attendue. Paris, 1955.

Lefranc, Georges. Les Expériences syndicales en France de 1939 à 1950. Paris, 1953.

—— Les Expériences syndicales internationales des origines à nos jours. Paris, 1952.

Lemin, I. "Mezhdunarodnye otnosheniia v 1945 godu" [International Relations in 1945], *Mirovoe Khoziaistvo i Mirovaia Politika*, Nos. 1–2 (January–February, 1946), 20–34.

—— "Poslevoennye tendentsii vneshnei politiki SShA" [Postwar Trends of United States Foreign Policy], *Bol'shevik*, No. 22 (November, 1946), 53–65.

Lemoine, Commandant. Vercors, citadelle de la Résistance. Paris, 1945.

Leonov, M. "Lenin o voine i roli moral'nogo faktora v nei" [Lenin on War and the Role of the Moral Factor in It], *Agitator i Propagandist Krasnoi Armii*, No. 6 (March, 1945), 19–32.

Lorwin, Val. The French Labor Movement. Cambridge, 1954.

Lozère, Henri "La Question coloniale," *Cahiers du Communisme*, No. 6 (April, 1945), 71–76.

Maclean, Fitzroy. Escape to Adventure. Boston, 1950.

McNeill, William Hardy. America, Britain, and Russia, Their Cooperation and Conflict, 1941–1946. London, 1953.

—— "The Outbreak of Fighting in Athens, December 1944," *The American Slavic and East European Review*, VIII No. 4 (December, 1949), 252–61.

Manusevich, A. Bor'ba za demokratiiu vo Frantsii [The Struggle for Democracy in France]. Moscow, 1947.

Marabuto, Paul. Les Partis politiques et les mouvements sociaux sous la quatrième République. Paris, 1948.

Marty, André. L'Affaire Marty. Paris, 1955.

—— "Les Conditions de la réconstruction," *Cahiers du Communisme*, No. 2 (December, 1944), 26–40.

Marty, André. "Idées sur la nouvelle constitution de la République française," *Cahiers du Communisme*, No. 7 (May, 1945), 17–36.

—— "Notre Avenir dépend de nous," *Cahiers du Communisme*, No. 3 (January, 1945), 25–32.

—— "La Question algérienne," *Cahiers du Communisme*, No. 8 (August, 1946), 678–705.

Massiet, Raymond. La Préparation de l'insurrection et la bataille de Paris, Paris, 1945.

Matthews, Ronald. The Death of the Fourth Republic. London, 1954.

Mauloy, J. F. Les Nouveaux Saigneurs. Paris, 1948.

Mauvais, Léon. Le Parti de la renaissance française: Rapport au comité central 22 janvier 1945 à Ivry. Paris, 1945.

—— Le PCF puissant facteur de l'union et de la renaissance de la France: Rapport au Xième congrès du PCF. Paris, 1945.

Mel'nikov, D. Bor'ba za edinuiu, nezavisimuiu, demokraticheskuiu, miroliubivuiu Germaniiu [Struggle for a United, Independent, Democratic, and Peace-loving Germany]. Moscow, 1951.

Michel, Henri. Histoire de la Résistance. Paris, 1950.

—— "Pour une Chronologie de la Résistance," *Revue Historique*, CCXXIV (July–September, 1960), 111–22.

—— "Quelques livres sur la Résistance française," *Revue d'Histoire de la Deuxième Guerre Mondiale*, No. 39 (July, 1960), 31–46.

——, and Boris Mirkine-Guetzévitch. Les Idées politiques et sociales de la Résistance: Documents clandestins 1940-44. Paris, 1954.

Mikolajczyk, Stanislaw. The Rape of Poland. New York, 1948.

Mirkine-Guetzévitch, Boris. La quatrième République. Paris, 1946.

Moch, Jules. Confrontations. Paris, 1952.

—— "La Politique des prix et le renforcement de l'autorité." *Bulletin Intérieur du Parti Socialiste SFIO*, No. 39 (February, 1949), 38–80.

Molotov, V. M. "28-aia godovshchina velikoi oktiabr'skoi sotsialisticheskoi revoliutsii" [The Twenty-eighth Anniversary of the Great October Socialist Revolution], *Bol'shevik*, No. 21 (November, 1945), 1–13.

—— Voprosy vneshnei politiki: Rechi i zaiavleniia, aprel' 1945–iiun' 1948 [Questions of Foreign Policy: Speeches and Statements, April 1945–June 1948]. Moscow, 1948.

Monin, D. "Krasnaia armiia sozdala fundament dlia pobedy svobodoliubivykh narodov" [The Red Army Has Laid the Foundation for Victory of the Freedom-loving Peoples]. *Bol'shevik*, No. 2 (January, 1943), 69–80.

—— "Na poroge 1945 goda" [On the Threshold of 1945], *Bol'shevik*, Nos. 23–24 (December, 1944), 61–69.

Monmousseau, Gaston. "Une nouvelle Etape de la lutte des classes," *Cahiers du Communisme*, Nos. 8–9 (June–July, 1945), 13–16.

Monod, Claude (Colonel Morait). Des maquis à l'armée regulière: Histoire des maquis de Bourgogne et Franche-Comté. N.d., n.p.

Morgan, Claude. Yves Farge. Paris, 1954.

Mosely, Philip E. "Dismemberment of Germany," Foreign Affairs, XXVIII, No. 3 (April, 1950) 487–98.

—— "Hopes and Failures: American Policy toward East Central Europe, 1941–47," in Stephen D. Kertesz, ed., The Fate of East Central Europe: Hopes and Failures of American Policy. Notre Dame, Indiana, 1956. Pp. 63–74.

—— "The Occupation of Germany; New Light on How the Zones Were Drawn," Foreign Affairs, XXVIII, No. 4 (July, 1950), 580–604.

—— "Peacemaking, 1946," International Organization, I (February, 1947), 22–31.

—— "Soviet-American Relations since the War," The Annals of the American Academy of Political and Social Science, CCLXIII, The Soviet Union since World War II (May, 1949), 202–11.

Mottin, Jean. Histoire politique de la presse, 1944–1949. Paris, 1949.

Mutter, André. Pourquoi faut-il dissoudre le parti communiste? Troyes, 1949.

Myers, E. C. W. Greek Entanglement. London, 1955.

Nardain, B. Les FTPF et l'insurrection nationale (juin, 1940–août, 1944). Paris, 1947.

Nazhenin, E. "O mezhdunarodnom edinstve profsoiuzov" [Concerning the International Unity of Trade Unions], Voina i Rabochii Klass, No. 1 January 1, 1945, pp. 4–7.

Négis, André. Marseille sous l'occupation. Paris-Marseilles, 1947.

"Obrashchenie tov. I. V. Stalina k narodu" (Statement of Comrade I. V. Stalin to the People), Bol'shevik, No. 9 (May, 1945), 4–5.

Oleshuk, F. "Razvitie demokratii v osvobozhdennykh stranakh Evropy" [The Development of Democracy in the Liberated Countries of Europe], Bol'shevik, Nos. 19–20 (October, 1945), 52–61.

"Opasnye tendentsii v mezhdunarodnoi politike" [Dangerous Trends in International Politics], Bol'shevik, Nos. 11–12 (June, 1946), 1–10.

Parazines, Louis. "Notes sur la Résistance." Unpublished memoirs.

Parti communiste français. Le Guide du militant communiste. Région communiste du Lot. July, 1944.

—— Des Témoins parlent. . . . du Vercors trahi. Paris, 1945.

Passy, Colonel (Dewavrin). Souvenirs. 2 vols. Monte Carlo, 1947.

Pauchou, Guy, and Dr. Pierre Masfrand. Oradour-sur-Glane. Limoges, 1955.

Penrose, E. J. Economic Planning for the Peace. Princeton, 1953.

Pickles, Dorothy. French Politics: The First Years of the Fourth Republic. London and New York, 1953.

"Pod znamenem Lenina—Doklad tov. A. S. Shcherbakova 21 ianvaria 1942 goda na torzhestvenno-traurnom zasedanii posviashchennom XVIII godovshchine so dnia smerti V. I. Lenina" [Under the Banner of Lenin—Report of Comrade A. S. Shcherbakov, January 21, 1942, at the Solemn Commemorative Meeting Dedicated to the Eighteenth Anniversary of the Death of V. I. Lenin], *Mirovoe Khoziaistvo i Mirovaia Politika,* Nos. 1–2 (January-February, 1942), 8–18.

Pogue, Forrest. The Supreme Command, United States Army in World War II: The European Theatre of Operations. Washington, D.C., 1954.

"Politika mezhdunarodnogo sotrudnichestva i ego vragi" [The Policy of International Cooperation and Its Enemies], *Novoe Vremia,* No. 22 (November 15, 1946), 1–2.

Polonski, Jacques. La Presse, la propagande et l'opinion publique sous l'occupation. Paris, 1946.

Ponomarev, B. "Natsional'no-osvoboditel'noe dvizhenie v okkupirovannykh stranakh Evropy" [The National-Liberation Movement in the Occupied Countries of Europe], *Bol'shevik,* No. 18 (September, 1943), 33–46.

Popova, N. Zhenshchiny v bor'be s fashizmom: Pervyi kongress Soiuza frantsuzskikh zhenshchin, Parizh, iiun' 1945 g. [Women in the Struggle with Fascism: First Congress of the Union of French Women, Paris, June, 1945]. Moscow, 1946.

"R." "The Fate of Polish Socialism," *Foreign Affairs,* XXVIII, No. 1 (October, 1949), 125–42.

"Rech' tovarishcha I. V. Stalina pri podpisanii dogovora o druzhbe, vzaim-noi pomoshchi i poslevoennom sotrudnichestve mezhdu Sovetskim Soiuzom i Polskoi Respublikoi" [The Speech of Comrade I. V. Stalin on the Signing of the Treaty of Friendship, Mutual Aid, and Postwar Cooperation between the Soviet Union and the Polish Republic], *Bol'shevik,* Nos. 7–8 (April, 1945), 1–2.

"Rech' tovarishcha I. V. Stalina na predvybornom sobranii izbiratelei Stalinskogo izbiratel'nogo okruga g. Moskvy, 9 fevralia 1946 g." [The Speech of Comrade I. V. Stalin to the Pre-election Meeting of the Electors of the Stalin Electoral District of Moscow, February 9, 1946], *Bol'shevik,* No. 3 (February, 1946), 1–2.

Renault, Gilbert. Mémoires d'un agent secret de la France libre, juin 1940–juin 1942. Paris, n.d.

"Résolution du comité central à Puteaux, 27 novembre 1946," *Cahiers du Communisme,* No. 11 (November, 1946), 1010–13.

Robinson, Donald B. "Blood Bath in France," *American Mercury,* LXII (April, 1946), 391–98.

Rochet, Waldeck. "Les Problèmes de la rénovation de l'agriculture française," *Cahiers du Communisme,* No. 3 (January, 1945), 59–70.

Rogé, Henri (Lt. Col. Etienne). "Les Forces françaises de l'intérieur FFI," in Claude Bourdet, ed., *Annuaire de la Résistance*. Paris, 1948. Pp. 102–19.

Romans-Petit, Colonel H., Les Obstinés. Lille, 1945.

Rossi, A. (Tasca, A.). Les Communistes français pendant la drôle de guerre. Paris, 1951.

—— La Guerre des papillons: Quatre Ans de politique communiste (1940–44). Paris, 1954.

—— La Physiologie du parti communiste français. Paris, 1948.

—— The Russo-German Alliance, August 1939–June 1941. London, 1950.

Rothstein, Andrew, ed. Soviet Foreign Policy during the Patriotic War. Vol. II. London, n.d.

Rougier, Louis, "Résponse à M. Teitgen sur les origines d'une insurrection," *Ecrits de Paris*, April, 1951, pp. 87–98.

Rozek, Edward J. Allied Wartime Diplomacy: A Pattern in Poland. New York, 1958.

Sainteny, Jean. Histoire d'une paix manquée: Indochine 1945–47. Paris, 1953.

Serezhin, K. "Problemy arabskogo vostoka" (Problems of the Arab East), *Novoe Vremia*, No. 3 (February 1, 1946), 12–15.

Sergeeva, N. "K voprosu ob anglo-amerikanskikh otnosheniiakh" [On the Question of Anglo-American Relations], *Novoe Vremia*, No. 15 (August 1, 1946), 6–9.

Sherwood, Robert E. Roosevelt and Hopkins: An Intimate Biography. New York, 1949.

Signor, Alain. "Déviation bolchévique?" *Cahiers du Communisme*, No. 4 (April, 1946), 442–52.

Slobodskoi, S. "O sostoianii italianskoi ekonomiki" [Concerning the Situation of the Italian Economy], *Novoe Vremia*, No. 11 (June 1, 1946), 3–5.

Soustelle, Jacques. Envers et contre tout. 2 vols. Paris, 1950.

Stalin, I. V. I. V. Stalin: Kratkaia biografiia (I. V. Stalin, Short Biography). Moscow, 1946.

Stavrianos, L. S. Greece: American Dilemma and Opportunity. Chicago, 1952.

—— "The Immediate Origin of the Battle of Athens," *The American Slavic and East European Review*, VIII, No. 4 (December, 1949), 239–51.

—— "The Mutiny in the Greek Armed Forces, April, 1944," *The American Slavic and East European Review*, IX, No. 4 (December, 1950), 302–11.

Taittinger, Pierre. . . . Et Paris ne fut pas détruit. Paris, 1948.

Tanant, Commandant Pierre. Vercors, haut-lieu de France. N.d., n.p.

Thorez, Maurice. Un grand français vous parle: Radio Moscou, mai-octobre, 1944. Paris [1944?].

—— Oeuvres de Maurice Thorez. La deuxième guerre mondiale. Book Five, Volume XIX (October, 1939–July, 1944). Paris, 1959.

—— Le Parti dans la préparation de l'insurrection nationale. N.d., n.p.

—— Produire, faire du charbon. Paris, 1945.

—— Travailler, se battre pour la victoire de la France. Paris, 1944.

—— S'unir, combattre, travailler: Rapport au comité central 21–23 janvier 1945. Paris, 1945.

—— S'unir pour vaincre le fascisme et pour reconstruire la France. Paris, 1944.

Trakhtenberg, I. A. "Perekhod kapitalisticheskikh stran ot voennoi k mirnoi ekonomike" [The Transition of the Capitalist Countries from a War to a Peace Economy], Prilozhenie k zhurnalu Mirovoe Khoziaistvo i Mirovaia Politika (Supplement to the periodical World Economics and World Politics), Nos. 4–5 (April-May, 1946), 1–32.

Truman, Harry S. Year of Decisions, 1945. New York, 1955.

Tsyrul'nikov N. G. "Parizhskoe vooruzhennoe vosstanie 19–26 avgusta 1944 goda" [The Parisian Armed Uprising, August 19–26, 1944], Novaia i Noveishaia Istoriia, No. 1 (January, 1959), 82–104.

Varga, E. "Osobennosti vnutrennei i vneshnei politiki kapitalisticheskikh stran v epokhu obshchego krizisa kapitalizma" [Peculiarities of Internal and External Policies of Capitalist Countries in the Epoch of the General Crisis of Capitalism], Mirovoe Khoziaistvo i Mirovaia Politika, No. 6 (June, 1946), 8–17.

—— "Pravitel'stvo Lavalia i polozhenie Frantsii" [The Laval Government and the Position of France], Mirovoe Khoziaistvo i Mirovaia Politika, Nos. 5–6 (May-June, 1942), 24–29.

Vasil'eva, V. "Frantsuzskii narod v bor'be" [The French People in the Struggle], Mirovoe Khoziaistvo i Mirovaia Politika, No. 8 (August, 1942), 18–28.

—— Indo-Kitai [Indo-China]. Moscow and Leningrad, 1947.

Viannay, Philippe (Indomitus). Nous sommes les rebelles. Paris, 1945.

Viret, Paul. Les 75,000 fusillés communistes. Paris, 1952.

Werth, Alexander. France, 1940–1955. London, 1956.

Woodhouse, C. M. Apple of Discord. London, 1948.

Wright, Gordon. "Communists and Peasantry in France," in Edward Mead Earle, ed., Modern France. Princeton, 1951. Pp. 219–31.

—— The Reshaping of French Democracy. New York, 1948.

Zhdanov, A. A. "29-aia godovshchina Velikoi Oktiabr'skoi Sotsialisticheskoi Revoliutssi" [The Twenty-ninth Anniversary of the Great October Socialist Revolution], Bol'shevik, No. 21 (November, 1946), 1–13.

NEWSPAPERS AND PERIODICALS

Agence France Press, Paris.
Agitator i Propagandist Krasnoi Armii [Agitator and Propagandist of the Red Army], Moscow, 1945.
L'Avant-Garde, [Paris?] 1944. Scattered numbers. Publication of the French Young Communists' League.
Bol'shevik (Bolshevik), Moscow. Theoretical journal of the All-Union Communist Party, 1941–59.
Cahiers du Bolchévisme, 1942–44.
Cahiers du Communisme, December, 1944–61. Theoretical journal of the French Communist Party.
Cahiers d'Histoire de la Guerre, Paris, 1948–50. Journal of the Committee of the History of the Second World War. In 1950 became *Revue d'Histoire de la Deuxième Guerre Mondiale.*
Cahiers Internationaux, Paris, 1949–60.
Le Cheminot Libéré, Paris, January, 1948. Non-Communist syndicalist publication.
Combat, Paris.
La Corrèze, Tulle, July, 1956.
Daily Worker, New York, 1945.
Le Drapeau Rouge, Brussels, November, 1944. The organ of the Belgian Communist Party.
L'Echo de Corrèze, October, 1944.
Ecrits de Paris, Paris, 1949–50.
L'Espoir, Toulouse, 1944. Scattered numbers.
L'Esprit, Paris.
Le Figaro, Paris, August 23, 1944–October, 1947.
Franc-Tireur, Paris.
L'Humanité, Paris, June, 1940–November, 1947. Scattered numbers 1952. Daily paper of the French Communist Party.
Izvestiia, Moscow, June 21, 1941–July 1, 1947. The daily paper of the Soviet government.
Les Lettres Françaises, 1947. A Communist publication.
Libération-Sud, 1943–44. A Left-wing Resistance journal.
La Marseillaise, February and July, 1944. A publication of the Front National.
Mirovoe Khoziaistvo i Mirovaia Politika [World Economics and World Politics], Moscow. The theoretical journal of the Institute of World Politics and World Economics, 1942–44.
Le Monde, Paris, December 19, 1944–October 20, 1947.
Novaia i Noveishaia Istoriia [Modern and Recent History], Moscow, 1959. Publication of the Institute of History of the Academy of Sciences of the USSR.

Novoe Vremia [New Times], Moscow, 1945–47.

L'Observateur, Paris.

Le Peuple, Paris, 1944–47. The daily paper of the CGT.

Le Populaire, Paris, August 30, 1944–October, 1947. The daily paper of the French Socialist Party, SFIO.

Pravda, Moscow, June 22, 1941–July 1, 1947. The daily paper of the Communist Party of the Soviet Union.

La Révolution Prolétarienne, Paris. The publication of French syndicalist groups.

Revue d'Histoire de la Deuxième Guerre Mondiale, Paris, 1950–61.

Revue de la Presse Communiste: Information de l'Etat Français, Vichy, August, 1943.

Les Temps Modernes, Paris.

La Terre, 1944. A French Communist publication devoted to peasant problems.

Le Travailleur du Centre et du Centre Ouest, Limoges, July, 1944.

La Victoire, Toulouse, August–November, 1944.

La Vie de la MOI, 1944. Scattered numbers. A publication of the *unitaire* faction of the CGT.

La Vie Ouvrière, Paris, 1944–47. A publication of the *unitaire* faction of the CGT.

La Vie du Parti, 1942–46. The organ of the Central Committee of the French Communist Party for Party militants.

Voina i Rabochii Klass [War and the Working Class], Moscow, 1944–45. (Became *Novoe Vremia* on June 1, 1945.)

Voprosy Istorii [Questions of History], Moscow, 1944–61.

Index